MOZART'S LETTERS,

MOZART'S LIFE

With greetings and best wishes,

Bob Spaethling

MOZART'S LETTERS,

MOZART'S LIFE

SELECTED LETTERS

EDITED AND NEWLY TRANSLATED BY

ROBERT SPAETHLING

W · W · NORTON & COMPANY

NEW YORK  LONDON

For information about permission to reproduce selections from this book, write to Permissions,
W. W. Norton & Company, Inc., 500 Fifth Avenue, New York, NY 10110

The text of this book is composed in 12.5/14 Centaur MT with the display set in Centaur MT
and Centaur MT Bold.
Composition by Sue Carlson
Manufacturing by Haddon Craftsmen Inc.
Book design by Margaret M. Wagner

Library of Congress Cataloging-in-Publication Data
Mozart, Wolfgang Amadeus, 1756–1791.
    [Correspondence. English. Selections]
    Mozart's letters, Mozart's life : selected letters / edited and newly translated by Robert Spaethling.
      p.   cm.
    Includes bibliographical references (p.) and index.
    ISBN 0-393-04719-9
    I. Mozart, Wolfgang Amadeus, 1756–1791—Correspondence. 2. Composers—Austria—
Correspondence. I. Spaethling, Robert, 1927– II. Title.

ML410.M9 A4 2000
780'.92—dc21
[B]   00-025530

W. W. Norton & Company, Inc., 500 Fifth Avenue, New York, N.Y. 10110
www.wwnorton.com

W. W. Norton & Company Ltd., 10 Coptic Street, London WC1A 1PU

1 2 3 4 5 6 7 8 9 0

for Ellen

Contents

Plates appear between pages 240 and 241

Preface

THE PURPOSE of this book is to present to the reader of English a new translation of letters written by Wolfgang Amadé Mozart. The let-ters are published here with annotations, commentaries, and introductions so as to place them within a biographical context and offer a chronicle of the composer's life as reflected in his correspondence. Spanning a period of over twenty years, the letters document, in Mozart's own words, his personal development and artistic growth, from his first journey to Italy, at age thirteen, to the final months of his life in Vienna.

Young Wolfgang never had any formal education; his only teacher was his father, who instructed him and his older sister, Nannerl, in music, arithmetic, history, German, and probably some Italian, French, and Latin. This lack of schooling is evident in Wolfgang's prose, especially in his early years, when the teenager wrote letters to his mother and sister with little concern about grammar and spelling. Even later, when he had become familiar with the epistolary conventions of his time, such as the formalities of court language and the learned styles of the Enlightenment, Mozart used these forms of writing primarily for jokes and parodies. His own expression remained personal, spontaneous, and "natural" (as he himself called it), like the rich and colorful Salzburg dialect of his mother.

Mozart spent a total of 3,720 days away from home (whether Salzburg or Vienna)—a staggering ten-plus years, or, in Mozart's case, nearly one-third of his life. Indeed, "Wolferl," as he was affectionately called, had been traveling with his family long before he wrote his first letter: the wunderkind of seven or eight was busy writing symphonies.

But beginning with his early teenage years, Mozart's travels to Italy, France, Bohemia, and some of the German states produced a considerable body of correspondence. Many of the letters were preserved by his father, Leopold, and more than half of them are housed today, together with other Mozart family letters, in the Mozarteum at Salzburg.

The original German texts of the letters written by Mozart and his family were published between 1962 and 1975 by Wilhelm A. Bauer, Otto Erich Deutsch, and Joseph Eibl in *Mozart: Briefe und Aufzeichnungen: Gesamtausgabe*. Its seven sizable volumes present the first complete critical edition of Mozart's letters in his own natural style, without deletions, additions, or embellishments. The Bauer/Deutsch/Eibl edition has served as the textual basis for this book, providing both invaluable critical information and the inspiration to attempt this rendering in English of Mozart's unique writing style.

Another work of fundamental importance for this book was Emily Anderson's classic translation, *The Letters of Mozart and His Family*. Anderson's research and understanding of Mozart's language provided much stimulation and guidance. The problem is, Anderson sought to render Mozart's letters into "impeccable" English;[1] Mozart wrote anything but "impeccable" German and, therefore, sounds much more eloquent and literate in Anderson's English than in his native tongue. In fact, Anderson's version has Mozart sounding more like his father than like himself.

IN THIS new translation, I have striven to bring out Mozart's own voice and diction by looking for close and suitable equivalents or approximations for his down-to-earth German vocabulary, the conversational structures of his sentences, and even his phonetic spelling. I have also kept his inspired language mixtures of German, Italian, French, and Latin. In all, I have tried to preserve the natural flow and flavor of Mozart's original style, the spoken character of his written language, so that his personality, which shines through vividly in his German, becomes evident in English as well.

The letters presented here make up about two-thirds of Mozart's surviving correspondence. They are arranged chronologically in eleven

1. See the London *Times* obituary for Emily Anderson (October 29, 1962, 12).

biographical chapters and were selected with one goal in mind: to provide a complete portrait and continuous account of Mozart the musician, Mozart the individual, and Mozart the writer. The letters are presented in full and in part; omitted passages are marked by ellipses. Comments on Mozart's style and diction are my own; however, I am indebted for numerous biographical and musicological data to the chronicles and editions listed below. Also, since I have limited my annotations to a bare minimum, I refer to these same sources the reader who wishes further information about names, events, and music mentioned in the letters.[2]

Emily Anderson, *The Letters of Mozart and His Family*
Bauer/Deutsch/Eibl, vols. 5 and 6 of *Mozart: Briefe und Aufzeichnungen: Gesamtausgabe*
Eric Blom, *Mozart's Letters*
Otto Erich Deutsch, *Mozart: A Documentary Biography*
Joseph Eibl, *Wolfgang Amadeus Mozart: Chronik seines Lebens*
Ruth Halliwell, *The Mozart Family: Four Lives in a Social Context*
Ludwig von Köchel, *Chronologisch-Thematisches Verzeichnis sämtlicher Tonwerke Wolfgang Amade Mozarts*, 6th ed.
The New Grove Dictionary of Music and Musicians

I WISH TO THANK Joachim Bumke, Steven Burger, William Kellogg, the late Alfred Hoelzel, Inge Hoffmann, Takenori Inoki, and Ray Pariser for their much needed support and encouragement. I thank Martine Bruel for helping me with Mozart's French and Antonio Carrara for guiding me through Mozart's Italian. Duc Truong helped me find recent medical literature on Mozart, and Ellen Anderson translated it from Swedish and Danish. Justin Vaïsse, who also assisted with the French, helped me conceptualize the commentaries, Cornelia Schacht contributed her knowledge of Prague's theaters, and Roye E. Wates added significantly to the bibliography.

Special thanks go to my wife, Ellen, as the ever willing and cheerful first reader of the manuscript, to Paul and Phyllis Deane for their unstinting moral support and stylistic help, to Richard Strager for his structural and stylistic suggestions, and to Michael Ochs, music editor at W. W. Norton, for his encouragement, patience, and guidance throughout.

2. Complete references to these works may be found in the bibliography.

Finally, I wish to thank Geneviève Geffray, librarian at the Mozarteum in Salzburg, for her friendly and efficient assistance in my wish to examine autograph letters in the Mozart collection at the Mozarteum.

A NOTE ABOUT THE TRANSLATION

Mozart uses no consistent pattern of spelling. The same word may appear in two or three different versions, particularly in his early years. I have tried to capture some of these variations by misspelling their English equivalents; for example, "remain" can also appear as "remein" or "remeine," "thanks" as "thancks," and "music" as "Musick" or "Musique." Mozart's spelling of city names varies as well; "Augsburg," for instance, can appear as "Ogsburg" or "Augspurg," "Strasbourg" as "Straßburg" or "Straßbourg." Names and places that Mozart heard for the first time are often spelled phonetically. Over the years, Mozart's spelling becomes a bit more conventional, but some of his spelling habits, such as the German *ß* instead of *ss*—he uses it even in French and Italian—never change.

Mozart's use of capitals is equally individualistic. In contrast to modern German writers, eighteenth-century writers did not always capitalize nouns, and Mozart is one of them—even "God" appears mostly as "god." Instead, Mozart uses capitals primarily for emphasis, an important and characteristic feature of his style that is largely retained in this translation. He also uses underlines to emphasize a word (underlines appear here as italics). I have tried to keep intact Mozart's sentence structure and punctuation, although his sentences are at times interminably long and his punctuation follows no discernible pattern. Mozart's use of Italian, French, and Latin is equally inconsistent and unruly. He is especially nonchalant in his placement of Italian and French accents: sometimes he writes "chèr papa" at other times "chér papa," and even his own name appears variously as "Amadé," "Amadè," and plain "Amade." To the extent possible, these idiosyncrasies have found their way into this translation.

Beginning with his journey to Mannheim in 1777, Mozart's style and grammar become relatively consistent with the common practices of eighteenth-century German writing. But the most essential features of his writing never change: his informality of style and individuality of expression.

EIGHTEENTH-CENTURY CURRENCIES

The most frequent currencies mentioned in Mozart's letters are the kreuzer, gulden, florin, and ducat.

1 kreuzer (kr. or xr.) = *4 pfennigs (smallest unit)*

1 gulden or florin (fl.) = *60 kreuzer*

1 ducat = *4½ gulden*

Also mentioned:

1 Bavarian thaler = *2–3 gulden*

1 carolin (southern and western states) = *10–11 gulden*

1 cigliato (Italy) = *4½ gulden (approx.)*

1 livre (= 20 sous; France) = *2 gulden (approx.)*

1 louis d'or, pistole, friedrich d'or, august d'or, max d'or (named after the ruler of the issuing state) = *7–10 gulden*

1 reichsthaler (northern Germany) = *1½ gulden (approx.)*

1 souverain d'Or (Austria and western states) = *13½ gulden (approx.)*

1 zecchino (Italy), a medieval gold coin = *6–8 gulden (approx.)*

None of the currencies listed above had an absolute value. Values and purchasing power changed from country to country and often from region to region, depending on where the thaler or gulden was minted. For instance, 12 "Salzburger" gulden were equal to only 10 "Viennese" gulden.

It is virtually impossible to calculate the value of eighteenth-century currencies in terms of modern money, but it has been speculated that 20 gulden in Mozart's time would have the purchasing power of $600 or £350 today.

PART ONE

THE EARLY YEARS

1 7 6 9 – 1 7 7 6

First Italian Journey

December 12, 1769–March 28, 1771

WOLFGANG MOZART was thirteen, going on fourteen, when he and his father, Leopold, set out for Italy on December 12, 1769. In spite of 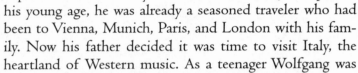 his young age, he was already a seasoned traveler who had been to Vienna, Munich, Paris, and London with his family. Now his father decided it was time to visit Italy, the heartland of Western music. As a teenager Wolfgang was no longer a wunderkind, but he was still young enough to be received as a musical sensation wherever he went. Leopold Mozart had counted on his son's fame to make the journey a lucrative enterprise, and he had guessed right. The concert tour was a splendid success. In Verona, where the young artist gave his first major concert in the Accademia Filarmonica, he was celebrated as *dulcissimo puero* (the sweetest child) and *vero Orfeo* (a true Orpheus). In Milan, where he composed an opera for the Teatro Regio Ducal, the audience affectionately shouted "Viva il maestrino" (long live the little maestro). In Rome, Pope Clement XIV honored him with the Speron d'Oro, the Order of the Golden Spur, and the Accademia Filarmonica of Bologna admitted the fourteen-year-old to membership in the select company of their Magistri Compositores. Even more valuable than the accolades and distinctions were the musical inspirations the young composer received along the way. Italian chamber music, Italian opera, and the smooth and flowing cantabile of Italian voices all had a deep effect on Mozart's own compositions and performances then and later. The same is true of personal contacts with famous artists and teachers. The violinist Pietro Nardini, the composers Niccolò Jommelli, Giovanni Paisiello, and Niccolò Piccinni, the singers Lucrezia Agujari, Giuseppa Useda ("La Spagnoletta"), Carlo Broschi ("Farinelli"), and Giovanni Manzuoli, and, most of all, the great theoretician and musicologist Padre Giovanni Battista Martini in Bologna—they all were part of young Mozart's artistic experience in Italy, and their influence would shape his musical language for years to come. Of incalculable importance for young Wolfgang's astonishing success in Italy was the generous support of noble families who took pride in providing a chain of glittering receptions and rewards that stretched from Milan to Naples.

In spite of an exhausting schedule, Wolfgang managed to write some forty letters to his mother and sister during this first journey across the Alps. Most of the communications, added to his father's letters, are postscripts addressed to his sister, Nannerl. They consist of hastily scribbled notes in a conversational, often chatty style. Dispensing serious information or writing formal letters was his father's job, and Leopold indeed wrote long, detailed, pedestrian accounts of travel routes, weather conditions, money matters, contracts, visits to noble families, the state of his digestion, and other daily affairs on and off the road. Should his reports not be detailed enough, Leopold wrote to wife and daughter in Salzburg, they might consult *Keyssler's Handbook on Travels in Europe* so that they could follow the journey on the map.[1] Wolfgang, on the other hand, was busy being a fourteen-year-old. He wrote about things he enjoyed, sometimes clearly and enthusiastically, at other times with a tired hand. Early on in the journey, he was happy, jolly, and full of fun and mischief, but toward the end he was, according to his father, serious and exhausted, falling asleep on a chair before dinner. The boy's writing style is expressive, creative, and personal, the language of someone who enjoys writing, loves the sounds of words, has a sharp eye for comical situations, and displays a penchant for verbal experiments, including some funny vulgarities. We also learn from these early letters that young Wolfgang was a loving, obedient, sweet-natured child. He was devoted to his father—"right after God comes Papa"—affectionate and respectful to his mother, and close to his sister. In company, he was open, friendly, and outgoing, prompting the German composer Johann Adolf Hasse to write that it was difficult not to love him.[2]

1. Johann Georg Keyssler, *Neueste Reisen durch Teutschland, Böhmen, Ungarn, die Schweiz, Italien und Lothringen.* 3 vols. (Hanover, 1751).
2. Letter to Giovanni Maria Ortes, September 30, 1769. (Deutsch, *Documentary*, 92).

When the two weary travelers returned to Salzburg at the end of March 1771, they had been on the road for fifteen months, during which they visited about forty towns, with major stops in Verona, Mantua, Milan, Bologna, Florence, Rome, and Naples. Wolfgang had given at least twenty-five public performances and written about twenty new pieces of music. The boy of thirteen had become a lad of fifteen, he had grown half a foot in height, and his voice was changing. His father wrote with some amusement that Wolfgang was highly annoyed because, for the moment at least, he had lost his singing voice: "He can reach neither high nor low notes, can't produce a pure sound, and cannot sing his own compositions, as he loved to." Yet for all the boy's growing, learning, and maturing, two things remained constant: his sweet, playful nature and his optimistic spirit.

Mozart's first communication from the journey is a postscript to his father's letter from Wörgl, a little town sixty-five kilometers east of Innsbruck, Austria. It shows him as a happy traveler who, like any thirteen-year-old, loved a fast ride.

To his mother, in Salzburg (postscript)*

Wörgl, December 14, 1769

My dearest mama,

My heart is filled with a alott of joy because I feel so jolly on this trip, because it's so cozy in our carriage, and because our coatchmann is such a fine fellow who drives as fast as he can when the road let's him. Papa has propably already given to mama the news of our trip, the reason I am writing to mama is to show that I know my duty, so I remein in deepest Respekt her devoted son

Wolfgang Mozart

Mozart added a second postscript for his sister, Nannerl, in Italian, which in content is much like the first: "Cariβima sorella mia. Siamo arivati à wirgel grazia iddio feliciβimamente . . . se tu vedi il signor de Schidenhofen, dice, che canto sempre: Tralaliera, Tralaliera." (Dearest sister. We have happily arrived in Wörgl,

---

*See facsimile, plate no. 2.

thank God. . . . When you see Herr von Schidenhofen[3] tell him that I am always singing: Tralaliera, Tralaliera.) Wolfgang had learned Italian from his father and the Italian musicians at Salzburg. "Tralaliera, tralaliera" could be his merry theme song for the early part of this journey.

To his sister, in Salzburg

Verona, January 7, 1770

Dearest sister.

I was really miffed because I had to wait so long in vain for an answer; and I had a good reason becaus I hadn't received your letter from the 1st. Now the German dope ends, and the little Italian dope begins. Lei è piu franco nella langua italiana, di quel che mi hò imaginato. . . . adeßo sentiamo sempre opere: che è Titulata: *il Ruggiero.[4]* . . . Between each act there is a ballet: they have a good dancer whose name is *Monsieur Ruesler;* he is a German, and his dancing is pretty good. When we were in the opera last time (but not the very last time), we sent for Monsieur Ruesler and asked him to come up to our box (we have free acess to the loge of Marquis Carlotti[5] and were given a key for it) and we talked with him: apropos,[6] everybody is wearing a mask now, and what is so great is that if you wear your mask fixed to your hat, you are not required to take it off when someone greets you, and you don't have to adress people by name, but simpy: *servitore umilißimo, giora Mascara.[7]* Holy smoke, that's real fun! but the most unusual thing is this: we go to bed already at 7 o'clock in the evening, maybe around half past 7 o'clock. se lei indovinaße questo, io dirò certamente, che lei sia la Madre, di tutti indovini.[8] Kiss mama's hand for me, and I kiss you a thousand times and assure you that I will remein allways your sincere, faithfull brother. portez vous bien, et aimez moi toujours.[9]

Wolfgang Mozart

3. Johann Joseph Ferdinand von Schiedenhofen, a friend of the Mozart family.
4. "You are more fluent in Italian than I thought. . . . we are always going to the opera, one of them is called *il Ruggiero.*" The opera Wolfgang is referring to is probably by Pietro Guglielmi.
5. Marchese Alessandro Carlotti, a Knight of the Maltese Order.
6. Mozart uses "apropos" mostly in the sense of "by the way."
7. "Your humble servant, dear Masque."
8. "If you can guess this, I will certainly say that you are the mother of all guessers." The riddle Mozart posed for Nannerl is based on a five-hour difference between German and Italian time telling in the eighteenth century. When Wolfgang says they are going to bed at 7 p.m., it is actually 12 midnight in Verona.
9. "Be well and love me always"; Mozart's first attempt to write in French, which he also learned from his father.

🐚 *After successful concerts in Verona and Mantua, the Mozarts proceeded to Milan by way of Cremona on "frozen roads," as Leopold reports. They reached Milan on January 23 and found comfortable quarters at the Augustinian monastary of San Marco, where Wolfgang was delighted to find a "pre-warmed bed." Wolfgang's first letter from Milan is amazing in its length and detail. We can feel the young musician's excitement about the wealth of musical life in Italy. Amazing, too, are the fourteen-year-old's observations as a music critic. His comments, which are neither polished nor polite, are sharp and humorous.*

To his sister, in Salzburg

Milan, January 26, 1770

I am truly delighted that you had such a good time at your sledding party, and I wish you a Thousand more such occasions for amusement so that you may be able to spend your life merrily. Only one thing troubles me and that is, you made Herr von Mölk[10] sigh and suffer endlessly, and you didn't go sledding with him so that he might have a chance to toss you into the snow. I wonder how many hendkerchifs he used up that day because of you to drie his tears; he propably took an ounce of Weinstein[11] beforehand to rid himself of all the horrible impurities of his body. I don't know anything new, exept that Herr Gelehrt,[12] the poet from Leipzig, died and after his deathe has written no more poetrie. Just before I began this letter I finished an aria from Demetrio,[13] which begins like this:

Misero Tu non sei:
Tu spieghi il Tuo Dolore;
e se non desti amore;
Ritrovi almen pietà.[14] . . .

10. Probably Franz von Mölk, a good friend of Nannerl's.
11. "Weinstein" is a kind of cleansing powder. Wolfgang uses the word as a pun on "to cry" (weinen).
12. "Herr Gelehrt" is the popular German writer Christian Fürchtegott Gellert, who died on December 13, 1769. Mozart's misspelling is an intentional pun, for *gelehrt* means "learned" and Gellert was known as a learned poet and admired by Leopold Mozart.
13. *Demetrio* is an opera by Johann Adolf Hasse that Wolfgang and his father heard in Mantua. Wolfgang wrote a new accompaniment to the aria "Misero Tu," but the composition is lost.
14. Wretched you are not/you show your pain;/and [even] if you do not arouse love;/you find at least pity.

The opera in Mantua was nice, they played Denetrio,[15] the prima Dona's[16] singing is good but too soft, and if you didn't see her act with her hands but only hearde her sing, you would think she is not singing at all becaus she doesn't open her mouth and just whines everything out very softly, but this sort of thing is nothing new for us. The seconda Dona looks like a grenadier and has a powerful voice to boot, her singing is really not bad at all, espessially since it was the first time she sang on stage. il primo uomo[17] il musico sings beautiful, but has an uneven voice, his name is Caßelli. Il Secondo uomo is pretty old, and I don't care for him. One of the tenors is called Otini, he doesn't sing badly but heavily like all Italian Tenors, he is also a good friend of ours; I don't know the name of the other one, he is still young but nothing spessial. primo ballerino: good. prima Ballerina: good. They say she is not at all bad looking, but I haven't seen her up close, the others are like everyone else. There was also a grotesco dancer[18] who jumps very well but can't write like me: as pigs piss.

The Orcchestro was not at all bad. The Cremona orcchestro is good, the first violinist is called Spangnoletto. The prima Dona, not bad, pretty old I think, and unattractive, and doesn't sing as good as she acts; she is the wife of one of the violinists who plays in the opera, her name is Masi. The opera is called "Le clemenza di Tito."[19] The seconda Dona is not bad looking on stage, young, but nothing spessial. The primo uomo Musico was Cichognani, a pretty voice and a beautiful Cantabile. The other two castrati: young and passable. . . . A grotesco dancer was there as well; he let out a fart each time he jumped. About Milano I can't tell you much, we haven't yet been to the opera, but we have hearde that it has not been sucesfull. Aprile, the primo uomo, sings well, his voice is very even, we heard him in a church where they just had a big celebration. Madame Piccinelli from Paris who sang at our Concert is here at the opera. Monsieur Bicch who danced in Vienna is also dancing here in Milano. The opera is called: "Didone abbandonata."

---

15. A misspelling of *Demetrio*.
16. Prima donna, the leading lady in an opera.
17. The male lead.
18. Derived from the Italian *grottesco* (grotesque, extravagant); here it means a humorous entertainer between acts.
19. The libretto of *La clemenza di Tito* is by Pietro Metastasio; it was set to music numerous times, including once by Mozart himself.

These performances will soon be over and Sig. Piccini[20] who will compose the next opera is already in Milano. I have hearde his opera will be called "Cesare in eccito." They also have dance festivals here, and as soon as the opera is over the dance fest starts. The wife of Conte de Firminan's stewart is Viennese, and last Friday she invited us to dinner; next Sunday we'll eat there again. Farewell and kiss mama's hands for me a Thousand times, I remein your brother true onto deathe,

> Wolfgang de Mozart
> Baron von Hochenthal
> Friend of the Countinghouse.

To his sister, in Salzburg (postscript)

Milan, February 10, 1770

Speak of the pig and it comes running:[21] I am well, praise and thancks be to the lord, and I can hardly await the hour when I will get an answer. I kiss mamas hand, and to my sister I send a smacker of a kiss and remein the same old—but who?—the same old buffoon.[22]

> Wolfgang in Germania, Amadeo in Italia De Mozartini.

March 3 was the last day of the carnival season in Italy. Wolfgang loved the colorful parades in Milan and at the end of the letter got into the spirit of things by creating his own fantasy language.

To his sister, in Salzburg

Milan, March 3, 1770

Cara sorella mia.[23]

It does my heart good to heare that you had such a good time. You may think that I didn't have fun here, but I did. I can't remember

---

20. Niccolò Piccinni was one of the most successful opera composers of that period; he gained additional notoriety in Paris as an opponent of the German composer Christoph Willibald Gluck; the name of the opera is *Cesare in Egitto.*

21. Wolfgang's German here is "Wenn man die Sau nennt so kommt sie gerent," a German peasant version of the English proverb "Speak of the Devil, and he'll appear."

22. Wolfgang is the star of the show, a celebrated teenage composer, yet he often applies deprecatory terms to himself, such as "dope," "blockhead," and "buffoon."

23. My dear sister.

exactly, but I'm sure we went to the opera at least 6 or 7 times, and then afterward to the festa di ballo,[24] which starts, just as in Vienna, right after the opera, but with the difference that in Vienna the dancing is more orderly. We also watched masked processions of the facchini and chiccherini.[25] They are a wonderful sight becaus people dress up in country costumes, they also come as porters or valets, and there was a boat with lots of people in it, and many others on foot, 4 or 6 bands of trumpeters and drummers, then severel bands of fiddlers and other musicians. . . . Today we are invited by the house-stewart of Count Firmian[26] to celebrate the last day of the festivities. We'll have a lot to *jabber* about; addio, farewell; next post day I'll write you a letter in Milanese. I remain your

Wolfgang Mozart

p.s. kiss mama's hands for me 1 000 000 000 000 times, greetings to all goode friends and a Thousand Compliments to you from ifyoucan-catchhimthenyougothim,[27] and from Don Cacarella,[28] espessially from the rear and[29]

The Mozarts left Milan on March 15, after Wolfgang had given a concert at the palace of Count Firmian for 150 invited guests, among them the duke of Modena and Archbishop Pozzonbonelli. On their way to Bologna, they stayed overnight at Lodi, where Wolfgang composed (or probably, completed) his first string quartet, K. 80. When they arrived in Bologna, Wolfgang immediately visited the famed composer and music theoretician Padre Giovanni Battista Martini, who was highly impressed with Wolfgang's fugue compositions.

To his sister, in Salzburg

Bologna, March 24, 1770

O, Thou Model of Diligence!

Because I've been so lazy for so long, I thought it wouldn't hurt if I got a bit more active for a while. Every Post Day, when the German

---

24. Dance festival.
25. A parade of people wearing workers' and domestics' dress, and other traditional masks and costumes.
26. Count Carlo di Firmian, governor-general of Lombardy, who had studied in Innsbruck, Salzburg, and Leiden, and was now in the service of the Austrian crown.
27. "wanstenderwischtsohastenschon."
28. "Don Cacarella" is Wolfgang's name for diarrhea.
29. The letter ends in midsentence.

Mail arrives, Eating and Drinking taste so much better. Please, write to me who is singing in the Oratorios;[30] and let me know the titles of the Oratorios. Also tell me how you like the Haydn Menuetts,[31] whether they are better than the earlier ones. . . . I'll soon send you a Menuett that Monsieur Pick danced onstage here and then, later on, everybody danced at the feste di ballo in Milan, so you can see how slowly people dance here. The Menuett itself is very beautiful. It is, of course, from Vienna, almost certainly by Teller or Starzer. It has a lot of notes. Why? because it's a Menuett for the theater that is danced slowly.[32] The Menuetti from Milan or from Italy have many notes, are slow, and have many bars. For instance, the first part has 16, the second 20 or 24 bars.

In Parma we got to know a singer and heard her sing in her own home: terrific! I'm talking about the famous Bastardella[33] who (1) has a beautiful voice, (2) a very agile throat, (3) an incredibly high range. When I was there, she sang the following notes and passages:

30. Oratorios that were regularly performed in Salzburg.

31. Minuets by Michael Haydn, concertmaster and organist at Salzburg; younger brother of Joseph Haydn. Nannerl had been copying the minuets; because she was very quick about it, Wolfgang addresses her as "O Thou Model of Diligence."

32. Years later, for *Don Giovanni*, Mozart wrote a similar minuet to be danced onstage.

33. "Bastardella" is the soprano Lucrezia Agujari.

🖎 *Before leaving Bologna, Wolfgang gave a well-attended concert for the high nobility of the region. On their way to Rome, the Mozarts stopped in Florence, where Wolfgang played at the Villa Poggio Imperiale, the summer residence of the grand duke of Tuscany, accompanied by the violinist Pietro Nardini. Wolfgang met the fourteen-year-old English violinist Thomas Linley, a student of Nardini's. After five days of drenching rain, Leopold and Wolfgang arrived in Rome on April 14. That same day they went to St. Peter's Basilica to observe Pope Clement XIV perform the traditional rites of Holy Week and hear the famous* Miserere *by Gregorio Allegri in the Sistine Chapel. The score of Allegri's* Miserere, *a setting of Psalm 50, was kept under lock and key by the Vatican, but Leopold writes to Maria Anna that Wolfgang wrote it down from memory after hearing it in the chapel. Leopold also reports that the papal guards mistook Wolfgang for a German prince and him, Leopold, for his tutor.*

To his sister, in Salzburg (postscript)

Rome, April 14, 1770

I am well, praise and thancks be to god, and so is my miserable pen, and I kiss mama and Nannerl one thousand or 1000 times. NB: I only wished my sister were here with us in Rome, for she would certeinly like this city, for Peter's church is very Regulair,[34] just as many other things in Rome are quite Regulaire. papa is just telling me that they are carrying the most exquisit flowers by our window. I am a fool, everybody knows that, but I do have a real problem, we have only one bed in our room, so mama can easily imagine that I can't get any rest sleeping in one bed with papa; I can't wait to get to our next quarters. I have just now sketched St. Peter with his keys, St. Paulus with the swordt, and St. Lucas together with my sister, etc. etc. I had the honour of kissing St. Peter's foot[35] at Sanct Pietro, and becaus I have the misfortune of being so small I, the same old numbskull,

Wolfgang Mozart,
had to be lifted up.

34. *Regulair(e)* probably means "evenly designed"; the word was a favorite of Leopold's, and Wolfgang is either imitating or mocking his father.
35. A statue from the thirteenth century in St. Peter's Basilica; kissing the statue's foot is a custom practiced by devout Catholics—and tourists.

To his sister, in Salzburg (postscript)

Rome, May 2, 1770

I am well, God be thancked and praised and, and I kiss mamas hand and my sisters face, nose, neck, and my wretched pen, and her rear end if it's clean.

Wolfgango Mozart.
Rome. 1770

The Mozarts left Rome on May 8 and traveled via Terracina, Sessa, and Capua to Naples, where they arrived on May 14 in the evening. Wolfgang's first letter from Naples is in two parts, both addressed to his sister. The first part is mostly in Italian and begins, "Alla vostra lettera non saprei veramente rispondere, perchè non avete scritta niente quasi" (I really do not know how to respond to your letter, because you did not write much). The second part is about first impressions of Naples. In spite of the crowds of beggars, Wolfgang and Leopold found Naples extraordinarily beautiful and its climate refreshing. One of the high points of their stay in Naples was a visit with Sir William Hamilton, the British ambassador, and his first wife, Catherine Barlow, who was an excellent pianist. Wolfgang and Catherine played for each other.

To his sister, in Salzburg

Naples, May 19, 1770

Cara sorella mia.

. . . On the 30th, an opera, one composed by Jomèlo,[36] will be performed. We saw the queen and the king during Maß at Porteci[37] in the court chapel, and we also saw Vesufius. Naples is beautiful, but it is crowded just like Vienna and Paris. and as far as impertinence of the people in London and Neapl is concerned, I'm not sure whether Naples doesn't have it over London, for here the beggars have their own chief, who gets 25 ducati d'argento[38] from the king every month, only to keep

---

36. Niccolò Jommelli, whose opera *Armida abbandonata* was performed at Teatro San Carlo in Naples.
37. The queen is Maria Carolina, a daughter of Maria Theresa; the king is Ferdinand IV, son of Charles III of Spain; Portici is the summer residence of the royal family of Naples.
38. "25 ducati d'argento" (silver ducats) equal about 45 gulden.

order among the laceroni.[39] De Amicis[40] is singing at the opera, we visited her and she recognized us right away. Càfaro is composing the second opera, Cicio de màjo the 3rd, and who will compose the fourth is not known. Do go as often as you can to heare the Litanies at the Mirabell, and also heare the Regina coeli or the salve regina, and sleep well, and have no bad dreams. Give H. von Schidenhofen some gruesome greetings from me, tralaliera, tralaliera, and tell him he should learn how to play the Repetiter menuet[41] on the Clavier, so he *does* not forget it, he must *do* it soon, and *do* me the pleasure that I *do* an accompaniment for him some day. *Do* give my greetings to all my other goode friends and *do* take care of yourselfe, and *do* not die, so you can *do* another letter for me, and I can *do* one more for you, and then we go on *doing* it until we are *doing* something out of us, but I am the one who wants to *do* all the *doing* until finally the *doing* is no longer *doable*, meanwhile I *do* remain,[42]

Wolfgang Mozart

    In the following linguistic gem, Mozart mixes three languages (German, Italian, French) and two dialects (Salzburgian, a bit of Swabian). Because of the rich, colorful, and often musical prose—it is great fun to read out loud—the letter is printed here in the original. The ensuing translation makes no attempt to render the letter's linguistic flavor into English; the translation is straightforward and literal.

To his sister, in Salzburg

Naples, June 5, 1770

Cara sorella mia.

    Heunt raucht der Vesuvius starck, poz bliz und ka nent aini. haid homma gfresn beym H: Doll, des is a deutscha Compositeur, und a

---

39. *Lazzaroni,* i.e., "beggars."
40. Anna Lucia de Amicis, a famous operatic soprano whom the Mozart family met in 1763; she would later sing in Mozart's *Lucio Silla*, in Milan.
41. "Repetiter menuet" has not been identified.
42. Wolfgang's final sentence is keyed on the verb "to do" (tun). In German the verb means to do or to make something, it can also mean to relieve yourself and even to have sexual intercourse. Wolfgang is here imitating songs that were current in Bavaria and Austria and that played on the latter two meanings. The end of Wolfgang's "to do" sentence reads in German (with his emphases): ". . . und *thue* gesund leben, und *thue* nit sterben, damit du mir noch kanst einen brief *thuen*, und ich hernach dir noch einen *thuen*, und dan *thuen* wir immer so vort, bis wir was hinaus *thuen*, aber doch bin ich der, der will *thuen* bis es sich endlich nimmer *thuen* läst, inzwischen will ich thuen bleiben."

brawa mo. anjezo beginne ich meinen lebenslauf zu beschreiben. alle 9 ore, qualche volta anche alle Dieci mi sveglio, e poi andiamo fuor di casa, e poi pransiamo d'un tratore e Dopo pranzo scriviamo et di poi sortiamo e indi ceniamo, ma che cosa?—Al giono di graßo, un mezzo pullo, overo un piccolo boccone d'un arosto, al giorno di magro, un piccolo pesce, e di poi andiamo à Dormire. est ce que vous avez compris? redma dofia Soisburgarisch don as is geschaida. wia sand got lob gsund, do Voda und i, ich hoffe du wirst dich wohl auch wohl befinden, wie auch die mama. se viene un altra volta la sig: alousia de scitenhofen fatte da parte mia il mio complimento. neapel und Rom sind zwey schlaffstätte, a scheni schrift, net wor? schreibe mir, und seye nicht so faul, altrimenti averete qualche bastonate di me. quel plaisir! Je te caßerei la tête. Ich freue mich schon auf die portrait, und i bi corios wias da glaich siecht, wons ma gfoin, so los i mi unden Vodan a so mocha. mädle, las da saga, wo bist dan gwesa, he! gestern waren wir in der compagnie mit den H: meuricofre, welcher sich dir und der mama empfehlt. Die opera dahier ist von Jomelli, sie ist schön, aber viel zu gescheid, und zu altvätterisch fürs theatro, die De amicis singt unvergleichich, wie auch der aprile, welcher zu mailand gesungen hat, die tänze sind Miserabl pompos, das theatter ist schön, der könig ist grob neapolitanisch auferzohen, und steht in der opera allkeizt auf einen schämerl, damit er ein bissel grösser als die königin scheint, die königin ist schön und höflich, indem sie mich gewis sechsmahl in molo (das ist eine spazierfahrt) auf das freundlichste gegrüsset hat. die herschaften geben uns alle abend ihren wagen mit ihnen in den molo zu fahren. sontag sind wir auf den Ball eingeladen worden, den der französisch gesandte gegeben hat. mehr kan ich nicht schreiben, an alle gutte freund und freundinen mein Compliment, leb wohl

p:s: kus
meinen handschus an die
mama.

Wolfgang Mozart
den 5 Juni 1770

My dear Sister, Vesuvius is really letting off steam today, holy smoke and lightning. Today we took our feed at Herr Doll's, he is a German composer, and a really good fellow. Now I will begin to describe my life here. I get up at nine, sometimes even at ten, then we leave the house and eat lunch at an inn, and after lunch we write, and then we go out and have supper, and what do we eat? On ordinary days half a chicken or a small slice of roast meat; on fast days a little fish; and then we go to bed. Have you understood it all? Let's talk Salzburgerian, that's more sensible. We are well, thank god, father and me, and I hope you, too, are in good health, and Mama as well. When Signorina Alousia de Schidenhofen calls on you again, give her my regards. Naples and Rome are good towns for sleeping. Beautiful my handwriting, isn't it!? Write to me and don't be so lazy. Otherwise I shall have to give you a thrashing. What fun! I'll break your head. I'm looking forward to your portrait, and I'm curious whether it really looks like you. If I like it, I'll have myself and father done also. Hey girl, let me ask, where have you been! Yesterday we were in the company of Herr Meuricofre who sends his regards to you and Mama. The opera playing here is by Jommelli, it's beautiful but too learned and old-fashioned for the theater. De Amicis sings beyond comparison, just like Aprile, who sang in Milan. The dances are miserably pompous, the theater is beautiful, the king has a crude Neapolitan upbringing, and in the opera house he always stands on a little stool so that he appears a bit taller than the queen. The queen is beautiful and courteous, she has greeted me at least six times at the molo (that is an outing by carriage) in the friendliest manner. Some nobles are sending us their carriages every evening so we can ride with them to the molo. Sunday we were invited to a ball given by the French ambassador. I can't write anymore for now, my greetings to all good friends. Farewell.

P.S. a kiss; I shoot a handkiss to Mama.

Wolfgang Mozart

Half a year into the journey, Wolfgang is not yet tired of traveling. On June 18 and 19, he goes sightseeing with his father to Mount Vesuvius, Pompeii, Herculaneum, Capodimonte, and, as he reports here, across the Mediterranean Sea to Baia to visit the famous baths of Nero.

To his mother and sister, in Salzburg (postscript)

Naples, June 16, 1770

I am also still alive and jollie as ever. And I love to travel: now I have also been on the Merditeranian sea.[43] I kiss mama's hand, and I kiss Nannerl 1000 times, and am

your son, Simple Simon and brother Jack

The Mozarts left Naples on June 25 by special "sedia" (a two-wheel coach with half-open top) and arrived in Rome in the evening of the 26th. On July 5, Pope Clement XIV conferred the Order of the Golden Spur on young Mozart, who received a golden cross on a red sash, sword, and spurs. Mozart was now a knight, which he is alluding to playfully, by calling himself "Chevalier de Mozart."

To his sister, in Salzburg (postscript)

Rome, July 7, 1770

Cara sorella mia!

I was truly amazed that you can Compose so well, in one word, the song you wrote is beautiful; you should try this more often. You probably received the Menuetts by Haydn;[44] send me the other 6 soon, please!

Farewell,

Wolfgang Mozart.

p.s. greetings to all good friends,
male and *female.*
a handkis for mama.
Mademoiselle, J'ai l'honneur d'etre votre tres humble
serviteur, e frere.[45]

Chevalier de Mozart.

---

43. Wolfgang spells Mediterranean as "Merditeranian" because he could not resist a pun: *merda* in Italian and *merde* in French mean "shit" so in Wolfgang's description the Mediterranean Sea becomes the "Shit Sea."
44. Dances by Michael Haydn that Wolfgang and Nannerl were arranging for piano, probably without Haydn's knowledge.
45. "I have the honor of being your very humble servant and brother."

Roma il sette di luglio anno
1770. addio statevi bene, e cacate nel letto che
egli fà fracasso.[46]

🐌 *The trip back to Bologna was difficult and took nearly ten days. The Mozarts trav-*
eled via Cività Castellana, Spoleto, Loreto, Ancona, and Rimini along the Adriatic
Coast. Leopold reports that they had to get up at three or four in the morning, trav-
el all day until eight or nine in the evening, and then struggle at night with an
"unbelievable multitude of fleas and bedbugs." So Wolfgang's remark about fleas is
indeed based on personal experience. The congratulatory note is on the occasion of
the feast day of Saint Anna and the corresponding name day for both Wolfgang's
mother, Maria Anna (also referred to as Anna Maria), and his sister, Maria Anne
(also called Marianne or Nannerl).

To his mother and sister, in Salzburg (postscript)

Bologna, July 21, 1770

I congratulate mama on her Name Day and wish that mama will
live many 100s of years, and remain healthy, something I shall always ask
for her from god and praye for every day, and I shall praye fervently
every day for both of you. I cannot present you with any gifts, except
with a few little Loreto bells and candles,[47] and some bonnets and fleas,
after I get home. In the meantime, I hope mama will stay well; I kiss her
hands 1000 times and remain until deathe

her obedient son
Wolfgang Mozart

Cara sorella mia:

lo vi auguro, che i dio vi dia sempre la salute e vi lasci vivere anco-
ra cento anni, e Vi faccia morire quando avrete mille anni.[48]

---

46. "Rome, July 7, 1770. Addio, be well and shit in your bed with a resounding noise." This is probably
Mozart's own translation of a German children's rhyme that is still current in south German language
areas today: "Gute Nacht, scheiß ins Bett daß' kracht" (Good night, shit in your bed with all your might).
Mozart and his mother were very fond of this little scatological verse, and he used it again in 1788 in his
comic canon "Bona nox!," K. 561.

47. Loreto, a town south of Ancona on the Adriatic Sea, is known for its pilgrimage church Della Santa
Casa, where religious objects such as Loreto bells and candles could be bought.

48. "My dear sister: I hope that God will always give you good health and let you live another hundred
years, and will not let you die until you have reached a thousand."

I received the Thousand and One Night in Italian[49] from our land-lady in Rome as a present; it makes for jollie good reading.

For the first time on this journey, Wolfgang hints of being tired. His father had written earlier that the boy had "visibly" grown in Naples; together with Wolfgang's demanding schedule, this growth spurt may well account for his constant sleepiness. It is not entirely clear which symphonies Mozart is referring to (probably K. 81, 84, 95, and 97). Some of the arias he mentions were written during his first stay in Milan for two young castrati who had become friends. Especially remarkable is K. 77, "Misero me—Misero pargoletto" (text from Metastasio's Demofoonte), which features Mozart's first dramatic recitative accompanied by instruments besides keyboard and bass.

To his sister, in Salzburg (postscript)

Bologna, August 4, 1770

I feel such deep sorrow in my heart about Miss *Martha* being so ill,[50] and I praye every day that she will recover; tell her for me she shouldn't move around too much, and always eat plenty of salty food. . . . I can't possibly write more clearly, because the pen I'm using is for writing music and not for writing letters. My fiddle has new strings now and I playe it every day; but I am saying this only because Mama wanted to know a while back whether I'm still playing the fiddle. At least 6 times I had the honour of visiting the Church here and its splendid Services all by myself. In the meantime I have already composed 4 Italian sym-phonies, quite apart from the arias of which I did at least 5 or 6, and then I did a motet as well. . . .

Italy is such a Sleepyland! I am always sleepy here! addio farewell!

Wolfgang Mozart

The letter of August 21 is an excellent early example of Mozart's descriptive humor and his sharp eye for comical situations. The gluttonous "holy man" seems like a fig-

49. The edition of *The Arabian Nights* that Wolfgang received from Signora Uslenghi, his very hospitable landlady in Rome, has not been identified.
50. Maria Martha Hagenauer, the nineteen-year-old daughter of the Mozart family's landlord in Salzburg, 225 Getreidegasse. She died on October 29, 1770, before Leopold and Wolfgang returned to Salzburg.

ure out of an opera buffa. Mozart's German spelling, always highly individualistic, is particularly adventurous here: for instance, the German word for peach is Pfirsich; Mozart spells it "sperschig," which is the way it sounded to him in his Salzburg dialect. When Mozart was unsure about the spelling of a word, he wrote it down as he heard it.

To his sister, in Salzburg (postscript)

Bologna, August 21, 1770

I am also still alive and very jolly indeed. Today I had a fancy of riding on a donckey, for it is costumary in Italia, and so I thought I should try it too. We have the honor of being aquainted with a certain Domenican who is said to be holy. I myself am not convinced of it, becaus he often consumes for breakfast a cup of ciocolata, right afterward a big glas of strong spanish wine, and I myself have had the honour of taking a meal with this saint, who imbibed heavily and at the end drank an entire glas filled with strong wine, in addition he ate two large slices of mellooni, peeches, pears, 5 cups of Coffée, a whole plate full of birds, two full saucers of milk with lemon. maybe there is some kind of plan behind it all, but I don't think so, because for one thing it's just too much, and for another, he takes quite a few morsels with him for an afternoon snack. addio. farewell. Kiss mama's hands for me. Greetings to all who know me.

Wolfgang Mozart, 1770

To his sister, in Salzburg (postscript)

Bologna, September 8, 1770

So that I won't fail again in my duty, let me add a few words. Please write to me which *brotherhood*[51] I am in and let me know what kind of required *prayers* I need to know. I am just now reading *Telemach*;[52] I'm in the second part already.

Farewell in the meantime.

My handkiss to mama.

Wolfgang Mozart.

---

51. "Brotherhoods" were church-based organization for the advancement of pious and ethical acts.
52. *Les Aventures de Télémaque, fils d'Ulysse,* the popular eighteenth-century adventure story by Francois de La Mothe-Fénelon. Wolfgang read the book in Italian; it must have made for good reading during the long hours on the road.

🐚 *The Mozarts had met Thomas Linley at the house of the poet Signora Corilla (real name: Maddalena Morelli-Fernandez) in Florence on their way to Rome. Here is what Leopold Mozart wrote about this encounter to Maria Anna Mozart on April 21, 1770: "In Florence we found a young Englishman who is a pupil of the famous violinist Nardini. This boy, who plays absolutely beautifully, and has Wolfgang's height and age, came to the house of the learned poetess Sgr. Corelli, where we happened to be visiting on the recommendation of M. L'Augier. The two boys took turns performing all evening while constantly embracing each other. The next day, the little Englishman, a most charming boy, brought his violin to where we stayed and played all afternoon with Wolfgang accompanying him on his violin. . . . Little Thomaso accompanied us home and wept the bitterest tears because we were leaving the next day." Thomas Linley, who later composed and concertized at Bath, England, accidentally drowned in a boating accident at the age of twenty-two. Wolfgang wrote his letter to Linley in Italian.*

To Thomas Linley, in Florence

Bologna, September 10, 1770

Dear Friend!

Finally a letter from me! I am answering your most kind letter sent to me in Naples, which however I only received two months after you had written it. My father's plan had been to take the Loretto road to Bologna; thence to go by Florence, Leghorn, and Genoa to Milano, and therefore to surprise you, showing up suddenly in Florence. But my father had the great misfortune of injuring his leg, which not only forced him to stay in bed for three weeks, but held us up in Bologna for 7 weeks; this nasty accident forces us to change our plans and go to Milan via Parma.

First of all we have lost too much time for taking such a trip; second, it's not a suitable season to take it, since everyone is away in the countryside and we could not even regain our travel expenses. Rest assured that we regret this accident greatly. I would do everything in my power to have the pleasure of embracing my dear Friend, and my Father, together with me, would wish very much to see Signor Gavard again, and his dear and most charming family, as well as Signora Corinna and Signor Nardini, and then return to Bologna. We would do this if there were any hope of recuperating at least the cost of our journey.

As for the lost engravings, my Father thought of being of service to you and ordered two of them which have now arrived. So, please let me know soon how to send them to you.

Keep me in your friendship and believe that, with unchanging affection, I am and will always remain

your most devoted servant and loving friend
Amadeo Wolfgango Mozart.

Leopold had injured his right shin on the way from Rome to Bologna when the two travelers were almost thrown from their sedia; he was now recuperating at Alla Croce del Biacco, the country estate of Count Giovanni Luca Pallavicini-Centurioni. The Mozarts stayed in that cool and luxurious environment from August 10 until the end of September.

To his sister, in Salzburg (postscript)

Bologna, September 22, 1770

I hope that Mama is well, and that you, too, are well, and I wished that you would answer my letters a little more fully in the future, after all, it's easier to give an answer than to have to think up something yourself. I like the 6 Menuetts by Hayden better than his first 12. We had to play them to the countess[53] several times, and we wished that we could introduce the German taste for menuetts to Italy because their menuetti last almost as long as a sinfonie. Forgive my poor handwriting, I could do mutch better, but I am in a hurry. We would like to have two small callendars for the new year. addio.

C. W. Mozart[54]

A handkiss for Mama.

After returning to Bologna, Wolfgang took the entrance exam to the Accademia Filarmonica, one of the oldest musical academies in Italy. The minimum age for admission to the academy was twenty; Wolfgang, fourteen, was admitted on the rec-

---

53. Contessa Pallavicini is the lady of the estate where Leopold and Wolfgang were staying.
54. The "C" in the signature probably means "Chevalier," the honorable title he had just received from the pope.

ommendation of his sponsor, Padre Giovanni Martini. For his exam, Mozart com-
posed "Quaerite primum regnum Dei," which is preserved as K. 86. Typically,
Wolfgang himself wrote nothing of the event, but Leopold reports on this "extraor-
dinary honor" in his letter to Maria Anna on October 20 from Milan: "We left
Bologna a few days late because the Accademia Philarmonica accepted Wolfgang
unanimously into its society and awarded him the diploma of the Accademico
Philarmonico. . . . He had to appear in the Hall of the Academy on October 9, in
the afternoon at 4 o'clock, where the Princeps accademiae and 2 Censores . . . hand-
ed him, in the presence of all members, an antiphona from an antiphonary that he
had to arrange for 4 voices in a separate room to which the custodian led him and
locked the door. After he had finished, all the Censores and Kapellmeisters and
Compositores examined it, and then gave their vote, which is done by white and black
balls. Because all the balls were white, he was called in, and everyone applauded
when he entered."

꩜ *Leopold and Wolfgang arrived in Milan, via Parma and Piacenza, on October 18.*
Young Mozart went to work immediately on Mitridate, rè di Ponto, *an opera*
he had been commissioned to write for the Teatro Regio Ducal.

To his mother, in Salzburg (postscript)

Milan, October 20, 1770

My dear Mama. I cannot write mutch becaus my fingers hurt terribly from writing so many Recitatives. I ask mama to praye for me that
my opera will go all right and that afterward we'll be happily together
again. I kiss Mama's hand a thousand times, and there is mutch I would
have to converse with my sister, but what? Only god and I know, if it is
god's will I can tell her soon myself, I hope. In the meantime I kiss her
1000 times. my greetings to all good friends. We have lost our good, sweet
Martha, but with god's help we shall see her again in another world.

꩜ *The following short note is perhaps Wolfgang's most poignant letter of the journey.*
He is trying to be funny, but he sounds exhausted; the many "tireds" at the end tell
the story.

To his sister, in Salzburg (postscript)

Milan, November 3, 1770

Dearest little sister of my heart.

I want to thank mama and you for your sincere wishes, I am burning with desire to see you both soon again in Salzburg. To come back to your congratulations, I must tell you that I almost suspected that Herr Martinelli helped you writing your wishes in Italian, but since you're always the smart sister and arranged it so cleverly that your own wishes in Italian were immediately followed by Herr Martinelli's greetings, which are written in the same hand, I didn't and couldn't possibly notice anything, and I said to papa right away: Ah! if only I could ever be so smart and clever! And papa said: Yes, that's true. Then I said: I'm getting sleepy, and he said just now: then stop writing. Addio. Praye to god that my opera will go well. My handkiss to Mama, my greetings to all our friends. I am, as always, Your

> brother wolfgang Mozart
> whose fingers are
> Tiherd Tiherd Tiredh
> tired from writing.[55]

🖎 *The opera seria* Mitridate, rè di Ponto *was premiered on December 26, 1770, with Wolfgang himself conducting from the harpsichord. He was dressed in a red coat with gold trim and light blue lining. Because of three intervening ballets (not composed by Mozart), the performance lasted six hours. The young composer received an honorarium of 100 cigliati (about 450 gulden) and free lodging for him and his father in Milan. Maestrino Amadeo, who was also affectionately called Il Sgr. Cavaliere Filarmonico, was the toast of music-loving Milan. To celebrate his success, Marianne d'Asti von Asteburg, a family friend, cooked his favorite meal for him: liver dumplings and sauerkraut. Wolfgang was appointed honorary Kapellmeister of the Accademia Filarmonica in Verona, and after a two-week stay in Turin, the Mozart's headed home via Brescia, Verona, and Venice.*

55. The German reads like this:

> "ich bin wie allzeit Dein
> bruder wolfgang Mozart
> dessen finger von schreiben
> Müdhe Müdhe Müedhes
> müde sind."

To his sister, in Salzburg (postscript)

Milan, January 12, 1771

Dearest sister!

I haven't written anything in a long time because I was busy with my opera. As I have more time now I want to be more attentive to my duties. The opera, thanck the lord, is a success as the theater is full every night, which astounds everyone and many are saying that as long as they have lived in Milano they have never seen a first opera so full. I and my papa are well, god be praised and thancked, and I hope to be able to tell mama and you at Eastertime everything in person. Addio, my handkiss to mama. Appropos, yesterday the Copyist came by and said that he has to make a copy of my opera right away for the court at Lisbon. In the meantime staye well, my dear Mademoiselle sister. I have the honor to be and to remein from now until all Eternity

Your obedient and faithful brother

🐙 *The Mozarts were in Venice visiting with the family of Giovanni (Johannes) Wider, a merchant who had moved there from Salzburg. His six daughters, apparently a rambunctious bunch, wanted to give Wolfgang the "treatment," which is known in southern Germany and Austria as* Arschprellen *(ass-bumping). In this treatment, which Wolfgang calls "attáca" in his letter, the victim is wrestled down, then held aloft by hands and legs and swung back and forth, bumping his or her bottom against the floor. Wolfgang must have been pretty agile to escape the attack of the "7 women," i.e., the six daughters plus Mrs. Wider.*

To his sister, in Salzburg (postscript)

Venice, February 20, 1771

I am also still alive and well, god be thanked and praised. De Amicis gave a recital here at the San Benedetto. Tell Herr Johannes[56] that the pearls of the Wider family[57] are always talking about him, most of all Mad.^selle Catharina, and he should come soon to Venice again to get, Nota Bene, "the treatment," which is to have your bottom bumped

---

56. A son of the Mozarts' landlord in Salzburg.
57. The six daughters.

against the floor to become a true Venetian. They wanted to do it to me too, and all 7 women got together and attacked me, but they couldn't get me down to the floor. addio. My handkiss to Mama, and Greetings from us both to all good friends. farewell. amen.

🐦 *Leopold and Wolfgang left Venice on March 12 and traveled to Salzburg via Padua, Verona, and Innsbruck, arriving home in the afternoon of March 28. They had been on the road for nearly sixteen months.*

Second Italian Journey

August 13, 1771–December 15, 1771

 LEOPOLD AND WOLFGANG had not yet reached home when a message arrived from Empress Maria Theresa, commissioning Wolfgang to compose a second opera for the Teatro Regio Ducal in Milan. The opera was to honor the marriage between Archduke Ferdinand, Maria Theresa's seventeen-year-old son, and Princess Maria Beatrice Ricciarda of Modena. The wedding would take place in October 1771 in Milan, the capital of Lombardy. The Austrian empress was commissioning two operas for the occasion: a grand opera seria from Johann Adolf Hasse, senior German composer in Vienna, and a short opera, a *serenata teatrale,* from Wolfgang Mozart, the youngest composer of the realm. Hasse would honor the festivities with *Il Ruggiero, ovvero L'eroica gratitudine,* which turned out to be his final stage work. Young Mozart's assignment was to set *Ascanio in Alba,* a work of the Milanese court poet Abbate Giuseppe Parini, to music. This *serenata* or *festa teatrale* was supposed not only to celebrate the union of the young couple but also to pay homage to Empress Maria Theresa, her wisdom, and her beneficence. The Mozarts, father and son, eagerly accepted the new commission; less than six months after returning home from their first Italian journey, they were on the road again, heading south across the Brenner Pass. In spite of the unusual summer heat, the journey proceeded without major incidents, and the Mozarts reached their destination after only eight days of travel. Although the young composer had come in haste, the libretto had not. The text for *Ascanio* did not arrive in Milan from the censors in Vienna until August 30, a week later than the Mozarts. But once the libretto was in hand, Wolfgang worked feverishly and completed the *serenata* in less than seven weeks. *Ascanio in Alba* had its scheduled premiere on October 17, 1771, at the Teatro Regio Ducal, two days after the wedding ceremonies of the Austrian archduke and the Italian princess in the cathedral of Milan. (Hasse's *Ruggiero* had been performed the preceding day, on October 16.)

"Our heads are spinning," Leopold reported on September 7 to his wife and daughter, who had remained in Salzburg. The statement is significant. The plural form indicates that Wolfgang was not the only one who felt the pressure of the close deadline but that Leopold, too, got caught up in the rush of things. We may assume, in fact, that much of Wolfgang's writing, if not all of it, passed under Leopold's vigilant eyes. But the statement has further implications. Leopold most likely regarded these commissions not only as family income or as fame and honor for his son but also as a kind of professional fulfillment for himself. This feeling was particularly acute in Milan, where people stopped the Mozarts in the street to offer their congratulations for the resounding success of the new opera. Leopold knew, of course, that the accolades were for Wolfgang, but who can blame him for basking just a little in his son's abundant glory?

When the royal newlyweds attended the performance of *Ascanio*, it is reported, they leaned over their loge, clapping, and shouting to the young composer: "Bravissimo maestro." It appears, too, that Archduke Ferdinand was so inspired by Mozart's *serenata* that soon after the festivities he asked his imperial mother in Vienna for advice whether he might offer the young composer a position at the court of Milan. Maria Theresa's answer was as prompt as it was negative: "You are requesting that I take the young Salzburger into your service. I don't know nor do I believe that you would need a composer or useless people. If that would give you pleasure, I don't want to keep you from it. What I am saying is to prevent you from being burdened with useless people and give titles to them. Having people like that in your service degrades such service, when they are going around the world like beggars." Such was the advice from Her Majesty, Empress of the German Empire, on the subject of hiring Wolfgang Mozart. If the statement seems crude and incredible today, it must be remembered that musicians at Mozart's time were considered little more than servants in the houshold of wealthy aristocrats. Mozart would learn this painful lesson later in a quarrel with the archbishop of Salzburg. As it was, the young archduke was not one to oppose his imperious mother. He admired Mozart's music but never offered him a position.

Mozart's second journey to Italy was short and intense. His letters—he wrote only twelve postscripts to his father's letters—are equally short and intense. Compared with his loquaciousness a year earlier, his terseness betrays hurry and weariness. Not even the completion of his assignment in Milan produced a rousing outburst from the teenager, who repeatedly proclaims in his letters that he knows nothing and has nothing to say. Although his natural urge for playfulness emerges once or twice in the form of language games, the basic theme of the fifteen-year-old is "always sleepy." On November 30, 1771, the Mozarts were received by Archduke Ferdinand and Princess Maria Beatrice for a farewell visit, and a few days later they started on their journey back to Salzburg along the route that had brought them there. They arrived in Salzburg in the evening of December 15. The very next day, Prince Archbishop Siegmund Christoph von Schrattenbach, spiritual leader and temporal ruler of Salzburg, died. This easygoing prince had allowed the Mozarts to travel and even contributed 120 ducats for their first trip to Italy. With the arrival of Schrattenbach's successor, Prince Archbishop Count Hieronymus Colloredo, things would be different.

A year and a half earlier, Wolfgang had given his first major concert in Verona. This time, however, the travelers did not linger but hurried on to Milan by way of Brescia. Wolfgang's first note home contains a row of synonyms, part of a verbal game he enjoyed playing and did so with skill and passion.

To his sister, in Salzburg (postscript)

Verona, August 18, 1771

My dearest sister.

I haven't slept more than half an hour because I don't like napping after a meal. you may hope, believe, think, be of the opinion, have an enduring expectation, find it quite in order, conjure up in your mind, imagine, assume with Confidence that we are well, but only I can tell you for shure. I'm in a hurry. addio. My regards to all goode friends. Wish Herr von Hefner[1] a good trip for me, and ask him whether he has seen Annamiedl[2] lately?

> Addio. be well. a handkiss for mama.
> terrific handwriting, isn't it?

The Mozarts arrived in Milan in the evening of August 21 and were given quarters in what seems like a lodging house for musicians. Wolfgang was delighted by all the sounds emanating from the rooms; only he could find such a musical mishmash inspirational and "fun for Composing."

To his sister, in Salzburg (postscript)

Milan, August 24, 1771

My dearest sister!

We suffered alott from the heat on our trip, and it was so dusty all along that we would have choked and died of thirst for sure, if we hadn't been smarter. there hasn't been any rain here for a whole month, that's what the people of Milano say; today it began to rain a few drops, but now the sun is out again and it's very warm. What you promised, you know what, you must keep;—what a dear you are!—you will oblige me very much. The princess[3] had the runs the other day—or a shit-fit. Apart from that I know nothing new, why don't you write me something new. My greetings to all goode friends and a Handkiss for Mama. I am panting it's so hot! I'm tearing open my waistcoat, right this minute!

Addio. Farewell.

Wolfgang

above us is a violinist, another one is below, next to us is a singing teacher giving lessons, in the last room across the hall is an oboist; it's all such fun for Composing! gives you lots of ideas.

At this point Wolfgang is working hard to finish his serenata teatrale, which he began on August 30, starting with the overture. Except for the recitatives, which he had

---

1. Heinrich Wilhelm von Heffner, a friend of Wolfgang's in Salzburg.
2. "Annamiedl," an unidentified girl in Salzburg.
3. Probably Princess Maria Beatrice of Modena.

composed earlier, he completed the three-hour opera in roughly three weeks. The "little opera," as Leopold called it, became the musical highlight of the festivities, while Hasse's opera seria, Il Ruggiero, *apparently failed to please. The "whistle call" Mozart mentions must have been a special signal between brother and sister. We cannot help thinking of Papageno's comic despair in* Die Zauberflöte *when no one answers his whistle call.*

To his sister, in Salzburg (postscript)

Milan, September 21, 1771

I am well, praise the lord. I cannot write alott. first: I don't know what. second: my fingers are so sore from writing. Farewell. my hand-kiss to mama. I often whistle my whistle call, but nobody answers me. now I need only 2 more Arias for the serenata,[4] then I'm all done. Regards to all goode friends. I have no desire to go to Salzburg anymore. I am afraid I might go crazzy, too.[5]

wolfgang.

To his sister, in Salzburg (postscript)

Milan, October 5, 1771

I am well, god be praised and thancked! but always sleepy. We paid two visits to Count Castelbarco and he came to my first rehearsal at the theater. I know nothing new, except that next Tuesday will be another rehearsal. Everything I wanted to write, papa has snatched from my pen and written already. Sig.ʳᵃ Gabrieli[6] is here, we will visit her soon so that we'll get to know all the distinguished singers who have come here.[7]

addio. Farewell. My greetings to all goode friends.

Wolfgang

---

4. Mozart's opera, *Ascanio in Alba,* K. 111.
5. This concerns a news item sent by Maria Anna according to which Salzburg had been hit by a wave of dysentery that had caused some people to lose their minds and had claimed several lives.
6. Catarina Gabrielli was one of the great prima donnas of the Italian stage. She had come to Milan to sing in a concert given in honor of the royal couple; Leopold and Wolfgang attended the concert.
7. For the wedding festivities.

To his sister, in Salzburg (postscript)

Milan, October 26, 1771

My dearest sister!

I am also well, thanck and praise the lord; because my work is now done, I have a little more time to write, but I don't know anything, papa has already written everything. I know nothing new, except that in the lotterie the numbers 35. 59. 60. 61. 62. were drawn, and if we had played those Numbers, we would have won; however, we didn't place a bet, so we neither won nor lost, but we laughed at the people who did. Of the 2 arias that were repeated in the serenata, one was sung by Manzoli,[8] the other by Gireli, the prima Dona. I hope you'll have fun in Triebenbach[9] with some rifle shooting and, if the weather permits, going for walks. We are about to go to the opera. My greetings to all goode friends . . . a handkiss for mama. farewell. I am as always your faithful brother.

Wolfgang

p.s. pardon my wild handwriting; I'm in a hurry.

Leopold was suffering from rheumatism and, therefore, decided not to attend that evening's performance of Hasse's Il Ruggiero. *Earlier he had written to Maria Anna with a bit of pathos, "I feel bad, Wolfgang's Serenata has so crushed the opera by Hasse that I cannot describe it." Wolfgang, however, who had seen Hasse's opera once or perhaps twice, knew all the arias by heart and was able to follow (and probably sing) the performance at home.*

To his mother and sister, in Salzburg (postscript)

Milan, November 2, 1771

. . . Today is a performance of Hasse's opera. But I can't go, because Papa isn't leaving the house. Fortunately, I know just about all the Arias by heart, so I can hear and see them at home in my imagination.

---

8. Giovanni Manzuoli, who sang the title role in *Ascanio.*
9. Triebenbach is a country estate near Salzburg owned by the Schiedenhofen family. The shooting here has nothing to do with hunting but is a form of target shooting with air guns called *Bölzelschießen,* a favorite pastime of the Mozart family and many of their friends.

🎵 *Mozart tells an interesting story about pride, vanity, and eighteenth-century pay scales. His remuneration for composing an opera was, at this time, about 100–150 Italian cigliati, which was equal to 450–675 gulden, plus free lodging and some sort of present. A castrato of Manzuoli's stature could command 500 cigliati for singing in one opera and settle for nothing less. It is amusing that Manzuoli, who was forty-six, was thought to be "old" by the fifteen-year-old Mozart.*

To his sister, in Salzburg (postscript)

Milan, November 23 or 24, 1771

My dearest sister!

Herr von Älfen is in Milan; he is still the same, just the way he was in Vienna and Paris. I know something else that's new: Herr Manzoli, who has always been thought of as the brightest among the Castrati, has now, in his old age, shown a bit of folly and conceit. He had been engaged for the opera[10] for 500 cigliati, and since nothing had been said in his contract concerning the serenata,[11] he demanded another 500 cigliati for the serenata, in other words, he wanted 1000 cigliati. The Milanese court gave him only 700 and a beautiful golden snuffbox. I thought this was quite enough. But he, the proud Castrato, returned the 700 cigliati together with the gold snuffbox, and left without anything. I don't know how this historie will come out in the end, I expect badly. I know nothing else. My handkiss to mama. Compliments to all goode friends. addio. farewell. I remain your

true and faithful brother
Wolfgang

🎵 *Wolfgang's last note from his second journey to Italy contains a brief, matter-of-fact observation about a hanging in Milan. His reference to Lyon indicates that he already witnessed such a public execution in 1766, at age ten.*

10. Hasse's *Il Ruggiero.*
11. Mozart's *Ascanio in Alba.*

To his sister, in Salzburg (postscript)

Milan, November 30, 1771

So that you won't thinck I am sick, I'll write these two lines. farewell to you all. a handkiss for mama. and greetings to all goode friends. I saw 4 fellows hanged here on the piazza del Duomo. They hang them here just as in Lyon.

Leopold had delayed the journey home twice because he was hoping that Archduke Ferdinand would offer Wolfgang a position at the court of Milan; but no offer was extended, and the Mozarts left Milan on December 5, 1771; they arrived home in Salzburg on December 15.

Third Italian Journey

October 24, 1772–March 13, 1773

IN LATE OCTOBER 1772, Wolfgang Mozart once again set off for Milan. It was his third trip to Italy in three years, and it would be his last. As in the year before, he had received a commission to write an opera for the Teatro Regio Ducal, albeit not from the Austrian empress but from the opera company itself. The commission, for a new opera seria to be performed during the carnival season of 1772–73, actually dated back to March 1771, when, after the success of *Mitridate, rè di Ponto*, the associates of the Milan opera house decided to sponsor a second opera by the young composer from Salzburg. So off to Italy they went once more, father and son, along the same well-known route, and mother and sister had again been persuaded to stay at home. Whether they remained behind for financial reasons as Leopold insisted, or for some other reason, we can be grateful to the extent that we would not be able to read Wolfgang's letters to Salzburg, which continue to give us a unique knowledge of the artist as a young man.

Mozart's letters from this journey do not differ radically from his previous communications; he still sounds jolly, witty, and quite unbusinesslike. Yet there are some variations on the theme. For one thing, his spelling is improving and, in general, his writing becoming more conventional and consistent. Another change derives from an increase in his hormonal activities. His thoughts no longer wander exclusively to mother and sister but to specific friends—girl friends. Wolfgang is sixteen now, and will have turned seventeen by the time he gets back to Salzburg. Although his body is small—he would never grow taller than five feet four inches—his physical maturation is in full swing. But the playfulness of his writing remains unchanged. Indeed, the letters from this journey give us two examples of Mozart's verbal play that belong to the most ingenious in his entire correspondence.

The new opera was titled *Lucio Silla*, and the star singers were the soprano Anna Lucia de Amicis, whom the Mozarts had known since 1763, and Venanzio Rauzzini, one of the most eminent castrati north or south of the Alps. Even though the premiere of the opera was delayed by three hours because Archduke Ferdinand first had to finish his correspondence—the six-hour performance concluded at two the next morning—the opera was both a critical and popular success. Leopold claimed later (in a letter of January 23, 1773) that it was performed twenty-six times to capacity crowds. Some of Mozart's biographers have described the opera as the composer's first romantic stage work; others have seen in it an example of musical Sturm und Drang, a work of individual expression similar to his earlier oratorio, *La Betulia liberata*, K. 118. However, there is general agreement that in *Lucio Silla*, Mozart went beyond the confines of the opera seria and, especially in his tonal colorations, took a first, daring step toward a more individualized style in opera.

Designations such as "romantic" or Sturm und Drang may be useful in categorizing certain literary and musical trends, but they are too abstract and ambiguous to help us understand Mozart's early operatic music. Although young Mozart's music does radiate a new lyricism and personal energy, it is still conventional music written to please a conventional audience. It may be forgivable to forgo learned categories at this juncture in Mozart's life and simply describe his music as inspired and enthusiastic. Beginning with the pulsating rhythms of K. 136, a divertimento Mozart wrote before starting on his third journey to Italy, and concluding with the dazzling "Exsultate, jubilate," K. 165, a motet he wrote after the premiere of *Lucio Silla*, Mozart's compositions radiated youthful joy and energy. Most telling in this regard are his vocal compositions. From early on, Mozart preferred to write vocal parts for singers whose voices and abilities he knew—doing so was a convention of the time and was expected of a young composer. For Mozart, however, it was more than convention; it was a fundamental practice he adhered to all his life. A composition, he explained later on in Mannheim, should fit a singer's voice like a well-tailored dress (February 28, 1778). Here, in Milan, he waited patiently (or maybe impatiently) for singers to arrive so that he could take the "measure" of their voice. Such personalized composing pleased the singers and often resulted in an artistic triumph. The motet "Exsultate, jubilate," for instance, not only allowed Venanzio Rauzzini to show off his vocal artistry; it also gave the world a new quality of sound that was at once formal and evocative.

Leopold delayed the journey home for several weeks in the hope of securing an appointment for Wolfgang at the court of Florence. He had sent a script of *Lucio Silla* to Archduke Leopold of Tuscany, but the archduke, third-eldest son of Maria Theresa, turned a deaf ear to the subtle pleas of Leopold, who finally faced reality and prepared for the trip back to Salzburg. His last letter to Maria Anna from Milan, written on February 17, 1773, tells his story: "With regard to certain matters, there seems to be no hope. I'll tell you more when we get home. God may have some other plans for us."

The Mozarts spent the fourth night of their trip in Bozen (now Bolzano), a charming little wine-growing Alpine town south of the Brenner Pass. Why Wolfgang calls the little town a "shit hole" (Sauloch) is hard to explain, except perhaps that he was, as he says, hungry, sleepy, and probably impatient. It had been raining heavily, and the Mozarts spent all afternoon and night in Bozen; "out of sheer boredom," as Leopold writes, Wolfgang composed a quartet (K. 155?).

To his sister, in Salzburg (postscript)

Bolzano, October 28, 1772

We are now already in Botzen. already? only! I'm hungry, I'm thirsty, I'm sleepy, I'm lazy, but I am well. At Hall we visited the convent;[1] I played the organ there. when you see Nanerl Nader, tell her I ran into Herr Brindl, her paramour; he asked me to send her his greetings. I hope you kept your promise and went to see D. N.[2] last sunday. farewell. write some news. Botzen is a shit hole.

---

1. Hall is a small town near Innsbruck, Austria; the "convent" is a cloister founded in the sixteenth century.
2. "D.N" has not been identified.

Here is a poem by someone who was totally fed up with Botzen, and angry:

Before I come back to this Botzen place,
I'd rather smack myself in the face.

🖎 *The little verse about Bozen at the end of the note has caused some problems in translation. Mozart's German is as follows: "soll ich noch komen nach botzen/so schlag ich mich lieber in d'fozen." The problem is* fozen, *which means "female genitals" (and has at times been translated as such); but in Bavarian/Austrian dialects,* fozen *also means "face," and that is definitely the meaning here.*

🖎 *The Mozarts arrived in Milan on November 4 and stayed for a few days with the d'Asti family. Marianne d'Asti von Asteburg, née Troger, was very helpful to the Mozarts whenever they were in Milan (even decades later, the d'Astis helped Carl Thomas Mozart, Wolfgang's oldest son, when he settled in Milan). The reference to war has to do with a conflict between the duke of Parma and Austria. Spain, aligned with Parma, threatened to send troops. Wolfgang is writing his letter as he is listening to the three men talking politics.*

To his mother, in Salzburg

Milan, November 7, 1772

Do not be alarmed when you see my handwriting instead of papa's. It's all because of the following: primo: we are staying with Herr von Aste, and Baron Christiani is here as well; they have so mutch to talk about that papa has no time to write; and secundo: he is too - - - lazy. We arrived here safely on the fourth at noon, and we are fine. All our good friends are either in the country or in Mantua, except Herr von Taste[3] and his wife who asked me to send greetings to you and my sister. Herr Misliveček[4] is also still here. About the Italian war which is so much talked about in Teutschland and the fortification of the castle

3. "von Taste" should be "von Aste." Wolfgang's confusion is either a misunderstanding or, more likely, a pun on the word *Taste*, which in German means "piano key."
4. Josef Mysliveček, a Czech composer, whom the Italians called Il divino Boëmo. He became a good friend of the Mozarts, and Wolfgang thought highly of his compositions.

here, none of it is true. Pardon my poor handwriting. When you write, write directly to us, for they don't have the custom here as in Germany that letters are carried out; here you have to fetch them at the Post office, and we go there every post day to pick them up. There's nothing new here, we are waiting for news from Salzbourg. We hope you received our letter from Botzen. I don't know anything else, so I am closing. Our greetings to all good friends; we kiss mama 100 000 times (I couldn't squeeze any more zeros onto the paper), and I kiss mama's hands, but I prefer to embrace my sister in persona rather than in my imagination.

Cariẞima sorella.
Spero che voi sarete stata dalla signora che voi gia sapete. Vi prego se la vedete di farle un complimento da parte mia . . . io sono sempre il vostro

fedele fratello amadeo Wolfgango
Mozart[5]

🐜 *Mozart is in a jolly mood. This postscript features some of his favorite language games: synonym rows, jumbled sentences, verbal mirror effects—"well fare" is, of course, "fare well," "oidda" is "addio," and "2771" is "1772." And when he says "my underprized friend," he really means "my highly prized friend."*

To his sister, in Salzburg (postscript)

Milan, November 21, 1772

I want to say my thanks; you know what for. My apologies to H. von Hefner that I haven't answered his letter yet. But it was impossible, and it still is because as soon as I get home there is always something I have to write, often it is already waiting for me on the table, and I can't very well write out of doors, in the street. When you see him, let him read this letter; I ask him to be content with it for right now. I will not take it amiss that my underprized friend hasn't replied to me. As soon

---

5. Mozart's Italian postscript to his sister is another indication that he now has not only music but females on his mind: "I hope that you have already seen the lady you know whom. Please give her when you see her my greetings. . . . I am as always your faithful brother Amadeus Wolfgangus Mozart."

as he has more time, he will certainly, doubtlessly, without any doubt, for sure, reply to me in a proper manner. Greetings to all good friends and I kiss Mama's hands. well fare, and new something to me soon write. Teutschland from the Post not yet has arrived.

Oidda.
Usual as am I

Milano à 2771 novembr. 12 the Mozart Wolfgang.

Once again, Mozart had to work under pressure, but his opera, Lucio Silla, *premiered on schedule, December 26, 1772. Leopold reports on January 2, 1773, that the opera was well received, but that it started with a three-hour delay caused by Archduke Ferdinand's late arrival. It appears that the archduke had been writing New Year's greetings and, as Leopold explains with a touch of sarcasm, "he writes very slowly."*

To his sister, in Salzburg (postscript)

Milan, December 5, 1772

Now I have to finish 14 more numbers, then I am done; of course, one could count the Terzetto and Duetto as four pieces. I can't possibly write mutch now, because I know nothing, and secondly I don't know what I'm writing, because my thoughts are always with my opera,[6] and I am running the danger of writing down, instead of words, a whole Aria for you. Herr and Frau Germani are sending greetings to mama, you, and Herr Adelgasser.[7] I have learned a new game here in Milan; it's called *Mercante in fiera*.[8] As soon as I get home, we'll play it. I have also learned a new language game from Frau v. Taste. It's easy to speak, but the writing part is hard, although not really bad; perhaps it is a bit —childish, but that makes it just right for Salzburg. Addio, farewell . . .

6. *Lucio Silla*, K. 135.
7. Anton Cajetan Adlgasser, court organist in Salzburg.
8. "Mercante in fiera" (Merchants in the marketplace) is a card game still played in Italy today.

The following letter may well include Wolfgang's most challenging language game. In the original every other line is written upside down; so Wolfgang had to move the page around each time he wrote a new line; Nannerl, in order to read the letter, had to do the same. The banner carried aloft by a little bird reads, "fly to my child and suck from front or behind" (flieg hin zu meinem Kind und saug' vorn oder hint!). This translation of Mozart's playful exercise is presented here without the turn-around challenge.

To his sister, in Salzburg (postscript)

Milan, December 18, 1772

I hope you are doing well, my dearest sister. By the time you receive this letter, my dear sister, on that evening my opera will go on. Think of me, my dear sister, and imagine, my dear sister, as hard as you can that you are seeing and hearing it as well, my dear sister.

Of course, it is hard because it's already 11 o'clock. Otherwise I believe and don't doubt at all that it is brighter during the day than at Easter. My dear sister, tomorrow we are eating at Herr v. Mayer's,[9] and why do you think? Guess. Because he invited us. Tomorrow's rehearsal is at the Teatro, but the Impressario, Sig. Castiglioni, has requested of me that I should say Nothing to anyone, otherwise too many people come in and we don't want that. Therefore, I beg you, my child, don't

9. Archduke Ferdinand's privy paymaster.

tell Anyone about it, my Child, for otherwise too many People will come running, my Child. By the way, do you know already the Historie that happened here? Well now, I will tell you.

We left today Count Firmian's place to go home, and when we came into our street, we opened the door to our house, and what do you think happened? we went inside. farewell, my little lung. I kiss you, my liver, and remain at all times, my stomach, your unworthy brother Wolfgang, frater, please, please, dear Sister, something is biting me, come and scratch me.

Three weeks after the premiere of Lucio Silla, *Mozart composed one of the great works of his youth: a three-movement piece of sacred music, "Exsultate, jubilate," K. 165. He wrote the motet for the castrato Venanzio Rauzzini, who was singing the role of Ceclio in* Lucio Silla. *The motet was first performed at the Church of the Theatines in Milan on January 17, 1773. Mozart must have known that this extraordinary vocal concerto with the jubilant "Alleluja" at the end was something very special, but instead of bragging to his sister, he kids around by jumbling his sentences.*

To his sister, in Salzburg (postscript)

Milan, January 16, 1773

I for the primo a homo motet to make had tomorrow that at the Theatines performed will be. Well be to you I ask. Farewell. addio.

Sorry, new nothing I know. Greetings to friends all good, male female, and my mama to handkiss, well fare, I kiss you times a Thousand and your brother remain as always,

faithful your Milano.

The letter is worth quoting in the original: "Ich vor habe den primo eine homo motteten machen welche müssen morgen bey Theatinern den producirt wird. seyet auf wohl ich eüch bitte. lebe wohl. addio.

mir leid ich neües meine an gutte und lebe meinen an mama küsse ist das nichts weiß, Empfelung alle freünde freudinen. wohl. handkus die ich dich zu und wie dein bruder Tausendmahl bleibe allzeit. getreüer Meyland."

Except for a note in Italian to his sister, this intriguing little word game is Wolfgang's last communication to Salzburg before he and his father returned home. They were back in Salzburg on March 13, 1773.

Interludes in
Vienna and Munich

VIENNA *July 14, 1773–September 24, 1773*

MUNICH *December 6, 1774–March 6, 1775*

UNSUCCESSFUL IN his efforts to secure a position for Wolfgang in Italy, Leopold Mozart set his sights on Vienna, the musical capital of continental Europe. After only four months at home, the two Mozarts were on the road again, this time to the Habsburg metropolis, where they arrived in the evening of July 16, 1773. Their primary mission, to get an audience with Empress Maria Theresa, was a success; Leopold's request was granted on August 5. But the visit produced neither any special recognition nor an appointment. "Her Majesty, the Empress, was very gracious," Leopold wrote to Maria Anna in Salzburg, "but that was all, I'll have to tell you more when we get back because one cannot put everything in a letter." Somehow, inexplicably, the Mozarts of Salzburg had become personae non gratae to the inner circle of the Habsburgs. It was not until the death of Maria Theresa in 1780 that Wolfgang Mozart received a modicum of recognition from her son and successor, Joseph II. For now, however, Leopold's hopes to see his son installed in a secure and profitable position at the Viennese court had come to naught.

Yet the time in Vienna was not wasted. There were friends to be visited, old ties to be renewed. The physician Dr. Franz Anton Mesmer, an amateur cellist and harpsichordist who was famous for his theory of healing through animal magnetism, invited the Mozarts to his stately house and gardens and encouraged Wolfgang to try out his most prized possession, a glass harmonica. Echoes from these cordial hours with

Dr. Mesmer can still be heard in Mozart's *Così fan tutte* (in the magnet cure of the "Albanians"), and in his two pieces for glass harmonica, the Adagio in C, K. 356, and the Quintet, K. 617. And there were other stimulating visits: Jean-Georges Noverre, the French ballet master at the Burgtheater, invited the Mozarts to dinner, and Johann Gottlieb Stephanie the Younger, actor and librettist, who would later collaborate with Mozart on *Die Entführung aus dem Serail*, enjoyed their company at the house of Dr. Mesmer. Most important, however, after so many years in Italy, young Mozart could renew his knowledge of the Viennese style of music, especially the quartets of Joseph Haydn. These works not only had a long-range effect on Mozart's chamber music, but they bore immediate fruit in six string quartets, K. 168–173, which Mozart composed while still in Vienna.

Characteristically, none of the political or musical happenings of the two-month stay in the Austrian capital are in any way reflected in Wolfgang's letters. As usual, Wolfgang left it up to his father to write about business. He concentrated on his language games, his wonderful *Sprachspiele*. None of his five letters, all of them postscripts to his father's letters, have any informational value; indeed, they invite speculation that the teenager was just whiling away his time. Nothing could be further from the truth. Wolfgang heard a lot of music, he listened and absorbed, and, after his return to Salzburg, he burst forth with immense productivity: he rewrote his String Quintet in B-flat, K. 174 (his first quintet), composed the Piano Concerto in D, K. 175, a favorite that he kept in his repertoire for many years, wrote his first sinfonia concertante, K. 190, and produced more than a dozen minuets. He also composed several symphonies, among them the "little" G minor, K. 183, a Sturm und Drang masterpiece.

There were other developments. Late in September 1773, the Mozarts moved from the Hagenauer house in Getreidegasse, the birthplace of Wolfgang and Nannerl, to the so-called Tanzmeisterhaus, on Hannibal Square (today Makartplatz); in other words, they moved from the narrow streets of medieval Salzburg to a modern section of town on the right bank of the Salzach River. The eight-room apartment on the second floor was spacious enough for them to have friends over for *Hausmusik* and for *Bölzelschießen* (target shooting). In late summer of 1774, a commission arrived from the court of Elector Maximilian III of Bavaria to write an opera buffa for the 1775 carnival season in Munich.

The libretto, *La finta giardiniera* (The Pretend Gardener), had already been selected. Both father and son were delighted and made instant preparations: Wolfgang began writing recitatives, and Leopold began dreaming of a permanent position for Wolfgang in the Bavarian capital. Early in December, they took a coach to Munich, where they stayed overnight in the charming town of Wasserburg, on the Inn River. Mozart's opera buffa premiered on January 13, 1775, but although it was declared a success, it was performed only twice more in Munich, and no appointment was forthcoming for the young composer. The Mozarts, including Nannerl, who had come to Munich for the premiere, returned to Salzburg fulfilled yet disappointed.

Mozart's first note from Vienna consists of one sentence written in Latin, French, German, and Italian. Like Mozart's other linguistic treasures, it loses everything in translation, so it is presented here in the original. The note was apparently written in Dr. Mesmer's garden, which was located on Landstraße, near the Prater amusement park.

To his sister, in Salzburg (postscript)

Vienna, August 12, 1773

hodie nous avons begegnet per strada Dominum Edlbach welcher uns di voi compliments ausgerichtet hat, et qui sich tibi et ta mere Empfehlen läst. Adio.[1]

W. M. Landstrasse den 12 aug.

Two days later Mozart engages in a different type of language game. This time it is a parody of the gallant writing style that was then customary in polite society, using modish references such as beauty, thought, and reason, and stringing them together in another modish feature: a German sentence of interminable length.

---

1. "Today we met Herr Edlbach in the street who brought us greetings from you and who wants to be remembered to you and your mama. Adio."

To his sister, in Salzburg (postscript)

Vienna, August 14, 1773

I hope, my queen, that you are enjoying the highest degree of health and yet now and then or rather once in a while or better occasionally or still better qualche volta, as the Italians say, you will sacrifice for me some of your deep and important thoughts, which always issue from that reasoning mind of yours, which is both pleasant and penetrating and which you possess in addition to your beauty, although you are so tender in years and so little is expected of the aforementioned things from members of your sex. O my Queen, you possess all this to such high degree that you put to shame the entire masculine gender, Yes, even those who are old and venerable.

Fare thee well.

Now here is something brilliant for you.

Wolfgang Mozart.

Mozart is still in his ironic mode, using words of the popular Enlightenment such as "natural reason" (natürliche Vernunft) and "benevolence, art" (gunst, kunst). He is clearly aware of the rhetorical culture of his time, but instead of using it, he makes fun of it. The greetings from "her majesty, the empress," are, of course, pure fiction; and he concludes in his favorite backward style: "oidda—gnagflow Trazom" is "addio—Wolfgang Mozart," and "neiw ned 12 tsugua 3771" is "Vienna, August 21, 1773."

To his sister, in Salzburg (postscript)

Vienna, August 21, 1773

If one contemplates the benevolence of Time while not completely ignoring the high esteem rendered by the sun, it becomes rather evident that I am well, god be praised and thanked. However, the second part of this sentence could also be written quite differently; instead of sun, let's put Moon, and instead of benevolence, art; now, anyone who is endowed with even a minimum of natural reason will have to conclude that I am a fool, especially since you are my sister. And how is

Miss Bimbes?[2] Please give her all kinds of messages. My regards to all goode friends, male and female. I have greetings from Herr and Frau Mesmer[3] . . . Stephanie[4] . . . as well as her majesty, the empress . . . oidda.
— gnagflow Trazom
 neiw ned 12 tsugua 3771

Wolfgang wrote the following postscript to his mother pretending that he is his father writing about Wolfgang. Wolfgangerl means "little Wolfgang"; it was one of his family nicknames such as "Woferl" or "Wolfi." It appears that he wrote the letter on some used music paper discarded by a friend, the composer Josef Mysliveček.

To his mother, in Salzburg (postscript)

Vienna, September 8, 1773

Wolfgangerl has no time to write because he has nothing to do, he paces around the room like a dog full of fleas.

Concerto
per violino obligato
è stromenti
del sig. giuseppe Misliwecek
detto il boemmo
= Baßo =

p.s. that's what it says on my writing pad.

In his last letter from this visit in Vienna, Wolfgang comes up with two different writing styles: the imperial chancellery style, complete with the imperial "we" used by princes and kings, and, in a second postscript, for his friend Heinrich von Heffner, an attempt at humorous rhyming. The note to Nannerl conveys the sad news that Dr. Franz Niderl, a family friend who came to Vienna for surgery, had died during the operation. Leopold Mozart, who was the same age as Dr. Niderl, was deeply affected by the death. Wolfgang, however, seems unable to get serious even

2. "Miss Bimbes" is Pimperl, the Mozarts' family dog, a female fox terrier.
3. Dr. Franz Anton Mesmer and Maria Anna Mesmer.
4. Johann Gottlieb Stephanie, Mozart's librettist for *Die Entführung* and *Der Schauspieldirektor.*

when the situation requires it. It could also be said that he often hides his true feelings in garbled language.

To his sister, in Salzburg (postscript)

Vienna, September 15, 1773

We are, Thank the lord, very well. And just this once we are taking time out to write to you, although there are many other matters to attend to. We hope that you, too, are in good health. Dr. Niderl's death has made us very sad, we can assure you, indeed we have wept, bawled, howled, and shed copious tears. Our regards to all good spirits who praise God the lord, and to all our goode friends. We remain graciously and favorably disposed to you.

> From our Residence in Vienna.
> Wolfgang.

To Herr von Hefner.
I hope we will still get to see you in Salzburg, my prizeless friend.
And I hope you are well and can see my predicament,
otherwise I'll buzz around you like a fly,
or love you as a bedbug.
So, then, let me advise you to write some better verse, *or*
I will visit the Cathedral in Salzburg no more,
for I am quite Capable to go
to Constantinople, a town all people know.
Afterward you won't see me and I won't see you, indeed,
but when the horses are hungry you give them oats to feed.
Farewell, my lad.   I will always endeavor
otherwise I'll go mad   to be yours now and forever.

After a brief stay in Salzburg, Wolfgang traveled on December 6, 1774, to Munich in order to stage his opera buffa La finta giardiniera. *He was accompanied by his father, who wrote back to Salzburg that the weather en route was so bitter cold that they had to use foot bags stuffed with hay to keep their feet from freezing. In Munich, Wolfgang developed a severe toothache (probably an abcess); for days, he had a badly swollen face and could eat only soup. In his dramatic announcement of his dental woes, he lists all of his baptismal names—including Amadeus, which he used very sparingly in his correspondence. "Freillibus" is his own latinization of "Fräulein" (Miss) and "S.P.D.," at the end of the note, is an abbreviation of the standard Latin formula "salutem plurimum dicit" (sends many greetings). The full text reads,* "I have a toothache. *Johannes Chrysostomus Wolfgangus Amadeus Sigismundus Mozartus sends many greetings to mother Maria Anna Mozart, and to sister, and to all the friends, and especially to pretty girls, and Fräuleins, and gracious Fräuleins."*

To his mother, in Salzburg (postscript)

Munich, December 16, 1774

Ich habe zahnwehe.

johannes chrisostomus Wolfgangus Amadeus Sigismundus Mozartus Mariae annae Mozartae matri et sorori, ac amicis omnibus, praesertimque pulchris virginibus, ac freillibus, *gratiosisque* freillibus

S.P.D.

In the following note Mozart once again asks Nannerl to act as go-between. The young lady in question is unknown. The departure Wolfgang is referring to is Nannerl's intended trip to Munich; she joined her father and brother for the premiere of La finta giardiniera, *which took place on January 13, 1775. The Mozarts enjoyed the opera and Munich's busy carnival season.*

To his sister, in Salzburg (postscript)

Munich, December 28, 1774

My dearest sister.

I beg you, don't forget to keep your promise before you leave, that is, to make a certain visit—for I have my reasons. Please convey my Compliments—but with real conviction—and great tenderneß—and—oh—well, I shouldn't worry so much, after all, I know my sister, tenderneß is her second nature; I know for sure that she will do all she can to do me this favor because she wants to know what's going on—I'm sorry, that was mean—let's quarrel about it in Munich. farewell.

To his sister, in Salzburg (postscript)

Munich, December 30, 1774

Please give my Compliments to Roxelana,[5] she is probably going to have tea this evening with the Sultan; and to Miss Mizerl[6] I send all sorts of regards, and tell her she must not doubt my love, I see her always before my eyes in her enchanting negligèe; indeed, I have seen quite a few pretty girls here, but I have not found a beauty such as hers.

My sister should not forget to bring the Variationes on the Menueto d'ecaudè by Ecart,[7] and my Variationes on the Menuet by Fischer.[8] Yesterday I was in the theater to see a comedy, "Mode nach der Haushaltung";[9] they performed it really well. My greetings to all good friends. I hope you will—fare well—I'll see you soon in Munich, I hope. . . . Adieu. I kiss mama's hands and that's how it stands. Keep warm on your trip, avoid the frost's nip, or you'll be sitting with a cold as the days unfold, behind a stove with shivers and sweat, and who will keep you from this dread? I don't want to get hot and talk more such rot, but just now on high I see lightenings in the sky. I remain always Your Munich. Brother, 1774th 30. Anno Decembre.

Mozart's following description of the premiere of La finta giardiniera *is rather touching because he usually does not write about his own successes. The remark about "how good it feels to breathe" is a cautious reference to the relative ease of life (and individual expression) in Munich as compared with the stifling atmosphere of Salzburg.*

5. "Roxelana" seems to have been some literary figure familiar to Wolfgang and Nannerl, perhaps from an oriental tale or play.
6. "Miss Mizerl" is Maria Anna Raab, the sixty-four-year-old landlady of the Tanzmeisterhaus, the Mozarts' new living quarters in Salzburg. Wolfgang is obviously having fun here at the expense of his new landlady.
7. "Ecart" is Johann Gottfried Eckard, a German composer living in Paris, who wrote variations on a minuet by André-Joseph Exaudet.
8. K. 179.
9. The play Mozart saw in Munich was not, as he writes, "The fashion according to the household" (Die Mode nach der Haushaltung), but "The household according to fashion" (Die Haushaltung nach der Mode). Just for fun, Mozart turned the title around.

To his mother, in Salzburg

Munich, January 14, 1775

Praise the Lord! My opera was performed yesterday, the 13th, and it was received so well that I can't possibly describe to Mama all the applause. First of all, the whole theater was so crammed full that many people had to be turned away. Then, after each Aria, there was a tumultuous storm of applause and shouts of "Viva Maestro." Her Highness, the Electress,[10] and the one who is widowed,[11] who were both sitting vis-à-vis from me, also called out bravo to me. Even at the end of the opera, when people usually quiet down until the ballet begins, there was nothing but clapping and shouts of bravo; it stopped for a while, then it started again, and so forth. After that I went with my papa to a certain room through which the Elector[12] and the entire court must pass, and there I kissed the hands of the Elector, the Electress, and the other highnesses all of whom were very gracious to me. Today, early in the morning, his princely Highness, the Bishop of Chiemsee,[13] sent me his congratulations saying that the opera was beyond comparison. As for our travel home, well, we're not in a hurry to come back, and Mama should not be impatient, for Mama surely knows how good it feels to breathe—we will be back soon enough. One other important reason is that next Friday the opera will be given again and I will be needed for its Staging—otherwise I might not recognize it anymore—strange things can happen here. I kiss Mama's hands 1000 times. My greetings to all good friends. Regards to Herr Andretter, and my apologies that I haven't answered him yet, but I had no time whatsoever, I'll write real soon. Adieu. 1000 smacks for Bimberl.

Mozart's last note from his 1774–75 trip to Munich is completely spurious, because it is addressed to his sister, who was at this time with him and his father in Munich. In other words, the note is really meant for his mother. It is a post-

10. Electress Maria Anna Sophie, wife of the elector (Churfürst) of Bavaria.
11. The elector's widowed sister.
12. Maximilian III, Joseph, elector of Bavaria.
13. Count Ferdinand Christoph Waldburg-Zeil, former dean of the cathedral in Salzburg. He was well disposed toward Mozart.

script to his father's letter, full of jokes and nonsense, particularly the date and signature: "franz v. Nasenblut. Mayland, den 5. May 1756" (the year, though not the
date, of Mozart's birth).

To his sister, in Salzburg (postscript)

Munich, January 18, 1775

My dear sister!

it isn't my fault that the clock has just struck a quarter past 7!—my
papa is not at fault either—all other things Mama will hear from my
sister. But traveling right now is not so great, because the Archbishop[14]
will not be here long—it is even said that he will stay only until he will
depart again.—I am only sorry that he won't be here for the first
Redoute.[15] My regards to Baron Zemen and to all good friends. I kiss
Mama's hands. farewell. I'll call for you very soon. Your faithful

Franz von Nosebleed.

Milan, May 5, 1756

The Mozarts returned to Salzburg on March 6, 1775. Wolfgang was nineteen now
and serving as a court musician and concertmaster in the orchestra of the archbishop, drawing a salary of 150 gulden a year. He remained in this employ for the
next two and a half years, honing his skills as pianist and violinist and writing
music. But he was also chafing at the bit, for he longed to be independent—and
away from Salzburg.

14. "The Archbishop" is Count Hieronymus Colloredo, prince archbishop of Salzburg.
15. "Redoute" is a festivity with dancing, here probably a masked ball.

PART TWO

IN SEARCH OF

INDEPENDENCE

1 7 7 7 – 1 7 8 1

The Journey to Mannheim

September 23, 1777–March 14, 1778

WHEN THE MOZART CARRIAGE rattled through Salzburg at six o'clock in the morning of September 23, 1777, on its way to Munich, Wolfgang Mozart, one of the passengers, was in the best of spirits. He was on the road again and ready to conquer the world. Surely there would be a prince, Maximilian III of Bavaria perhaps, or Karl Theodor of the Palatinate in Mannheim, who would wish to have him as Kapellmeister or court composer. After all, he had been to Italy and Vienna; he had written operas, masses, church sonatas, piano sonatas, and serenades. In 1775, within the space of eight months, he had composed four brilliant violin concertos; and in January 1777 he had produced his Piano Concerto in E-flat major, K. 271, a uniquely personal and passionate work inspired by Mademoiselle Jeunehomme, a French pianist. Young Mozart, who now called himself Wolfgang Amadé, had reasons to be optimistic.

The other passenger in the carriage was Wolfgang's mother, Maria Anna Mozart, who was taking the place of Leopold as Wolfgang's travel companion. Leopold, to his chagrin, had been compelled to stay in Salzburg or else lose his position as deputy Kapellmeister in the archbishop's orchestra. Wolfgang, although he had never been on the road without his father, was undaunted by this change. To the contrary, it gave him a chance to be "the secondt Papa" (*der anderte Papa*), as he wrote in his first letter back to Salzburg; and while Maria Anna had been sent along to take care of her son's personal needs, it was actually the twenty-one-year-old who felt empowered to take care of his mother. The journey to Munich, Augsburg, and Mannheim, planned by Leopold as a search for employment, turned out to be Wolfgang's journey into adulthood. Little did the young musician know that it would also become a journey of frustration and calamity, for the sixteen-month tour brought neither employment nor financial success, but brought instead the death of his mother.

The immediate goal was Munich and the court of Elector Maximilian III of Bavaria. Despite Mozart's impressive credentials and energetic efforts, the elector offered nothing but a shrug of his shoulders: "But my dear child, there is no vacancy." Next on the itinerary was Augsburg, an imperial city ruled by a merchant patriciate. It was Leopold Mozart's birthplace, but the city officials offered the same snubs and shrugs that Wolfgang knew from Munich. Only his eighteen-year-old cousin, Maria Anna Thekla Mozart, offered a more pleasing welcome. The two cousins obviously enjoyed each other; indeed, they seem to have had a rollicking good time. What has baffled readers and biographers, however, was not so much the two youngsters' fun and games in Augsburg, but Wolfgang's subsequent letters to his cousin, letters that have become notorious because of their, well, bathroom humor. The letters, known in German as the *Bäsle-Briefe* (letters to the little cousin), were cleansed and altered in early editions, if they were printed at all. When they were finally published in full, they were promptly psychoanalyzed and, most recently, subjected to medical diagnosis as possible evidence that Mozart suffered from Tourette's syndrome.[1] There is no question that Mozart's Bäsle letters are replete with bawdy language, but its usage is hardly a neurotic malfunction; rather, it was meant to be funny, and the cousin in Augsburg seemed an ideal partner for Wolfgang Amadé's natural silliness. The bawdy language served yet another purpose. As the frustrations increased during his difficult journey, the obscenities became a valve through which the young musician was able to release some of the mounting pressures.

The most voluminous and, in many ways, most important correspondence was that exchanged between Leopold and Wolfgang Mozart. The letters between father and son contain the essential personal and professional information, such as descriptions of travel routes, income and expenses, appointment schedules, compositions, and performances;

1. Tourette's Syndrome is a neurological disease characterized by involuntary facial tics, spasmodic body jerks, and uncontrollable eruptions of verbal obscenities. The medical research referred to is by Dr. Rasmus Fog of Denmark, Dr. Lars Gunne of Sweden, and Dr. Benjamin Simkin of California. See the bibliography.

they are also filled with messages of love, tears, and anger. In the beginning, the tone between father and son is jocular and jovial, even affectionate. Naturally, Leopold was deeply pained by his son's absence.
"What saddens me most," he wrote poignantly to Wolfgang, "is that I
can't hear you play Clavier or violin anymore." But as the journey wore
on with no practical success, Leopold became increasingly irritated,
suspicious, and dictatorial. Wolfgang, on the other hand, grew more and
more uncertain, confused, and ambivalent in his feelings toward his
father. In one important aspect, however, Wolfgang kept a steady pulse
of communication with his father: his thoughts about music. Although
fragmentary and often indirect, the comments are frequent and contain
the rudiments of his aesthetics.

Mannheim with its famous court orchestra was, initially at least, the
main destination of the Mozarts after Munich and Augsburg. The elector of the Palatinate, Karl Theodor, seemed encouraging at first, but
ultimately offered nothing more than the familiar shrug of the shoulders. So, after a long winter of fruitless waiting, Leopold declared that
Wolfgang and his mother were to go to Paris. Not the least reason for
this paternal decision was an affair of the heart. Wolfgang had met a
young singer in Mannheim, Aloysia Weber, who enchanted him with
her youth as well as her beautiful voice. Leopold, alarmed and angry,
reminded his son by express mail that the purpose of the journey was
"to find a steady and good appointment, or, if that should fail, go to a
place where good money can be made"; and in an emotion-packed letter, he practically shouted at his son: "Off with you to Paris!"

🕮 *Wolfgang Amadé and Maria Anna Mozart set out for Munich on September 23,*
1777. Before he could travel, Wolfgang had to get permission from the archbishop of
Salzburg, so he submitted the following petition. The letter was signed by Wolfgang
but written by Leopold, who was better versed in the convoluted style of eighteenth-
century court language.

To Prince Archbishop Count Hieronymus Colloredo, in Salzburg

August 1, 1777

Your Princely Grace
Most Worthy Prince of the Holy Roman Empire,
Most Gracious Ruler and Lord!

I shall not importune Your Princely Grace with a cumbersome description of our sad circumstances as my father has already detailed them in a petition humbly submitted to Your Princely Grace on March 14 in all honor and conscience and with every reason for truth. Since, however, the desired favorable decision from Your Princely Grace was not forthcoming, my father would have most submissively requested already in June that Your Grace kindly allow him a journey of several months in order to help our situation, if Your Grace had not graciously given orders that all members of the orchestra were required to hold themselves in readiness for the impending visit of His Majesty, the Emperor.[2] Still, my father submissively requested permission for travel, but Your Princely Grace refused him and graciously suggested that perhaps I, being employed only part-time, should travel alone. As our situation is urgent, my father resolved to send me off by myself. But then Your Princely Grace made some gracious objection to that resolution as well. Most Gracious Ruler and Lord! Parents make great efforts to enable their children to go out and win their own bread; they owe that to themselves and to the welfare of the state. And the more children are blessed with talent by God, the more they are obliged to make use of it and improve their own as well as their parents' lives, to help their parents and take their own progress and future in hand. The Gospel teaches us to take advantage of our talent. Therefore, before God and my conscience, I owe it to my father, who has untiringly given all his time for my education, to be thankful to him with all my strength, to ease his burden, and to take care of myself as well as my sister, for it would be a pity for her to have spent so many hours at the harpsichord without making good use of it.

Your Princely Grace, will You graciously permit that I ask Your

2. Emperor Joseph II of Austria, who had been on a visit to Paris under the pseudonym of Count Falkenstein and was now on his way back to Vienna via Salzburg.

Highness submissively for my discharge from service as I am forced to make use of the coming month of September in order to avoid the severe weather of the following cold months. Your Princely Grace will not, I trust, take this submissive request amiss, since Your Highness graciously declared already three years ago, when I sought permission to travel to Vienna, that I had nothing to hope for and would do better to seek my fortune somewhere else. I am grateful to Your Princely Grace in profoundest humility for all the high and gracious favors I have received, and in the most selfish hope that I can serve Your Princely Grace better and with greater approbation in my adult years, I commend myself to the highest favor and good will of

Your Princely Grace
Most Gracious Ruler
and Lord,
in greatest humility and obedience
Wolfgang Amade Mozart.

The archbishop granted Wolfgang's petition with a somewhat ironic remark: "Father and son have permission to seek their fortune elsewhere, according to the Gospel." Since this meant dismissal for both Mozarts with no financial support, Leopold decided to stay and reapplied for his position as deputy Kapellmeister. His application was accepted.

Wolfgang's first letter from the journey is from Wasserburg, on the Inn River. It is also his first letter ever to his father, without whom he had never traveled before. Wolfgang is obviously exuberant about leaving Salzburg, but he also wants his father to know that he is responsible and will look after his mother.

To his father, in Salzburg

Wasserburg, September 23, 1777

Mon trés cher Pére

We have arrived safely, God be thancked and praised, at Wagin, Stain, Ferbenthain,[3] and Wasserburg. Now for a little description of our

---

3. That is, Waging, Schign, and Frabersham.

trip. Right at the start, when we came to the city gate, we had to wait nearly a quarter of an hour until the gate was opened for us; they were doing some sort of work there. Before we arrived in Schinn we saw a herd of cows, and one of them was very Strange—she was *one-sided*, something we had never seen before.[4] When we finally got to Schinn, we noticed a coach that had stopped there and Ecce—our Positilion called out immediately—this is where we're going to change horses—all right with me, I said. Mother and I were talking when a stout gentleman came up to our carriage whose Sinfonie[5] was right away familiar to me—he was a merchant from Meiningen. He looked at me for quite a while, finally he said: you are Herr Mozart, aren't you? At your service. I know you, too, but not your name. I saw you a year ago in a concert at Mirabell.[6] Whereupon he revealed his name to me, but thanck the Lord, I have forgotten it. . . . At Wagin I was alone for a moment with the clergyman. He made big eyes. He had no idea about our situation. From Stain we had a Postiglion who was an absolutely dreadful phlegmaticus; Nota Bene, *as far as his driving was concerned.* We didn't think we would get to the next Post station anymore. Finally, we did arrive. (Mama is now already half asleep) N.B. while I'm writing this letter. From Ferbertshaim to Wasserburg everything went well. Viviamo come i Principi.[7] we lack nothing but Papa, ah well, it is god's will. all will turn out well in the end. I hope Papa is in good spirits and as cheerful as I am; I am quite well adjusted to it all. I am the secondt Papa; I'm looking after everything. In fact, I am insisting on paying the Postiglions, after all, it's easier for me to talk to these fellows than it is for Mama. In Wasserburg, at the Hotel Stern, the service is beyond compare. I am sitting here like a Prince. Half an hour ago, (Mama was just in the t-let) the porter knocked at the door, well, he was curious about all sorts of things, and I answered him in full Earnestness, just the way I look in my Portrait.[8] I must close now; Mama is undressed already. We both beg Papa to take good care of his health, not to go out too early, not to let himself get

---

4. The "one-sided cow" is probably a cow that stood perfectly still and parallel to the road.
5. Mozart writes "Sinfonie," but what he means is "face."
6. The summer residence of the archbishop of Salzburg.
7. "We live like princes."
8. The mocking reference to "my Portrait" is to a painting by an unknown artist, which Leopold had commissioned in 1777 for Padre Martini in Bologna. Young Mozart is shown in that portrait as a Chevalier of the Golden Spur; he looks old beyond his years and, indeed, deadly serious. See facsimile plate no. 7.

upset, to have a good laugh and be merry and always remember, joyfully, as we are doing, that the Mufti H. C.[9] is an ass, but god is gracious and loving. I kiss Papa's hands 1000 times, and embrace my sister the Canaglie,[10] as often as I have taken—snuff today.

<table>
<tr><td>P.S. my pen is coarse
and I am not polite.

Wasserburg, 23 sept[ber]. 1777.
undecima hora nocte tempore.[12]</td><td>I believe I forgot my diplomas
at home?[11] —Please send them
soon. Early in the morning at
half past six. 24th sept[br]
Most obedient son
    Wolfgang Amadé Mozart</td></tr>
</table>

The departure from Salzburg may have cheered Wolfgang, but it was a traumatic event for his father and sister. Nannerl wrote in her diary that she got sick to her stomach and spent the rest of the day in bed. Leopold described his bewilderment in a letter to Maria Anna: "In my stupor I forgot to give my son my fatherly blessing. I ran to the window and sent my blessings after you both, but I did not see you drive through the gate." It is the beginning of a lonely and painful time for Mozart's father. The image of Leopold standing at the window trying to catch a glimpse of the carriage going through the city gate (probably the Klausentor) and mumbling a blessing is quite moving.

Wolfgang's first letter from Munich is long, detailed, and affectionate. Wolfgang seems to understand his father's pain about having to remain in Salzburg, for at the end of the letter he calls him "My most cherished Papa."

To his father, in Salzburg

Munich, September 26, 1777

Mon trés cher Pére.

We arrived safely in Munich on the 24th in the evening at half past 4 o'clock. What was new to me was that we had to drive to Customs

---

9. The "Mufti H. C." is Archbishop Hieronymus Colloredo.

10. "My sister the Canaglie" (*canaille* means "riffraff" in French); it is Wolfgang's brotherly way of being sweet to Nannerl.

11. Wolfgang's diplomas from the academies of Bologna and Verona.

12. "Eleven o'clock at night."

right away, accompanied by a grenadier with a fixed bayonette. The first familiar person we saw while we were still driving into the city was Sig.ʳᵉ Consoli[13] who recognized me right away and was exceedingly happy to see me; he came to visit the very next day. I cannot fully express Herr Albert's[14] joy in seeing me; he is a thoroughly Sincere Man and such a good friend. After our arrival I played the Clavier until it was time to eat. Herr Albert had not come home yet, but after he came we wendt downstairs to have supper together. . . .

Today, Friday, the 26ᵗʰ, I went to see Count Seeau[15] at half past 8 o'clock; here is what happened: I walked into his house and Mad. Nießer, the Actress, was just coming out and said to me, you probably want to see the count? Yes! He is still in his garden, god knows when he'll get back. I asked her where the garden was, she said, I need to see him also, so let's go together. We had hardly gone outside the gate, when the count came toward us, and he was about 12 paces away when he recognized me and called out my name. He was very courteous and knew already what had happened. We walked up the stairs just the two of us, slowly, and I told him briefly what was on my mind. He said I should straight away request an audience with his Highness, the Elector, but should I not be able to get through to him, put my case before him in writing. I begged him to keepe all of this private—he promised. When I said to him that a really good Compositeur was lacking here, he said: I am well aware of it! After that I went to see the Bishop of Chiemsee and spent half an hour with him. I told him the whole storie; he promised to do his best for me in this matter. He was going to Nümpfenburg[16] at 1 o'clock and promised to speak with her Highness, the Electress. . . .

I am truly in the best of spirits. Ever since I left that Chicanery in Salzburg, my heart feels as light as a feather.—I have also gotten fatter. Herr von Wallau talked to me at the theater today, and I went to the loge of Countess Laroso and paid my respects. Now I have to leave a

---

13. Tommaso Consoli, a castrato at the Munich court theater, who had sung in Mozart's Munich performance of *La finta giardiniera* and in *Il rè pastore* in Salzburg.

14. Franz Joseph Albert, proprietor of the inn Zum schwarzen Adler, 19 Kauffinger Straße, in Munich (the inn is no longer in existence).

15. Count Joseph Anton von Seeau, privy councillor, who was also manager of opera and drama at the Munich court.

16. "Nümpfenburg" is the castle of Nymphenburg, summer residence of the elector of Bavaria.

little room for Mama. Please give our salutations to our highly Distinguished Compagnie of Marksmen from three of its members, that is from Mama, me, and Monsieur *Novac*[17] who comes to Albert's every day. Farewell in the meantime, my Most Cherished Papa; I kiss your hands countless times, and to my sister, the Canaglie, I give a hug.

Wolfg. Amadé Mozart

Wolfgang's letter includes a postscript from his mother, whose writing is amazingly similar in style, humor, and grammar to Wolfgang's: "We lead a charming life, early to rise, late to bed, all day we have visitors. We live a life of princely clout/until the knacker comes to put it out. adio ben mio. stay well in body and mind/and try to kiss your own behind./I wish you a good night/shit in your bed with all your might,/it's already past one, so now you can make your own rhymes."

Wolfgang liked it in Munich and wanted to stay. His efforts to gain some kind of appointment at court were tireless. But while the court was cool and political— political in the sense that Elector Maximilian probably did not wish to annoy the archbishop of Salzburg by offering Mozart a position—Franz Joseph Albert, who was known in Munich as the "learned innkeeper," came up with all sorts of schemes to keep Mozart in Munich.

To his father and sister, in Salzburg (postscript)

Munich, September 29, 1777

I was at Count Seau's yesterday at half past 10 o'clock and found him much more serious and not quite as open as the first time. But it only seemed that way. Then today I was at Prince Zeil's[18] who told me, in all politeness, the following: I believe there is not much we can do. I have spoken privately with the Elector at table in Nümphenburg; he said to me: it's still too early, let him travel a while, let him go to Italy and make a name for himself, I refuse him nothing, but now is too early.

---

17. "Our highly Distinguished Compagnie of Marksmen" refers to a group of family friends who were regulars in the game of target shooting at the Mozart residence in Salzburg. M. Novac seems to have been a member of the group.
18. The bishop of Chiemsee.

So, there we have it. Most of these bigwigs have such an insane obsession with Italy. However, he also advised me to go to the Elector anyway and put my case before him. I talked with Herr Wotschicka[19] secretly at table today; and he said I should come tomorrow at 9 o'clock, he will get me an audience for sure. . . . I like it here. I am of the opinion, as are many of my good friends, that if I stayed a year or two I could gain income and respect through my work, and the court would more likely come after me rather than me going after them. Ever since I came here, Herr Albert has had in mind a Project that seems, as far as I am concerned, not impossible to carry out. He would get 10 good friends together who would each contribute a Ducat per Month, that makes 10 Ducats a Month or 50 gulden, or 600 gulden a year.[20] If I could get just 200 gulden a year from Count Seau, that would make 800 gulden.—now how does Papa like such an idea?—is it not a sign of true friendship?—and wouldn't it be acceptable if indeed it would become a serious thing?—I am completely happy with the plan; I would be living near Salzburg, and if you, My dearest Papa, had the urge to leave Salzburg, as I wish with all my heart, and live your life in Munich, it would be such a jolly and easy thing to do. We had to live on 504 gulden a year in Salzburg, so we could certainly live in Munich on 600 or 800 gulden.—

🜲 *Second postscript:*

Today, the 30th, I went to court at 9 o'clock as I had agreed with Monsieur Wotschicka. Everybody was there and dressed for the hunt. Baron Kern was the officiating chamberlain. I would have gone there already yesterday evening, but I didn't want to hurt the feelings of Herr Wotschicka, who had come to me on his own and offered to make it possible for me to speak with the Elector. At 10 o'clock he took me to a narrow little room where his Highness, the Elector, must pass through to hear Mass before the hunt. Count Seau walked by and greeted me quite cordially: at your service, my dear Mozart. When the Elector came, he walked up to me and I said: With your Highness's permission,

19. Franz Xaver Wotschitka, a cellist in the court orchestra and personal valet of the elector.
20. Mozart gets a bit carried away in his calculations; normally a ducat was worth only 4½ gulden.

may I humbly lay myself at your feet and offer you my services? Well now, so you are gone from Salzburg for good? yes, Your Highness, for good. But why? did you have a quarrel with him?[21]—Not at all, your Highness, I only requested permission to travel, but he refused it; so I was forced to take this step; although I had wanted to leave anyway for quite some time. Salzbourg is no place for me; no, absolutely not! My god, what a young Man! but your father is still in Salzbourg?—Yes, Your Highness, and he too throws himself most humbly, Etc. I have been to Italy Three Times, have written 3 operas, I am a Member of the accademie of Bologna, I had to take a Test at which many maestri had to work and sweat 4 to 5 hours, but I did it in one hour. That may serve as proof that I am able to serve at any court. But my one and only wish is to serve Your Highness, who himself is a great—But my dear child, there is no vacancy. I am sorry, if only there were a vacancy. I can assure Your Highness, I would bring great Honor to Munich. Yes, but it's of no use; there just isn't any vacancy. He said this as he was walking away already. I then commended myself to his good graces. Herr Wotschicka advised me to make myself a bit more visible around the Elector. . . .

Now I beg you to take real good care of your health, I kiss Papa's hands 100 000 times, I am and remain

your most obedient son
Wolfgang Amadé Mozart

Third postscript:

P.S. Ma trés chere soeur,
next time I'll write
a letter just for you.
My greetings to A. B. C. M. R. and
other such letters. Addio.
Some fellow built a house here and wrote on it:

---

21. Mozart quotes this phrase in Bavarian dialect, "häbts eng z'kriegt?" *(habt Ihr Euch zerstritten?)* and thereby adds color and personality to the otherwise colorless elector.

When I built my house, I was very glad,
when I knew its cost, I got very sad.
(During the night somebody scribbled right under it):

Building a house takes a lot of loot,
and you should have known it, you nincompoop.

To his father, in Salzburg

Munich, October 2, 1777

Yesterday, October 1st, I was again at Count Salern's house,[22] and today, the 2nd, I even had dinner there. I played a lot these 3 days; and I enjoyed it. . . . I played quite a bit from memory at Count Salern's these last 3 days, I did the 2 Cassations I wrote for the countess[23] and at the end the finalmusick with the Rondeau,[24] all from memory. You cannot imagine how delighted Count Salern was: he certainly knows his Musique because he kept saying Bravo when other gentlemen would take a pinch of snuff—blow their nose, clear their throat—or start a conversation—I told him, I only wished the Elector were present so he could hear me play—he knows nothing about me; he doesn't know what I can do. Why do these gentlemen always believe others, but don't want to find things out for themselves. *It's always that way.* I would be glad to put it to a Test. Let him bring on all the Composers from Munich, he can even invite some from Italy and France, Germany, England, and Spain; I am willing to compete with any one of them. I told the count what I had done in Italy and asked him to mention this whenever people were talking about me. He said: I have very little influence, but what I can do, I will do gladly, and with all my heart. He, too, is of the opinion that, if I could stay here for a while, things would work themselves out. For me alone it would not be impossible to manage because I would probably get at least 300 gulden from Count Seau; about meals I wouldn't have to worry because I get invited out a lot and whenever I didn't, Albert would be delighted to have me at his table. I

22. Count Joseph Ferdinand Maria Salern, former director of music and opera in Munich.
23. The two cassations to which Mozart refers are the Divertimentos K. 247 and 287, which he dedicated to Countess Antonia Lodron.
24. The "finalmusik with the Rondeau" is probably Divertimento no. 11, K. 251.

eat very little, drink water and only at the end of the meal a small glass of wine with my fruit. I would set up a Contract with Count Seau (all this is on the advice of my friends) that would look something like this: to write 4 German operas a year, some of them buffo, some seria; and I would get the income of one benefit performance for myself;[25] that is, after all, the custom. That alone would bring me at least 500 gulden, which would be, with my salary, 800 gulden, but probably more. Because Reiner, the Actor and singer, took in 200 gulden on his benefit night and I am *very popular* here; and just imagine how much more popular I would become if I helped build up the German National Music Theater?—I have no doubt that I could really do something like this. My enthusiasm for composing was already fired up by simply attending a German singspiel here. The name of the Leading singer is Keiserin; she is the daughter of a cook and a count. a very pleasant girl; good-looking on stage, but I haven't seen her up close; she was born here. when I heard her sing she had been on stage only for the third time; she has a beautiful voice; not strong but not weak either; very pure, with good intonation. . . .

Postscript to his own letter:

Today at 8 o'clock in the morning I visited Count Seau; I made it very brief and said only: I have come, Your Excellenz, to explain myself and my situation to you. The suggestion has been made that I should travel to Italy. Well, I've been in Italy for 16 Months, I have written 3 operas, everybody knows that. and I did other things which your Excellenz can read in these papers. I showed him my *Diplomata.* I share and say all this to Your Excellenz only in case there is any talk about me and any injustice done to my name, so your Excellenz can take my side with confidence. He asked me whether I was now headed for France, I said, I want to stay in Germany for right now. But he understood *Munich* and said laughing with delight: oh, so you are staying on here? I said no, I would have liked to stay; and to tell the truth, I would have

25. Mozart is referring to the custom, prevalent at the time, of giving the receipts of one peformance to the composer.

liked to get some financial support from the Elector just so I could present a composition to Your Excellence without any further reward; to do that would have been a pleasure for me. He tipped his cap when I said that. . . .

Afterwards I lunched with the Brancas. Privy Councillor von Branca had been invited by the French ambassador and was, therefore, not at home; one addresses him as "Your Excellence." His wife is French. she speaks almost no German. I spoke French with her all the time I was there, and I spoke with great élan. She told me that my French was not bad at all, and that I had the good habit of speaking slowly and thereby made myself easily understood. She is a great lady, with most pleasant manners. . . . Tomorrow we're going to have a little schlackademie[26] just for ourselves, with that Wretched Clavier, nota bene! auweh! auweh! auweh![27] Now I wish you a restful night and to feel better a good wish, to hear healthy hope that completely is the Papa. I your pardon beg for my writing terrible hand, but also for Inck, Hurrydness, Sleep, Dream, just about everything.—I my Papa kiss with handkiss gracefulness, with dearest 1000 times, and my heart with all embrace, sister of my Canaglie, and I remain from now until Eternity, amen

Wolfgang most obedient your
Amadé Mozart son.

🖎 *Josef Mysliveček, Wolfgang's Bohemian composer friend, whom he had met in Bologna and Milan, was in Munich to be treated for venereal disease. Mozart's hesitation to visit him at the hospital has to be understood in light of the fact that venereal disease was as scary in the eighteenth century as AIDS is in our time; besides, Mysliveček was disfigured, because the doctors had burned off part of his nose. He suggested that Mozart go back to Italy, possibly to Naples. Given his lack of success in Munich, it is not surprising that Mozart was interested.*

---

26. "Schlackademie" is Mozart's fun word for academy, i.e., a musical get-together, in this case a group of musicians having a musical session at Albert's. Mozart played his Piano Concerto in E-flat ("Jeunehomme"), K. 271, and the violin parts of his Divertimentos K. 287 and 254. "I played," he wrote subsequently to his father, "as if I were the greatest fiddler in all of Europe."
27. *Auweh* is a German expression of pain, sometimes used mockingly. It has the same origin and function as the Yiddish *oy vay.*

To his father, in Salzburg

Munich, October 11, 1777

Mon trés cher Pére!

Why I haven't written about Misliwececk until now?—because I was glad that I didn't have to think about him—every time when people told me about him, they also told me how much he is always praising me and what a good and true friend he is! Put that together with my feeling of sympathy and pity for him; and then they described him to me; I was so beside myself, I didn't know what to do. . . . Then I resolved to go and see him. I went to the director of the Herzogsspital the day before and asked him whether he could arrange it so I could visit Misliwetcek in the garden, because although everybody tells me, including the doctors, that I couldn't be infected, I still did not want to see him in his room; it's very small and smells terribly. The doctor agreed with me entirely and told me that he usually strolled in the garden between 11 and 12 o'clock. . . . When he came up to me, I took him by his hand and he took mine, in friendship. Just look, he said, how unfortunate I am! His words and and his appearance, which Papa knows already from earlier descriptions, touched me so deeply that I couldn't say anything, except, half crying: my dear friend, I feel for you with all my heart. . . .

I've been told that Misliwetcek gets very puzzled when they talk here of Beeché[28] or other such Clavier virtuosi; he always says that no one should feel superior, for no one plays like Mozart. In Italy, where the greatest masters are, they talk of no one but Mozart. When his name is mentioned, they all fall silent. He says he could write a letter to Naples whenever I want him to; but the sooner, the better. But before I do anything, I want to hear what that very wise Hofkapellmeister, Herr von Mozart, has to say about it. The thing is I have an inexpressible desire to write an opera again; . . . it would make me so happy because it gives me something to Compose which is my real joy and Passion. . . . whenever I hear people talk about an opera, whenever I'm in the theater and just hear the tuning of the instruments—oh, I get so excited, I'm totally beside myself. . . .

28. Notger Ignaz Franz von Beecke, pianist and composer, with whom Mozart had a piano competition at Albert's inn in 1775-76, at the time of the premiere of *La finta giardiniera.*

🔖 *Postscript to his own letter:*

A certain Court Councillor Effele[29] is sending his humblest Regards to Papa. He is one of the best court councillors here and could have made chancellor long ago, if it wasn't for one thing: the bottle. When I saw him for the first time at Albert's, I thought, and so did Mama, Ecce! what a perfect Simpleton! Just imagine a very large man, strongly built, Corpulent, with a ridiculous face. When he walks across the room to greet people at other tables, he puts both his hands on his stomach, pushes in, then thrusts his whole body upward, produces a nod with his head, and when that is accomplished, he jerks his right foot backward; and he goes through all this motion anew for each Person. He says he remembers Papa for a thousand reasons. I'm now going to the Theater for a little while. I'll write more soon, today I can't write any more; my fingers are aching.

Wolfgang Mozart

🔖 *Wolfgang's letter contains two postscripts by his mother. Maria Anna tells her husband that she is busy packing and that she has to do it all by herself "since Wolfgang is not able to help me in the slightest." Wolfgang gets back at his mother—all in good fun—telling his father that he and his mother had been invited out to coffee, but instead of coffee she drank two bottles of Tyrolian wine. In her second postscript, Maria Anna complains, "I'm sweating that the water is running down my face with all this packing. The devil take all this traveling. I feel like shoving my feet into my mouth, that's how tired I am." Like her son, Maria Anna has a strong and colorful language, and she speaks her mind. While she was packing, sweating, and cursing, Wolfgang claimed his hands were hurting and he went to see a late show, a pantomine by the name of* Girigarikanarimanarischariwari.

🔖 *Wolfgang and his mother left Munich on October 11, 1777, at noon and arrived in Augsburg at nine o'clock that same evening. They took a room at the inn Zum weißen Lamm (The White Lamb), and immediately after their arrival Wolfgang*

---

29. "Hofrath Effele" is Court Councillor Andreas Felix Oefele, of whom Mozart gives a humorous description. The good councillor had a drinking problem and had suffered a stroke, but young Mozart saw primarily the theatrical possibilities.

was making a round of visits in his father's native town. First on his list was the city magistrate, Herr von Langenmantel.

To his father, in Salzburg (postscript)

Augsburg, October 14, 1777

Actually we did not make an error about the date of our departure;[30] the fact is we wrote to you before noon; I also think we'll be leaving again next friday, that is the day after tomorrow; just listen how grand and generous these noble Augspurgers are! Nowhere have I been honored with greater Distinction.[31] My first visit was to Herr Longotabaro,[32] the City Magistrate. My uncle,[33] who is a very sincere and amiable man, and a Respectable citizen, accompanied me and then had the honor of having to wait in the antechamber like a lackey until I would emerge again from my visit with the Arch-magistrate. I did not forget to convey, right at the beginning, the humblest greetings from Papa. He, graciously, remembered everything about you and then asked me: *how has the gentleman fared all this while?* I replied at once: very well, praise and thank the lord; and you?, I trust you have been in good health as well?—He began to be a little more polite and addressed me with "Sie";[34] I continued to address him with "Your grace," as I had done from the start. He then insisted that I come upstairs with him to visit his son-in-law[35] on the 3rd floor,[36] and my uncle had the honor of waiting all the while downstairs in the foyer. I had to control my temper with all my might, otherwise I would have said something, in all politeness. Upstairs, I had the honor of playing about ¼ of an hour on a good Clavicord by Stein[37] in the presence of his rather foppish son, the son's

30. Mozart is continuing a thought from his mother's letter.
31. Mozart is being sarcastic here.
32. "Longotabaro" is Mozart's own ironic rendering of the name Langenmantel (longcoat) of the city magistrate whose full name was Jakob Wilhelm Benedikt Langenmantel von Westheim and Ottmarshausen.
33. Mozart's uncle is Franz Alois Mozart, a bookbinder in Augsburg.
34. "Sie" is the polite form of address in German. Mozart's remark indicates that at the beginning the magistrate had addressed him as "Er" (He), i.e., in the third person, which was the customary address of a highborn to a lowborn.
35. Mozart seems to have made an error here; he probably means "son" rather than "son-in-law."
36. Mozart writes "2. Stock," which is "third floor" in American English.
37. Johann Andreas Stein was considered the best piano maker in Germany in the second half of the eighteenth century.

long-legged young wife, and the Simple-minded old lady of the house. I played some Phantasies and finally everything I could find there, prima vista.[38] Among other things I found some very nice pieces by a certain Edlmann. Afterward they were all exceedingly polite, and I was also very polite; after all, it is my habit to treat people just the way they treat me. It's best for everybody. I mentioned that I would visit *Stein* after lunch; so the young man of the house immediately offered to take me there. I thanked him for his courtesy and promised to be back in the afternoon at 2 o'clock. I came, and we went off together accompanied by his brother-in-law, who looks very much like a young student. Although I had asked them not to divulge who I was, Herr von Langenmantel thoughtlessly blurted out to Herr Stein: I have the honor of presenting to you a virtuoso on the Clavier, and he grinned. I immediately raised my voice in Protest and declared that I was only an unworthy pupil of Herr Sigl in Munich, from whom I was bringing 1000 greetings.—He shook his head—and then—finally: is it possible that I have the honor of seeing Herr Mozart before me?—Oh No, I replied, my name is Trazom, and here I have a letter for you. He took the letter and wanted to open it right away; but I didn't give him time to do it and said: why do you want to read the letter out here, why don't you open your door instead so we can go inside; I am very eager to see your Piano fortes. All right, then, if that's what you wish; but, still, I don't think I'm mistaken. He opened the door. I ran straight to one of the 3 Claviers that were in the room. I started playing; and he could hardly manage to open the letter, he was so eager to prove himself right; he read only the signature. Oh, he cried, and embraced me, crossed himself, made faces, and was absolutely delighted. I shall give you a report on his instruments later. He then took me to a Cofféhaus,—where, when I entered, I thought I would be blown backward from all the stink and smoke of Tobacco. But I had to put up with it for an hour, in god's Name. I accepted it all in good humor, although I thought I had come to Turkey. He then spoke with great enthusiasm about a certain Graf,[39] a Compositeur, and his flute concertos. He said, well now, that is something very special, and all the *exaggerated* things you hear people say. My

---

38. At sight.
39. Friedrich Hartmann Graf, music director in Augsburg and a highly regarded composer and flutist. Mozart obviously was not impressed.

head, hands, and my entire body were sweating I was so impressed by all this. This Graf is a brother of the two Grafs who live in The Hague and Zurich. Stein insisted on taking me to see him right on the spot. And what a Noble Gentleman he is indeed. He was wearing a dressing gown, which I wouldn't mind wearing in public; he pronounces his words as if they were sitting on stilts, and, for the most part, he opens his mouth before he knows what he wants to say—and sometimes it falls shut again without anything having emerged from it. He performed, after much coaxing, a concert for 2 flutes. I had to play the First violin. The concert was like this: not good for the ear; not natural; he often marches into his tones with too much—Heaviness; and everything was without the slightest bit of magic. When it was over, I paid him many compliments because he actually deserved it. The poor Fellow must have had plenty of trouble writing it all, he probably had to work on it quite a bit. At last, they brought out a Clavicord from a backroom, one built by Herr Stein, it was good, but full of dirt and dust. Herr Graf, who is music Director here, stood there like Someone who had always thought that he was somebody special in his Journey through music, and now finds out that somebody else can be even more special, and that without assaulting anyone's ears; in one word, they were all quite amazed. Now I must close, otherwise I will miss the Post which leaves already at 4 o'clock. In my next letter I will tell you more of my Augspurg storie. I kiss your hands 1000 times and remain

Wolfgang Mozart

Mozart's prose is full of dialogue and verbal gestures, and his first letter from Augsburg is no exception. The letter is of musical interest as well because it is the first time that Mozart uses the word "natural" to describe his idea of good music or music making. By "natural music" he means unexaggerated sound, clear structures, simple melodic lines, and a truly singing cantabile.

To his father, in Salzburg

Augsburg, October 16, 1777

Mon trés cher Pére.

As far as the daughter of War-Secretaire Hamm[40] is concerned, all I can say is that she must have some real talent for music because she has been studying it only for 3 years but already playes a number of pieces very well; but when I'm asked to give my impressions of how she plays, I don't know exactly how to put it—curiously stiff, that's how she seems to me—she stalks with her long bony fingers so oddly all over the Clavier; of course, she's never had a really good teacher, and if she stays in Munich she will never be what her father wants her to be; he would like her to become an outstanding Pianist. . . .

Let me finish as briefly as I can my Augspurg storie that I began last time. . . . First I must tell Papa that the young Herr von Langenmantel said, when we were together at Stein's, that he wanted to do everything possible to organize an concert for me at the *Stube*,[41] it would be something unusual for me that would bring me honor, he told me, and it would be only for the Patricians. . . . In the morning he sent me a message requesting that I come to his house at 11 o'clock and bring some music; he had invited a few members of the Orchestra, and they wanted to do a little music together. I sent something over right away, and I myself arrived there at 11 o'clock; but he gave me a lot of lame excuses and said, with an air of indifference, listen, the concert is off; oh, I myself was so annoyed about this yesterday, but the Patricians told me that their funds were very low, and that you are not the kind of virtuoso one can offer a mere souvrain d'or.[42] I grinned and said, I don't think so either. . . . Then he said to me, friendly-like, let's do something together today; let's go to the theater and then have supper here. We were all very jolly. When we came back from the theater, I played until it was time to eat, then we went to supper. He had asked me already in the morning about my cross.[43] I told him exactly what it was all about.

40. Maria Anna Josepha Aloysia von Hamm; she was Mozart's pupil in Munich and was thinking of taking lessons with Leopold in Salzurg. Leopold had inquired about her musical skills.
41. The *Stube* was a small concert hall opposite the city hall in Augsburg that was used by the patricians for their musical events. "Young Herr von Langenmantel" was the organizer of these musical events.
42. Approximately 12 to 13 gulden.
43. The "cross" is the Order of the Golden Spur, which Pope Clement XIV had conferred upon Mozart on July 5, 1770, in Rome. Mozart was very proud of the order and so was his father, who had in fact advised him to wear it especially in Augsburg.

He and his brother-in-law said repeatedly: we want to send away for such a cross so that we can be in one league with Herr Mozart. I paid no attention to them. They kept addressing me as "Sig. Cavalier," "Herr Spur." I said nothing. But during the soupée it got a bit too much for me. I wonder what it would cost? 3 Ducats—does one need permission to wear it?—does the permission cost anything? Let's send away for a cross. A certain Officer who was present, Baron Bach, said: Oh, phooey, you ought to be ashamed of yourselves, just what would you do with the cross? The young Ass von kurzenMantl[44] winked at him with his eyes. I saw it, he noticed; after that it was quiet for a little while. Then he offered me tobacco and said: there, take a pinch of snuff on it. I remained silent. Then he started again, full of mockery: so then, tomorrow, I'll send someone over to you and I hope you'll be good enough to lend me your cross for a short while. I'll return it to you promptly. All I want is to talk to the goldsmith about it; I'm sure if I ask him how much he would estimate its value, he will probably say (he is a very Funny Man) about one bavarian thaler[45] It can't be worth much more because, after all, it's not made of gold but of copper, Ha! Ha! I said, oh heavens no, it's made of tin. Ha! Ha! I was now getting hot under the collar with rage and Anger. But tell me, he said, if need be, could I leave off the spur?—Oh definitely, I said, you don't need a spur, you already have one in your head. I have one in my head as well, but there's certainly a difference, and I truly wouldn't want to exchange mine for yours. Here, take a pinch of snuff on that. . . . and I got up. Everybody rose in greatest embarrassment. I took my hat and sword[46] . . . *and left.* . . .

The other day, when young Herr von Langenmantel . . . told me that the Patricians are inviting me to their Concert next Thursday, I told him I would come just to listen. Ah, but will you give us the pleasure of playing something?—*well who knows, why not.* But now, after being so affronted the following evening, I decided not to go and have the entire Patrician lot kiss my ass, and then get out of here. . . . I am so sick of it all, I can't tell you. I will be so glad to get back to a place that has a Court! I can tell you this: if it weren't for such a great uncle and aunt, and such a dear cousin, I would have as many regrets about coming to

---

44. "kurzenMantl" (shortcoat) is Wolfgang's part whimsical, part angry translation of Langenmantel (longcoat).
45. Roughly 2 to 3 gulden.
46. The papal order had elevated Mozart to the rank of a knight with the privilege of wearing a sword.

Augsburg as I have hair on my head. Now I must tell you something about my dear Mademoiselle Bäsle.[47] But I will wait till tomorrow because one should be in a cheerful mood if one wishes to praise her as she deserves.

Today, the 17th, early in the morning, I write and declare that our Bäsle is pretty, sensible, charming, talented, and jolly; and that is because she's been out in the world a bit and even spent some time in Munich. The fact is, the two of us are just made for each other, because she too is a bit of a rascal. We both play tricks on people and have a jolly good time. . . . Next time I will tell you about Stein's Piano fortes, his organs, and about the concert at the "Stube." A goodly number of high Nobility was present: the Duchess Kickass, the Countess Pisshappy, also the Princess Smellshit with her 2 daughters, who are married to the 2 Princes of Mustbelly von Pigtail. Farewell, everyone, everywhere. I kiss Papa's hands 100 000 times and I embrace my sister, the canaglie, with the Tenderness of a bear, and I remain your obedient son,

Wolfgang Amadé Mozart

After first refusing to play at the Stube, Mozart finally did perform there, on October 16, 1777, and he also gave a public concert at Fugger Hall on the following day. But he never quite recovered from the insults he had received from the Langenmantels and at the end of his letter vents his anger in a sarcastic description of the Augsburg audiences. Mozart's German names are most imaginative: Duchess Kickass is "Ducheße arschbömerl," Countess Pisshappy is "gräfin brunzgern," and Princess Smellshit is "fürstin riechzumtreck."

The Mozart letter that follows, about piano making in the eighteenth century, is well known and much quoted. Johann Andreas Stein of Augsburg built the first pianoforte (or fortepiano) with an escapement action, and his pianos had a light touch that allowed great rapidity of action. Mozart's enthusiasm for the instrument is obvious. He concludes his fairly serious and factual letter with the description of a prank. Here the victim is Pater Aemilian Angermayr, professor of theology, whom Mozart judged pompous and ignorant—and therefore a good target for his ever-ready scatological humor.

47. Wolfgang's cousin, Maria Anna Thekla Mozart, the eighteen-year-old daughter of Franz Alois (Leopold's brother) and Maria Viktoria Mozart, with whom he had such a memorable time in Augsburg. The word *Bäsle* is Swabian and means "little female cousin."

To his father, in Salzburg

Augsburg, October *17, 1777*

Mon trés cher Pére!

Let me start right off with Stein's Piano forte. Before I had seen Stein's work, I favored Spät's Claviers.[48] But now I must give Stein's Claviers preference because they have a much better damper than the Regensburg instruments. If I strike the key hard, I may keep my finger down on it, or lift it up, the sound stops the instant I produced it.[49] No matter how I play the keys, the tone is always even. There is no jangling noise, the sound will not get louder, or softer, or stop altogether, in one word: everything remains even. It is true, he won't sell a Piano forte like this for under 300 gulden, but the effort and care he puts into the instruments is beyond any price. What distinguishes his instruments from all others is that they are built with an escapement. Not one in a hundred will bother about this, but without escapement action you cannot possibly have a Piano forte that will not have a clangy and vibrating after-effect. When you press down on the keys, the little hammers fall back the moment they have struck the strings, no matter whether you keep the keys down or release them. He told me himself that after he has finished a Clavier, he will first of all sit down and try all sorts of passages, runs and leaps, and then he goes on filing and fitting until the Clavier does everything he wants it to. He works truly for the Good of Musique, and not alone for profit, otherwise he would finish them much more quickly. He often says: if I were not such a Passionate lover of Musick and were not able to play a little on the Clavier myself, I would have long ago lost my patience for this kind of work. But I love instruments that are reliable and wear well. And indeed, his pianos really last. He guarantees that the soundboard will neither break nor crack. When he has finished a soundboard for a Clavier, he puts it outside and exposes it to the weather, to rain, snow, the heat of the sun, and all the Devils of hell, so that it will crack; he then inserts a wedge and glues it in to make it all strong and firm. He actually likes it when the wood cracks; it gives him the assurance that nothing else can happen to it. Sometimes he cuts into the wood himself, glues it together again, and

48. Franz Jakob Späth was a well-known piano maker in Regensburg.
49. Apparently Mozart meant "or lift it up and the sound stays the instant I do so."

thereby strengthens the whole thing. He has three Piano fortes finished; I just played them again today. . . .

At 4 o'clock the Herr Capellmeister came and then, shortly after, Herr Schmittbauer, the organist at St. Ulrich, a sweet and courteous old gentleman. I was just playing a sonata by Becché prima vista; it was quite difficult, miserable al solito.[50] I can't tell you how the Capellmeister and Organist kept crossing themselves. I have played my 6 sonatas[51] from memory several times both here and in Munich. The 5th, in G, I played in that fancy Stube-Academie,[52] the last one, the one in D,[53] sounds absolutely great on Stein's Piano forte. The device by which you control the action by pressing with your knee is so much more perfect in his pianos than in the instrument of anyone else. All I need to do is touch it, and it works instantly; and the moment you remove your knee even a little, there's not the slightest vibration of sound. Maybe tomorrow I'll be able to get to Stein's organs, I mean get *to tell you about them;* and then, at the very end, I want to write something about his little daughter. When I told Herr Stein I would love to try out his organ because organ playing was my real Paßion, he was a bit skeptical, and said: what? a man like you? such a great Clavierist, wants to play an instrument that has no *douceur,* [54] no Expression, no piano, no forte, but always sounds the same?—That makes no difference. The organ is in my eyes and ears the king of all instruments. Well, all right then. So off we went. I could tell from his comments that he believed I would not be able to do much with his organ; I would, for example, play it like a Clavier. . . . I said nothing but this: Herr Stein, do you really think I will just run hither and thither all over the organ?—Well, in your case it may be different. We got to the choire, I began a Praeludium, he broke into a broad smile; then I played a fugue. I can well believe it, he said, that you love playing the organ; when one plays like you. . . .

Afterward, we were all ushered, that is my mother, my cousin, and Herr Stein, into a guest lounge. A certain Pater Emilian, a conceited ass and simpleminded clerical wag, was there, full of sweetness. He wanted

---

50. Wretched as usual.
51. The "6 sonatas" Mozart says he played in Munich and Augsburg are his first piano sonatas, nos. 1–6, K. 279–284, which he had composed in Munich between January and March 1775 at the age of eighteen and nineteen.
52. K. 283.
53. K. 284.
54. Gentle action.

to flirt with Bäsle, but she instead had her fun with him—but when he got tipsy, which happened very quickly, he was getting into Musick. He sang a Canon and said, in all my life I have never heard anything more beautiful. I told him I was sorry but I couldn't sing along with him, because Nature had not endowed me with the gift of carrying a tune. That doesn't matter, he declared. He started the canon, I was third in line to sing. But I sang a whole different text: "P. E., oh you prick, why don't you kiss my ass." I sang it *sotto voce*[55] to my Bäsle. We were laughing for half an hour. Then he said to me, if we only could stay together a little longer. I would love to discuss composition with you. Well, I said, that would be a very short discussion. *Swallow that, you imbecile!* To be continued soon.

W. A. Mozart.

Mozart's two concerts in Augsburg were artistic successes—the reviews were excellent—but they brought in only 10 gulden and 90 gulden, respectively, not enough to please Papa in Salzburg. Of particular interest in this letter are two descriptions of music making. One is Mozart's mocking description of Nanette Stein's piano playing as a child, which says, in effect, "Put your strength and expression in your fingers, not in your arms, body, and face." The other describes his own playing. Mozart talks about his improvisations as if they were live beings. For instance, instead of writing that he was improvising, he says he took a theme "for a walk" (ich führte es spazieren) and returned it "assbackwards" (arschling); and one of his musical figures is a "merry little thing" (das scherzhafte wesen). It is an endearing characteristic of Mozart that he describes music in nontechnical language and relates it to human activities.

To his father, in Salzburg (postscript to his own letter)

Augsburg, October 23–25, 1777

. . . Last Sunday I went to Mass at Holy Cross Church. At 10 o'clock, this was on the 19th, I went to Herr Stein's house. We rehearsed a couple of Sinfonies for the Concert; then I lunched with my uncle at the Holy Cross Convent. While we were at table, they played some Musique for us; their fiddles were pretty bad, but, as bad as they were,

---

55. Softly.

I still prefer the Musique in the convent to that of the Augspurg orchestre. We did a sinfonie and then I played the violin Concerto in B by Vanhall;[56] everyone applauded. The Herr Dechant is a nice and convivial man, he is a cousin of Eberlin, his name is *Zeschinger*.[57] He says he remembers Papa well. In the evening, at supper, I played my Strasbourg Concerto.[58] It went like oil. Everyone praised my beautiful, pure tone. Then they brought in a small Clavichord. I played a Praeludium, after that a sonata and my Fischer Variazionen.[59] Somebody whispered into the Dechant's ear that he should really hear me play in the organ style; so I asked him to give me a theme, he didn't want to, but one of the clergymen did. I took the theme for a walk, then in the middle of it— the fugue was in g minor—I changed it to major and came up with a very sprightly little tune, but in the same tempo, then I played the theme again, but this time assbackwards; in the end, I wondered whether I couldn't use this merry little thing as a theme for the fugue?—Well, I didn't stop to inquire, I just went ahead and did it, and it fit so well as if it had been measured by Daser.[60] The Herr Dechant was quite beside himself with joy. You have done it, that's all I can say, I would not have believed what I just heard, what a man you are. . . .

Apropós Herr Stein's little girl.[61] Whoever can see and hear her play the piano without laughing must be like her father—made of *Stone*.[62] You must not place yourself in the middle of the piano, but way up at the trebles, for in this way you have a better chance of flinging your body around and making all sorts of grimaces. You roll your *eyes* and smirk. When a passage occurs twice, you play it slower the 2nd time; if it comes around a 3rd time, you play it slower still; and when playing a Passage you must lift your arm as high as as you can, and if the Passage requires emphasis, the arm and not the fingers must do this and do it

56. Johann Baptist Vanhal, a Bohemian composer and music teacher who lived in Vienna.
57. P. Ludwig Zöschinger, deacon of the Holy Cross Convent, was a composer in his own right; he and Johann Andreas Stein were practically the only positive musical contacts Mozart had in Augsburg.
58. The "Strasbourg Concerto" is usually identified as Mozart's Violin Concerto no. 4 in D major, K. 218, but according to the musicologist Dénes Bartha it is actually the Concerto no. 3 in G major, K. 216 (Zaslaw, *The Compleat Mozart*, 141).
59. "Twelve Variations on a Theme by Johann Christian Fischer," K. 179.
60. Johann Georg Daser was a tailor in Salzburg.
61. Nanette Stein was a prodigy pianist in Augsburg. After her father's death, she carried on the family piano business; she later married the piano maker Johann Andreas Streicher and moved to Vienna.
62. "Stone," in German, *Stein*, as in Johann Andreas Stein.

with great purpose and heaviness. . . . She is eight and a half years old and she is now learning everything by heart; she has a chance of getting somewhere, for she has real talent; but she won't succeed if she continues this way, she simply won't get the necessary rapidity, because she does everything she can to make her hand heavy. She will never be able to get what is most essential and difficult and the principal thing in Musique: the right tempo, for she has, since her earliest youth, completely neglected to play in time. Herr Stein and I have talked at least 2 hours about this very point. I have pretty much convinced him. He now asks my advice in everything; he used to be very taken by Becché, now he sees and hears that I can do better than Becché, and that I am not making any grimaces when I play, and yet I play with much expression; and no one—these are his words—has ever played his Piano forte as well as I have, and, besides, I always keep correct time. They are all wondering about that. They simply can't believe that you can play a Tempo rubato in an Adagio, and the left hand knows nothing about it but goes on playing in strict time. As far as they know, the left hand always follows the right. . . .

What does Papa think came right after the Sinfonie?—The Concerto for *3 pianos*:[63] Herr *Demler* played the first, I played the second, and Herr *Stein* played the third piano. Then I did something alone, I played the last sonata, in D, the one I wrote for Dürnitz,[64] after that my Concerto in B♭,[65] then again alone and in organ style: a fugue in C minor, and suddenly a Magnificent sonata in C major popped right out of my head with a Rondeau at the end.[66] There was a regular uproar and tremendous applause. . . . The 24 oct. 1777 augusta vindelicorum.[67]

Wolfgang Amadé Mozart

. . . Tomorrow we'll travel to Wallerstein straight as ——> an arrow. I think it'll be best if Papa continues to send his letters to my uncle until we stay put long enough in one place but, mind you, not in jail.[68]

---

63. K. 242.
64. K. 284.
65. Piano Concerto no. 6 in B-flat, K. 238.
66. The "Magnificent sonata in C major" is most likely the Piano Sonata in C major, K. 309, which Mozart completed in Mannheim.
67. The original name of Augsburg as a Roman fortification.
68. This is another Mozartian pun. He writes in German, "bis wir einmahl in einem ort sizen bleiben. aber nicht in Arrest, versteht sich." *Sitzen* means to sit or stay but also to be locked up in jail.

My dear Bäsle, who sends regards to both of you, is not at all a *Pfaffenschnitzl.* [69] Yesterday she dressed up in the French fashion just to please me. She was 5 per cento more beautiful. Addio for now. I kiss Papa's hands once again, I embrace my sister and send greetings to all my goode friends, and now I'll go to the privy, and try to shit in a jiffy, and I remain the same old anus, Wolfgang et Amadeus Mozartianus, augspurg, the 25th octoberani, 1700 and seventy-seven anni.

The Mozarts left Augsburg on October 26 and arrived in Mannheim on October 30, 1777, at six o'clock in the evening. They took quarters at the Pfälzischer Hof (The Palatine Court). Their travel had taken them through some of the most charming hill country in southwest Germany—Donauwörth, Nördlingen, Hohenaltheim, Schwäbisch Gmünd, Schwetzingen, Mannheim—but Mozart says nothing about the scenic beauty along the way. As in his earlier years, when he traveled to Italy, he seems to have been oblivious to the landscape outside his coach.

To his father, in Salzburg (postscript)

Mannheim, October 31, 1777

Please accept my mediocrity as well. [70] Today I went with Herr Danner [71] to see Monsieur Canabich. [72] He was extremely polite. I played something for him on his piano forte, a very good instrument. Then we went to rehearsal together; when I was introduced to the people there, I thought I wouldn't be able to keep from laughing; some, who knew me by reputation, were very courteous and respectful; but others, who didn't know anything about me, stared at me with big eyes and a certain sneer. They probably think because I am so small and young, nothing of greatness and class can come out of me; but they shall soon find out. Tomorrow, Herr Canabich will take me to Count Savioli, [73] the Director

---

69. Mozart is defending Bäsle against Leopold's insinuations that she was altogether too friendly with the Augsburg clergy. He called her "Pfaffenschnitzl," which might be freely translated as "a tasty morsel for a priest." It turns out that Leopold was right: in 1784 Maria Anna Thekla gave birth to an illegitimate child whose father was an Augsburg clergyman.

70. Mozart is continuing the sentence his mother had written to Leopold: "today you'll have to be content with 'little old me.'"

71. Christian Danner was a young violinist in the Mannheim orchestra.

72. Christian Cannabich was a violinist and concertmaster of the orchestra.

73. Count Louis Aurèle de Savioli, manager of the orchestra.

of Musique here. It's a very good thing that the Name Day of the Elector is coming up just now.[74] The oratorium they were rehearsing is by Händl;[75] but I didn't stay, because they were first rehearsing a Psalm, a Magnificat, by *Vogler,* [76] the Vice-Kapellmeister of the orchestra here; and that took nearly an hour. Now I must close because I still have to write to my Baasle. I kiss Papa's hands, and I embrace my love of a sister without muss or fuss, in whatever way it's possible.

+ Joannes Chrisostomus **sigismundus

Wolfgang gottlieb Mozart

Today is my Name Day!   ** This is my confirmation name!

+ My birthday is on 27 January!

Between October 1777 and October 1781, Mozart wrote twelve letters to his cousin at Augsburg, Maria Anna Thekla, whom he calls Bäsle. Nine of these so-called Bäsle-Briefe *have survived and appear in this volume.*

To Maria Anna Thekla Mozart, in Augsburg

Mannheim, October 31, 1777

That's so strange! I'm supposed to write something sensuble, but nothing sensuble comes to my mind. Don't forget to remind Herr Dechant to send me the Music soon.[77] And don't forget your Promise; I certainly won't forget mine. How could you have doubted it, very soon I'll write to you a letter all in French, which you can have yourself translated by the Postmaster;[78] I hope you have already begun to learn some? well, now I don't have enough space left to write anything sensible, besides to be always sensible gives you a Headache. Anyway, this letter is already crammed full with sensible and learned Things; if you have finished reading it, you'll have to admit as much, and if you haven't read it yet, then I beg you to read it forthwith; you will gain much Profit from it, some lines will make you shed bitter Tears.

74. The elector is Karl Theodor, whose name day was on November 4.
75. "Händl" is George Frideric Handel, and the "oratorium" being rehearsed was part 1 of *The Messiah*.
76. Abbé Georg Joseph Vogler was the deputy Kapellmeister of the court orchestra.
77. Mozart is referring to some handwritten compositions (e.g., the two masses K. 192 and K. 220) that he had lent to Herr Zöschinger, the music-loving deacon of the Holy Cross Convent in Augsburg.
78. Mozart writes *Forstmeister* (forester), presumably meaning *Postmeister* (postmaster).

📖 *The Mannheim court orchestra was famous throughout Europe for its disciplined and dynamic playing. The orchestra had been founded by Johann Wenzel Stamitz, a Czech violinist and composer, and continued by his sons Carl and Anton Stamitz. One of the reasons Mozart had wanted to come to Mannheim was to hear the orchestra perform.*

Mozart to his father, in Salzburg

Mannheim, November 4, 1777

Monsieur mon trés cher Pére.

We wrote to you on the day before our departure from Augsburg; . . . so this is actually my second letter to you from Mannheim. I am at Canabich's every day; today Mama came along too. He is so different from the way he used to be, everyone in the orchestra is saying it; and he has taken a liking to me. He has a daughter who plays the clavier quite well, and in order to win his friendship I am working on a sonata for his Mad.ᵉˡˡᵉ daughter;[79] it is finished, except for the Rondeau. After I had finished the first Allegro and the Andante, I took it over to them and played it. Papa cannot imagine the applause with which the sonata was received. Some members of the orchestra happened to be there, young Danner, a horn player by the name of Lang, an oboist whose name I don't remember anymore, but he plays very well and has a beautiful pure tone. I made him a Present of my Hautbois Concerto;[80] it's being copied right now in a room at Canabich's. The man is beside himself with joy. . . .

Herr Kapellmeister Holzbauer[81] himself took me to Count Savioli, the Manager, today. Canabich happened to be there as well. Herr Holzbauer told the count in Italian how honored I would be if I were allowed to play before his Grace, the Elector. I had been here, at this court, already 15 years ago, I was 7 years old then, but now I am older and grown up, and so is my Musick. Ah, said the count, so that is—God knows who he thought I was; but then Canabich spoke up; I acted as if I didn't hear it, and entered into a conversation with some of the

79. Cannabich's fourteen-year-old daughter, Rosina, called Rosa.
80. The oboist is Friedrich Ramm; the concerto Mozart gave him was probably the Concerto for Flute or Oboe, K. 314, which he had written in Salzburg prior to the journey.
81. Ignaz Jakob Holzbauer, composer and Kapellmeister in Mannheim.

other guests. I noticed that he talked quite seriously about me. After a while the count said to me, I hear you play the Clavier quite passably? I bowed.

Now let me tell you about the Orchestra here. Saturday, on All Saints Day, I was at High Mass in the Chappel. The orchestra is very good and strong. On either side there are 10 to 11 violins, 4 violas, 2 oboes, 2 flutes and 2 Clarinetti, 2 horns, 4 violoncellos, 4 bassoons, and 4 double basses, there are also trumpets and Drums. They can really create some beautiful sound, but I wouldn't want to produce any of my Masses here, why?—because of their brevity?—No, here they like things short as well.—because of the church style?—no, not at all. but because, as things stand here right *now*, you have to write primarily for instruments, because the singing here is unimaginably poor. 6 soprani, 6 alti, 6 tenori, and 6 Baßi, against 20 violins and 12 basses is just like 0 to 1. n'est-ce pas, Herr Bullinger?[82]—It's because the Italians are in bad repute here; there are only 2 Castrati and both are old, they will probably be allowed to just die off. At any rate, the soprano would much rather sing alto, he can't reach the high notes anymore, the few boys they have are terrible, and the tenor and bass are like the funeral singers in Salzburg. Herr Vice-Kapellmeister *Vogler,* who composed the music for the Mass the other day, is nothing but a joke; he is very conceited but has little ability. The whole orchestra dislikes him. But today, Sunday, I heard a Mass by Holzbauer, which he wrote 26 years ago, but it's really good. Now here is a good composer, he has a good church style, is good at writing for voices and instruments, and fugues. . . .

Mama wants Nannerl to know that the lining for the jacket is in the large chest, toward the right, way at the bottom. There are probably all sorts of pieces of material lying on top of it: black and white ones, yellow, brown, red, green, blue ones, etc. Mama sends her regards to everyone, but she can't write at the moment, she still has to do her evening prayers; we came home real late from a dress rehearsal at the opera. Also, the yarn is not in skeins but rolled up in balls or bells or bolls, wrapped in a blue scarf. Well, that's the way it is and not any other way. Tomorrow, after Mass, I am required to go and see the stern Frau

---

82. Franz Joseph Johann Nepomuk Bullinger, an ex-Jesuit who was tutor of the young Count Leopold Arco and whom Mozart called his "very best friend."

Churfürstin;[83] she is determined to teach me how to knit a filet. I am truly worried about it; because she as well as the High-noble Herr Churfürst have expressed the wish that next Thursday evening, in the grand gala schlacademie, I should give a public knitting.[84] . . .

Postscript to his own letter:

. . . As for the shooting targets,[85] if it's not too late, I would like you to paint the following scene: a small man with fair hair is standing there bent over and showing his bare ass. Out of his mouth come the words: *Bon appetite, have a good meal.* A second man is to be shown in boots and spurs wearing a red coat and a beautiful wig à la mode. He should be of medium height and shown as he is just licking the other man's ass. Out of his mouth come the words: *Ah, nothing could be finer.* So, please, if it's possible; but if it's too late, maybe we can use this idea some other time.

The following letter, a classic, is one of Mozart's epistolary creations that made the Bäsle-Briefe famous. It contains about 20 percent information and 80 percent Spiel—i.e., Mozartian play. From the charming alliteration of the initial greeting to the mirror construct at the end, the letter is a veritable singsong of internal rhymes, synonyms, echo effects, and earthy lyrics. It is also one of the letters that some medical scientists cite as evidence that Mozart suffered from Tourette's syndrome.

Mozart to Maria Anna Thekla Mozart, in Augsburg

Mannheim, November 5, 1777

Dearest cozz buzz!

I have received reprieved your highly esteemed writing biting, and I have noted doted that my uncle garfuncle, my aunt slant, and you too,

---

83. Electress Elisabeth Aloysia Auguste.
84. Wolfgang has just answered some domestic questions from Nannerl concerning the whereabouts of certain knitting materials. His imagination is immediately set in motion by this request and instead of saying he is expected to play in a "gala academie," festivities associated with the elector's name day, he writes that he has to do some "public knitting" at the "gala schlacademie."
85. The "shooting targets" (Scheiben) are targets painted by members of the rifle club in Salzburg. These targets were often done with humor and imagination; Mozart's suggestion here certainly fits both categories.

are all well mell. We, too, thank god, are in good fettle kettle. Today I got the letter setter from my Papa Haha safely into my paws claws. I hope you too have gotten rotten my note quote that I wrote to you from Mannheim. So much the better, better the much so! But now for something more sensuble.

So sorry to hear that Herr Abbate Salate has had another stroke choke. But I hope with the help of God fraud the consequences will not be dire mire. You are writing fighting that you'll keep your criminal promise[86] which you gave me before my departure from Augspurg, and will do it soon moon. Well, I will most certainly find that regretable. You write further, indeed you let it all out, you expose yourself, you let yourself be heard, you give me notice, you declare yourself, you indicate to me, you bring me the news, you announce onto me, you state in broad daylight, you demand, you desire, you wish, you want, you like, you command that I, too, should could send you my Portrait. Eh bien, I shall mail fail it for sure. Oui, by the love of my skin, I shit on your nose, so it runs down your chin.

apropós. do you also have the spuni cuni fait?[87]—what?—whether you still love me?—I believe it! so much the better, better the much so! Yes, that's the way of the world, I'm told, one has the purse, the other has the gold; whom do you side with?—with me, n'est-ce pas?—I believe it! Now things are even worse. apropós.

Wouldn't you like to visit Herr *Gold*-smith again?—but what for? —what?—nothing!—just to inquire, I guess, about the Spuni Cuni fait, nothing else. nothing else?—well, well, all right. Long live all those who, who—who—who—how does it go on?—I now wish you a good night, shit in your bed with all your might, sleep with peace on your mind, and try to kiss your own behind; I now go off to never-never land and sleep as much as I can stand. Tomorrow we'll speak freak sensubly with each other. Things I must you tell a lot of, believe it you hardly can, but hear tomorrow it already will you, be well in the meantime. Oh my *ass* burns like fire! what on earth is the meaning of this!—maybe *muck* wants to come out? yes, yes, *muck*, I know you, see you, taste you—and—what's this—is it possible? Ye Gods!—Oh *ear* of mine, are you deceiving me?

86. A Mozartian pun; he writes *Verbrechen* (crime) instead of *Versprechen* (promise).
87. The meaning of "spuni cuni fait" is unclear.

—No, it's true—what a long and melancholic sound!—today is the write that I fifth this letter. Yesterday I talked with the stern Frau Churfürstin, and tomorrow, on the 6th, I will give a performance at the big gala-academie; and afterward I will give a special performance in her chambers, as the Fürstin-Chur said to me herself. Now for something real sensuble!

1. A letter or letters addressed to me will come into your hands, and I must beg of you—where?—well, a fox is no hare—yes there!—Now, where was I?—oh yes, will come,—yes, yes, they will come—well, who?—who will come?—oh yes, now I remember: letters, letters will come—but what kind of letters?—well now, letters for me, of course, I want to make sure that you send these to me; I will let you know where I'll be going from Mannheim. Now Numero 2: I'm asking you, why not?—I'm asking you, dearest numbskull, why not?—if you are writing any-way to Madame Tavernier in Munich, please include regards from me to the two Mad.[selles] Freysinger,[88] why not?—Curious! why not?—and to the Younger, I mean Fräulein Josepha, tell her I'll send my sincere apolo-gies, why not?—why should I not apologize?—Curious!—I don't know why not?—I want to apologize that I haven't yet sent her the sonata I promised, but I will send it as soon as possible. why not?—what—why not?—why shouldn't I send it?—why should I not transmit it?—why not?—Curious! I wouldn't know why not?—Well, then you'll do me this favor;—why not?—why shouldn't you do it for me?—why not, it's so strange! After all I'll do it to you too, if you want me to, why not?—why shouldn't I do it to you?—curious! why not?—I wouldn't know why not?—and don't forget to send my Regards to the Papa and Mama of the 2 young ladies, for it is a terrible thing to be letting forgetting one's father and mother. Later, when the Sonata is finished,—I will send you same, and a letter to boot; and you will be so kind as to for-ward same to Munich. Now I must close and that makes me morose. Dear Herr Uncle, shall we go quickly to the Holy Cross Convent and see whether anybody is still up?—we won't stay long, just ring the bell, that's all. Now I must relate to you a sad story that happened just this minute. As I'm in the middle of my best writing, I hear a noise in the street. I stop writing—get up, go to the window—and—the noise is gone—I sit down again, start writing once more——I have barely writ-ten 10 words when I hear the noise again—I rise—but as I rise, I can

88. Juliana and Josepha Freysinger; the sonata Mozart is referring to is K. 311.

still hear something but very faint—it smells like something burning—wherever I go it stinks, when I look out the window, the smell goes away, when I turn my head back to the room, the smell comes back—finally My Mama says to me: I bet you let one go?—I don't think so, Mama. yes, yes, I'm quite certain. I put it to the test, stick my finger in my ass, then put it to my nose, and—Ecce Provatum est![89] Mama was right! Now farewell, I kiss you 10000 times and I remain as always your

old young Sauschwanz,[90]
Wolfgang Amadé Rosenkranz.

From us two Travelers a thousand
Regards to my uncle and aunt.

To every good friend I send
My greet feet; addio nitwit.
Love true true true[91] until the grave,
if I live that long and do behave.

Miehnnam eht [ht]5 fo rebotco 7771.[92]

🐦 *Because* Bäsle-Briefe *were not available in print until well into the twentieth century, the German novelist Stefan Zweig arranged for a private printing of the above letter in a 1931 facsimile edition. Zweig presented copies of the numbered edition to his friends, including one copy to the composer Richard Strauss, who, like Zweig himself, loved Mozart, his music, and his* Bäsle-Briefe.

🐦 *Mozart had high hopes of getting an appointment at the Mannheim court. He felt wanted and respected; his letter and the congratulatory note to his father at the end show him in a joyous mood. Unfortunately, he was easily fooled, and within a month he would be getting the same treatment he received in Munich: a shrug of the shoulders.*

---

89. Should be "Ecce probatum est" (There is the proof).
90. *Sauschwanz* (pig's tail) rhymes with Rosenkranz.
91. Mozart actually writes "333," which in German is "drei, drei, drei" and in Mozart's dialect can also be "treu, treu, treu" (true, true, true).
92. The phrase, written in mirror language, means "Mannheim the 5th of October 1777," though it should say 5th of November.

Mozart to his father, in Salzburg (postscript)*

Mannheim, November 8, 1777

At Kanabich's, this morning, I wrote the Rondeau for the Sonata for his Mad.^selle daughter;[93] no wonder, they wouldn't let me go anymore, afterward. The Elector, the Electress, and the entire court are well pleased with me. In the Academie, the two times I performed, both he and she came right up to me and stood next to me at the Clavier. After the concert Canabich arranged it so I could be introduced to the rest of the court. I kissed the Elector's hand; he said, it must be 15 years now that you were here last. Yes, Your Highness, it is 15 years that I didn't have the honor—Your play is beyond comparison. And the Princess, when I kissed her hand, said, "Monsieur, je vous aßure, on ne peut pas jouer mieux."[94]

Yesterday . . . I talked with the Elector as if he and I were the best of friends. He is a gracious and good lord. He said to me: I hear you have written an opera in Munich. Yes, Your Highness, I commend myself to your Highness's grace, my greatest desire is to write an opera here. I beg his Highness not to forget me completely; and, thank god, I also know German, *and I grinned.* Well, that's quite possible. He has a son and three daughters, the oldest daughter and the young Count play piano. The Elector wanted to know, confidentially, how his children were doing. I answered very honestly but without putting down their music teacher. Kanabich agreed with me. When he left, the Elector thanked me very cordially. Today, after lunch, at 2 o'clock, I went with Canabich to the flutist Wendling.[95] They were all extremely nice to me. His daughter, who had once been the Maitresse of the Elector, plays Clavier quite well. Then I played. I was in such high spirits today, I cannot describe it. I played everything from memory, also three Duetti with violin that I had never seen before, from a composer I had never heard of. Everybody was so delighted with me that I had to—kiss all the ladies present. With the daughter this wasn't hard at all, she is anything but ugly.

* See facsimile, plate no. 9.

93. The "Rondeau" is the last movement of the Piano Sonata in C major, K. 309.
94. The "Princess" is Countess Karoline Luise, one of four "natural" (i.e., illegitimate) children of the elector. She addresses Mozart in French (I assure you one cannot play any better), for French was the language of German courts in the eighteenth century.
95. Johann Baptist Wendling, flutist in the Mannheim court orchestra.

Afterward, we spent some more time with the Elector's natural children. I played some more, and I played from the heart. Actually, I played 3 times. The Elector himself asked me again and again; he sat right next to me and sat perfectly still. I also asked a certain Profeßor to give me a theme for a fugue, which I developed. Now my congratulations:

My dearest Papa!

I cannot write Poetically; I am not a Poet. I cannot arrange my words so artfully that they reflect shadow and light; I am not a painter. I cannot even express my feelings and thoughts through gestures and Pantomimes; I am not a dancer. But I can do it with the sounds of music; I am a Musikus. Tomorrow at Cannabich's I will play a whole congratulatory arrangement on the Clavier for both your Name Day and Birthday. Today I can only wish you with all my heart, Mon trés cher Pére, what I wish for you every day, mornings and evenings: goode health, a long life, and a cheerful heart. I also hope that you feel less burdened these days than when I was still in Salzburg; for I must say that I was the sole cause of our problem. They treated me badly, which I didn't deserve; and you, naturally, took my side—but too much. Believe me, that was the primary and most important reason why I was in such a rush to get away from Salzburg. I do hope that my wish is now fulfilled. I will close now with a Musical wish. I wish that you will live as many years as it takes until nothing new can be done anymore in Musick. Farewell for now! I ask you most humbly to continue loving me a little, and to be content for the moment with this token of a con-gratulation until new drawers can be made for my small little brain box, so I have a place to put the brain that I still hope to acquire. I kiss Papa's hands 1000 times and I remain until Death,

Mon trés cher Pére,
your most obedient son,
Wolfgang Amadé Mozart

Mozart to his father, in Salzburg

Mannheim, November 13, 1777

Mon trés cher Pére!

. . . Now for some news from here. Yesterday I had to go with Canabich to the Manager Count Savioli to fetch my Present. It was just as I had thought: no money, but a beautiful gold watch. Right now I would rather have 10 Carolins[96] than the watch, which is, with its chain and inscription, valued at about 20 Carolins. What one needs on a journey is money. Now I own, con permissione, 5 watches. I have a mind to have an extra watch pocket put on each of my trousers, so when I come before one of these great lords I can wear two watches (which is the fashion anyway), so that they don't get the idea of bestowing on me yet another watch. . . .

Yes, I am familiar with the sonatas of Misliwetceck.[97] I played them in Munich. They are quite easy and good to listen to. My advice to my sister, to whom I commend myself humbly, is to play them with much expreßion, temperament, and fire; and to learn them by heart. They are sonatas that are bound to be popular with audiences, they are easy to memorize, and if played with the proper Precision, they draw attention. I kiss Papa's hands and remain his devo-son.[98]

Wolfgang Amadé Mozart.

The letter begins with an admonishment, probably from Mozart's mother, to write a nice, friendly letter to the helpful cousin in Augsburg who has been forwarding the Mozarts' mail to Mannheim. But the suggestion is hardly down on paper when it gets blown away by a barrage of mock curses leveled at poor Bäsle, simply because she neglected to include her portrait in the "Paquet" she sent. What is fascinating here is Mozart's obvious delight in word associations, alliterations, and parodies. All these elements come to life if the letter is read aloud.

Mozart to Maria Anna Thekla Mozart, in Augsburg

Mannheim, November 13, 1777

now write her a sensible letter for once, you can still write all that funny stuff, but be sure to tell her that you have received all the mail, so she won't be concerned about it, and worry.

Ma trés chére Niéce! Cousine! fille!

Mére, Sœur, et Epouse!

---

96. Approximately 100 gulden.
97. Probably the *Six Easy Divertimentos for the Harpsichord or Pianoforte*, which appeared in London in 1777.
98. Mozart concludes his letter, "bin dero gehors-sohn," which is a contraction of *gehorsam* (devoted, obedient) and *Sohn* (son).

Heaven, Hell, and a thousand sacristies, Croatians damnations, devils, and witchies, druids, cross-Battalions with no ends, by all the elements, air, water, earth, and fire, Europe, asia, affrica, and America, jesuits, Augustins, Benedictins, Capucins, Minorites, Franciscans, Dominicans, Carthusians, and dignified Holy-Crucians, Canons regular and irregular, and all hairy brutes and snitches, higgledy-piggledy castrates and bitches, asses, buffaloes, oxen, fools, nitwits, and fops! What sort of manner is this, my dear? 4 soldiers and only 3 gear?—such a Paquet and no Portrait?—I was already filled with high expectations—I thought for sure—for you wrote it to me yourself not long ago that I would receive it soon, very soon. Are you perhaps doubting whether I will keep my word?—I certainly hope that you have no doubts! Well then, I beg you, do send it to me, the sooner, the better. And I hope it will portray you the way I requested, I mean in french fashion.

How I like Mannheim?—as well as one can like any place without Bääsle. Pardon my poor handwriting, the pen is already old; now I have been shitting for nearly 22 years out of the same old hole and yet it's not torn a whit!—although I used it so often to shit—and then chewed off the muck bit by bit.

I hope, on the other hand, that you have been receiving my letters, as it so happens, one from Hohenaltheim, 2 from Mannheim, and now this one. As it so happens, this one is the third from Mannheim, but all in all it's the 4th, as it so happens. Now I must close, as it so happens, because I am not dressed yet, and we'll be eating soon so that afterward we can go and shit again, as it so happens. Do go on loving me as I love you, then we'll never stop loving each other. . . . Adieu, j'espére que vous aurés deja pris quelque lection dans la langue française, et je ne doute point, que—*Ecoutés:* que vous saurés bientôt mieux le français, que moi; car il y a certainement deux ans, que je n'ai pas ecrit un môt dans cette langue. adieu cependant. je vous baise vos mains, votre visage, vos genoux et votre—afin, tout ce que vous me permettés de baiser. je suis de tout mon cœur

votre

Mannheim le 13 Nov. 1777.

trés affectioné Neveu et Cousin
Wolfg. Amadé Mozart

Mozart concludes his letter in French. He insists that his cousin learn the language, but most likely he himself had begun to study French again because it was almost certain at this point that he would go on to Paris. The mistakes in the French quotation are Mozart's; here is a translation: "Farewell, I hope that you would already have taken some French lessons, and I wouldn't doubt that—Listen—you would know better French than I because I certainly haven't written a word in this language in two years. Farewell. I kiss your hands, your face, your knees and your— at any rate, all that you permit me to kiss. I am with all my heart your very affectionate Nephew and Cousin."

Mozart's begins his next letter with a parody of the Catholic confessional prayer, "Ich, johannes Chrisostomus Amadeus Wolfgangus sigismundus Mozart giebe mich schuldig," and then accounts for his sinful life. He obviously enjoyed the easygoing atmosphere in the Cannabich household. However, of more significant interest are his comments on the pianistic abilities of young Rosa Cannabich, age fourteen. Mozart's various descriptions and suggestions reveal him as a strict taskmaster in the fundamentals of piano playing; they also convey an idea of his own pianistic technique, which featured precision and cantabile.

Mozart to his father, in Salzburg (postscript)

Mannheim, November 14, 1777

I, Johannes Chrisostomus Amadeus Wolfgangus Sigismundus Mozart, am guilty of not coming home until 12 o'clock midnight, the day before yesterday and yesterday, and often times before, and that from 10 o'clock until said hour at Canabich's, I did some rhyming in the presence and company of Canabich, his wife and daughter, the *Treasurer,* and Messrs. *Raam and Lang,*—nothing too serious but rather light and frothy, actually, nothing but crude stuff, such as Muck, shitting, and ass licking, all of it in thoughts, words—but not in deeds. I would not have behaved so godlessly if our ringleader, known as Lisel, namely Elisabetha Cannabich, had not inspired and incited me to such high degree; I must also confess that I thoroughly enjoyed it all. I confess all these my sins and transgressions from the bottom of my heart, and, in the hope that I can confess them more often, I am fully committed to perfecting the sinful life that I have begun. I, therefore, beg for holy dispensation if it can be obtained easily; if not, well, it's all the same to me because the play must go on. "Lusus enim suum habet ambitum,"[99] says the late singer Meissner, Chap. 9, page 24.[100] Furthermore we can read it in the words of the holy *Ascenditor*,[101] patron saint of burnt and soupy Coffé, rancid Limonade, almond milk without the almonds, and, especially, frozen strawberries full of ice chunks, all because he himself was such a great connoisseur and artist of frozen matter. The sonata, which I wrote for Mad.^selle Canabich,[102] I will have copied as soon as possible on smaller paper and send it to my sister. 3 days ago I started to teach the sonata to Mad.^selle Rose; today we finished the first Allegro. The Andante will give us the greatest trouble because it is full of expreßion and has to be played exactly in the dynamics of forte and piano, just as they are marked. She is very skilled and learns quickly; her Right hand is very good, but her left hand has been completely ruined. I must say, sometimes I feel quite sorry for her when I see that she must work so hard that she actually gets short of breath, not because she is not skilled enough but because she doesn't know how to play any different; it's become a habit now, because she has never been taught any other way. I told her mother and said it to her, too, if I were her regular teacher, I would lock up all her Notes, cover the Clavier with a handkerchief, and make her practice with her right hand and then with her left, slowly in the beginning, nothing but Passages, Trills, and Mordants, Etc., until her hand would be totally reconditioned. I believe that I could, after that, make a true Clavier player out of her. It's a pity, she has so much talent, reads quite well, has a naturally light touch, and plays with a lot of feeling. They both agreed with me. Now a word about the opera;[103] very briefly. The Musick by Holzbauer is very beautiful. The text is not worthy of such music. What surprises me the most is that an old man like Holzbauer still has so much esprit; it's hard to believe how much fire he has in that Musick. Madame Elisabetha Wendling was the Prima

99. The Latin version of Mozart saying, "The play must go on."
100. Nikolaus Meissner, a Salzburg court musician and father of Joseph Nikolaus Meissner, famous bass singer. Mozart's reference here is parodistic.
101. *Ascenditor* is Mozart's Latin version of the name Steiger. Anton Steiger was the owner of a well-known café in Salzburg.
102. Piano Sonata in C major, K. 309.
103. The opera is *Günther von Schwarzburg*, by Ignaz Jakob Holzbauer; it is still performed today and was recently reissued on a CD. Mozart's remark about Holzbauer's music being too beautiful for the worth of the text is not without irony, for the same criticism was leveled against him and his German-language opera *Die Zauberflöte* in 1791.

donna, this is the wife not of the flutist but of the violinist. She tends to be somewhat sickly and what's more, the role was not written for her but for a certain Danzi, who happens to be in England at the moment; in other words, the role was not suited for her voice, it was too high. Herr Raaf[104] sang 4 Arias, about 450 measures, in such a way that one could hear that his voice is actually the biggest reason why he is singing so poorly. When you hear him begin an Aria and you don't think right away that this is Raaf, the once so famous tenor, you can't help bursting out laughing. That's just the way it is. I thought just like this to myself: if I didn't know that this is *the* Raaf singing, I would bend over with laughter. As it was—I just pulled out my handkerchief and giggled. Besides, he has never been, as people here tell me, a good Acteur. It was better just to hear him but not see him; he doesn't have a good stage presence at all. In this opera he had to die and die while singing a long and slow Aria; well, he died with a smile on his face; but toward the end of the aria his voice faded so fast that one could hardly stand it. I sat next to Wendling, the flutist, in the orchestra; and I said to him—because he had made a remark earlier that it was unnatural to go on singing while one is dying, because one can hardly wait any longer— so I said to him: just be patient a little more, he'll soon be dead, I can hear it. I can too, he said and laughed. . . .

There is a German National Theater in residence here,[105] just as in Munich. They put on a German singspiel once in a while, but the singers, both male and female, are Wretched. . . .

🐚 *Abbé Vogler, deputy Kapellmeister, continues to be a target for Mozart's criticism. His music, Mozart says, is "plump," which means clumsy, unrefined, unfinished. "Vogler is a fool," he wrote to his father on November 13, 1777, "who thinks that there is no one better and more perfect than he is. . . . His book is of more use for learning how to count than to compose." Vogler's book, dedicated to Elector Karl*

104. Anton Raaff, a well-known tenor who was sixty-three at the time and obviously past his prime. Leopold had advised Wolfgang to seek him out in Mannheim because he thought of him as a "God-fearing honorable man who loves Germans." In spite of his unflattering comments here, Mozart would write the tenor role of *Idomeneo* for him in Munich in 1780.

105. The German National Theater was established in Mannheim under Elector Karl Theodor between 1775 and 1777. Its director was Wolfgang Heribert von Dalberg, whom Mozart would meet in 1778. The Mannheim theater attained fame in 1782 when it performed Friedrich von Schiller's explosive Sturm und Drang play *The Robbers (Die Räuber)* .

Theodor and published in 1776, is titled, Tonwissenschaft und Tonsetz-kunst (The Science and Art of Composition).

Mozart to his father, in Salzburg

Mannheim, November 20, 1777

Mon trés cher Pére.

Today I will have to be brief because I am out of writing paper. Yesterday, Wednesday, the 19ᵗʰ, the gala celebrations got under way again. I attended the service; the mass was brand-new, composed by Vogler. I had already been to the rehearsal the day before yesterday in the afternoon, but I left right after the Kyrie. I have never heard anything like this in my life. Sometimes it doesn't even sound right. He attacks the music in such a way that one must fear he wants to drag you in by your hair; not that he makes it all worthwhile in some interesting way, no, it's all so Clumsy. I don't even want to talk about the execution of his ideas. I say only this much: it's not possible that a mass by Vogler could ever please a Compositeur who is worthy of the name. Briefly: for a moment I hear an idea that is not at all bad—well, it doesn't stay *not at all bad* for very long, it quickly becomes—beautiful?—god forbid!—it becomes bad and indeed dreadfully bad; and he does this in 2 or 3 different ways; for instance, one idea has hardly been introduced when another one comes along immediately and ruins it; or he doesn't conclude his idea in a natural enough manner that one could keep it as it is; or the idea does not appear in the right place, or, finally, it gets ruined by his instrumentation. That's the Musick of Vogler. Cannabich is now a much better composer than when we met him in Paris. But what I noticed about the Sinfonies here, right from the beginning, and Mama did too, they all begin in the same manner, always in a slow tempo and in unisono. . . .

Adieu. I kiss Papa's hands 100000 times, and I embrace my sister with all my heart and remain your obedient son,

Wolfgang Amadé Mozart

🖎 *As Wolfgang's situation in Mannheim is still without tangible results, the atmosphere in the correspondence between him and his father is getting tense. To begin with, Mozart's humorous exactitude in the dating of his letter—"at the stroke of ten"—*

is in response to his father's constant nagging to be more precise in his communications, including the time of writing. Mozart's funny references to Herr Schmalz, the reluctant banker, were, of course, products of his natural humor, but they are also designed to make light of the fact that he had borrowed money without Leopold's permission. Indeed, Leopold did not approve of it after he found out. It is unclear what Mozart had in mind with his "oracles." It may have something to do with Aloysia Weber, a young singer whom he had probably just met in Mannheim; it may also have something to do with his secret hopes for employment at the Mannheim court. Mozart liked oracles; his father did not. Predictably, Leopold responded ironically, almost cynically, in his letter of December 1, calling them "Thunderous oracles and no end in sight."

To his father, in Salzburg

*Mannheim, November 22, 1777
in the evening or rather Nocte
temporis Puncto and exactly
at the stroke of 10 o'clock.*

Mon Trés cher(e) Pére!

I almost slipped into the feminine.

The first thing I want to report is that my *truth-full* letter to Herr Herzog[106] in Augspurg in puncto Schmalzii[107] had very good results. He answered me very politely and expressed his annoyance that I had been received with such coolness by Herr Butter. A few days ago, he sent me a sealed letter addressed to the above mentioned Herr Milk, including a draft of 150 gulden for said Herr Cheese. You need to know that I could not refrain from asking Herr Herzog in a letter, although I had met him only once, whether he might send me a money order for Herr Schmalz or Butter, Milk, Cheese, or for whomever he wished. Well, this little venture actually worked; so no need to knock at my door and offer condolences. Today, the 21st, in the morning, we received your letter of the 17th. I was not at home but at Cannabich's, where Monsieur

---

106. "Herr Herzog," a banker in Augsburg, who helped Mozart get a loan.
107. "Schmalzii" (here used in a Latin genetive) is Dietrich Heinrich Schmalz, a merchant and banker in Mannheim. He was at first very reserved toward Mozart, and since his name is Schmalz, meaning "lard" in German, Mozart shows his indignation by referring to him as butter, milk, cheese, and assorted milk products.

Wendling was working on a concerto that I had orchestrated for him; then today at 6 o'clock we had a gala performance.[108] I had the pleasure of hearing Herr Fränzl,[109] who is married to a sister of Mad.^me Cannabich, play a violin concerto. I like him very much. You know that I am not a great lover of difficulties; and he does play difficult stuff; but one is not aware that what he plays is difficult, one has the feeling one can play the same things immediately, and that's the real thing. He also has a beautifully rounded tone; he doesn't drop a note, you can hear everything; it's all very Precise. And he has a beautiful staccato, plays it with a single bow, up or down, and I have never heard a double trill executed as well as he does it. In a word: he may not be a wizard, but he is a very solid violinist. . . .

What you are writing about Mannheim, I know already—but I don't want to talk about things before their time. Everything will turn out fine. Maybe I can report to you in my next letter about something that is *very good* for you but only *good* for me, or something that is *very bad* in your eyes, but *Acceptable* in mine, perhaps also something *Acceptable* to you, however, *very good, dear,* and *precious* for me! This is all rather like an oracle, isn't it?—well, it sounds mysterious but can be understood. . . . One of these oracular sayings will have to come to pass.—I think it will either be the one in the middle or the last one—it doesn't matter which; because it's one thing whether I eat the muck or Papa shits it —it seems I can never get this thing right! I wanted to say: it's one thing whether Papa shits the muck or I eat it!—now I better quit, I can tell, it's useless for me to try. . . .

"Rosemunde" will be given here this coming carnival season; it's a newly Composed text by Herr Wieland with newly Composed Musique by Herr Schweizer.[110] They will both be here. I have seen parts of the opera already and played them on the piano, but I don't want to say anything about it yet. The shooting target you had painted on my behalf as Master of the Shoot[111] is wonderful, and the verses are beyond compare. Now I have nothing left to write, except to wish everybody a pleasant

108. These "gala performances" were in honor of Electress Elisabeth Augusta, whose name day was on November 19.
109. Ignaz Fränzl, a violinist whom the Mozarts had already met in 1763 in Schwetzingen.
110. *Rosamunde* is a singspiel by Anton Schweizer; the libretto is by Christoph Martin Wieland.
111. The ad hoc president of a shooting event.

rest, a good sleep for all until this letter of mine will wake you up. Adieu. I kiss Papa's hands 100000000 times and my sister, that darling twister, I embrace with my love true, with my love blue, just a whit, or not a bit. I am your most obedient son, you see, please don't run away from me.

Wolfgang Amadé Mozart
Knight of the golden Spur
and of two Horns if I should err
and get married.
Member of the great Academie,
of Verona and Bologna,
oui mon ami.

🐚 *The target Mozart is referring to here depicts Wolfgang and Bäsle taking leave of each other, drying their copious tears with two giant handkerchiefs. In the background one can see the panorama of Augsburg. It appears that Wolfgang's story with his cousin had in a real sense become a target for fun and games. The scatological proverb Mozart is trying to remember is "It is one thing to shit the muck and another to eat it," but once he gets his father mixed up in the saying, he cannot get it straight anymore. At the end of the letter, Mozart paraphrases the German version of a charming little children's oracle, "He (she) loves me, loves me not" (meine Schwester, den lieben Polester umarme ich von herzen, mit schmerzen, ein wenig, oder gar nicht).*

🐚 *Leopold is pressing Wolfgang to move on. He thinks his son is wasting time in Mannheim and suggests Mainz, Frankfurt, Koblenz, and Paris as further destinations. On November 20 he writes, "I wonder where you will read this letter?— probably in Maynz. For heaven's sake—you must try to earn some money." But Wolfgang, reluctant to leave Mannheim, subtly opposes his father. At the end of the letter, he comes up with a long list of friends in Salzburg to whom he sends regards; it must have annoyed Leopold that Wolfgang claims to be out of room (and out of paper) and then proceeds to add a lengthy alphabetical register of all the Salzburg friends he can think of. The list not only provides an interesting index of friends of the Mozart family but highlights yet another aspect of Mozart's verbal humor. Mozart's final sentences are a jumbled apology to "Hapa," his father, which is of more than passing interest. Mozart meant it to be funny, but it seems that when he fractures his language, something else is fractured within him.*

To his father, in Salzburg (postscript)

Mannheim, November 26, 1777

The reason why we are still here is that I'm thinking of staying here for the winter; I'm only waiting for some word from the Elector. Count Savioli, the Manager, is an honest Cavalier, and I told him he should let the Elector know that, since right now the weather is bad for traveling anyway, I would consider staying here and giving lessons to the young count. He promised to do his utmost, but he also said that I should be patient until the gala celebrations are over. All this happened with the knowledge and at the *instigation* of Cannabich. When I told him that I had seen Savioli and what I had said to him, he told me that he would sooner believe it will happen than not. Cannabich had spoken about this matter even before Savioli had seen the Elector. Now I just have to wait. Tomorrow I'll fetch my 150 gulden from Herr Schmalz, for our landlord will undoubtedly prefer the sound of cash to that of musick. Of course, I would never have thought that my honorarium here would be a watch, but that's how it is. I would have left long ago, but they are all saying: where do you want to go, now that it is winter?—it's not a good thing to be on the road at this time of year. Stay here! Cannabich has expressed much the same sentiment. That's why I put out these Feelers, and since you can't hurry something like this along, I have to be patient and wait. I hope to be able to give you some good news soon. I can count on 2 pupils already who will bring me, more likely than not, 1 louis[112] each per month, and that's without the *Arch-pupil*;[113] but I admit, I cannot do it without the Arch. Well now, let's leave this as it is and as it will be; what use are these idle speculations, we don't know what will happen anyway, yet—we do know!—it's all in god's hands. So, let's cheer up, Allegro style, "non siate so Pegro."[114] If we should leave here after all, we'll go straight to—where?—to Weilburg, or whatever the name is, to the Princess, the sister of the Prince of Orania; the one who was so friendly to us à la Haie.[115] And there we will stay, Nota bene, as

112. "1 louis" is 1 Louis d'or, worth 8 to 10 gulden.
113. The "Arch-pupil" is young Count Karl August, who would bring in the highest fee.
114. "Don't be so lazy."
115. The "Princess" is Caroline von Nassau-Weilburg, whom the Mozarts had met in 1767 in Holland; she now resided in Kirchheimbolanden, a day's travel to the northwest of Mannheim; "la Haie" is The Hague.

long we are well fed at the officer's table; and we might still earn at least 6 Louis d'or. . . .

Now I must close because I have no more room left to write, and I can't write lying down, and I don't want to stay up with a frown—for I'm sleepy. I'll write much more in my next letter, but today I can't any-more for lack of space, you understand. Next time I write I'll prepare a stack of paper. Adieu. Holy Thunder, there's still something I need to write. I kiss Papa's hands.

and I embrace my sister with all my heart, and remain faithfully your obedient son. Wolfgang Amadé Mozart

Mannheim, 26[the] Nov.[b] 1777.

If I can find any more room, I would like to add 100000 Greetings from us two, that means from the two of us, to all good friends, espe-cially to all the *As:* the Adlgassers, Andretters, and Arco (count); the *Bs:* Herr Bullinger, Barisani, and Beranitzky; the *Cs:* Czernin (count), Cußetti, and the three Calcanten;[116] the *Ds:* Herr Daser, Deibl, and Dommeseer; the *Es:* Mad.[selle] Eberlin Waberl, Herr Estlinger, and all the Esln[117] in Salzburg; the *Fs:* Firmian (count and countess and their little funny-bunny), little Franz, and the Freyhof[118] at St. Peter's; the *Gs:* Mad.[selle] and Madame et deux Ms. Gylofsky, and the Councillor, and Herr Gretri and Gablerbrey; the *Hs:* the Haydns, Hagenauers, and Höllbrey Thresel; the *Js:* Joli (Sallerl), Herr Janitsch the violinst, and Jacob at the Hagenauers; the *Ks:* Herr und Frau von Kürsinger, Count and Countess Kühnburg, and Herr Kassel; the *Ls:* Baron Lehrbach, Count and Countess Litzauw, Count and Countess Lodron; the *Ms:* Herr Meissner, Medlhammer, and Moserbrey; the *Ns:* Nannerl, the court jester Pater Florian, and all Nightwatchmen; the *Os:* Count Oxenstirn, Herr Oberbreiter, and all the oxen of Salzburg; the *Ps:* the Prexi family, Count Pranck the head cook, and Count Perusa; the *Qs:* Herr Quilibet, Quodlibet, and all the quackers; the *Rs:* Pater Florian Reichsigel, the Robinig family, and Maestro Rust; the *Ss:* Herr Suscipe, Herr Seiffert, and all Swines in Salzburg; the *Ts:* Herr Tanzberger our

---

116. Organ blowers.
117. "Esln" is *Eseln* (asses).
118. "Freyhof" is *Friedhof* (cemetery).

Butcher, Thresel, and all the trumpet players; the *Us:* the cities of Ulm and Uttrecht, and all the Uhren in Salzburg, especially if you add an H in front;[119] the *Ws:* the Wiesers, Wurstmacher Hans, and Woferl;[120] the *Xs:* Xantipe, Xerxes, and all whose names begin with X; the *Ys:* Herr Ypsilon, Herr Ybrig, and all whose names begin with Y. Finally the *Zs:* Herr Zabuesnig, Herr Zonca, Herr Zezi at the castle. Adieu. If I had more space, I would write something more, at least a few Greetings to my good friends, but, as it is, it can't be done, I wouldn't know where to put it all. I sensible things cannot write today, because my track off am I. Hapa not must wrong it pake, this way simply am I today. Help myself I not can. well thee fare. I good a night wish. Well geslaaf. Sensible I write again time nextly.

🐚 *Leopold's annoyance at what he perceived as his son's failings, such as imprecise reporting, overspending, and lack of income, is getting more and more obvious. In his letter of November 27, he lectures his son: "The purpose of this journey, that is the necessary purpose, was, is, and must be to find employment or earn money. So far there doesn't seem to be a prospect for one or the other." Mozart, in turn, is getting edgy about his father's continual badgering. It must be said, however, Leopold was a more realistic judge of the situation in Mannheim than Wolfgang. He understood correctly that Wolfgang was too naive and gullible, too easily influenced by flatteries and empty gestures. Wolfgang wanted people to like him and listen to his playing; and nothing could please him more than when people sang, fiddled, and whistled his melodies.*

To his father, in Salzburg

*Mannheim, November 29, 1777
in the evening*

Mon trés cher Pére!

I received your letter of the 24th this morning, and I could see from it that it is not easy for you to adjust to the inevitable when things, as it sometimes happens, take a downturn. Until now, the four of us, such as we are, have been neither completely happy nor unhappy and I thank

---

119. If you put an *H* in front of *Uhren* (clocks), you get *Huren* (whores).
120. Mozart includes himself as Woferl.

god for that. Now you are reproaching the two of us for a number of things, none of which we deserve. We don't spend money unnecessarily, and what one needs on a trip you know as much as, indeed better than, we do. The fact that we stayed so long in Munich is no one's fault but *mine*; and if I had been alone, I would most certainly have stayed there; but why did we stay two weeks in Augspurg?—I should almost think you didn't get my letters from there?— . . . and that we traveled straight to Mannheim?—I answered this question in my last letter; and why are we still here?—well—do you really think that I would stay anywhere without a reason?—but I could have informed you?—all right, I will tell you what's what, yes, the whole course of events; but, by god, I did-n't want to say anything about it, because I couldn't be specific then any-more than I can be specific today, and consequently I could have given you only the *vaguest* report, which, as I know you, would have caused you worries and grief, which is something I always try to avoid. But if you attribute my silence to negligence, carelessness, and laziness, then I can only thank you for your high opinion of me and regret with all my heart that you do not really know your own son.

I am not careless, I am only prepared for whatever lies ahead and can, therefore, anticipate and endure anything with patience—as long as my Honor and my good Name, Mozart, are not affected. Well then, since I must say it, let it be said; but I beg you beforehand, do not be happy or sad prematurely, for no matter what happens, all's well as long as we have our good health; after all, happiness exists—only in our imagination. . . .

I saw Canabich in the afternoon and since he had advised me to talk to Count Savioli, he asked me right away whether I had been to see him.—I told him everything; he said: I would be so glad if you would stay here for the winter, but I would like it even more if you could stay here for good and have a regular appointment. I said: I could not wish for anything better than to be around you always, but to do that on a permanent basis, I really would not know how that could be done. You already have two Kapellmeisters, so I really don't know in what capaci-ty I could stay here. . . . Well, the Elector could appoint you as court composer; just be patient a little, I will take it up with the count. The following Thursday we had a big gala concert. When the count saw me, he apologized that he had not yet talked to the Elector, because the gala days were still in full swing, but as soon as they are over, which will be on Monday, he will bring up the subject for sure. I waited for 3 days, and when I heard nothing, I went to see him to find out what happened. He said: My dear Mozart (that was Friday, yesterday) today was a hunting day, so it was impossible for me to speak to the Elector, but tomorrow at this time I will most certainly be able to give you an answer. I asked him not to forget! but to tell you honestly, I was rather upset when I left him; at any rate, I decided to take the 6 easiest variations of the Fischer Menuett, which I had copied out for this very purpose, and bring them to the young count so I would have an opportunity to talk with the Elector myself, . . . for the Elector is fond of me, he thinks highly of me and knows what I can do. So I hope to be able to give you some positive news in my next letter. But I beg you once again not to rejoice or worry too early, and don't tell anybody, except Herr Bullinger and my sister. I'm including the allegro and Andante of the Sonata for Mad.^{selle} Cannabich for my sister. The Rondeau will follow soon; the parcel would have gotten too heavy if I had mailed everything together. I hope you don't mind my sending you the original, it's easier for you to have it copied for 6 kreutzer a sheet than for me to pay 24 kreutzer.[121] Don't you think that's pretty expensive?—adieu. I kiss your hands 100000 times and embrace my sister with all my heart. I am your obedient

Wolfgang Amadé Mozart

You must have heard a little
about my sonata because at Canabich's it's being
sung, strummed, fiddled, or whistled at least 3 times a day!—Only sotto
voce, of course.

Mozart says, "I love to work"; this is as true and typical of him as his desire to have fun. Indeed, he worked tirelessly when he felt appreciated.

---

121. A kreutzer was the smallest denomination of money in German states, comparable to a penny; 1 gulden was worth 60 kreuzer. Mozart wants to impress his father with his thriftiness by sending the original score of his Piano Sonata in C major, K. 309, to Salzburg because copying cost less there than in Mannheim.

To his father, in Salzburg

Mannheim, December 3, 1777

Monsieùr, mon trés cher Pére.

I still can't write anything definite about my situation here. Last Monday I had the good luck of finally seeing the Elector after I had visited his natural children 3 days in a row, mornings and afternoons; we all thought that my efforts to see the Elector would be fruitless once again, because it was already getting late, but at last we saw him coming. The governness immediately called the young countess to the piano, I took my place next to her to give her a lesson; and that's how the Elector saw us when he came in. We all rose, but he told us to carry on. When she had finished her piece, the governness spoke up and said that I had composed such a beautiful Rondeau. I played it; he liked it very much; then he asked, will she be able to learn it? Oh yes, I said; I only wished I could be fortunate enough to teach it to her myself. . . . How long do you intend to stay here?—*My answer:* as long as Your Highness commands; I have no engagement elsewhere, I can stay as long as it pleases Your Highness. So, there I had said it. This morning I went there again; they told me the Elector had said several times yesterday: Mozart is going to stay here for the winter. So now we are right in the middle of this thing, and I must wait and see. Today I ate at Wendling's, it was the fourth time. Before table Count Savioli came with Kapellmeister Schweitzer, who had arrived last night. Savioli said to me: I spoke with the Elector again yesterday evening, but he has not yet made up his mind. . . . I begged him to use his influence so that the Elector would give me a permanent appointment, I was afraid that he would give me so little to do during the winter that I couldn't afford to stay. I really want him to give me work, for I love to work. . . . Well, whatever happens, happens. If he won't keep me here, I will insist that he give me some *travel money* because I do not intend to make him a complete present of the Rondeau and the variations.[122] . . . Who knows!—maybe— by the time Papa reads this letter, god willing, everything has been decided. In the event that I will stay, it has been suggested that I go to Paris during Lent with Herr Wendling, Raam the oboist who plays

---

122. Mozart had made a present of six of his Fischer Variations, K. 179, to Count Karl August, and he had composed a "Rondeau" for Countess Karoline Luise; the "Rondeau" has not been identified.

beautifully, and Monsieur Lauchery the ballet master. Herr Wendling assures me that I shall not regret it. He has been to Paris twice and has just returned from there; he says it's really the only place where you can make money and a good reputation for yourself. You are a man who is able to do just about everything, and I'll show you how to find your way around, you'll have to write opera seria, opera Comique, oratories, anything you can think of; but once you have done a couple of operas in Paris, you will have something for sure all year long. Then there is the Concert spirituell,[123] the accademie des amateurs,[124] where you'll earn 5 louis d'or for a Sinfonie. If you give lessons, the customary fee is 3 louis d'or for 12 lessons. Afterward, you can have your sonatas, trios, or quartets engraved for Subscription. Cannabich and Toeschi send a lot of their compositions to Paris; Wendling is a man who knows how to travel. Let me know what you think about all of this. Please. To me it seems quite useful and it all makes sense. I would be traveling with a man who knows Paris as it is today, he knows it inside out; after all, there have been many changes. I wouldn't spend any more money than I am spending now, indeed, I think I would need less than half because I would have to pay only for myself, since Mama would stay here, possibly with the Wendling family. . . .

I kiss Papa's hands 100000 times and embrace my sister with all my heart. And I hope that my Sonata will please you, my sister, Herr Bullinger, and everyone who will hear it as much as it pleases everyone who has heard it here. Adieu. I am your obedient son

Wolfgang Amadé Mozart

The thought of going to Paris was becoming more and more acute, although Mozart remained ambivalent about his future. The same evening that he wrote to his father, he also wrote to his cousin in Augsburg—albeit in a very different tone.

Mozart is playing the clown. The beginning of this letter to Bäsle reads like the opening scene of a commedia dell'arte piece: the main character appears only to announce that he "has to go." Still, the letter contains some interesting truths about Mozart's writing style, for he did use different styles for different people. To his father, for instance, he wrote mostly in a "straight" and "serious" manner, to his sis-

123. The Concert Spirituel was founded in 1725; the orchestra usually performed at the Tuileries in Paris.
124. The Concert des Amateurs, founded in 1769, was the second-most prominent orchestra in Paris.

*ter, Bäsle, and sometimes his mother, he preferred to be "crooked" and "jolly."
Mozart's statement "I have not taken off my pants since I left Augsburg" is inter-
preted by some Mozart scholars to suggest that Mozart and his cousin had engaged
in sexual intercourse and that this remark was meant to assure Bäsle that he was
remaining true to her. Most biographers think that the two cousins simply had fun
together but no sexual relations. Beginning with the sentence "Mannheim will soon
depart," Mozart goes into one of his language games; here he is exchanging subject
and object.*

To Maria Anna Thekla Mozart, in Augsburg

Mannheim, December 3, 1777

Ma très chère Cousine!

Before I start writing to you, I have to go to the john — — — well
now, that's over with! Ah!—now my heart feels so much lighter again!—
it's like a big stone is off my chest—now I can go and indulge myself
again! Well, it's true, after you have completely emptied yourself, life is
twice as much fun. . . . Hussa-sa, Coppersmith, hold the wench for me,
but don't squeeze her, hold the wench for me, but don't squeeze her;[125]
kiss my Ass, Coppersmith, and yes, it's true, whosoever believes it will
be blessed, and who doesn't believe it will also go to heaven; but in a
straight line and not the way I write. You can see now that I am able to
write any way I want to, beautifully and wild, straight and crooked. The
other day, I was in bad humor, so my writing was beautiful, straight, and
serious; today I'm in a good mood, and my writing is wild, crooked, and
jolly. Now it all depends on what you would rather have—you must
make a choice between the two because I have nothing in between, it can
only be beautiful or wild, straight or crooked, serious or jolly; the first
three words or the last three.[126] I expect your decision in you next letter.
My mind is made up: if I have to go, I go; but it all depends, if I have
the runs, I must run; and if I can't hold it any longer, I'll shit in my
pants. God be with you, foot, your heel lies on the windowsill. . . . A
propos, I have not taken off my pants since I left Augsburg—except at
night before going to bed. I wonder what you think about the fact that

---

125. "Hussa-sa Coppersmith" appears to be a local folk song.
126. The first three words Mozart has in mind are "beautiful . . . straight . . . serious;" the last three, "wild
. . . crooked . . . jolly."

I am still in Mannheim, really in it. That's because I haven't gone anywhere, nowhere! But now I think that Mannheim will soon depart. But Augsburg can, through you, still write to me and address any letters to Mannheim until further notice. Herr Uncle, Frau Aunt, and Mad.^selle Bäsle are sending their regards to Mamma and me. You were worried already that we might be ill because you didn't get a letter from us for such a long time. The day before yesterday you could finally rejoice in receiving our letter from 26th November and today, the 3rd of December, you are pleased to answer me. So I will keep my promise to you?—Well, that makes you happy. Just don't forget to compose Munich for the Sonata, for what you have kept, you must also promise, you always have to be a word of your man. . . .

Do stay well and always keep your love for me; do write soon because we have a cold moon, keep your word, or I'll be hurt, adieu, mon Dieu, I kiss you forever and remain always your clever

Mannheim	Ma très chère Cousine
without slime	Were you ever in Berlin?
the 3rd of Decembr.	I'm your honest trustworthy relation
today is not Quatembr.	In a good or bad situation
at night in 1777	W. A. Mozart
from now until we go to heaven,	Sh: to take a shit: that's so hard.
Amen	

The letter of December 6 contains Mozart's often quoted comparison between the Andante of his Piano Sonata in C major, K. 309, and the character of young Rosa Cannabich. To render human portraits in music was not new, but Mozart's musical character study has a special charm. It is part of his "humanistic" aesthetics. There has been no agreement, however, on the interpretation of the Andante. One writer thought that, judging by the dynamics of the piece, the girl must have been quite a rascal. Another, though, suggested that the movement was tender and sensitive and so, presumably, was young Rosa. Both views may be valid. Rosa was a teenager, and her temperament may well have been dynamic *and* sensitive.

To his father, in Salzburg

Mannheim, December 6, 1777

Mon trés cher Pére!

I still can't tell you anything definite. I'm slowly getting tired of this joke. I'm only Curious now to see how it will end. Count Savioli has spoken 3 times with the Elector, and each time the answer was a shrug with the shoulders and then the reply: I will give an answer in due time but—I haven't made up my mind yet. My good friends all share the opinion I have, namely that this unwillingness and reserve is a good rather than a bad sign; because if the Elector had no intention of keeping me here, he would have told me so right away; as it is I attach to these delays no other motif than—*denari.* siamo un poco scrocone.[127] Besides, I know for sure that the Elector likes me. . . .

Cannabich's daughter, who is 15 years old and the eldest of his children, is a very beautiful and well-mannered girl; she is very thoughtful and self-assured for her age, she is serious, doesn't talk too much, but when she speaks—she speaks with graciousness and friendliness. Yesterday she gave me once again an indescribable pleasure, she played My sonata—exquisitely. She plays the Andante, which must not be played *too fast,* with the greatest sensitivity; besides, she loves to play it. You remember that I had the first allegro finished the 2nd day I came here, consequently I had seen Mad.selle Cannabich only once. It was then that young Danner asked me how I would compose the andante; I want it to be entirely like the Character of Mad.selle Rose. Then when I played it, it was a huge success; and young Danner said afterward: it is true, she is just like the andante. I hope you received the sonata safely?—This morning we received your letter of 1st Dec. Today I had my 6th meal at Wendlings' and my 2nd at Herr Schweizer's. . . .

But now I must go to sleep. I wish you a good night.

Both Leopold and Wolfgang suspected that Abbé Vogler had worked behind the scenes to prevent Mozart's appointment at the court of Mannheim. Leopold wrote to Maria Anna on December 18, "No one has intrigued more against Wolfgang than Vogler." One thing is certain: Mozart had been highly critical of Vogler, a fact

127. "We are a bit stingy with cash."

that was undoubtedly well known around Mannheim. However, in spite of being "shrugged off" by Elector Karl Theodor, Mozart wanted to compose a mass for him.

To his father, in Salzburg

Mannheim, December 10, 1777

Mon Trés cher Pére!

There's nothing doing here with the Elector at this time. The day before yesterday I went to a concert at court to get an answer. I could see that Count Savioli tried very much to avoid me, but I went right up to him; when he saw me, he shrugged his shoulders. What, I said, still no answer?—Please forgive me, he said, but unfortunately, there is nothing.—eh bien, I said, the Elector could have told me that some time ago. Yes, he said, and he would not have made a decision even now if I had not urged him and made it clear to him that you have been sitting around here for a long time, eating up your money at the inn. Indeed, that's what annoys me the most, I replied, the whole thing is not very civil; however, I am much obliged to you, Herr Count—one doesn't call him Excellency—that you have taken such trouble on my behalf and I beg you to thank the Elector in my name for his gracious although rather late reply, and assure him that he would never have regretted employing me. Oh, he replied, of that I am more convinced than you might imagine.

I then informed Herr Wendling of the decision, he turned quite red and said angrily: we'll have to find another way; we have to keep you here, at least for two months, until we can go to Paris together. Tomorrow Cannabich will come back from the hunt, then we'll talk some more about this. After that, I left the academie concert and went directly to Mad.^{me} Cannabich. . . . I told her the whole story; she knew of similar stories that had happened here before. When Mad.^{selle} Rose, who had been 3 rooms away taking care of the linen, came into the room, she said to me: Is it convenient now to begin?—because it was time for her lesson. I am at your service, I replied. Then she said: let's have a really good lesson today; by all means, I said, for we won't be able to continue much longer.—how so?—what do you mean?—why?—She went to her Mama, who told her. What?—she said, is it really true—I can't believe it. Yes, yes, it's true, I said. She then sat down and played my sonata with great seriousness. I must confess, I could not keep my tears back. . . .

The other day I had lunch with Wendling, as usual, when he said: our Indian, actually a Dutchman of independent means,[128] who is a lover of all sciences and a great friend of mine, is indeed a rare individual. He is offering to pay you 200 gulden if you will compose for him 3 short, easy concertos, and a pair of quartets for the flute.[129] Moreover, with Cannabich's help you can get at least 2 pupils who will pay well; then you compose several Duetti for Clavier and violin for subscription and get them engraved; meals you can have at noon and evening at my house; lodging for yourself you can have at the house of Herr Court Councillor,[130] so all this won't cost you a thing; for your mother we'll find an inexpensive lodging where she can stay for 2 months, until you have heard from home; then your Mama can travel home, and we go to Paris. Mama is quite satisfied with this plan, now all that's needed is your consent, but I'm so confident that you will give it that if it were time to travel now I would depart for Paris without even waiting for your answer. . . . As we will not leave before the 6th of March, I would like to ask you to arrange for me, if it's easily possible, through Herr Messmer in Vienna or someone else, a letter of introduction to the Queen of France;[131]—but only if it can be done without great effort!—not that it is of utmost importance, but it is undoubtedly better to have such a letter. . . . Now I must go to sleep. I shall have plenty to do for the next 2 months: 3 concertos, 2 quartets, 4 or 6 Duetti for piano, and then I have in mind to write a New Grand Mass and present it to the Elector.[132] adieu. please let me have an answer to all my questions very soon. I kiss your hands 100000 times and embrace my sister with all my heart. I remain your most obedient son

Wolfgang Amadé Mozart

---

128. Ferdinand Dejean (or Dechamps) was a doctor in the Dutch East India Company and an amateur flutist.

129. The exact terms of the commission are not known, but when Dejean left for Paris Mozart had composed two flute quartets, K. 285 and 285a, an incomplete flute quartet, K. 285b, and two flute concertos, K. 313 and 314. Dejean considered it half of the commission and paid only 96 gulden.

130. Court Councillor Serrarius offered Mozart free lodging in his house in exchange for music lessons for his fifteen-year-old stepdaughter, Therese Pierron.

131. The queen of France, Marie Antoinette, was a daughter of Maria Theresa of Austria; Joseph Mesmer, a cousin of the physician Dr. Anton Mesmer, had been her tutor in calligraphy in Vienna.

132. The mass was never completed.

Baron Dürnitz[133] was not in Munich when I was there.

Next post day I will write to Prince Zeil[134] to keep things going in Munich. If you would write as well,

I would appreciate it. But be to the point.

Don't grovel; that's something I can't stand. . . .

The postscript shows that Mozart still had hopes of getting an appointment in Munich but, at the same time, he tells his father, "Don't grovel."

Wolfgang's New Year's greetings to his father give a good account of his busy schedule in Mannheim. His mother confirms it: "Wolfgang is so busy that he doesn't know what to do first." She adds proudly, "They all agree, he has no equal, they completely adore his Compositions." It is also interesting to note that Wolfgang reacts with great sensitivity to Leopold's allegation that he might have become a bit lax about going to confession. In fact, Leopold wanted to know and control everything. In one of his letters, he even inquired about the growth of Wolfgang's beard: "Is his beard going to be cut off, or singed off, or perhaps even shaved off?" Maria Anna replied that Wolfgang's whiskers could still be handled with a small pair of scissors, but a trip to the barbershop would soon become inevitable.

To his father, in Salzburg (postscript)

Mannheim, December 20, 1777

I wish you, dearest Papa, a very happy New Year, and that your health, so dear to me, will get better from day to day, all for the benefit and joy of your wife and children, for the pleasure of your true friends, and to the annoyance and anger of your enemies!——I beg you to grant me the same fatherly love for the coming year that you have always bestowed on me! I, for my part, will make every effort to earn more and more the love of so excellent a father. You have made me quite happy with your last letter, the one of 15 Dec.[bre], because I could see from it that you are in good health, god be praised and thanked. We too are fine, with god's help; in my case it can hardly be otherwise because I certainly get enough Exercise. I'm writing this at 11 o'clock at night, for

133. Thaddäus Freiherr von Dürnitz, for whom Mozart had composed the Piano Sonata in D major, K. 284.
134. The bishop of Chiemsee, a supporter of Mozart.

there's no other time. We can't get up before 8 o'clock, because we have no daylight in our room until half past 8, since it is situated on the ground floor. I get dressed quickly, at 10 I sit down to Compose until 12 or half past 12 o'clock; then I go to Wendling's, where I write a little more until half past 1 o'clock, after that we take our noon meal, which lasts until almost 3 o'clock when I have to go to the inn Mainzischer Hof, in order to give lessons to a Dutch officer in galanterie playing[135] and thoroughbass for which I receive, if I remember correctly, 4 ducats for 12 lessons. At 4 o'clock I need to be back home to give a lesson to the daughter of the house; although we never begin before half past 4 o'clock, because we have to wait for the lights to come on. At 6 o'clock I go to Cannabichs' to give a lesson to Mad.^selle Rose; I stay there for supper, after which we talk—or sometimes they play a game; and when that happens, I pull a book out of my pocket and read—just as I used to do in Salzburg.

I said earlier that your last letter made me quite happy; that is the truth! One thing, however, bothered me a little—your question whether I am perhaps getting forgetful about going to confession?—not that I want to object to this, but I will make one request and that is: don't think so badly of me! I like to have fun, but be assured that in spite of it all, I can also be Serious. Since I left Salzburg, and even in Salzburg itself, I have come across people who would have made me be ashamed if I had talked and acted like them, although they were 10, 20, and 30 years older than I am!—I do ask you, therefore, again and humbly, to have a better Opinion of me. Please give my regards to Herr Bullinger, my very best friend, and convey to him my most cordial New Year's wishes, and Regards to all good friends, male and female. Nota bene: also to Pater Dominicus.[136]

🙰 *The question of Mozart's reading habits comes up again and again. It is a frequent assumption that Mozart did not read much, because he was too busy composing. Such assumptions are contradicted by Mozart's own statement that once in a while he liked to pull a book out of his pocket and do some reading. The books*

---

135. The "Dutch officer" is Ferdinand Guillaume Duval de la Pottrie, and "galanterie playing" is an eighteenth-century term for playing short, gallant pieces in a nonfugal style.
136. "Pater Dominicus" is Kajetan Rupert Hagenauer, one of the sons of the Mozarts' former landlord.

found in his library were of a wide variety: works by Ovid and Molière in trans-
lation, Ewald Kleist, C. M. Wieland, Moses Mendelssohn (Phaedon),
Metastasio, etc.

🕮 *Although he had reason to be depressed because he did not receive an appointment at*
the Mannheim court, Mozart nevertheless sounds optimistic, especially as he was
able to arrange a free apartment for himself and his mother. Maria Anna describes
the apartment as a "clean room with two beautiful beds and an alcove." Naturally,
Wolfgang wanted to impress his father with his good business sense.

To his father, in Salzburg

Mannheim, December 27, 1777

Mon très cher Pére!

Terrific paper, isn't it?—Well, I wished I could make it more beautiful!—but it's too late now to get some other kind. You know already
from previous letters that Mama and I now have much better quarters
to live in. I never thought for a moment that she and I should live apart.
So when Herr Court Councillor Serarius kindly offered that I could
stay at his house, I *thanked him* but did not say yes right away. A few
days later, I went to see him, together with Herr Wendling and M. De
Champs, the gallant Dutchman, and sort of waited until he himself
would bring up the subject. At last, he did renew his earlier Proposition
and I thanked him with the following words: I realize what a sign of
friendship it is when you Honor me with an invitation to stay at your
house, but I am sorry I cannot accept your kind offer—and I don't
think you will take it amiss when I tell you—I don't want my mother
to be separated from me without a good reason; and I can't think of a
good reason why my mother should live in one part of town and I in
another.—Of course, when I go to Paris it will be a big advantage for
me when she is not with me, but for the two months that we'll be here
together, it won't matter whether we are spending an extra gulden or
two. With this speech I achieved a *complete* realization of my wish, namely that for both of us neither lodging nor meals will cost anything and
make us any—poorer. Now I must hurry upstairs for supper.—

We've been playing cards till now, and it's half past 10 o'clock. A few
days ago we went to the Reformed Church with the Dutch officer,

Monsieur La Pautri,[137] who is my student, and I played the organ for an hour and a half. The playing just flowed from my heart. In the next few days we, that is the Cannabichs, the Wendlings, the Serarius family, and the Mozarts, will visit the Lutheran Church, where I am going to have some fun with the organ. I tested its full power already at the recent try-out I told you about, but I didn't play much, only a Prelude and then a fugue. I also have finally met Herr Wieland.[138] He doesn't know me as well as I know him, because he hasn't heard anything about me. I would never have imagined that he would be the way he was when I saw him. His speech is somewhat stilted; he has a somewhat childish voice, and is constantly scrutinizing you through his glasses, he has a certain learned rudeness about him and yet, now and then, an air of stupid condescension. But I am not surprised that he acts in such a way here, he may be different in Weimar or elsewhere; for the people here stare at him as if he had come straight down from heaven; they are actually embarrassed to be in his presence, no one says a word, everyone is hushed; all pay close attention to each word he utters;—it's a pity they often have to wait so long because he has a speech defect and, because of it, speaks very slowly and can't say 6 words without coming to a halt. Apart from that he has, as we all know, a superb mind, though his face is really ugly, full of pockmarks, and he has a rather long nose. As to his height, I would guess, he is a little taller than Papa. You must not be in doubt about the 200 gulden from the Dutchman. Now I have to close because I would like to Compose a little more. One more thing: it's probably better if I don't write to Prince Zeil right at this moment!—you undoubtedly know the reason why, after all, Munich is closer to Salzbourg than to Mannheim—I'm saying that Elector Maximilian[139] is dying of smallpox.—It's true. This will upset things quite a bit. Now I wish you farewell. As far as Mama's journey home is concerned, I think it could be done easiest by having her travel with merchants during the

---

137. "Mr La Pautri" is Ferdinand Guillaume Duval de la Pottrie.
138. Christoph Martin Wieland, a popular writer of the German Enlightenment, who had come to Mannheim for the premiere of *Rosamunde*, a singspiel (music by Anton Schweitzer) for which he had written the libretto. Wieland lived in Weimar, where he was engaged as tutor to the princes of Sachsen-Weimar. Together with Goethe and Schiller, he is associated with "Weimar Classicism." Wolfgang's description of him is humorous, ironic, and wonderfully theatrical.
139. Maximilian III, Joseph, elector of Bavaria.

time of Lent!—but that's only what I think; I know for sure, that what-ever you think is best for her, for you are the Herr Hofkapellmeister with the best brain of all!

I kiss 1000 times the hands of Papa, if you happen to know him, and I embrace my sister with all my heart and remain in spite of my scratch-patch writing your most obedient son and faithful brother

Wolfgang Amadé Mozart

ⓘ *Maximilian III, elector and duke of Bavaria, died in Munich on December 30, 1777, of smallpox. Leopold gives a detailed account of his death in his letter of January 5, 1778. Since Maximilian was without heirs, the legal succession to Bavaria fell to the elector of the Palatinate, Karl Theodor, because both lines, the Bavarian and the Palatine, descended from Ruprecht of the Palatinate. The urgency of Count Daun, chief equerry in Munich, to proclaim Karl Theodor as the right-ful successor was an important political move because the Austrian emperor, Joseph II, was poised to march into neighboring Bavaria, annex the state, and declare it a protectorate. As Frederick II of Prussia was strongly opposed to such a move by Austria, there was tension throughout southern Germany, especially in Salzburg, which is located between Bavaria and Austria. The conflict was finally settled in 1779 through arbitration by Empress Catherine of Russia.*

To his father, in Salzburg (postscript)

Mannheim, January 3, 1778

I hope that both of you are well; I am in good health and spirits, thank the lord; but you can readily imagine that I am quite sad that the Elector of Bavaria died. My wish is now that our Elector here will suc-ceed to all of Bavaria and move to Munich—I think you, too, would be happy about such an outcome. Today, at 12 noon, Karl Theodor was proclaimed Duke of Bavaria at court here. In Munich, Count Daun, the chief equerry, declared his allegiance to our Elector here right after Maximilian's death; and he had the dragoons ride through Munich with trumpets and drums shouting: "Long live our Elector Karl Theodor!" If all goes according to plan, as I hope it will, Count Daun is in for a sizable present. His adjutant, Lilienau by name, whom he sent here with the news of Maximilian's death, received a present of 3000 gulden from our Elector here. Farewell for now. I kiss your hands 1000 times and sincerely embrace my sister and remain

Wolfgang Mozart

à tous mes amis des Compliments.[140]

🖎 *In December 1777, Emperor Joseph II established a German opera at the Burgtheater in Vienna; it was called the National Theater (Nationalbühne). The theater, which produced about thirty German plays and singspiele in its short life, lasted until April 1783 when the Italian opera returned to the Burgtheater. Mozart was interested in being appointed director or Kapellmeister of the German opera, but Leopold's inquiries established that a director had already been chosen and no new Kapellmeister was needed.*

To his father, in Salzburg (postscript)

Mannheim, January 10, 1778

I, too, wish for peace with all my heart.[141] I have told you already what I would truly wish for. Anyway, it's time to think seriously about Mama's return trip. Although we had numerous Rehearsals of the opera all along, it's not at all certain whether the opera will actually go into production;[142] if it doesn't, we'll probably be leaving on 15th feb^{ro}. This would not be difficult if one could get prepared ahead of time. I will certainly find out how to go about it. I cannot use the big suitcase; I want to take as little stuff as possible; and the things I don't need right away, such as a pile of Sinfonies, Etc., also some of my clothing, I will store here at the house of Herr Court Councillor, where they would certainly be safe. Then, after receiving your advice on the matter, I will follow the example and advice of my Fellow Travelers and have a black suit made for myself; I will save my clothes with braided borders for Teütschland because in Paris they are out of fashion. . . . Please let me know in your next letter whether I should go ahead with it. Now something else: Herr Wieland, now that he has heard me play twice, is total-

---

140. "Greetings to all my friends."
141. Maria Anna had ended her letter by saying, "May god keep the peace."
142. The singspiel *Rosamunde*, by Anton Schweitzer. Its performance was in doubt because of the death of Maximilian of Bavaria and the obligatory period of mourning.

ly enchanted with me. Last time he said to me, after giving me all sorts of compliments, I feel so fortunate to have met you here, and he pressed my hand. Today they rehearsed "Rosamund" in the theater. It is—good, but nothing more. If it were really poor, they wouldn't perform it? or would they? . . .

🐦 *Second postscript:*

. . . I know for sure that the emperor[143] has in mind to establish a German opera in Vienna; and that he is seriously looking for a young Kapellmeister who knows German, is talented and capable of producing something novel in the world. Benda, who is at Gotha,[144] is interested and Schweizer is determined to get the post. I think it would be the right thing for me, but only, of course, if it pays well. If the emperor gives me a Thousand gulden, I will write him a German opera; and if he doesn't wish to keep me, it's all right with me. Please write to all our good friends in Vienna that I am quite capable of bringing honor to the emperor; if he thinks it necessary, let him Try me out with one opera —then he can decide as he wishes, it'll all be the same to me. adieu. But please, get this thing going right away, otherwise someone else might get there first. I kiss your hands 1000 times and I embrace my sister with all my heart, and remain

Wolfgang Mozart

🐦 *The name of Aloysia (Luise) Weber comes up for the first time in Mozart's letters. Wolfgang had probably known her for a while but had not mentioned her to his father; now he does so with studied innocence. Wolfgang's infatuation with her would become a sore subject for Leopold and a truly painful experience for Wolfgang himself.*

143. Emperor Joseph II of Austria.
144. Georg Benda, composer and court Kapellmeister at Gotha, the capital of Sachsen-Gotha (now part of Thuringia).

To his father, in Salzburg (postscript)

Mannheim, January 17, 1778

Next Wednesday I will be going to Kirchheim-Poland[145] for a few days to present myself to the Princess of *Oranien*. I heard so many good things about her that I finally decided to go. A Dutch officer,[146] a good friend of mine, was terribly scolded by her for not bringing me along when he went to offer his New Year's wishes to her. I should earn at least 8 louis d'or,[147] for, as she is extremely fond of singing, I had four arias copied for her, and I shall bring her a sinfonie as well because she has a pretty good orchestra, which performs every day. The copying of the arias didn't cost me much either, because it was done by a certain Herr Weber, who will accompany me on the trip.[148] I'm not sure whether I have mentioned his daughter to you—she sings superbly and has a beautifully clear voice. The only thing she lacks is some experience in acting, but once she has mastered that she can be a Prima donna in any theater. She is only sixteen. Her father is a good, honest German who is raising his children properly, and that's the very reason why everyone is after the girl. Herr Weber has 6 children, 5 girls and one son;[149] for 14 years he, his wife, and his children had to get along on an income of 200 gulden, but because he always did his work well and provided the Elector with a talented 16-year-old singer, they finally doubled his salary to a paltry 400 gulden. She sings my aria, the one I wrote for De Amicis[150] with those horrific Passages, exceedingly well; and she will sing the aria also at Kirchheim-Poland. She is well capable of teaching herself, she accompanies herself quite well, and she plays galanterie quite Passably. The best thing for her at Mannheim is that she is well respected by all Honest and kindly-thinking people; even the Elector and the

---

145. "Kirchheim-Poland" is the town of Kirchheimbolanden, situated in the Rhineland, north of Mannheim and west of Worms.
146. The "Dutch officer" is probably Ferdinand Guillaume Duval de la Pottrie.
147. Between 56 and 80 gulden.
148. Fridolin Weber, bass singer at the Mannheim theater and copyist. He was the father of Aloysia, with whom Wolfgang fell in love, and uncle of the composer Carl Maria von Weber.
149. Mozart says there were five girls, but there were probably only four: Josepha, Aloysia, Constanze, and Sophie. They were all talented musicians, three of whom (Josepha, Aloysia, and Sophie) became professional singers.
150. Mozart met Anna Lucia de Amicis, the great Italian soprano, in May 1770 in Naples.

Electress are well disposed toward her, provided it doesn't cost them anything; she is allowed to visit the Electress any time, any day; and that is because of her excellent manners.

You know what I would like to ask you?—that you would send me whenever you have a chance, *but as soon as possible,* and little by little in separate mailings, the 2 sonatas for 4 hands and the Fischer Variations!—I could really use them in Paris.

I think we'll be leaving here on 15 feb.ᵗᵒ at the latest, as there will be no opera performance here. Now for something different. Last Wednesday they had a big party here at the house, I was there too. 15 guests were invited, and the Mad.ˢᵉˡˡᵉ of the house was to perform the Concerto I taught her.[151] At 11 o'clock in the morning, the Herr Court Councillor came to my room with Herr Vogler. He *absolument* insisted on making my acquaintance. . . . After dinner he had 2 Claviers, which were tuned to each other, fetched from his house, plus his engraved and ever-so-boring Sonatas. He insisted that I play them, and he accompanied me on the second clavier. Then, on his urging, I had to fetch my own sonatas. N.B., before dinner he raced prima vista through my concerto, the one the Mad.ˢᵉˡˡᵉ of the house had learned and which I wrote for the Countess Litzau. He played the first movement *Prestißimo,* the Andante *allegro,* and the Rondeau truly *Prestißißimo.* The Bass he played mostly quite different from the way it is written, and once in a while he came up with entirely different Harmonies and Melodies. Of course, at that speed it's inevitable, for the eyes cannot follow the notes fast enough, and the hands cannot execute them. So then, what do you call this?—to play prima vista like this and to take a shit is one and the same to me. The listeners, I mean those worthy of the name, can't say anything, except that they have—*seen* Musique and Clavier being performed. They hear, think—and *feel* as little as—*he* does. You can well imagine that it was hard to take, especially since I couldn't say to him: *much too fast!* Besides, it is so much easier to play a piece fast than to play it slowly; in fast Passages you can drop a note or two without anybody noticing; but is it beautiful?—When you play with such rapidity you can make changes in your right and in your left hand without anybody seeing or hearing it; but is it beautiful?—And what does the art of

151. Piano Concerto no. 8 in C major, K. 246.

Prima vista consist of? it is this: to play the piece in correct time, just the way it is supposed to be, and to play all the notes, appogiaturas, Etc., with all proper expression and feeling, just as it says on the page, so that one could have the impression that the one who is playing the piece had actually Composed it. . . . Addio. . . .

Wolfgang Amadè Mozart.

Please write down an A b c for me, both large and small letters, clearly written; and send it to me.

Mozart did not like Vogler as a person and even less as a pianist. Most interesting, however, are Mozart's views on how one should play prima vista. It is easy to imagine that Mozart's own playing was just the way he described it. At the end, Mozart requests a neatly written alphabet from his father. All his life he was bothered by his poor handwriting; here he wants to do something about it. Leopold finally obliged him by writing an alphabet on the outside of a letter to Paris (April 12, 1778).

Mozart writes his mother a rhymed letter from his journey to the princess of Nassau-Weilberg at Kirchheimbolanden. Although the letter-poem is full of humor and bathroom jokes, it contains one serious message: Wolfgang is distancing himself from the musician friends with whom he had wanted to go to Paris. He was most certainly influenced in this decision by the Webers, father and daughter, with whom he was traveling and whom he adopted as his new friends.

To his Mother, in Mannheim

Worms, January 31, 1778

Madame Mutter!
I like to eat Butter.
We are, Thank the Lord,
Healthy and never bored.
Our trip is bright and sunny,
Though we haven't any money;
We enjoy the company we keep,
We are not sick, we do not weep.

Of course, the people I see
Have muck in their bellies, just like me,
But they will let it out with a whine,
either before or after they dine.
There's a lot of farting during the night,
And the farts resound with thunderous might.
Yesterday, though, we heard the king of farts,
It smelled as sweet as honey tarts,
While it wasn't in the strongest of voice,
It still came on as a powerful noise.
We have now been here for over a week,
Shitting muck upon muck in a steady streak.
Herr Wendling has reason to be angry with me,
For I haven't written any of the quartetti;
But when I get back to the bridge o'er the Rhine,
I will travel homeward in one straight line,
And write the 4 quartets without any sass,
So he has no reason to call me an ass.

The Concerto I'll write him in Paris, it's fitting,
For there I can dash it off while I'm shitting,
To tell the truth, I'd rather go with these people here
Into the world both far and near,
Than with those music men I thought I knew,
When I think of them now, I feel so blue;
I may have to do it, but now it's a dread,
For Herr Weber's ass is better than Ramm's head.
Indeed, a small slice from the ass of Herr Weber
I prefer to the whole Wendling endeavor.
We don't insult God when we sit down and shit
Or if we eat muck, chewing off every bit,
We are all honest folk, birds of a feather,
And have summa summarum 8 eyes all together.
That's not counting the one on which we sit.
But now I'd better stop this Poesie of wit.
Just one more thing allow me to add
Monday coming, please don't be sad,

For I'll have the Honor of kissing your hands
Though before I see you, I'll shit in my pants.
à dieu Mamma

Worms, 1778th of January   Yours,
Anno 31.   with deep Respect and Allegiance,
                                   and full of scabs and obedience
                                   Trazom.

The "quartetti" and "Concerto" mentioned in the letter are most likely the flute pieces commissioned by Dejean that the flutist Baptist Wendling had helped him obtain. What is puzzling, however, is his reference to "4 quartets." In his letter of December 10, 1777, to his father, Mozart spoke of "a pair of quartets for the flute."

Mozart has fallen madly in love. Whether it was Aloysia's youthful charm or the way she sang his arias, the fact is that she completely turned Wolfgang's head. As a result, he has suddenly lost interest in writing a German opera for Vienna, or in going to Paris; he now wants to go on tour with Aloysia. To make his change of plans palatable to Leopold, he advances the most incredible reason: the Mannheim musicians with whom he was to go to Paris, particularly the flutist Johann Baptist Wendling, do not have enough religion. It is an argument designed for Leopold, who was, however, not fooled for a moment. He knew right away that Wolfgang had fallen in love, that his plans of going to Italy with the Webers were totally unrealistic, in addition, he feared that his own hold on his son was slipping. It did not help matters that Mozart's mother added a postscript to Wolfgang's letter in which she wrote, "My dear Husband. You can see from this letter that Wolfgang, when he makes new acquaintances, is immediately ready to offer to these people everything he has: life and property."

To his father, in Salzburg

Mannheim, February 4, 1778

Monsieur mon trés cher Pére!

I could not possibly have waited for our usual post day on Saturday, because I haven't had the pleasure of conversing with you in writing for so long. The first thing I want to report to you is how I and my good friends fared in Kirchheim-Poland.[152] It was a vacation trip, nothing

---

152. Kirchheimbolanden.

more. We left here on a Friday morning at 8 o'clock, after eating breakfast at the Webers', then we traveled in an elegant, covered four-seater, and at 4 o'clock we were already at Kirchheim-Poland. We were requested to report our names to the castle right away. Next day, early in the morning, Herr Concert-Meister Rothfischer came to greet us; he had been described to me in Mannheim as a man of sterling honesty; and that's what I found him to be. In the evening we were received at court, that was on Saturday; Mad.^selle Weber sang 3 *arias;*[153] I don't want to go into details about her singing—just this one word: excellent!—. . . The following Monday we had another evening of Musique, Tuesday as well, and then again Wednesday. Mad.^selle Weber sang altogether 13 times and played the Clavier twice; her playing is not bad at all. What amazes me most is her ability to read music; just imagine, she played my difficult sonatas at sight, *slowly* but without dropping a note. In all honesty, I'd rather hear my sonatas played by her than by Vogler. I myself played altogether 12 times and once, by request, on the organ in the Lutheran church. I presented the Princess four of my sinfonies, but I did not receive more than seven louis d'or, NB in silver coins, and my dear poor Weber girl only got five. I was not prepared for that, honestly. Not that I expected a lot, but at least Eight louis d'or for each of us. Basta! we didn't lose any money. I still have a Profit of 42 gulden and the indescribable pleasure of having become acquainted with such thoroughly Honest and good Catholics and Christians. I am only sorry that I did not get to know them long ago. Now I have to tell you something urgent for which I need an answer right away.

My mother and I have talked about it and agree that we don't like the conduct of the Wendling family. Wendling is an Honest and good man, but he has no Religion and neither does his family. It is enough said when I tell you that his daughter was a mistress. And Ramm is a good person but a libertine. I know who I am, I know that I have enough religion in me that I would never do anything that I could not do before the whole world; just the idea to be alone on a trip with such men whose way of thinking is so different from mine and different from that of all honest people, is scary to me. They are, of course, free to do as they please, but I don't have what it takes to travel with them; I probably wouldn't have a single enjoyable hour; I wouldn't know what to say

---

153. The three arias are from Mozart's opera *Lucio Silla*.

to them. In a word, I don't really trust them. Friends who have no Religion do not last. . . .

Right now my thinking goes like this: I'll stay here and finish the Musique for De Jean without haste. It will bring me 200 gulden; besides I can stay here as long as I want to without having to pay for food or lodging. During this time Herr Weber will attempt to organize some concert tours for me and him; we want to go on tour together. For when I travel with him it's just as if I were traveling with you. That is why I like him so much because, apart from his outside appearance, he is so much like you, he has your Caractére and your way of thinking. . . .

I am so fond of this unfortunate family that I wish nothing more than to make them happy; and maybe I can do that. My advice to them is to go to Italy. Therefore, I would like to ask you to write—the sooner, the better—to our good friend Lugiati, and ask him what the top salaries are these days for a Prima donna in Verona?—of course, the more, the better, one can always come down—perhaps one could also try to get the Ascenza in Venice.[154] I can guarantee the quality of her singing with my life; I know she would do me great honor. She has already learned a lot from me in a short time, there's no telling what she might still Learn until then.—About her acting ability, I am not worried. If our plans could be realized, we, that is Monsieur Weber, two of his daughters, and I, will have the honor of visiting my dear Papa and my dear sister on the way to Italy for 2 weeks. My sister will find a friend and companion in Mad.^selle Weber, for she has the same Reputation here as my sister enjoys in Salzburg on account of her proper behavior, her father is like my own father, and the whole family is like the Mozart family. . . . I beg you, do whatever you can to get us to Italy. You know my biggest desire: to writes operas. . . .

My mother pretty much agrees with my way of thinking. I can't possibly travel with people, one man especially, who live a life that would make the youngest traveler feel ashamed; and the thought of helping a poor family, without doing harm to myself, gives me a happy feeling deep in my soul. I kiss your hands 1000 times and remain until death

Your most obedient son
Wolfgang Amadé Mozart.

154. Ascenza is the theatrical and operatic season in Venice during the Festival of Ascension.

🖎 *It would be difficult to find another letter in Mozart's correspondence that shows him quite as impressionable, vulnerable, unrealistic, and transparent. Leopold's reaction was as harsh as it was predictable; he answered his son on February 12 with an emotion-packed letter that begins, "My dear Son! I have read your letter of February 4 with amazement and horror. I am only now, on the 11th, beginning to answer it: but I have not slept all night and I am so weak that I have to write very slowly, word by word. . . . Your proposal to travel about with Herr Weber and, Nota Bene, 2 of his daughters has almost driven me to insanity." Leopold's lengthy letter culminates in an angry command: "Off with you to Paris!"*

🖎 *Mozart's reflections on love, poverty, and money marriages are probably influenced by his feelings for Aloysia Weber and the poverty of her family. But his comments have broader implications. Although he was not a revolutionary or a fervent critic of the upper classes, he does come forth on occasion with a critical remark about the nobility. The second interesting point here is Mozart's self-assessment. He has a good judgment of himself as being a composer rather than a performer, and he understands his unique gift of being able to compose in any style.*

To his father, in Salzburg (postscript)

Mannheim, February 7, 1778

Herr von Schidenhofen could have let me know through you long ago that he was planning to get married soon. I would have Composed some new Menuetts for the occasion. I wish him the very best with all my heart. It is, of course, a money marriage, nothing more. I wouldn't want to enter into this kind of marriage. I wish to make my wife happy and not make my happiness through her. That's why I want to stay away from it all and rather enjoy my golden freedom until I am able to support a wife and children. For Herr von Schidenhofen it was necessary to choose a wealthy woman; after all, he is a nobleman. People of noble birth cannot marry out of inclination or love, they have to marry out of material interest and other such motives. It wouldn't fit the image of such high and noble Personages if they loved their wives in addition to having fulfilled their obligation of bringing a Plump scion into the world. But we poor common folk not only have to take a wife we love and who loves us, but we are permitted, able, and willing to take such a wife precisely because we are not aristocratic, highborn, Noble, and rich, but indeed lowborn, humble, and poor, in other words, we are not in need of a rich wife, for our riches die with us because we carry them in our heads;—and no one can take that away from us, unless someone chops our head off, in which case—we won't need anything anyway. We have received your letter of 2ⁿᵈ feb.ᵗᵒ safely.

The main reason why I am not going to Paris with Wendling and the others, I already told you in my last letter. The 2ⁿᵈ reason is this: I have given some thought to what I could possibly do in Paris. There is really not much I could do for a living, except to find some pupils, but I am not well suited for that kind of work. . . . I want to leave this sort of thing to people who can't do anything but play the Clavier. I am a Composer, and I was born a Kapellmeister. I must not and cannot bury my Gift for Composing, that a benevolent God has bestowed upon me in such rich a measure—I may say so without arrogance because I am aware of it now more than ever before; and I would indeed bury it if I had lots of pupils, for it is a very hectic business. I would rather, *as it were,* neglect the Clavier than Composition. For the Clavier is essentially a sideline for me, but, thank god, a very strong sideline. My third reason is: I am not sure whether our friend Grimm is in Paris.[155] If he is there, I can always follow the others in a mail coach. . . . Indeed, I would be glad to follow, provided all else is fine, especially if I would do an opera. Writing operas is a desire deeply ingrained in me; French rather than German, and Italian rather than German and French. In the *Wendling* family they are all of the opinion that I would do extremely well with my Compositions in Paris. I certainly am not worried about that, for I can, as you know, pretty much adopt and imitate any form and style of composition. . . .

📰 *Second postscript:*

I forgot to mention Mad.ˢᵉˡˡᵉ's Weber's greatest talent in my last letter: she sings a superb *Cantabile.* Please don't forget about Italy. I recom-

---

155. "Our friend Grimm" is Friedrich Melchior von Grimm, minister plenipotentiary of Sachsen-Gotha and, later, secretary of the duc d'Orléans. He had been helpful to the Mozarts when they visited Paris in 1763.

mend the poor but honest Mad.^{selle} Weber with all my heart. Caldamente[156] as the Italians say. . . . Addio, I am your obedient son

WMzt

Thank you for sending the sonatas for 4 hands and the Fischer Variations.

At this time, Mozart is still pursuing his plans of traveling with Aloysia to Italy, perhaps to Switzerland; he is dreaming of making her a star—and maybe his wife. He has not yet heard from his father (a letter from Mannheim to Salzburg took about six days), who will put a stop to his unrealistic plans. The letter also contains a most puzzling remark about the flute: "Besides, my mind gets easily dulled, as you know, when I'm always supposed to write for an instrument that I can't stand." The remark is puzzling because, as most flutists would agree, Mozart composed some excellent flute music, not only the flute quartets and two concertos he wrote (or rewrote), but his Flute and Harp Concerto, K. 299, the Andante for Flute, K. 315, and, of course, the flute music in Die Zauberflöte. *Mozart's remark probably reflects not so much his disdain for the flute as his irritation at being pressured by Dejean and his father to finish the assignment. Mozart seems to be musically and emotionally at a point where he wants to explore new things in his life and in his music. He is getting irritable and impatient.*

To his father, in Salzburg (postscript)

Mannheim, February 14, 1778

Monsieur mon trés cher Pére!

I can see from your letter of 9th feb.^{ro} that you have not yet received my last two letters. Herr Wendling and Herr Ramm are leaving early tomorrow morning. If I knew that you are very unhappy about my not going to Paris with them, I would feel badly that I stayed here; I do hope you're not. After all, the road to Paris is not closed to me. Herr Wendling promised to inquire about Monsieur Grimm right away and to send me word about him immediately. If this good friend of ours should be in Paris, I'll go there for certain; for he will probably be able to arrange something for me. The biggest reason why I didn't go with the others was the following: we haven't been able to find an appropriate

---

156. "Warmly."

transportation to get Mama to Augsburg. How could she have stayed here, in the house, without me?—So I'm asking you to try and find a way for her to get from Augsburg to Salzburg; once I know for sure you have done that, I will see to it that she will get safely to Augsburg—and if there is no other way, I will take her there myself. . . . Herr de Jean, who is also leaving for Paris tomorrow, paid me only 96 gulden because I don't have more than 2 Concerti and 3 quartetti ready for him;[157] even for giving me only half the sum, he was still short 4 gulden; but he will have to pay me the whole amount because I talked to Wendling about it and we agreed that I will send the rest to Paris.

The fact that I could not finish the assignment can easily be explained. I never have a quiet hour around here. I cannot compose, except at night; which means, I also can't get up early in the morning. And then, one isn't always in the mood to write. Of course, I could scribble all day long, and scribble as fast as I can, but such a thing goes out into the world; so I want to make sure that I won't have to feel ashamed, especially when my name appears on that page; besides, my mind gets easily dulled, as you know, when I'm supposed to write a lot for an instrument I can't stand. So, for a change of pace, I've been working on something different now and then, for instance, Clavier duetti with violin, and a Mass[158] . . .

I beg you most sincerely, do take an interest in the Weber girl; it would mean much to me if she could make her fortune; just think: Husband and wife, 5 children and 450 gulden salary!—and don't forget about Italy, and don't forget about me, for you know my true desire and Passion. I hope all will go well. I have confidence in god, he will not forsake us. Now I wish you all well, keep in mind my requests and Recomendations. I kiss your hands 100000 times and remain your most obedient son,

Wolfgang gottlieb Mozart
Mannheim, 14th feb.ro 1778

157. Mozart writes he finished three "quartetti," but apparently he completed only two: K. 285 and 285a. He wrote a new flute concerto, K. 313, but the second flute concerto, K. 314, was a rearrangement of his Oboe Concerto, K. 271k, composed a year earlier in Salzburg. Clearly, Dejean felt he had received only half of the music he had commissioned.
158. Mozart wrote four sonatas for piano and violin in early 1778 in Mannheim: K. 301, 302, 303, and 305. He would later add two more, K. 304 and 306, and dedicate the six sonatas to Electress Elisabeth Auguste of the Palatinate, who had by then moved from Mannheim to Munich.

📖 *Leopold's angry and dictatorial response to Wolfgang's plans to go on tour with Aloysia threw Wolfgang into complete disarray. Clearly, he was no match for his father. To prevent losing his son to someone else, Leopold had pulled out all the stops. He reminded Wolfgang of how he had been totally devoted to his father, singing to him as a child before going to bed and wishing to keep him alive forever in a glass case; and, in a second line of attack, Leopold disparaged all the female company Wolfgang had ever had. He put it to Wolfgang crudely but effectively: Do you want to become a famous Kapellmeister about whom posterity will read in books, or do you want to wind up on a sack of straw having to feed a bunch of hungry children? Wolfgang had very little choice but to give in to his father and his powerful arguments.*

To his father, in Salzburg

Mannheim, February 19, 1778

Monsieur mon trés cher Pére!

I hope you have received my last two letters safely; in the last one I told you my thoughts about my Mother's trip home, but now I see from your writing of the 12th that it was quite unnecessary. I never expected anything else but that you would disapprove of my traveling with the Webers, because I couldn't quite put it together in my own mind, *given our present situation;*[159] but I had given my word of honor that I would write to you about it. Herr Weber does not know about our circumstances, and I will certainly not tell anybody. I wished that we could be in a position where such things didn't matter and we could all be happy together, I forgot in my intoxication that, for the time being, the whole thing was impossible and also—to let you know that I was thinking that myself; at any rate, that's what I am doing right now. You have read often enough in my last two letters why I haven't gone to Paris. If my Mother hadn't started raising questions about it, I would certainly have gone with the others. But when I noticed that she felt uneasy about it, I began feeling uneasy about it myself; as soon as someone loses confidence in me, I lose confidence in myself too. Indeed, the days are gone when I stood on a chair and sang the "oragna fiagata fà"[160] and kissed the tip of your nose; but does it mean that my Respect, love, and obedience for

---

159. Leopold had just written how much in debt the family was on account of Wolfgang's trip.
160. "Oragna fiagata fà" seems to be a children's nonsense song that Wolfgang loved to sing to his father when he was little.

you have diminished?—I will say no more. In reference to what you are saying about the young singer in Munich, I must confess that it was stupid of me to write such an obvious lie.[161] She doesn't even know yet what real *singing* is. It is true that she sang extremely well for someone who had studied Musick for only 3 months, and, besides, she had a very pleasant and pure voice. . . .

What you are saying in such a biting way about the merry time I had with your brother's daughter, has hurt me deeply;[162] but as it was not at all the way you think it was, I have nothing more to say about it. . . . What you are saying about Mad^selle Weber is quite correct; and when I wrote to you about her I knew as well as you that she is too young and needs to learn about acting; . . . and while my letter was on its way to Salzbourg I kept telling her to be patient, and that she was still too young, etc. they do accept my advice readily, for they really think highly of me; and her father followed my advice and talked with Mad.^ame Toscani, an actress, to give his daughter acting lessons. . . . Farewell. I kiss your hands 100000 times and remain your most obedient son

wolfgang Amadé Mozart

I'm so hungry now,
I can't write any more.

My Mother will open our big Cash Box for your inspection.[163] I embrace my sister with all my heart, but she shouldn't cry about every little sh(it),[164] otherwise I'll never come back. Regards to all good friends, especially Herr Bullinger.

Mozart is still reeling from the effects of his father's letter of February 4. His reaction to Leopold's aggressiveness is typical: he withdraws, gets sick, and loses his self-esteem. Only two weeks earlier, he had prided himself on being a born composer;

161. Margarethe Kaiser in Munich. Wolfgang had exaggerated her talent as a singer, which made Leopold suspect that they had had an amorous relationship.
162. Maria Anna Thekla Mozart, the *Bäsle* in Augsburg.
163. Wolfgang and his mother were ordered by Leopold to account for their remaining travel money. The box contained 140 gulden in cash.
164. Leopold had written that Nannerl had cried for two days because of Wolfgang's association with the Webers, to which Wolfgang reacts with great irritation: "sie soll nicht gleich über jeden Dr(eck) weinen."

now he ridicules himself as a born "wood tapper" (Holztapper) who cannot do anything but pound the clavier. In letters to come, Mozart would try to make his peace with his father, to be polite and conciliatory, but it is very obvious from the following letter that his father wounded him to the quick.

To his father, in Salzburg

Mannheim, February 22, 1778

Monsieur mon trés cher Pére.

I've been at home for 2 days now and have been taking Anti-spasmodics and black Powder and elderberry tea to make me sweat, because I've been suffering from Catharr, a runny nose, headaches, a soar throat, eyeaches, and earaches; but now I feel better, thank god, and tomorrow I hope to be able to go out again, as it is sunday. I received your letter of the 16th, including the two unsealed letters of introduction for Paris, in good order. I am glad you liked my French aria.[165] Please forgive me if I'm not writing a whole lot today, but I simply can't. I'm afraid my headache may come back, besides, I'm just not in a very good mood for writing today—anyway, one can't write all the things that go through one's mind—certainly I can't. It's better to say things in person than in writing. You will have read in my last letter how things stand here. I beg you, think of me whatever you like, but don't think anything bad. There are people who believe that it is impossible to love a poor girl without having bad intentions; and that pretty word maitreße, h——e in German,[166] oh, it's so charming and convenient!—but I am no Brunetti and no Misliwetcek![167] I am a Mozart, a young and decent-minded Mozart; therefore, I hope you will forgive me if I get carried away sometimes in my excitement—for I have to say it this way, although I would rather say it in my own natural way. There is much I could write on this subject, yet I can't; in fact, it's quite impossible for me, for among my many faults I also have the following: I always believe that my friends who know me, really know me!—and it is not necessary to use many words; and if they don't know me, oh, where should I take

---

165. The aria titled "Oiseaux, si tous les ans" (Birds, if every year), K. 307.
166. "h——e" is *Hure* in German, or "whore."
167. Antonio Brunetti, a violinist in the Salzburg orchestra, had fathered an illegitimate child; Josef Mysliveček, Mozart's Bohemian friend, was suffering from venereal disease.

all the words needed to explain! It's bad enough if one requires words and letters for this. I am not writing these things with you in mind, my dear Papa, No! You know me too well, and you are too decent to make judgments that would dishonor anyone!—I only mean those—and they know that I'm talking about them: people who do that sort of thing.—

I have decided to stay home today after all, although it's Sunday, because it's snowing so hard. But tomorrow I will have to go out because our House Nymph, Mad.^selle Pierron, who is my Highhonorable pupil, will be dashing off my Highnoble Litzow Concerto at the French Academy, which meets every Monday. I too shall ask them to let me bang out something on the piano, prostituting myself all the way, so I can thump something out prima *fista*;[168] for, after all, I am a born wood tapper who can do nothing but pound the Clavier a little! Now I'm asking permission to stop writing, my mood is not good for writing letters today, but more for composing. . . .

Wolfgang Amadé Mozart

🖎 *Mozart's aria for Aloysia Weber—the first of eight he would write for her—is filled with tender expression but also technical difficulties. If she sang the coloratura parts as cleanly as he seems to indicate, she had, indeed, an excellent voice. Most interesting, however, is Mozart's statement that he loves to compose for the voice so that it fits like a well-tailored dress. It is this "human" factor that gives Mozart's voice compositions a special warmth and brilliance.*

To his father, in Salzburg

Mannheim, February 28, 1778

Monsieur mon trés cher Pére!

. . . Yesterday I visited Raff[169] and I brought him an aria that I had written for him these past few days. The words go like this: "se al labro mio non credi, bella nemica mia," etc., etc.[170] I don't think the text is by Metastasio. He was absolutely delighted with the aria. . . . When I left he thanked me very warmly; and I assured him in return that I will

---

168. "Prima fista" is a pun on "prima vista," i.e., sight-reading with a fist.
169. The tenor Anton Raaff, whom Mozart met in Mannheim.
170. "If you do not believe my lips," K. 295.

arrange the aria for him in such a way that he would certainly enjoy singing it; for I love it when an aria is so accurately measured for a singer's voice that it fits like a well-tailored dress. I also set, as a kind of exercise, the aria "non sò d'onde viene" etc, to music, which has already been so beautifully composed by Bach;[171] and I did it for the following reason: I know the aria by Bach so well because I like it very much and can always hear it in my head. So I wanted to see whether I would be able, in spite of all this, to write an aria that was completely different from the one by Bach;—and indeed, my aria does not resemble his at all, not at all.

At first, I thought it would be a good aria for Raff, but already the beginning seemed too high for him, and yet I liked it too much to make any changes; . . . so I resolved to compose the aria for the Weber girl, and make it as accurate for her voice as possible; it is an Andante sostenuto, preceded by a short Recitative, then comes the middle section, "nel seno à destarmi,"[172] then again the Sostenuto. When I had finished it, I said to Mad.^selle Weber, learn the aria by yourself, sing it according to your own feelings, then let me hear it and I will tell you afterward honestly what I like and what I don't like. After 2 days I went to her, and she recited the aria for me, accompanying herself. I had to admit that she sang it exactly as I had wished and as I would have taught her. It is now the best aria she has in her repertoire; she will most certainly gain honors with it wherever she goes. . . .

I beg of you, don't let the thought come into your head that I shall ever forget you!—I cannot bear it. My main goal was, is, and will always be to strive for a speedy and happy reunion—but it means to be patient; you know better than I how things sometimes go awry—but they also straighten out again. Just be patient. Let's put our trust in god, I am sure he will not forsake us; I certainly will do my part; how can you possibly have any doubts about me?—Is it not to my own advantage that I would work with all my strength so I can, the sooner, the better, have the good fortune and pleasure to embrace my best and most beloved father with all my heart?—there you see!—nothing in the world is free

171. "Bach" is Johann Christian Bach, whom young Mozart met in London. The aria is the Recitative and Aria for Soprano, K. 294, "I confess to you, Alcandro . . . I know not whence comes this tender feeling" (Alcandro, lo confesso . . . Non sò d'onde viene); the text is by Pietro Metastasio.
172. "In my breast awaken . . ." (second part of "Non sò d'onde viene").

of self-interest!—if there should be war in Bavaria,[173] then, I beg you, come to us at once. There are 3 friends I trust, they are strong and indomitable friends: namely god, your head, and my head; our two heads are, naturally, different, but each is in its own way very good, useful, and practical; and in time I hope that my head will gradually come up to the level of yours in the area where yours is stronger than mine. Now fare well! Be merry and enjoy yourself; keep in mind that you have a son who has never knowingly forgotten his filial Duties, and who will strive to become more and more worthy of such a good father, and who will never change, your most obedient

Wolfgang Mozart

It is difficult to say whether the following letter, Mozart's fifth to his cousin in Augsburg, is his funniest or saddest. He appears to be in high spirits, producing his patented nonsense verse, rhythmic prose, and what might be called an Ode to Muck. But underneath his lyrical scatology, underneath his humorous conjugation of the verb "to be," one senses tension, frustration, and anxiety; the jolly face he wants to show Bäsle contains a strain of sadness.

To Maria Anna Thekla Mozart, in Augsburg

Mannheim, February 28, 1778

Mademoiselle ma trés chére Cousine!

you may perhaps believe or even think that I am dead!—that I Croaked?—or kicked the bucket?—not at all! Don't think it, I beg of you; for thinking and shitting are two different things!—how could I write such a beautiful letter if I were dead?—how would that be possible?—I won't even begin to excuse my long silence, because you wouldn't believe me anyway; but what's true is true!—I've been so terribly busy that I had time to think of my Bäsle but not to write to her, so I needed to defer.

But now I have the honor to query how you are and whether you are weary?—whether your bowels are solid or thin?—whether you have scabs on your skin?—whether you are still a little fond of this here gawk?—whether you sometimes write with a chalk?—whether you now

173. The threat of war over the succession in Bavaria was still in the air.

and then think of me?—whether at times you'd like to hang yourself from a tree?—whether perhaps you are angry at me, fool that I'll always be; whether you won't make peace in your heart, or, by my honor, I'll crack a big fart! now you're laughing—victoria!—our asses shall signal the tidings of peace!—I knew you couldn't resist me any longer; yes, yes, I am absolutely sure of this, even if today I still have to shit and piss, but in 2 weeks I'll be off to Paris; so if you want to find me hither with an answer from Augsburg thither, hurry up with your letter, send it, the sooner, the better; for if I have already left this place, instead of a letter I'll get muck in my face. muck!—muck!—oh muck!—o sweet word!—muck!—chuck! That's good too!—muck, chuck!—muck!—suck—oh charmante!—muck, suck!—love this stuff!—muck, chuck and suck!—chuck muck and suck muck!—Now let's talk about something else; have you had some good fun in this year's carnival? I think one can have more fun in Augsburg than around here. I wished I could be with you so I could hop, skip, and dance with you. My Mama and I send greetings to your Father and Mother, and, of course, to Bäsle, and we hope that all 3 of you are well and in good spirits. We are just fine, god be praised and thanked. Don't believe it. So much the better, better the much so. apropós: how are you coming with your French?—may I soon write a complete letter in French?—from Paris, n'est-ce pas?—tell me, do you still have the spunicunifait?—I believe it. Now I must tell you something before I close because I have to stop soon, for I am in a hurry, as I have absolutely nothing to do right now; and then, too, because I have no more space left, as you can see, I am just about out of paper; besides I'm tired, my fingers are aching from writing so much, and, finally, I wouldn't know, even if I had more room to write, what else I could tell you? except perhaps the story that I'm going to tell. So listen! It didn't happen so very long ago, and it happened here somewhere out in the country; it created a big stir because it's almost unbelievable. Nobody knows, just between you and me, how this thing will end. So then, to make a long story short, it happened about 4 hours from here, I don't remember the name of the place—it was a village or something like that; at any rate, it doesn't really matter whether it was Tribsterill, where the shit runs into the sea, or Burmesquick, where they make the crooked assholes; in other words, it was some kind of a place. Well then, there was once a herdsman or shepherd who was already quite old but looked still rugged and strong;

he was unmarried and well off, and he enjoyed life. Oh yes, there's one more thing I must tell you before I go on with my story: the sound of his voice was terrifying, people always got scared when they heard him speak. Well now, to be brief, you should know further that he had a dog called Bellot; it was a very beautiful, big dog, white with black spots. So, one day, the man came wandering along with his sheep, he had about 11 thousand, and he was carrying in his hand a stick that was decorated with a beautiful rose-colored ribbon. He never went anywhere without his stick; it had become a habit with him; but let's continue: after he had walked a good hour, he got tired and sat down by a river. At last, he fell asleep, and he dreamed he had lost his sheep; in his fright he woke up and to his great joy he saw that his sheep were all there; finally, he got up and went on his way, but he didn't get very far, for scarcely half an hour had gone by when he came to a bridge that was very long and had railings on both sides, so no one would fall off; well now, he looked at his flock and because he had to cross over, he began to usher his 11 thousand sheep across the bridge.

Now will you please be so kind and wait until the 11 thousand sheep are on the other side, then I will finish my story. I told you beforehand that no one knows how this thing will end. I do hope, however, before I write again, the sheep will all have crossed the bridge; if not, it really doesn't matter much; as far as I am concerned, they could have all stayed on this side; at any rate, you'll have to be satisfied with what I know and what I told you; it's better I stop here rather than add to the story by making things up. In that case you might doubt the whole shistori[174] as it is now—you probably don't believe half of it, anyway. Now I must close, though it makes me morose, but if you start something, you must know when to stop, for if you don't you'll be considered a flop, to all my friends my Compliment, and who doesn't believe it can kiss my rear end, from now until eternity, or until I regain my sanity, in which case he will have to lick and lick, and I must worry myself quite sick that there won't be sufficient muck and he won't have enough to suck. adieu, Bäasle! I am, I was, I were, I have been, I had been, I would have been, oh if I were, oh that I were, I wished to god I were, I would be, I shall be, if I should be, oh that I would be, I might have been, I shall have

---

174. "Shistorie" is Mozart's own creation combining the German words *Schiss* (shit) and *Historie* (story).

been, oh if I had been, oh that I had been, I wished to god I would have been, what?—a numbskull.[175]

adieu, my Cousine dear, where do we go from here?—I am the same old cousin,

Wolfgang Amadé Mozart

🔖 *Mozart's Ode to Muck deserves to be quoted in the original: "dreck!—dreck!—o dreck!—o süsses wort!—dreck!—schmeck!—auch schön!—dreck, schmeck!— dreck!—leck—o charmante!—dreck, leck!—das freüet mich!—dreck, schmeck und leck!—schmeck dreck, und leck dreck!"*

🔖 *A kind of emotional battle is going on between Wolfgang and Leopold Mozart. Wolfgang has not yet given up on his plan to marry Aloysia Weber, but first he tries to reestablish good feelings with his father and then ask "a big favor," which is to get permission to marry. Leopold, on the other hand, tries to tie his son firmly to him by reminding him how much he has sacrificed and is sacrificing still for his son's career. In a letter of February 25–26, Leopold painted an effective picture of personal suffering: "I look like poor Lazarus, my morning coat is in tatters . . . my flannel vest . . . is so torn that it can barely stay on my body . . . since your departure I had no new shoes made." The message worked; it moved Wolfgang to tears.*

To his father, in Salzburg

Mannheim, March 7, 1778

Monsieur mon trés cher Pére!

. . . Once I am safely in Paris and our situation is somewhat settled, with the help of god, and we're all a bit more relaxed and in better spirits, I want to convey my thoughts more fully and ask a big favor of you. But right now I must tell you that I was greatly alarmed, indeed, tears came to my eyes, when I read in your last letter that you have to go about in tattered clothes. My dearest Papa! it's not my fault—you know that; we are saving here as much money as we possibly can, food and lodging, firewood and light, is not costing us anything here; and that's all we can expect to get free; and as far as clothes are concerned, you know very well that, when you are out in the world, you can't walk about

---

175. Mozart's German word here is *Stockfisch*, which means "dried cod"—and is often translated as such— but the colloqial meaning, and certainly Mozart's meaning, is "numbskull" or "simpleton."

poorly dressed; you always have to pay attention to your appearance. I have now put my entire hope on Paris, for the German princes are all penny-pinchers. And I will work as hard as I can to soon have the pleasure of getting you out of your distressing situation. Now about our trip. We shall leave a week from today, that is the 14th; we're having big problems selling our carriage; so far we didn't have a single inquiry. If we get 4 louis d'or for it, we'll be lucky. People are advising us to hire a driver and have him take us to Strassburg in our own carriage, if we can't sell it here; we might be able to sell it more easily in Strassburg. However, it is less expensive to go by mail coach, so I'll probably end up leaving the carriage here, with honest people, who will sell it for us. . . . Now I must close so Mama has a little room to write. adieu. I kiss your hands 100000 times and remain your most obedient son

wolfgang Mozart

To his father, in Salzburg

Mannheim, March 11, 1778

Monsieur mon trés cher Pére!

I have received your last letter of March 5th and read to my greatest delight that our good and most excellent friend Baron Grimm is in Paris.[176] Yes, you are right, we shall be leaving here next Saturday, the 14th; but we are not yet sure whether we'll take the diligence[177] or not and whether we'll travel via Strassburg or Metz; all these things will be decided tomorrow morning. . . . I apologize that I am writing so poorly and so little today, but there's so much to do that I don't know where to begin. Farewell in the meantime; two weeks after you receive this letter, I hope you'll be receiving my first letter from Paris. I kiss your hands 1000 times and embrace my sister with all my heart and remain until death, your most obedient son

Wolfgang Amadé Mozart

P.S. apropòs. Let me ask you for something that I had requested some time ago, and that is an Abc, written in your hand, large and small

---

176. Baron Grimm wrote to Leopold on February 21, 1778, that he would be glad to help Wolfgang in Paris.
177. The "diligence" was an express coach service (*Eilpost* in German).

letters. Please don't forget. . . . Just this moment we worked out a contract with the driver. He will take us to Paris for 11 louis d'or in our own chaise, which he has bought from us for 40 gulden. Tomorrow we'll put in writing that I need to pay him only 7 louis d'or and 4 gulden when we get to Paris, because I didn't insist that he pay me for the chaise immediately.

Paris et Retour

March 14, 1778—Mid-January 1779

ON A SUNNY MORNING in March 1778, Wolfgang and his mother set out for Paris. The weather remained pleasant for most of the journey, but two days before reaching their destination, the travelers were overwhelmed by a powerful spring storm. Wet, tired, and with little money, they arrived in the French capital on March 23 and found temporary quarters at the house of Herr Mayer, a German business agent, in the rue Bourg l'Abbé. Nannerl had given fifty gulden, her entire savings, as security for an additional loan to finance the trip, and Leopold had sent a list of Parisian friends who had, fifteen years before, been helpful to the Mozarts on their first visit to Paris. La Duchesse de Bourbon and Baron von Grimm topped the list of fifty-one distinguished names.

Wolfgang, who had been glum and bored throughout the nine-day trip, leaped into action as soon as he reached Paris. Within days he contacted Baron von Grimm, who helped with introductions, and Monsieur Legros, director of the Concert Spirituel, who helped by giving Mozart some instant work. Indeed, a few weeks later, Legros commissioned Mozart to write a "grand symphony" for the Concert Spirituel. The new symphony, which was performed "on Corpus Christi Day," June 18, 1778, at the Palais des Tuileries, was Mozart's Symphony in D major, K. 297, appropriately nicknamed "the Paris."

In spite of these promising beginnings, Mozart failed to achieve a decisive breakthrough. For one thing, the Paris music world was just then preoccupied with a musical feud between the composers Niccolò Piccinni, who favored Italian opera buffa, and Christoph Willibald Gluck, who favored the French *tragédie lyrique*. Few music connoisseurs took time to pay attention to a newcomer who would not even take sides in the dispute. But perhaps even more damaging for Mozart was his own attitude toward the French and their musical taste. His criticism may well have been based on emotions, for Mozart had wished to go on tour with Aloysia Weber to make her a star. When his father ordered him to Paris, he took it as a form of banishment, and his immediate reaction was a thorough dislike of everything French. Only at the end of his stay, when his father required him to return to Salzburg, did he find that Paris held great promise after all.

Equally disastrous was Mozart's political ineptitude. He had never been skilled in the world of courtly politics or in the art of self-promotion, but in Paris he seemed particularly clumsy. He was, as Baron von Grimm observed, "zu treuherzig," that is, too trusting. Grimm used the same German phrase in a letter written in French to Leopold Mozart in July 1778: "He is *zu treuherzig*, too inactive, too easy to catch, too little intent on the means that may lead to fortune. To make an impression here one has to be artful, enterprising, daring. To make his fortune I wish he had but half his talent and twice as much shrewdness, and then I should not worry about him."

The story of Mozart in Paris is filled with pain, ambivalence, and miscalculation, and the story of Mozart's mother is even more so. Maria Anna, who spoke no French and was in awe of big cities, would have much preferred to travel home to her beloved Salzburg. Instead, dedicated and uncomplaining as she was, she accompanied her son to Paris and suffered the consequences. "As far as my life is concerned," she wrote to Leopold shortly after their arrival, "it's not very pleasant. All day I sit in my room alone as if it were a prison cell; the room is dark and faces a little courtyard where you can't see the sun all day and one doesn't know what the weather is like. There's just enough light coming through the window that if I try very hard I can do a little knitting. We have to pay 30 livres a month for this room. Entrance and staircase are so narrow that it is not possible to bring a clavier up into our room. So Wolfgang has to do his composing at the house of Monsieur le Gros because there he has a clavier. I don't see him all day and may well forget how to talk." Things got a bit more bearable when Madame d'Epinay, Baron von Grimm's friend, succeeded in finding better and less expensive quarters for the Mozarts in the rue du Gros Chenêt, not far from the Paris opera house. Maria Anna began to venture out a little along the "broad and shiny" boulevards, taking in the wondrous sights of the city, including the latest Parisian fashions. The hairstyles were so high, she reported to Leopold and Nannerl with a blush of humor, that the carriages would have had to be raised if the ladies had desired to sit upright. For a short while, it seemed as if both Wolfgang and Maria Anna would make their adjustments to the big city, but three months into their stay, tragedy struck. "After lunch I went walking in the Luxembourg Garden," wrote Maria Anna, "afterward I looked at the beautiful pictures in the Palace, but when I got home I felt strangely tired." Two weeks later, on July 3, 1778, Maria Anna Mozart succumbed to typhus, her life "went out like a light," as Wolfgang wrote to his father in sorrow and complete bewilderment.

After six months in Paris, Leopold decided it was time for Wolfgang to return home to Salzburg, find employment, and help pay off the family debts, which by now were considerable. Wolfgang was reluctant. Ultimately, he had no choice but to obey his father, but he stretched the journey, which should have taken about two weeks, into nearly four months, giving his father fits of anger and anxiety. When he finally arrived in Salzburg, in the middle of January 1779, Wolfgang felt thoroughly defeated.

Mozart's letters to his father, which constitute the bulk of his Parisian correspondence, are lengthy, detailed, poignant, and dramatic. One event naturally stands out: the death of Maria Anna. Mozart's description of his mother's final hours are filled with pain and unacknowledged guilt. But the name that gives him hope throughout this mournful experience is not Leopold in Salzburg but Aloysia Weber in Mannheim. His search for the young singer concludes this long and painful journey from Salzburg to Paris and back, but of all the disillusions and false hopes that accompanied the trip, Mozart's fervent hope of being reunited with Aloysia proved to be the most painful disillusion of them all.

Mozart's first letter from Paris shows that he may have arrived there physically but not mentally. With the help of Baron von Grimm, he made contacts very quickly, but his thoughts were still with his friends in Mannheim and his real wish was to be on tour with Aloysia.

To his father, in Salzburg

Paris, March 24, 1778

Mon Trés cher Pére.

Yesterday, Monday, the 23ʳᵈ, we arrived here safe and sound at 4 o'clock in the afternoon, god be praised and thanked; so we were on the road for 9½ days. For a while we thought we couldn't take it anymore. I've never been so bored in all my life. You can easily imagine what it is like to leave Mannheim and so many dear and close friends, and then not only be without those good friends for ten and a half days, but have no company at all, not a single soul to talk to. But now, thank the lord, we have reached our destination. I hope that with god's help all will turn out for the best. Today we'll take a cab and visit Grimm and Wendling; tomorrow morning I will call on Herr von Sückingen,[1] the Palatine minister here, who is a great connoisseur and Passionate lover of Musick; I have two letters for him, one from Herr von Gemmingen[2] and one from Monsieur Cannabich. Before leaving Mannheim I had the Quartett I wrote one evening at the inn at Lodi, the Quintett, and the Fischer Variations[3] copied out for Herr von Gemmingen. He sent me a very dear thank-you note and told me how delighted he was that I was leaving him such a fine remembrance; he also gave me a letter to his very good friend Herr von Sückingen, saying that he was sure I myself would be a better recommendation for the letter than the letter could be for me, and to reimburse me for the cost of copying he sent me 3 Louis d'or. He assured me of his friendship and asked for mine. I must say that all the Gentlemen who knew me, the privy councillors, chamberlains, and other worthy people, including the members of the court orchestra, were all very indignant and sorry about my leaving. That's the absolute truth. We left Mannheim on Saturday, the 14ᵗʰ, and the Thursday before we had a musical get-together in the afternoon at Cannabich's, where my Concerto for 3 pianos was performed.[4] Mad.ˢᵉˡˡᵉ

---

1. Count Karl Heinrich Joseph von Sickingen, Palatine ambassador, was not only a music connoisseur but also a reputable scientist.
2. Baron Otto Heinrich von Gemmingen-Homburg, a government official (and dramatist) in Mannheim whom Mozart would meet again in Vienna as the grand master of the Masonic lodge For Beneficence (Zur Wohltätigkeit).
3. The quartet written at Lodi, Italy, is K. 80, Mozart's first quartet, written when he was fourteen; the quintet is K. 174, written in 1773; the Fischer Variations are K. 179, written in Salzburg, 1774.
4. The Triple Piano Concerto in F ("Lodron"), K. 242.

Rosl Cannabich played the first, Mad.^selle Weber the second, and Mad.^selle Piérron Serarius, our house nymph, the third Clavier. We had 3 rehearsals, and it all went quite well. Mad.^selle Weber also sang 2 of my arias, the "Aer tranquillo" from Rè Pastore,[5] and the new one, "Non sò d'onde viene."[6] With this last aria my dear Weber girl brought extraordinary honor to herself and to me; everybody was saying that no aria had ever moved them as much; and indeed, she sang it just the way it ought to be sung. As soon as the aria had ended, Cannabich shouted loudly, bravo, bravißimo, maestro; veramente scritta da maestro.[7] It was the first time I heard the aria with orchestral accompaniment; I only wished you could have heard it just the way it was played and sung here, with this kind of precision in its interpretation, just the right piano and forte. But who knows, maybe some day you'll hear it just this way—I do hope so. The musicians kept praising the aria and couldn't stop talking about it. I do have so many good friends in Mannheim, even friends of rank and wealth—they all would have liked me to stay. Well, I hold with those who pay me well; but who knows, it may happen still; I certainly wish it; and I always have this—feeling of hope. . . .

Mad.^selle Weber has crocheted two pairs of lace cuffs for me, out of the goodness of her heart. She presented them to me as a keepsake and a modest gift of gratitude. Also her father copied everything I needed without charging me for it and, in addition, he gave me some music paper; he also presented me with the comedies of Molière, because he knew I had never read them, with the following inscription: Ricevi, Amico, le opere del moliere in segno di gratitudine, e qualche volta ricordati di me.[8] When he was alone with my Mama he said to her: now our best friend is leaving us, our benefactor. It's true, if it hadn't been for your son, he has done so much for my daughter, he took an interest in her, and she cannot thank him enough. . . . When I left, they all wept. You must excuse me but tears come into my eyes when I think about it. He escorted me down the stairs and stood at the door until I turned the corner, and even then he still called after me: Adieu!

5. *Il rè pastore, dramma per musica*, K. 208, written in Salzburg, 1775.
6. K. 294, an aria specifically composed for Aloysia Weber.
7. "truly written by a maestro."
8. The inscription reads, "Accept, my friend, the works of Molière as a sign of my gratitude, and think of me sometimes." The third volume of this German Molière edition was found in Mozart's library after his death.

The expenses for our trip, food, beverages, lodging, and tips run a little over 4 Louis d'or;[9] the farther into France we got, the more expensive things became. Just this minute I received your letter from the 16th. You don't have to worry, I'll be doing just fine. I have only one request: please be more cheerful in your letters; and if war comes and gets too close to you,[10] come and join us! My greetings to all good friends, I kiss your hands 1000 times and embrace my sister with all my heart and remain your most obedient son

Wolfgang Amadè Mozart

On April 5, Maria Anna wrote to Leopold, "Wolfgang is extremely busy and . . . so well known here and popular that it is hard to describe." Indeed, Mozart had thrown himself into all kinds of projects: writing new parts for a choral work by Ignaz Holzbauer, composing a sinfonia concertante for winds, and making plans for an opera. Unfortunately, none of these projects materialized.

To his father, in Salzburg (postscript)

Paris, April 5, 1778

I want to explain a little more clearly what Mama told you already but not very accurately.[11] Herr Kapellmeister Holzbauer had, indeed, sent a "Miserere" here; but because the choruses at Mannheim are weak and poorly manned, whereas here they are good and strong, his choruses would not have been very effective here; therefore, Monsieur Le Gros, the director of the Concert spirituel, asked me to compose some new choruses. . . . I must say that I am glad to be done with this kind of busywork. If you can't write at home and you have to do things in a hurry, it's damned hard. But now I am finished with it, god be praised and thanked; and I hope it will have the desired Effect. Monsieur Goßec,[12] whom you no doubt know, told Le Gros, after he had looked at my first chorus—I wasn't there at the time—that it was Charmant and would certainly make a good Effect. He said the words were well

---

9. About 44 gulden.
10. There was a threat of war between Prussia and Austria over the Bavarian succession.
11. Maria Anna had written to Leopold that Wolfgang had to compose a "Miserere" (i.e., Psalm 50), one act of an opera, and two concertos.
12. François-Joseph Gossec, operatic composer and founder of the Concert des Amateurs in Paris.

arranged and beautifully set. He is a good friend of mine, and very matter-of-fact. Also, I will not just write one Act for an opera, a *whole* opera will be done by me, en deux acts. The Poet has already finished the First Act. Monsieur Noverre,[13] at whose house I can eat as often as I want to, is in charge of the project and came up with the idea. I think the title is "Allexandre and Roxane."[14] Also Mad.^me Jenomè[15] is here in Paris. And I am about to write a sinfonia concertante for *flute* (Wendling), *oboe* (Ramm), *waldhorn* (Punto), and *bassoon* (Ritter).[16] Punto plays Magnificently. I have just come back, this moment, from the Concert spirituel. Baron Grimm and I are often venting our indignation about the state of Musick here; nota bene: just between ourselves; because in Public one must applaud: Bravo, Bravißimo, and clap until one's fingers hurt. Now fare well, I kiss your hands 100 times and remain your

Wolfgang Amadè Mozart

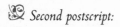 *Second postscript:*

Monsieur Raff is here and he is staying with Monsieur Le Gros. We see each other almost daily. Now, my dearest Papa, I must beg you not to be so worried and anxious, for you have no reason whatsoever. I am now in a place where one can most certainly make money. To be sure, it all costs a terrible amount of effort and work; but I am willing to do whatever it takes to make you happy. What is most annoying in all this is that these French gentlemen have improved their taste only to the point that they are now capable of appreciating good music; but would they understand that their own Musique is poor, or at least notice a difference? Not on your life! And their singing—oimè![17]—if only the French sopranos wouldn't sing Italian arias; I would forgive them their

---

13. Jean-Georges Noverre, ballet master; Mozart had met him in Vienna; now he was maître des ballets at the Paris opera.
14. This opera was probably never written.
15. "Mad.^me Jenomè" is most likely Mademoiselle Jeunehomme, the French pianist whom Mozart met 1776 in Salzburg; he wrote for her his Piano Concerto in E-flat, K. 271.
16. Johann Baptist Wendling, Friedrich Ramm, and Georg Wenzel Ritter are soloists from the Mannheim orchestra, "Punto" is actually Jan Václav Stich, one of the greatest horn virtuosos of the time, who had assumed the Italian name Giovanni Punto.
17. "oimé" appears to be a Mozartian word creation; it sounds like a mix of Italian *ahimé*, South German *o mei*, and Yiddish *Oy vay*, all meaning "Good grief!"

screeching in French, but to ruin good Musick!—it's unbearable. Here is our new address:

> Rue gros chenet, vis à vis celle du Croißant.
> à l'hôtel des 4 fils emont.
> It is important to write the number 4, it's written that way
> on the building.

Mozart's early days in Paris were filled with misunderstandings, aggravations, and a certain hostility toward the French music world. Nothing seemed to go right for him. His "sinfonia concertante" is a case in point. Little is known about the actual circumstances of its disappearance; was Legros pressured not to perform it? was it stolen? was it simply lost? Mozart's unhappy mood was fueled by his desire to go to Italy with Aloysia, but his plea to his father elicited a very sober reply: first we must pay off our debts; then perhaps you can think about Italy.

To his father, in Salzburg

Paris, May 1, 1778

Mon Trés cher Pére!

We received your letter of April 12th safely. I did not write to you for such a long time, because I was waiting for a letter from you; please don't take it amiss if I let you wait once in a while with my answer, because it's quite expensive to send a letter from here and if there's nothing urgent to report it doesn't make sense to pay 24 sous and sometimes even more; therefore, I thought I should wait with my letters to you until I have something new to say about our situation here; but at the moment I have to write to you anyway, although there's not much to report and what there is, is not at all definite.

The little cellist Zygmontofscky is here with that no-good father of his, maybe I wrote it to you already—I'm mentioning it only in passing because I just remembered seeing him at a place I wanted to talk to you about; the place in question is the residence of Mad. La Duchße de Chabot.[18] Monsieur Grimm had given me a letter of introduction, so I went to see her. The subject of the letter was mostly to recommend me

---

18. Elisabeth-Louise de la Rochefoucauld, duchess of Chabot, wife of Louis-Antoine-Auguste de Rohan.

to the Ducheße de Bourbon,[19] who was in a convent the last time we were in Paris; he wanted to bring me to her attention so that she would remember me again. A week went by without any reply; but she had informed me to come and see her in a week's time, so I kept my word and went to see her on that day. I had to wait for half an hour in a large, ice-cold, unheated room that didn't even have a fireplace. At last, the Ducheße de Chabot came in and asked me, with the greatest politeness, to use the Clavier that was in the room because none of her own pianos were in good enough condition to be played; I should just try it out. I said: I would be very happy to play something, but that at this very moment it would be quite impossible, for in this cold I could not even feel my fingers; I asked her whether someone could show me to a room that had a fire place with a fire in it. O oui, Monsieur, vous avés raison.[20] That was all the answer I got. Then she sat down and began to draw for an entire hour in the company of gentlemen who sat in a Circle around a large table; I had the honor of sitting there for a whole hour. Windows and doors were open. Not only my hands but my whole body and my feet were freezing cold, and my head began to ache. In the room was altum silentium.[21] I didn't know what to do for all the cold, headache, and boredom. Several times I thought, if it weren't for Monsieur Grimm, I would leave this place in a minute. At last, to make a long story short, I did play on that miserable, Wretched Pianoforte. And what really galled me was that Mad.[me] and her gentlemen never interrupted their drawing for one moment, they just continued, and I had to play for the chairs, tables, and walls. Given these miserable conditions, I finally lost my patience—I had begun to play the Fischer Variations and I had played about half of them when I stood up. They immediately showered me with compliments; but I said what had to be said, namely that I could not do myself justice on this Clavier, and I would be happy if Madame would choose another day when a better Clavier would be available. But she wouldn't hear of my leaving and I was obliged to wait another half hour until her husband came. He, however, sat down next to me and listened to me very attentively, and I—I forgot the cold and the headache, and played in spite of the

19. Louise-Marie-Thérèse-Bathilde d'Orléans, daughter of the duc d'Orléans.
20. "Yes, Monsieur, you are quite right."
21. "utter silence."

Wretched clavier—the way I play when I am in the best of spirits. Give me the best Clavier in Europe, but an audience that either doesn't understand, or doesn't want to understand, people who do not connect with me and my playing, and I will lose all joy in performing. I told the whole story to Monsieur Grimm afterward.

You are writing that I should go out and visit people so I can make new contacts and renew old ones. But that's quite impossible. Everything here is too far to walk—or too muddy; for the dirt in Paris is beyond all description. And to go by cab—there you have the honor of spending about 4 to 5 livres a day, and all *in vain*. They give you many Compliments, but that's it. They send for me to come on a certain day, I come and play, then they exclaim: O c'est un Prodige, c'est inconcevable, c'est étonnant.[22] And afterward it is: Adieu! I lost a lot of money here in the beginning, just to get around—and often with no results, because the people weren't home. If you are not here yourself to experience these things, you cannot possibly imagine how dreadful it is. Paris has changed quite a bit. The French are by far no longer as Polite as they were 15 years ago; their manners now border on rudeness, and they have become terribly conceited.

Now for a description of the Concert Spirituel. First let me tell you quickly and *en passant* that my chorus work was pretty much a waste of time. The "Miserere" by Hozbauer is quite lengthy and was not well received; so instead of the 4 choruses I wrote, they used only 2, leaving out the better ones. But it doesn't mean much anyway, because many in the audience were not aware that some of the music was by me and many others didn't even know me. However, there was a lot of applause during the rehearsal, and I myself am very satisfied with my chorus work, but I don't count on any praise by the Parisians anyway. As far as the Sinfonie Concertante is concerned, well, there we have another hitch. I believe there are some strange things going on; it would seem that I have enemies here as well; but where did I not have them?—I think it's a good sign. I had to write the Sinfonie Concertante in the greatest hurry, I really worked very hard, and the 4 soloists[23] were and still are quite in love with the piece. Le Gros had it for 4 days so it could

---

22. "Oh, what a prodigy, this is extraordinary, it is amazing."
23. Wendling, Ramm, Punto, Ritter. Robert Levin has reconstructed the Sinfonia concertante, K. 297b; it is available on a Philips CD.

be copied. Yet I always found it lying there in the same place. Finally, the day before yesterday I didn't see it anymore—I look under a pile of Music—and there it is, out of sight. But I pretend not to have noticed and ask Le Gros: apropós, have you sent out the Sinf. Concertante for copying?—No—I forgot. Of course, I can't order him to have the piece copied and get it ready, so I didn't say anything. But I went to the Concert on the 2 days it should have been performed. Ramm and Punto came up to me all worked up and asked why my Sinfonie Concerto was not on the program?—I don't know. It's the first I've heard about it. I know nothing about it. Ramm was absolutely furious; he railed against Le Gros in French right in the Music Room, saying that it was a dirty trick, etc. What bothers me the most in all this is that Le Gros never said a word to me, I alone was to be kept in the dark— if he had given me some kind of excuse, such as the time was too short, or something of the sort, but nothing at all—I do think, however, the reason behind it all was *Cambini*, [24] an Italian maestro here, because when we first met at the house of Le Gros, I inadvertently put him down. He has composed quartetti, and I heard one of them in Mannheim; they are quite pretty, and I praised them to him; then I proceeded to play the beginning of the one I had heard, but then Ritter, Ramm, and Punto insisted that I continue playing and invent something for the part of the piece I couldn't remember. So that's what I did, and Cambini was quite beside himself; he couldn't contain himself and blurted out: questa è una gran Testa! [25] Well, I guess he didn't appreciate what I did. Now, if I were in a place where people had ears to hear, hearts to feel, and had some small understanding of Musique, if they had a modicum of taste, I should heartily laugh about all these things; but as it is, I am living among brutes and beasts as far as Musique is concerned; but how can it be otherwise; after all, that's precisely what they are in their behavior, sentiments, and Passions.—There is no place in the world like Paris. But don't think that I am overstating things when I am speaking like this of the Musique here; ask whom you want—except a native French-man—if they know anything about this subject, they will tell you the same thing. But I am here. I have to live with it, for your sake. I'll thank god, the almighty, if I come out of here with my taste still intact. I pray

24. Giuseppe Maria Cambini.
25. A rather ambiguous statement; it can mean either "What a great mind!" or "What a swelled head!"

to god every day to bestow on me the strength to endure it all, to grant me the ability to bring Honor to myself and the German Nation, as it all reflects on god's own highest Honor and Glory; and that he will enable me to make my fortune, plenty of money, so that I can get you out of your dreadful situation and make it possible that we can soon live together happily and comfortably. Let His will be done on Earth as it is in heaven. But I entreat you, dearest Papa, do all you can, in the meantime, to help me get back to Italy soon, so I can live and breathe again. Please do this favor for me, I beg you.

Now I ask you to be of good cheer—I shall fight my way through this as best I can. If only I can get out of here in one piece. Adieu. I kiss your hands 1000 times and embrace my sister with all my heart, and I am your obedient son.

Wolfgang Amadè Mozart

The letter of May 14 allows yet another glimpse of Mozart as a teacher, this time a teacher of composition. Although he appears quite patient and inventive, his expectations of his French pupil may have been too high. Certainly his father thought so, for he replied to Wolfgang's vivid description of his lesson, "Do you think all people have your genius?"

To his father, in Salzburg (postscript)

Paris, May 14, 1778

I have so much work to do already, what will it be like in the winter season?—I believe I told you in my last letter that the Duc de Guines,[26] whose daughter is my Composition student, plays the flute extraordinarily well and her harp playing is magnifique; she has a lot of talent and ability, especially a superb memory, for she plays all of her pieces by heart, and she knows about 200. But she has serious doubts whether she has any talent for Composition, particularly as far as inventions—ideas—are concerned. Her father, who dotes on her a little too much—this is just between you and me—says that she does have ideas

---

26. Adrien-Louis Bonnières de Souastre, Comte de Guines, later governor of Artois. He had also served as French diplomat in Berlin and London.

all right, but she is too shy—what she lacks is self-confidence. Well, we shall see whether she can develop any musical ideas or themes; right now she really has none—none whatsoever—and if she can't, all effort is in vain; for god knows, that's something I cannot give her. . . . Today I gave her the 4th Lesson, and as far as rules of Composition and harmony are concerned, I am fairly satisfied with her—she did quite well in writing a bass line for the First Menuett that I had written down for her. Now she is beginning to write for 3 voices; she can do it all right; but she gets easily bored; and I can't help her there. The problem is, I cannot move ahead. It would be premature, even if she had some real talent, but alas she has none—it looks like we'll have to do everything by the rules. She simply has no inspiration of her own; nothing comes out of her; I have tried all sorts of methods. Among other things I tried the idea of writing down a simple Menuett to see whether she could do a variation on it?—Well, that didn't work.—Then I thought, maybe she doesn't know how to get started—so I began to write a variation on the first bar, and told her to continue in this manner and stick with the basic idea—that went fairly well. When it was finished, I asked her to begin something of her own—just the first voice, a melody—well, she thought about it for a quarter of an hour—nothing happened. Then I wrote down 4 bars of a Menuett and said to her—look, what a stupid fellow I am, I started a Menuett and can't even finish the First part—please be so kind and finish it for me. She thought she couldn't possibly do it; but finally, with much effort—she put something together; and I was happy that just once she came up with something. . . .

Noverre is planning a new ballet, and I will write the music for it.[27] Also, Rudolph, a horn player in the royal orchestra here, who is a good friend of mine (he has a thorough understanding of Composition and writes beautifully), well, he has offered me the position of organist at Versailles, if I want it. It pays 2000 liv.[res] for the year; I would have to be in Versailles 6 Months, the other 6 in Paris or wherever I wish. I don't think I will take it, but first I want to hear the opinion of some good friends about it. 2000 liv.[res] is not such a big offer, maybe it would be in German money, but here it is not. It amounts to 83 louis d'or and 8 liv.[res] a year, that's 915 gulden and 45 kr. in German money; that, of course,

---

27. Among Mozart's sketches for Noverre's new ballet were the charming ballet pieces *Les Petits riens*, K. Anh. 10.

sounds like a considerable sum, but here it is only 333 Thaler and 2 liv.ʳᵉˢ—and that's not much. It's just terrible how fast a thaler disappears around here. I'm not surprised that a louis d'or is not considered to be of such great value here, it just doesn't go very far. 4 thaler or one Louis, which is the same, are gone very quickly. Adieu for now. Farewell. I kiss your hands 1000 times, and I embrace my sister with all my heart, and I remain your most obedient son,

Wolfgang Amadè Mozart

Leopold reacted with skepticism to Monsieur Rudolph's proposal that Mozart become the organist at Versailles. Who is this Rudolph, Leopold wanted to know, that he can make you such offers? Apart from that, Leopold was all for accepting the offer, but Wolfgang did not want it. In earlier times, for instance in Munich, Mozart might have thought that 915 gulden for half a year's work was pretty good; but at this moment in his life, all his arguments and calculations point toward leaving Paris and being reunited with Aloysia.

*Leopold Mozart had published a method book for playing the violin (*Versuch einer gründlichen Violinschule*) in 1756, the year of Wolfgang's birth. When Wolfgang discovered a copy of a French translation of the* Violinschule *in a bookstore in Paris, Leopold reacted with great interest. He wrote to Wolfgang on June 11, 1778, "As to my Violinschule.——If my name is printed on it, try to buy it and send it to me through the mail. Since I have the Dutch translation, I would like to have the one in French as well."*

To his father, in Salzburg (postscript)

Paris, May 29, 1778

I am tolerably well, god be thanked and praised; but at times my life seems to be without rhyme or reason.——I feel neither hot nor cold—and take little joy in anything. What keeps me going and gives me strength is the thought that you, dearest Papa, and my dear sister, are in good health, that I am an Honest German, and that even though I cannot always say what's on my mind, I can at least think what I want. But that's all. Yesterday I paid a visit to Count Sückingen, the Palatine Ambassador, for a 2ⁿᵈ time; I had already been at his house previously for lunch with Herr Wendling and Raaff. I don't remember whether I told you already, but the count is a charming man, a Passionate lover and true connoisseur of Musique.

I spent 8 hours alone with him at his house, we were at the clavier in the morning, afternoon, and evening until 10 o'clock; we paged through all kinds of Musique—praised, admired, reviewed, debated, and criticized. He owns about 30 opera scores.

Now I wish to tell you that I had the Honor of seeing your Violinschule in a French translation.[28] I think the translation is from at least 8 years ago. I just happened to be in a Musick store to buy a book of sonatas by Chobert[29] for a pupil. I want to go back to the store in the next few days to take a better look at your edition and tell you about it in greater detail. When I saw it the other day, I didn't have enough time.

Farewell for now, I kiss your hands 1000 times and embrace my sister with all my heart. Mes Complimens à tous mes amis, particulierement à M. Bullinger.[30]

Wo A Mozart

Mozart's letter of June 12 is a gold mine for his aesthetics. In characteristically simple language, he talks about some important principles of music: singers should avoid artificial quavers and virtuosic effects; cantabiles should be smooth, sustained, and stay within the natural limits of the voice. Mozart's advocacy of "natural" music and unaffected performance is the beginning of his classical aesthetics of musical balance and proportion.

To his father, in Salzburg (postscript)

Paris, June 12, 1778

I need to say a few words about our Raaff.[31] You will undoubtedly recall that I didn't write too favorably about him from Mannheim, that I wasn't very positive about his singing, . . . but here, when he made his

---

28. Leopold Mozart's method book for the violin, which was translated into French and Dutch, established his reputation as a theoretician for the violin. It also appeared in Russian in 1804.

29. "Chobert" is Johann Schobert, A German composer and pianist living in Paris.

30. "Greetings to all my friends, particularly Herr Bullinger."

31. Mozart had met the German tenor Anton Raaff in Mannheim and written the aria "Se al labbro mio non credi," K. 295, for him.

debut at the Concert Spirituel, he sang the scena by Bach, "non sò d'onde viene,"[32] which is my favorite anyway, and for the first time I truly heard him sing—and I liked it—I mean in this particular style of music. The style itself—the Bernachi school[33] —is not to my taste; and Raaff tends to go overboard with the Cantabile. I admit that when he was younger and in his prime, he probably made a good impression with it, he probably took his listeners by surprise; I do like his cantabile, but he overdoes it, and sometimes he even sounds funny to me. What I like best in his singing is when he does short pieces, some andantinos, for instance. . . . His voice is beautiful and very pleasing; when I close my eyes and listen—I hear a lot that reminds me of Meissner,[34] only that Raff's voice appears to be even smoother. . . . Meissner has, as you know, the bad habit of giving his voice an extra tremolo—entire quarter notes—even eighth note quavers when the music is marked for sustained singing—and that's something I could never stand in his singing. It's dreadful. It is a style of singing entirely contrary to nature. The human voice vibrates naturally—but in such a way—to such a degree that it all sounds beautiful—it is the nature of the voice. We imitate such effects not only on wind instruments, but also with violins—even on the clavier—but as soon as you go beyond the natural limits, it no longer sounds beautiful—because it is contrary to nature. It reminds me a little of the organ when the bellows are quaking.—Well, Raff doesn't sing like that, in fact, he can't bear it either. But as far as real Cantabile is concerned, I do like Meissner, even though I still have a few reservations, for he also exaggerates, but still, he is better than Raff. On the other hand, Raff has totally mastered the bravura aria, Passages and Roulades.[35] He is masterful in these things—and then there is his precise and clear articulation—that is beautiful. . . .

Today I was with Raff at Count Sückingen's again. I brought along various things I had composed because he had asked me for it some time ago. So today I brought my New Sinfonie,[36] which I had just fin-

32. "Bach" is Johann Christian Bach, "the London Bach"; the aria "Non sò d'onde viene" is from his opera *Ezio*. Mozart used the same theme for an aria (K. 294) he wrote for Aloysia Weber.
33. The Bernacchi school is a bel canto singing method made popular by Antonio Bernacchi.
34. Joseph Nikolaus Meissner, a bass singer from Salzburg.
35. "Passages and Roulades": passages are lengthy vocal runs that display virtuosity; roulades are rapid ornamental vocal figures.
36. "My new Sinfonie" is Mozart's "Paris" Symphony, K. 297.

ished and which is scheduled to open the program of the Concert Spirituel on Corpus Christi Day. Both of them liked it very much. I, too, am very happy with it; but whether others like it, I don't know— and to tell you the truth, it doesn't matter much to me, for who, after all, are these people who wouldn't like it?—I can vouch for a *few* perceptive French listeners who will be there; but the dumb ones, well, it won't be a big misfortune if they don't find it to their liking—but I do hope that even the stupid asses will find something they can like; after all, I made sure to include the Premier Coup d'archet,[37] and that's enough to please them. . . . Now I must close; please give my greetings to all friends, especially Her Bullinger. . . .

Wolfgang Amadè Mozart

During the night of July 3, 1778, Mozart wrote three letters: one to his father, one to Abbé Bullinger, his friend in Salzburg, the third to Fridolin Weber, Aloysia's father, in Mannheim. The message to his father contained a gentle lie, namely that his mother was gravely ill; the message to Abbé Bullinger contained the painful truth, namely that his mother had died a few hours ago; and Mozart requested that his friend immediately visit his father and sister and prepare them for the unexpected sad news; the letter to Herr Weber, which is lost, presumably conveyed the news of Mozart's calamity to Aloysia. The two surviving letters are masterpieces of painful diplomacy, self-control, and thoughtfulness. Peter Gay (Mozart, 42) calls it "a curious game of denial."

To his father, in Salzburg

Paris, July 3, 1778

Monsieur mon trés cher Pére!

I have to bring you some very distressing and Sad news, which is also the reason why I couldn't reply earlier to your most recent letter, the one dated on the 11th.—

My dear Mother is very ill—she was bled, just as she had it done always, and it was indeed necessary; afterward she felt somewhat better—but a few days later she complained of chills but at the same time she seemed to have a burning fever—then she came down with diarrhea,

---

37. "Coup d'archet" is a strong tutti opening of a symphony. Mozart's remark is sarcastic because French audiences liked and expected a *coup d'archet*.

headaches—in the beginning we used only our own home remedies, Antispasmodic Powder, we would have liked to use black powder as well, but we had none left, and we couldn't get any; it is not known here, not even under the name of Pulvïs epilepticus.[38] As her condition grew steadily worse—she could hardly speak anymore and lost her hearing, one had to shout to reach her—Baron *Grim* sent his physician.—She is very weak, still feverish, and Delirious.—They are giving me hope, but I don't have much—I have been between fear and hope for several days and nights now—I have now surrendered myself entirely to the will of god—I hope that you and my dear sister will do the same; what other way is there for staying calm—calmer, I should say, because one can never be completely calm. I am comforted, come what may, because I know that god, who arranges things for our best—even if we don't always understand it fully—wills it so. I believe, and I won't be dissuaded from this belief, that no physician, no human being, no misfortune, no accident, can give life or take it away, only god alone can do that—everything else serves as his instruments, at least most of the time—although not always. We see people collapse, stricken down, fall over dead—when their time is at hand nothing can help, often they hasten death rather than prevent it—we have seen it with my dear departed friend Hefner.[39] —I don't mean to say with all this that my Mother will have to die, that all hope is lost—she may recover and be well again, but only if god wills it so—those are the consoling thoughts I like to engage in after I prayed to god for the health and life of my dear mother; I find myself uplifted, calmer, and consoled afterward,—for you can easily imagine that I need some such comfort right now!—but now for something else; let's leave these mournful thoughts, let's turn to hope, although not too much; . . .

I had been requested to compose a sinfonie for the opening of the Concert spirituel.[40] It was performed with great applause on Corpus Christi Day. I am told that there was even a notice about it in the

38. Pulvis epilepticus niger is a powder consisting of desiccated earthworms and ground charcoal, which the Mozarts used as a purgative. (Davies, *Mozart in Person*, 13.)
39. Heinrich Wilhelm von Heffner, Mozart's friend, died in 1774.
40. Symphony no. 31 in D major ("Paris"), K. 297; it was performed for the first time on June 18, 1778, at the Palais de Tuileries.

Couriere de L'Europe,[41] which means it was exceptionally well received. During rehearsals I was extremely worried because I had never heard a worse performance in all my life; you can't imagine how they bungled and scratched their way through the Sinfonie—twice in a row.—I was truly worried—I would have liked to have one more rehearsal; but because they are always rehearsing so much stuff all at once, there was no more time. I had no choice but go to bed with a troubled heart and a dissatisfied and angry mind. The next day I decided not to go to the concert at all; but then, in the evening, the weather turned nice and I decided to go, but with the firm resolve that if things went as poorly as during rehearsal, I would walk straight up to the orchestra, snatch the violin out of the hand of Herr Lahousè, *the First violinist*, and conduct myself. I prayed to god to be merciful and let it all go smoothly, as it is all for His highest Honor and Glory; and *Ecce*, the Sinfonie began, Raff was standing next to me, and right in the middle of the First Allegro came a Passage that I knew would please, and the entire audience was sent into raptures—there was a big applaudißement;—and as I knew, when I wrote the passage, what good effect it would make, I brought it once more at the end of the movement—and sure enough there they were: the shouts of Da capo. The Andante was well received as well, but the final Allegro pleased especially — because I had heard that here the final Allegros begin like the first Allegros, namely with all instruments playing and mostly unisono; therefore, I began the movement with just 2 violins playing softly for 8 bars—then suddenly comes a forte—but the audience had, because of the quiet beginning, shushed each other, as I expected they would, and then came the forte—well, hearing it and clapping was one and the same. I was so delighted, I went right after the Sinfonie to the Palais Royale—bought myself an ice cream, prayed a rosary as I had pledged—and went home.—Most of the time I enjoy simply being at home, indeed, I will always prefer to be at home—or else be in the company of a good, truthful, honest German who leads the life of a good Christian if he's unmarried and, if he's married, loves his wife and brings up his children properly.

41. The *Courrier de l'Europe* (London) reported on June 26, 1778, in French, "The Concert spirituel on Corpus Christi Day began with a symphony by M. Mozart. This artist, who from the tenderest age made a name for himself among harpsichord players, may today be ranked among the most able composers." (Deutsch, *Documentary*, 176.)

Now I have an item of news that you may have heard already, namely that the godless Arch-culprit Voltaire has kicked the bucket—like a
dog,[42] so to speak—like a beast—so that's his reward! . . .

As far as the opera is concerned, the situation at the moment is like
this: it's very difficult to find a good libretto. The old texts, which are
best, are not adaptable to the Modern style and the new ones aren't any
good. The quality of poetic texts, the one thing the French could be
proud of, is getting worse every day—and yet it is the poetry that has
to be good here—because they don't understand the Musique.—There
are at present two operas that I could compose, one en deux actes, the
other en trois. The one en deux is "Alexandre et Roxeane"—but the
Poet who is writing the libretto is still in the country—the one en trois
is "Demofont" by Metastasio (translated); it is interspersed with choruses and dances and by and large arranged for the French Theater. I
haven't been able to see any of this text either.—

Please let me know whether you have Schrötter's[43] concertos in
Salzbourg?—and the sonatas by Hüllmandel?[44] I thought I might buy
them and send them to you. Both œuvre are very beautiful.—As to
Versailles, I never considered the offer seriously—I did seek the advice
of Baron Grimm and other good friends—they all thought as I did.
The money is not much, you have to languish in a place for 6 months
where you can't earn anything else, where you must bury your talent, for
whoever enters the royal service is forgotten in Paris—and then as an
organist!—I should very much like a good appointment, but nothing
less than Kapellmeister, and well paid.

Now fare thee well!—Take care of your health and trust in god—
you will surely find comfort in Him. My dear Mother is in the hands
of the Almighty—if he will let us keep her, as I pray he may, we shall
thank him for such grace, if he will call her to Himself, then all our anx-
iousness, worry, and despair won't change anything—it's better to be
strong and submit to his divine will, knowing fully that it will be for
our good in the end, for he does nothing without purpose—so be well,
dearest Papa, take good care of your health for my sake; I kiss your

42. François-Marie Arouet Voltaire died in Paris on May 30, 1778; "kicked the bucket like a dog" presumably means without the blessings of the church. Mozart's negative remark is probably prompted by
what he thinks his father wants to hear.
43. Johann Samuel Schröter, a German composer and pianist who lived in London.
44. Nicolaus-Joseph Hüllmandel of Strasbourg, a composer, had also settled in London.

hands 10000 times, and I embrace my sister with all my heart and remain your devoted son,

Wolfgang Amadè Mozart

🎵 *To divert Leopold's attention from the sad news, Mozart reports other items of interest, such as the death of Voltaire and the premiere of his Symphony in D major, K. 297. Mozart's report about the reception of his symphony allows two interesting insights. One is that Mozart candidly admits that he composed parts of the symphony with certain calculated effects in mind; the other concerns the habits of eighteenth-century audiences: they applauded not only at the end of a performance but anytime they felt like it.*

🎵 *Mozart's letter to Joseph Bullinger, written in the night of his mother's death, has an extraordinary poignancy, which is deepened by the simplicity of his language. "Trauern sie mit mir, mein freünd!—dies war der Traurigste Tag in meinen Leben—. . . meine Mutter, Meine liebe Mutter ist nicht mehr! . . . sie starb ohne das sie etwas von sich wuste—löschte aus wie ein licht."*

To Joseph Bullinger, in Salzburg

Paris, July 3, 1778

My very dear friend!
for you alone.

Mourn with me, my friend!—This was the Saddest Day of my life—I am writing at 2 o'clock in the morning—and I must tell you that my Mother, My dear Mother, is no more! God has called her to Himself—it was his will to take her, I can see it clearly—therefore, I have resigned myself to god's will.—He gave her to me, he could also take her from me. Just imagine all the turmoil, the anxiety and worries that I endured these last 2 weeks—she died without regaining consciousness—she went out like a light. 3 days earlier she made her last confession and received Extreme Unction—but the last 3 days she was delirious throughout, and today, at 21 minutes after 5 o'clock, her breathing became convulsive, she lost her senses and perception, I pressed her hand, spoke to her—but she did not see me and did not hear me, she felt nothing anymore—she lay like this until she died five hours later, at 21 minutes after 10 o'clock at night—no one was present but I, Herr Haina,[45] a good friend of ours, whom father knows, and the

45. Franz Joseph Haina, a Czech horn player, ran a small hotel in Paris and a shop for musical instruments. He was very helpful to Mozart in his hour of need.

nurse—I cannot describe to you right now the whole course of her illness—I am of the opinion that her time had come—god willed it so. At this time, I am asking you for only one service as a friend and that is to prepare my dear father very gently for this sad news—I have written him today as well—but only that she is gravely ill—now I am waiting for an answer so I can be guided by it. May god give him strength and courage!—My friend!—I am not only consoled at this moment, I have been consoled for a while!—I have been able, by a special act of god's grace, to bear it all with fortitude and resignation. When her condition got serious, I prayed to god for only 2 things, namely a peaceful last hour for my mother, and strength and courage for myself—and our gracious Lord heard my prayer and granted me both blessings in rich measure.

I beseech you now, dearest friend, watch over my father, inspire him with courage so that, when he hears the worst, the blow won't be so hard and unbearable. I also commend my sister to you with all my heart— perhaps you can go and see them right away, I beg you,—don't tell them yet that she is Dead, but just prepare them for the news as best you can.— Do whatever you feel is right—do whatever you have to—only put my mind at ease so I need not fear another blow.—Save my dear father for me and my dear sister; and write to me at once, I beg of you.—Adieu, I remain your

most obedient and grateful servant
Wolfgang Amadè Mozart.

in the event you don't have my address:
Rue du gros chenet
vis à vis celle du croißant
à l'hôtel des quatre
fils aimont.

Maria Anna was buried on July 4, 1778, in the cemetery of Saint-Eustache in Paris. The cause of her death is not entirely clear, but Dr. Peter J. Davies, physician and Mozart scholar, contends that the symptoms of her death are "compatible with epidemic louse-borne typhus" (Mozart in Person, 49).

Mozart wrote a lengthy letter filled with details of his life in an obvious attempt to distract his father from the news of his mother's death. It was a good plan, but the psychology did not work. In his return letter, Leopold insisted that Wolfgang give him a full account of Maria Anna's death.

To his father, in Salzburg

Paris, July 9, 1778

Monsieur mon Trés cher Pére!

I hope you are now ready to receive this Saddest and most painful news with fortitude—my last letter to you, from the 3ʳᵈ of the month, will have prepared you to expect the worst—that very same day, on the 3ʳᵈ, at 21 Minutes after 10 o'clock at night my Mother passed on peacefully to the Lord.—When I wrote to you she was already partaking of the Heavenly joys—it was all over by then—I wrote to you late that night—and I hope that you and my dear sister will forgive me for this small but necessary deception—when I thought about my own pain and sadness in relation to how it might affect you, I simply could not bring myself to overwhelm you with this distressing news. . . . You can easily imagine what I went through—what courage and fortitude I needed to endure it all with composure when things got increasingly stressful and difficult—and yet, god in his mercy bestowed on me the grace I needed—I felt such terrible pain, cried and cried—but to what avail?—I had no choice but to console myself; and I beg you, dear father and sister, to do the same! . . . Now, His divine and most holy will is fulfilled—let us pray a deeply felt Paternoster for her soul—and then turn our thoughts to other matters, for there is a right time for everything.—

I am writing this letter in the house of Mad.ᵐᵉ d'Epinai[46] and Monsieur Grimm, where I am staying at present and where I have a pretty little room with a very pleasant view—and where, as much as my emotional condition permits, I feel quite cheerful. A big help for me in regaining my tranquillity would be if I could hear that my dear father and my dear sister are facing the will of the Lord with calmness and fortitude,—that they trust in him with all their heart and in the firm belief

---

46. Louise Tardieu d'Esclavelles d'Epinay, a French writer, friend of Diderot, d'Alembert, Grimm. She lived with Grimm in the rue de la Chaussée d'Antin, where she and Grimm had offered Mozart a room after his mother died.

that he arranges everything for our best!—Most beloved father! Take care of yourself! dearest sister!—take care of yourself—you have not yet experienced the true kindness of your brother — because up to now he lacked the opportunity to show you—My two dearest! Be mindful of your health—and remember you have a son—a brother—who will use all his strength to make you happy—well knowing that some time hence you will not deny him his own wish and fulfillment (which will be completely honorable) and that you will do all you can to make him happy—oh, then we'll live as contentedly, honestly, happily as it is possible in this world—and finally, if it's god's will, to be reunited in the hereafter—for which we are destined and created.

I received your last letter from June 29ᵗʰ safely, and I read with pleasure that you are both well, god be thanked and praised. About Hayden's drunkenness,[47] I had to laugh out loud;—had I been there, I would most certainly have whispered into his ear: *Adlgasser.*[48] It's a real shame when such a talented man incapacitates himself by his own folly to the point where he can no longer fulfill his duties—during a church service in god's honor—in the presence of the Archbishop and the whole court—the church full of people—it's disgusting—but it's also one of the things I hate about Salzburg—the coarse, slovenly, run-down Court Orchestra—no decent man who has any self-respect can live with such musicians;—instead of being honored to associate with them, one has to be ashamed!—besides, and perhaps for this very reason, the orchestra is not well liked in Salzburg, it's not held in high esteem—if only it were as well organized as the one in Mannheim! What discipline they have in that orchestra!—and what authority Cannabich has—everything they do is done with real dedication. Cannabich, who is the best music director I have ever seen, commands the love and respect of his musicians.—he is well liked in town, and so are his Soldiers[49]—and that's because they behave properly, have decent manners, are well dressed, and don't spend their time in local inns getting drunk—but none of this is possible in Salzburg, unless the prince would give you or me his trust and let us have whatever authority is *necessary for maintaining a good orchestra*—otherwise all is in vain. . . .

47. Michael Haydn; Leopold had written that he had been drunk while playing the organ during church service.
48. Anton Cajetan Adlgasser, court and cathedral organist, suffered a stroke while playing the organ.
49. Mozart is referring to Cannabich's highly disciplined players in the Mannheim orchestra.

Apropos: the Elector[50] is back in Mannheim at the moment—I am corresponding with Mad.^me Cannabich as well as her husband—if what I fear will *not* happen (if it were to happen it would be a terrible shame) namely that the orchestra will be reduced in strength—I would actually have some hope for an appointment there—you know that I wish for nothing more than a good position, good in quality and good in pay— no matter where it is—provided it is in a Catholic area. . . . Even if I would get all I want in Salzburg, I would rather be anywhere but there.— Anyway, there's no need to worry because they would hardly grant me all the things I want—for it's quite a bit—of course, nothing is out of the question—if all my conditions were met, I would not mind— if only to have the pleasure of being with you—but if they wish to have me in Salzburg, they'll have to meet all my demands—or they can't have me. . . .

My friend Raaff will leave Paris tomorrow; he will travel via Brussels to Aix la Chapelle and Spa—and then on to Mannheim. He will notify me of his arrival immediately because we agreed to correspond—he sends his greetings to you and my sister, even though you never met him. You write that you haven't heard anything for a long time about my Composition student?[51] —it's quite true, but what can I tell you? She will never be a composer—in her case, all effort is in vain. To begin with she is totally stupid and, in addition, thoroughly lazy!—And as to the opera? I told you already in my last letter!—And as far as Noverre's Ballet is concerned, I never said anything, except that he wanted to arrange a new one—right now he needed only half a ballet for which I did the Musique—6 pieces are from other composers, consisting of Wretched old French airs; and I did the Overture, the Contredanses, altogether I think I contributed 12 pieces.[52] —The Ballet has been performed 4 times already —with the greatest applause—but now I will accept no new commission unless I know ahead of time how much I will get for it. . . . Kapellmeister Bach[53] will be here shortly—I believe he's going to write an opera—the French are such asses, they are

50. Elector Karl Theodor.
51. The daughter of the comte de Guines.
52. *Les Petits Riens,* K. Anh. 10.
53. Johann Christian Bach.

truly inept, for they have to go abroad for help. I talked with Piccini[54] in the Concert spirituel—he is very polite to me, and I am polite toward him, when we meet on occasion—but I don't seek any closer acquaintanceship, not with him or any other composer—I know what I am doing, and they know what they are doing—and that's just fine. . . . Monsieur Le Gros, the Director, is very much taken with me; you should know that, although I had previously been with him every day, I have not gone to see him since Easter, because I was so annoyed that he did not perform my sinfonie concertante; I did go to his house quite often but only to visit Monsieur Raaff; I had to pass by his rooms—his servants and maids would see me, and I asked them to communicate my compliments to him.—It's such a pity he didn't have it performed, it would have had a great effect—now the chance is pretty much gone; where and when can one find 4 such soloists again? . . . My symphony was highly applauded—and le Gros is so happy with it that he says it's his best Sinfonie—the Andante, however, was not so fortunate as to find his approval—he says it has too many modulations—and it's too long—but the real reason is that the audience neglected to make the same strong and sustained noise by clapping their hands as they did for the first and last movement—but the andante has the greatest applause *from me*, from all experts and connoisseurs, and from most of the audience, in fact, it's just the opposite of what le Gros says, for it is natural—and short—but to please him and some others, as he claims, I wrote a second andante—each is good in its own way—for each has a different Caractére—but the last one I like the best—I shall send you the Sinfonie and your Violinschule, some piano pieces, and Vogler's book, "Tonwissenschaft und Tonsezkunst," as soon as I find a good opportunity—and then I would like to hear what you have to say about it—on August 15ᵗʰ—the Feast of the Assumption—the Sinfonie will be performed a second time and with the new andante—the Sinfonie is in Re and the Andante in Sol—here you can't say D or g.—Le Gros is now completely on my side.—But now it's time to come to an end—when you write to me I think it's best if you write to: chez Monsieur Le Baron de Grim, chaußèe d'antin prés le Boulevard—Monsieur Grim has in mind to write to you soon himself. He and Mad.ᵐᵉ d'Epinay send greet-

54. Niccolò Piccinni, one of the two dominant composers in Paris at the time, the other being Christoph Willibald Gluck.

ings as well as their heartfelt condolences—they both hope, however, you will have resigned yourself to accepting a situation that cannot be altered. . . .

Adieu. I kiss your hands 100000 times, and I embrace my sister with all my heart; I am your most devoted son

Wolfgang Amadè Mozart

Mozart continues to bring up a topic he knows his father is reluctant to hear about: Aloysia Weber. One has to admire his tenacity and talent in finding ways of confronting his father with the subject. The following three letters show just how methodically and seriously Mozart pursued his plans of winning Aloysia.

To Mozart his father, in Salzburg

Paris, July 18, 1778

Monsieur mon Trés cher Pére!

I hope you received my last two letters all right.—Let's not talk about their main subject anymore—it's over now—even if we were to write pages and pages about it, we cannot change things anymore!—

The main purpose of this letter is to congratulate my dear sister on her Name Day; but before I do I want to have a little chat with you first;—what terrific writing, isn't it?—Well, just be patient—I'm in no mood today to take pains in writing clearly—this will have to do, that is if you can manage to somehow understand what I want to tell you. I think I wrote to you already that Monsieur Raaff has left Paris—but I could not possibly have told you that he is my true and very special friend—and that I can fully rely on his friendship—because I didn't know myself that he is so very fond of me. . . . I can't remember what day it was—some day in the middle of the week—I happened to be sitting at the Clavier, at his place,—and Ritter—our good wood biter,[55] sat next to me; . . . when I finished playing, during which Raaff had shouted Bravo again and again—with an expression that showed his complete inner delight, I entered into a conversation with Ritter; among other things I said that I wasn't particularly happy here—mostly on account of the Musique—and then, too, I have no real relaxation here,

55. I.e., bassoon player.

no good diversions,—no pleasant and decent social life—especially with women—most of them are whores—and the few who are not, lack in social graces.—Ritter could not help agreeing with me—but then Raaff said with a smile—yes, I believe it—Herr Mozart is not a *hundred percent* here to admire all the local beauties—half of him is still where I just came from[56]—of course, there was a good deal of laughing—and joking—but in the end Herr Raaff said in a more serious tone—you are right—and I can't blame you—she deserves it; she is a well brought up, good-looking, Honorable Girl, and she always gives a good account of herself—she has great skills and lots of Talent—Now I had the best opportunity to recommend my dear Weber girl to him with all my heart—but I didn't really need to say much, he was already quite taken with her.—He promised that as soon as he would get back to Mannheim he would give her singing lessons and take an interest in her. . . .

Now farewell; take care of your health—and Cheer up—think that maybe soon you'll have the pleasure of joyfully emptying a glass of Rhine wine with your son, a son completely happy and content. Adieu. I kiss your hands a Thousand times, and embrace my dear sister with all my heart, and as long as I can draw breath I will remain your most obedient son

Wolfgang Amadè Mozart

🖾 *Mozart wrote four letters to Fridolin Weber from Paris. The one printed here is the only one surviving, and it is fortunate that Leopold never got to see it, because it would have confirmed his worst suspicion, namely that Mozart was more concerned about the debts of Herr Weber than about those of his own father. In fact, Mozart shows signs that he already considers himself Weber's son-in-law.*

To Fridolin Weber, in Mannheim

Paris, July 29, 1778

Monsieur mon Trés cher et plus cher Amy!

I have received your letter of July 15th this very moment—indeed, I've been eagerly awaiting it and had gotten a bit concerned! Basta!—

---

56. I.e., Mannheim.

but now, thanks to your most cherished letter, my mind is somewhat at ease—except for your principal news, which made my blood boil so that—well, I better stop right now—you know me well enough, my friend,—and I think you know what kind of feelings I had while I was reading your letter—therefore, I cannot delay, I must answer you at once, for I think it's very important.—But first let me ask you whether you received my letter of June 29th?—I sent you 3 letters in a row;—one on the 27th, addressed to you directly; another on the 29th, addressed to Herr Heckmann, and one on July 3rd, again addressed to the latter. Now to the matter at hand:—did I not always tell you that the Elector will establish his Residence in Munich?—I even heard that Count Seau has been appointed Manager for both Munich and Mannheim!—Now let me tell you something very important—something I cannot say openly—but I'm sure you will understand what I'm saying. I wish in the meantime—whether the court will go to Munich or stay in Mannheim—that you will get an increase in your salary and that your Mad.selle daughter will get a reasonable salary as well and that you can completely pay off your debts and begin to breathe a little easier. . . . But now listen: I was going to use my influence here, and perhaps not without success, that you and your Mad.selle daughter could come to Paris this winter—just the two of you; but, here is the situation: Monsieur Le Gros, Directeur of the Concert spirituel, with whom I have talked already about my friend,[57] cannot invite her for this winter—because Mad. Le Brun has already been engaged for this season—and he is really not in such good circumstances *at the moment,* that he could pay 2 such singers what they deserve—as *I would certainly insist on;* so there wouldn't be any income here—however, this plan could be made to work for next winter. . . . In the meantime you must press on *forcefully* for an increase in your own salary as well as a good salary for your daughter—submit it in writing and more than once—and, Nota Bene, whenever our heroine is supposed to sing at court—and *you* have not been given an answer to your request—or at least not a favorable one;—then you simply won't let her sing—pretend she is not well—and do it several times— I beg you;—and then when you have done this a few times, you suddenly allow her to sing again—you'll see how Effective such a little trick

---

57. Mozart is using the feminine here, *meine Freundin* (my female friend); he is referring to Aloysia.

can be—but you have to do it with finesse and cunning. . . . Oh, Dear god, if only I were in fortunate circumstances and could support you wholly on my own—then you could come here without the slightest fear that it would be dishonorable for you, for I swear by my honor that no one but you and I would know about it. . . . Now a few words about my own affairs—I am having such a hard time here that I can't describe it to you—everything is slow here; until you are well enough known, you can't do anything with your Compositions—I told you already in my last letter how difficult it is to get a good text—and after I told you what I think of the Musick here, you can easily imagine that it is not a great joy for me to be here—and so I am trying to get away as soon as I can—this is just between you and me. Herr Raaff will unfortunately not be in Mannheim until the end of August—but once he is there, he will *get busy* on my behalf—and one can hope that maybe something will come of it—if nothing turns up, then I'll probably go to Maynz more likely than not. Count Sückingen, whom I visited yesterday and with whom I had a really good talk about you, has a brother in Maynz—he himself brought up the idea—therefore, I think this possibility is real. So, there you have my prospects, which I have kept a secret from every-one, except the count, you, and me.—By the way, in spite of all the sad-ness of my present situation, nothing pains me as much as the fact that I am unable to help you as much—as I would like to—I swear it upon my honor.—Adieu, my very best friend, farewell. . . . If I didn't have a father and sister for whom my life is more important than for myself, whose livelihood is my responsibility, I would gladly neglect my own future plans and concentrate my efforts entirely on yours.—Your well-being, your peace of mind, your happiness would give me, if I had only myself to think about, all the happiness I need—farewell—

your unalterable
Mozart

Mozart's Paris correspondence contains his only surviving letter to Aloysia Weber. Given the fact that he was deeply in love with her, it seems strange that the letter is completely devoid of any familiarities; it is a model of courtesy, tact, and respect-fulness. The language has nothing of the clownishness that Mozart loved to exhibit to other women, especially his sister, cousin, and even his mother. His instructions on how to perform the Andromeda scene ("Ah, lo previddi") indicates that, apart *from his personal affection, he also wanted to be Aloysia's teacher. Why he wrote the letter in Italian is not clear; Italian was the language of musicians, and perhaps he wanted to approach her on a professional basis. The translation of the letter is followed by the original to allow readers to see that Mozart's Italian is not flawless, though still very good.*

To Aloysia Weber, in Mannheim

Paris, July 30, 1778

Dearest friend!

I beg you to forgive me for failing to send you at this time the variations that I have composed for the aria you sent me—but I thought it was necessary to reply as quickly as possible to your esteemed Father's letter, so I did not have time to write them down and, therefore, it was impossible to send them to you—but you shall certainly have them with my next letter. I hope that my sonatas will be Printed very Soon—and together with them you shall also have the "Popolo di Teßaglia," which is already half completed—if you are as pleased with it as I am—I shall consider myself very happy; meanwhile, until I have the pleasure of learning directly from you whether you really like this scena, since I have composed it solely for you—I desire no other Praise but yours; I can only say that of all my compositions of this kind—I must admit that this scena is the best I have composed in all my life—you will make me very happy if you apply yourself Completely to the scena of Andromeda "Ah lo previddi" for I assure you that this scena will suit you eminently—and that you will derive great credit from it—I particularly advise you to pay attention to the expression marks—to think carefully about the meaning and the force of the words—to put yourself with all seriousness into Andromeda's situation and position!—and to imagine yourself to be that very person. By doing this, with your beautiful voice—your beautiful way of singing—you will become unfailingly Excellent within a short Time! . . .

Dearest friend! I hope that you are in excellent health—I beg you to always take care of it—this being the best thing we have in the world; as far as my own health is concerned, thank God I am well, because I take care of my health—but my mind is not at ease—and it will not be until I have the comfort of knowing for certain that, for once, your merit has been recognized.—yet the happiest condition and situation for me will be on the day when I will have the great pleasure of seeing and embracing you with All my heart—but this too is All I can long for and desire—only in this desire and wish do I Find my consolation and peace of mind;—please write to me often—you cannot imagine what pleasure your letters bring to me. . . . Farewell for now, my Dearest friend! I am extremely anxious to get a letter from you, I beg you therefore not to keep me waiting too long and not keep me longing too much—in the hope of having news from you soon, I kiss your hands, I embrace you with all my heart and I am, and ever shall be, your true and sincere friend

WAMozart

Cariβima Amica!

La prego di pardonarmi che manco questa volta d'inviare le variazioni per l'aria mandatami—ma stimai tanto neceβario il rispondere al più presto alla lettera del suo sig.ⁿ Padre, che non mi restò poi il Tempo di scriverle, e perciò era impoβibile di mandargliele—ma lei le avrà sicuramente colla proβima lattera; Adeβo spero che ben Presto saranno Stampate le mie sonate—e con quella occasione avrà anche il Popolo di Teβaglia, ch'è già mezzo Terminato—se lei ne sarà si contenta—comme lo son io—portrò chiamarmi felice;—intanto, sinchè avrò la sodisfazione di sapere di lei steβa l'incontro che avrà avuta questa scena apreβo di lei s'intende, perchè siccome l'hò fatta solamente per lei—così non desidero altra Lode che la sua;—intanto dunque non poβo dir altro, che, Trà le mie composizioni di questo genere—devo confeβare che questa scena è la megliore ch'hò fatto in vita mia—Lei mi farà molto piacere se lei vuol mettersi adeβo con Tutto l'impegno sopra la mia scena d'Andromeda, Ah lo previddi! perchè l'aβicuro, che questa scena le starà aβai bene—e che lei sene farà molto onore—al più le raccomando l'espreβione—di rifletter bene al senso ed alla forza delle parolle—di mettersi con serietà nello stato e nella situazione d'Andromeda!—e di figurarsi d'eβer quella steβa persona;—Caminando in questa quisa colla sua belliβima voce—col suo bel methodo di cantare—lei diventerà in breve Tempo infalibilmente Eccelente. . . .

Cariβima amica!—spero che lei starà d'ottima salute—la prego di averne sempre cura—eβendo questa la miglior cosa di questo mondo; io, grazie à Dio stò bene, toccante la mia salute, perchè ne hò cura—mà non hò l'animo quieto—e non l'avrò mai sinchè non avrò la consolazione di eβere accertato che una volta si hà reso giustizia al di lei merito—ma lo stato e la situazione più felice per me sarà in quel giorno in cui avrò il sommo piacere di rivederla, e di abbracciarla di Tutto il mio

*cuore—mà questo è anche Tutto ch'io poßo bramare e desiderare—non Trovo che
in questo desiderio ed augurio l'unica mia consolazione, e la mia quiete;—la prego
di scrivermi speßo—lei non si può immaginare quanto piacere mi fanno le sue let-
tere. . . . Addio, fràtanto, Cariſſima amica!—sonoanziosiſſimo d'avere una lettera
di lei, la prego dunque di non farmi troppo aspettare, e troppo languire—speran-
do di aver ben presto delle sue nuove, le baccio le mani, l'abbraccio di core e sono e
sarò sempre il di lei vero e sincero amico*

WAMozart

Leopold's request that Wolfgang give him a detailed description of his mother's death
resulted in a vivid and dramatic rendering of what must have been the most terrifying event in Mozart's young life. The letter, which is of considerable length, affords
an interesting view of the state of medicine at the time, but it also testifies to Mozart's
uncertain and confused state of mind. He wanted to leave Paris but did not wish
to return to Salzburg, he wanted to be with Aloysia but could not be sure of her
love, he disliked the French but wished to be accepted by them. And buried in all the
disconcerting messages is a brief reference to Mozart's Concerto for Flute and Harp,
K. 299, which had been commissioned by the comte—not duc, as Mozart writes—
de Guines for himself (flute) and his daughter (harp). The concerto is written in
the style of French salon music, but, as so often in his compositions, Mozart far
transcended the formal requirements of the commissioned work and created a masterpiece of precision and lyricism.

To his father, in Salzburg

Paris, July 31, 1778

Monsieur mon trés cher Pére!

I hope you have safely received my last two letters, one from the 11th,
the other from the 18th, I think;—In the meantime I have received 2
from you, that's from the 13th and the 20th.—The first letter brought
tears of anguish to my eyes—because it brought back the memories of
the sad day of my dear mother's passing—everything stood before me
once again in full vividness; I shall not forget it as long as I live—you
know I had never seen anybody die, although I had wanted to,—and
then, when I experienced it for the first time, it had to be my mother—
it was a moment I dreaded most of all—and I fervently prayed to god
to give me strength—and he heard me—he gave me the strength I need-

ed.—Sad as your letter made me, I nevertheless was beside myself with joy when I read that you had taken the news as it must be taken—consequently I felt I did not need to worry anymore about that very best father of mine and my dearest sister. As soon as I had finished your letter, I fell to my knees and thanked god from the bottom of my heart for the mercy he had shown me;—Now I am entirely at ease,—for I know that I need not worry about the two Persons who are dearest to me in all the world—for such a worry would be the greatest misfortune for me right now—it would most certainly crush me.—So, both of you, please take care of your health, it is so very precious to me—I beg of you—and please give him, who is flattering himself that he is now the most beloved person for you in the world, the happiness, pleasure, and joy of embracing you both very soon. . . .

You are asking for a short description of the illness and all the details?—I shall give it to you, I ask only that I may be brief and give you only the essentials; for one thing, it's all behind us now and cannot be changed anymore—and, for another, I must save a little room for writing about things that concern our present situation. So then, first of all, let me tell you that my dear mother *had* to die—no physician in the world could have saved her this time—it was clearly god's will; her time had come—and god wished to call her to him. You think she put off being bled until it was too late?—Maybe that's true; she did put it off a little; but I share the opinion of some people here who advised her against being bled and tried to persuade her to have an enema instead—but she didn't want it—and I didn't dare say anything, because I don't understand these things and consequently would have had to take the blame if the procedure hadn't been good for her—if it had been for myself I would have consented immediately—because this sort of thing is much in vogue here—if there's any sign of an inflammation, an enema is administered—and the cause of my mother's illness was nothing but an internal inflammation; at any rate, such was the diagnosis. How much was she bled? I can't say precisely, because here the blood is not measured by the ounce but by the plateful—and she was bled not quite 2 platefuls; the surgeon said that it had been very necessary—but as it was such a dreadfully hot day, he thought it best not to bleed her too much; she felt better for a few days but then she started to have diarrhea—no one gave it much thought, because it's so common here, all foreigners who drink a lot of water find it works like a laxative; and it's true enough! I, too, had it the first few days, but ever since I stopped drinking plain water and began mixing a little wine into it, I've been fine; but since I can't live without plain water, I purify it with ice and drink it *en glace*; I drink two glasses before going to bed.—

But to continue: on the 19ᵗʰ she complained of headaches—so I kept her in bed all day for the first time—on the preceding day, the 18ᵗʰ, she was up for the last time. On the 20ᵗʰ she complained of chills—then of being hot; so I gave her some Antispasmodic Powder; all this time I wanted to send for a doctor—but she didn't want one; when I insisted she told me that she had no confidence in French doctors—so I started looking for a German—but, naturally, I could not go out and leave her alone—I waited anxiously for Monsieur Heina, who came to see us every day without fail—except, of course, just this once, he stayed away for 2 days.—At last Haina came, and because the doctor was unable to come the next day, we couldn't have his help right away. He finally came on the 24ᵗʰ. The day before, when I had waited for him so eagerly, I got very worried—because she suddenly lost her hearing—the Doctor, an elderly German of about seventy, gave her some rhubarb powder stirred into wine—it's something I can't understand—for it is said that wine increases your body heat—but when I said that, they all shouted—Not at all; what are you saying?; wine doesn't make you hot—wine only strengthens the body; it's the water that creates the heat—and all the while the poor patient was desperately longing for a little fresh water—how much I would have liked to give her some—dearest father, you cannot imagine what I went through—but there was no other way, I had to leave her, in god's name, in the hands of the doctor.—the only thing I was able to do in good conscience was to pray to god and pray continuously that he would turn everything to the best—I walked about as if I had lost my mind—there would have been time for composing, but— I would not have been able to write a single note. The doctor didn't come on the 25ᵗʰ—he came again on the 26ᵗʰ, and just put yourself in my position when he quite unexpectedly said to me—"I fear she will not live through the night"— . . .

Monsieur Grimm said the other day to me, what should I write to your father?—what are your plans now?—will you stay here, or will you go to Mannheim? I couldn't keep from laughing—what should I do in Mannheim now?—if I had never come to Paris—but as it is, I am here now and have to try as hard as possible to make my way—I know, he

said, but I can hardly believe that you can make it here—why?—I see a
lot of Miserable bunglers who can make a living here, and I, with my
talent, should not be able to do so?—I can assure you that I would love
to be in Mannheim—I wished I could be in service there—but only in
an Honorable and Reputable position—and I must make certain of it,
otherwise I won't move one step. Well, he said, I'm afraid you are not
active enough here—you are not getting out and about enough—yes, I
said, that's indeed the hardest thing for me—besides, I couldn't go anywhere these days, because of the long illness of my mother—and 2 of
my pupils are in the country—and the third, the daughter of the Duc
de Guines, is about to be married and will not continue, which, I must
admit, won't harm me much. I won't lose any money in her case, for
what the Duc is paying me—I can get from anybody here. Just imagine,
the Duc de Guines, to whose house I was required to come every day
and stay for 2 hours, let me go on teaching 24 lessons, although it is customary to pay after 12, then he went to the country and came back 10
days later without letting me know—if I hadn't gone there and inquired
out of sheer curiosity, I would still not know that they are back;—
the housekeeper finally pulled out her purse and said: pardon me for
paying only for 12 lessons right now, I don't have more money on
hand—now there's *noblesse* for you!—and then she counted out 3 louis
d'or—and added—I hope this is satisfactory for you—if not—please
tell me—so Monsieur le Duc has no honor either;—he must have
thought: this is a young fellow and a stupid German besides—that's just
how all French speak of the Germans—he will be quite content with
this—but the stupid German was not content—and didn't accept the
money either—in other words, the Duc wanted to pay only one lesson
for 2, and this although he has had a Concerto for flute and harp[58] from
me already for 4 months without paying for it—so, I'm going to wait
until the wedding is over, then I'll got to the housekeeper and demand
my money. What annoys me most is that these stupid Frenchmen think
I am still just seven years old—because that was my age when they first
saw me—it's absolutely true; Mad. d'Epinai told me so herself in all
seriousness—they treat me here like a beginner—except the musicians;

58. Concerto for Flute and Harp in C major, K. 299.

they know better. But it's the general public that counts. After my conversation with Grimm I went to see Count Sückingen the very next day—he agreed entirely with me—namely I should be patient until Raff is back in Mannheim—for he will do his utmost for me there—his very best—and if nothing comes of it, Count Sückingen himself offered to get me an appointment at Maynz.—So then, these are my prospects;—I will now do my utmost to continue here with teaching and making as much money as I can—and I am doing it in hopeful anticipation of a change I hope will be forthcoming soon, for I can't deny it and must confess to you that I'll be glad to be liberated from here; for to give lessons here is no fun—you wear yourself out doing it, and if you don't take *many* pupils, you cannot make much money; you must not think that it's laziness on my part—No!—but it is totally contrary to my talent, contrary to my whole being—you know that I am, as it were, completely immersed in Musique,—it is on my mind all day long—I love to plan—study—reflect on it—But I am unable to do so in my present circumstances—to be sure, I would have a few free hours, but I would need these more for rest than for work.—About the opera, well, I talked about it in my last letter. I cannot help it, but I must write a grand opera or none at all; if I write a short opera, I'll earn very little; for here they weigh and measure everything, and if the opera is unfortunate enough not to appeal to these stupid Frenchmen, then all is lost—for I wouldn't get a chance to write another one—I would have gained little—and my reputation would have suffered—but if I'll write a grand opera—the money is better—and I'll be in my element, which makes me happy—I could also expect greater approbation because in a larger work you have a better opportunity to make your reputation—I can assure you that if I get to compose an opera, I will have no fear—the language, it's true, was made by the devil—and I do recognize the difficulties all Compositeurs have to face in this regard, but still, I feel capable of overcoming these and all other difficulties—au contraire, whenever I imagine, as I do once in a while, that I will be able to go ahead with my opera, I feel a veritable fire in my body, and my hands and feet tremble with impatience to teach these French how to appreciate the Germans better—how to value them and how to be in awe of them. . . .

Farewell in the meantime, and continue to love me—my heart is laughing with joy when I think of the day when I'll have the good fortune of seeing you again and embracing you. Adieu. I kiss your hands 100000 times, and I embrace my sister with

brotherly love; I remain your most obedient son

Wolfgang Amadè Mozart

In a letter to his friend Abbé Bullinger, Mozart pokes fun at the musical life in Salzburg. His underlying theme is the stinginess of the archbishop and the resultant low quality of the court orchestra. The archbishop's search for a new Kapellmeister is a related subject. It was particularly painful for the Mozarts that Leopold, who was deputy Kapellmeister and had applied for the vacant position, was not appointed to the post. Mozart's remark that the Salzburg court orchestra had a head, but what it really needed was "an ass" (einen arsch), is a unique characterization of the orchestra's lack of completeness. Mozart's lively language, his sarcastic jabs, and his imaginative signature are indications that his trauma of the past few weeks is abating and his natural humor and verbal play are coming back.

To Abbé Joseph Bullinger, in Salzburg

Paris, August 7, 1778

My very dearest friend!

Allow me to thank you first of all wholeheartedly for yet another proof of your friendship, which you have rendered me by taking such wonderful care of my dear father; first preparing him so well, then consoling him like a true friend;—you have played your role superbly— these are my father's own words. Dearest friend!—how can I ever thank you enough!—you have saved my most beloved father for me!—Thanks to you—I still have him. I won't say any more about it right now, because I can't even attempt to express my full gratitude to you; I actually feel too weak, too incompetent, too worn-out—dearest friend!—I will be in your debt always. . . . You undoubtedly know that the best and truest friends are the poor—rich people know nothing about friendship!—especially those who are born rich;—and even the ones who become rich by circumstances often lose their way and succumb to their fortune. . . . You are writing that I should now think only about my father, I should tell him frankly what my thoughts are, and put my trust in him completely;—how unfortunate would I be, if I needed to be reminded of that!—It is certainly appropriate that you are telling me this;—however, I am quite happy —and you can be too—that I'm not in need of this advice. In my most recent letter to my father I told him already everything I know myself up to now—and I assured him that I will always keep him informed about the details of my life and always tell him honestly what I think, because I have complete confidence in him and I am certain of his fatherly concern, love, and goodness—knowing full well that one day he will grant me fulfillment of a request on which the happiness and joy of the rest of my life depend, which will be an honest and reasonable request, as expected of me, and which he will not deny me.[59] Dearest friend, don't let my dear father read any of this;—you know how he is; he would start to think and worry about it—to *no good purpose!*—

Now let me turn to our Salzburg story! You know, my dear friend, how I hate Salzburg!—not only on account of the injustices that my father and I have suffered there, which would be reason enough to forget such a place altogether, indeed wipe it from your memory!—but let's leave that as it is—after all, things should always be worked out so that we can all live *respectably* with each other—but to live respectably and to live happily are two different things,—and the latter I couldn't manage without some witchcraft! . . . Well, no matter what happens,—it will always be my greatest pleasure to embrace my dearest father and sister, and the sooner the better; but I can't deny the fact that my pleasure and joy would be twice as much—if this could happen somewhere else—because I have far *more* hope to live a pleasurable and happy life anywhere else!—Perhaps you misunderstand me and think that I feel Salzburg is too small for me?—if you think that, you are quite mistaken;—I told my father some of the reasons already; let me tell you just one: Salzburg is no place for my talent!—First of all, the court musicians do not enjoy a good reputation, second, there's nothing going on musically; there is no theater, no opera!—and even if they wanted to stage one, who would be there to sing?—for the last 5 or 6 years the Salzburg orchestra has always been rich in what is useless and unnecessary—and very poor in what is essential;—and essential things that are indispensable, they don't have at all;—in fact, we have such a situation

59. Probably a reference to Mozart's intention of marrying Aloysia Weber.

right now!—The cruel French are suddenly the reason why the orchestra has no Kapellmeister![60] . . . Well, that's the way it goes if you don't plan ahead!—One should always have half a dozen Kapellmeisters in reserve, so if one drops out, you can instantly call upon another—but, pray, where to get one now? . . . I will do my best to lend a hand;—Tomorrow, first thing, I will hire a carriage for the whole day and make the rounds among the hospitals and infirmaries to see whether I can't find one. . . . Yet, it is more useful and reasonable to look for a Kapellmeister, since they really have *none* at present, than to write all over creation, as I've been told they are doing, to hire a good female singer; I can hardly believe it!—A female singer!? When we have so many already!—and all of them first-rate; if they went after a tenor, I could understand it, although we don't really need one either; but a female singer, a Prima donna!—after all, we have a castrato now!—It's true, Mad. Haydn is sickly,[61]—she has gone too far with her austere religious life; but anyway she is a rare case!—I'm surprised that she hasn't long since lost her voice with all her constant flagellations and whippings, her posturing in a hairy shirt, her unnatural fasting and nightly praying!—she will probably keep her voice for a while yet—indeed, instead of getting worse, it will probably get better in time—but if it should happen that god, at last, will place her among his saints, then we still have 5 female singers left who can all compete for first place! So you can clearly see how unnecessary it is to hire a new one!—but let me take my argument to the extreme: let's just imagine that, apart from the weeping Magdalena,[62] we had no other female singers, which, of course, is not the case, but let's nevertheless pretend that one of them suddenly gets pregnant, another one is taken to jail, the 3rd is going to be flogged, the 4th perhaps beheaded, and the 5th—snatched up by the devil!—what then?—well, nothing!—after all, we still have the castrato!—and you know what kind of an animal that is?—he can sing in the high register and would, therefore, be excellent in a woman's role; of course, the chap-

---

60. The Salzburg court Kapellmeister, Giacomo Rust, was in poor health, and an effort was under way to replace him with maestro Giuseppe Bertoni. But Bertoni favored an offer from Paris.
61. Maria Magdalena Haydn, wife of Michael Haydn, was a singer at the Salzburg court. Mozart's remarks about her austere religious practices are completely ironic; apparently she was fond of the bottle.
62. "The weeping Magdalena" is Madame Haydn.

ter[63] would object, but objecting is not as bad as rejecting—besides, no one worries much about the gentlemen of the clergy. So then, in the meantime, we'll allow Herr Ceccarelli[64] to change back and forth between his male and female roles. In the end, because I know at Salzburg they love variety, change, and innovation, I can see before my eyes a large field of opportunities whose realization can truly make History. My sister and I practiced it a little when we were children, just imagine what adults can do with this idea?—Oh, there are no limits to those who think imaginatively;—I'm certainly not worried—and I will gladly take on the task of bringing Metastasio from Vienna, or at least make him an offer, to write several dozen operas in which the male lead and the female lead never encounter each other on stage, for in this way the castrato can play both the male and the female lover in one performance, and the piece would be found especially interesting because it allows us to admire the virtuousness of the two lovers, which goes so far that they deliberately avoid speaking with each other in public.— There you have the opinion of a true Patriot!—now you had better see to it that the orchestra will soon get an ass—because that's what it needs most of all; it has only a head at present—but that's just what's wrong with it.—Unless there is some change in this scenario, I shall not come back to Salzburg. . . .

Adieu, I continue to pray for your good friendship, and I assure you that I will be Forever your

> true friend and closest servant
> Wolfgang *Romatz.*

To his father, in Salzburg

St. Germain, August 27, 1778

Mon trés cher Pére!

I'm writing to you in greatest haste—you can see that I am not in Paris—Monsieur Bach of London is here and has been here for the last

---

63. The "chapter" (in German, *Domkapitel*) is the clerical hierarchy of Salzburg. The chapter founded the cathedral as well as the town of Salzburg in the eighth century and remained the constituted body to elect the archbishop.
64. Francesco Ceccarelli was a castrato singer in Salzburg and a good friend of the Mozarts.

two weeks; he is going to write a French opera—and has come to hear the singers, after that he will go back to London, write the opera, and then return here to oversee its production;—you can easily imagine his joy as well as my joy in seeing each other again—maybe his joy isn't quite as genuine as mine—but you have to grant him that he is an Honorable man and fair to everyone; I love him, as you know, with all my heart,—I have the highest respect for him, and one thing is certainly true: he has praised me not only to my face but also to others—not exaggeratedly as some have, but Seriously and truthfully.—Tenduci[65] is here as well—he is a very close friend of Bach's—he was overjoyed to see me again—Now let me tell you how it happened that I came to St. Germain. The home of the Marechal de Noaile is here, as you probably know, and they tell me that I had been here 15 years ago—but I don't remember anything about it.—Tenduci is a great favorite of his—and because Tenduci is very fond of me also, he wanted me to make his acquaintance. I probably won't gain anything by being here—maybe a small present—but I won't lose anything either, for it's not costing me anything—and even if I don't receive anything—I will have made a useful contact.—The reason I'm in a hurry: Tenduci has asked me to write a scena for him—for Sunday—a piece for piano forte, oboe, French horn, and bassoon;[66] it's for the Marechal's own orchestra, all Germans who play very well—I would have written to you long ago, I started a letter and now it's lying in Paris, unfinished. I drove to St. Germain thinking that I would come back to Paris the same day—but now I've been here a week already.—I will return to Paris as soon as I can,—even though I'm not losing out on anything there—I have only one pupil, the others are in the country. . . . France is quite similar to Germany—they are good in dishing up compliments but little else—still—there's always hope that one can make one's fortune somehow. . . . I will soon write more—1000 greetings from Mr. Tenduci. . . . Adieu, farewell, I kiss your hands 1000 times and embrace my dear sister with all my heart, I remain your obedient son

Wolfgang Mozart

65. Giustino Ferdinando Tenducci, a male soprano, whom the Mozarts also knew from London.
66. There is no trace of this composition; it is assumed that Tenducci took it with him to London.

🐚 *In his last letter from Paris, Mozart is full of ambivalences and rationalizations. He understood his father's financial predicament, and it was certainly one of the reasons why he overcame his distaste for Salzburg and agreed to return home. It is not without irony, however, that the man he disliked most in Salzburg, the prince archbishop, is the only person who offered him a firm salary. Yet the ultimate motivation for Mozart's return is the chance of being close to Aloysia; he knew that she would be singing in Munich, perhaps even in Salzburg. Clever Leopold dangled this possibility like a carrot before Wolfgang's eyes: "The Prince and all the others are intrigued by Mad.^selle Weber, they all want to hear her" (August 31, 1778).*

To his father, in Salzburg

Paris, September 11, 1778

Mon Trés cher Pére!

I have received your 3 letters of August, 13th, 27th, and 31st in good order, but at the moment I will just answer the last one, because it is the most urgent; when I read it through—Monsieur Heina, who sends his regards to you both, happened to be here with me—I was trembling with joy, for I saw myself already in your arms; it's true, what awaits me in Salzbourg is not a great fortune[67]—and you would be the first to tell me so—but when I imagine myself kissing you, my dear father and my dear sister, I cannot think of any greater happiness. And it's the only real excuse I can offer to anyone here who is filling my ears with shouts that I should stay. For I keep telling them: but what do you want?—I'm happy with this arrangement, and that settles it. I will have a place that I can call my home,—live in peace and quiet with my beloved father and dear sister—I can do as I please—and, apart from my duties, I am my own master—with a Permanent income—can leave when I want to—travel every 2 years—what more can I possibly want?—The only thing that bothers me about Salzbourg—and I'm telling you this straight from the heart, is that one is so restricted in one's social life—and that the members of the orchestra are held in such low esteem—and—that the Archbishop doesn't take advice from knowledgeable people who have been out in the world, for I can assure you that without traveling

---

67. The archbishop had agreed to reemploy Mozart as court organist and concertmaster with an annual salary of 500 gulden. Together with Leopold's c. 400 gulden a year, it was a good enough income, Leopold felt, for the family to live on.

one remains a poor creature; that goes especially for people in the arts and sciences!—And I'm serious when I say that if the Archbishop doesn't allow me to take a trip every 2 years, I cannot possibly accept the Engagement; a person of mediocre talent will always be mediocre; whether he travels or not—but a person of superior talent,—and it would be impious of me to say I am not—will wither away if he keeps staying in one and the same place. If the Archbishop would give me his confidence, I would soon bring his Orchestra to fame; and that's the truth.—I can tell you that this particular journey has not been without its gains for me—I am talking especially about Composition, because as far as the Clavier is concerned—I'm playing as well as I ever will. But there's one other condition for my return to Salzbourg: I don't want to be only a violinist as I was before—I'm not a fiddler anymore—I want to conduct from the piano—and accompany arias; it would have been a good thing if I could have had a written guarantee, specifying that I will be in line for the position of Kapellmeister; otherwise I may have the honor of doing duties for two posts—but getting paid for only one—and in the end I will have some stranger appointed over my head. Dearest father! Let me confess, if it weren't for the pleasure of seeing both of you again, I really couldn't decide to come back—yet, I do wish to get away from Paris, a city I can't stand—although my situation here has begun to improve steadily, and I don't doubt that if I could only make up my mind to hold on for a few years longer, I could do well indeed; at any rate, I'm now fairly well known here—I don't know people as well as they know me, but I have made a good name for myself with my 2 Sinfonies; the last one was performed on the 8th of this month.[68] . . . If I wanted to tell you all that's on my mind—my fingers would hurt from writing. I will tell you everything in person and explain to you also that Monsieur Grimm is capable of helping *children* but not adults.—and, but no, I had better not write this—and yet—I must say it. Don't think that Monsieur Grimm is the same man he once was; were it not for Mad.^me d'Epinay, I wouldn't be in their house; at any rate, he need not be so proud of his hospitality—for there are 4 other places where I could have had a room—and board; the good man has no idea that *if I had stayed here*, I would have moved out next month and gone to

---

68. The "Paris" Symphony, K. 297, is one of the two mentioned by Mozart; the other has not been identified.

a place where they are not as smug and dumb as in this house—where they don't always rub it in when they have done you a favor—his behavior can really make me *forget* that he ever did anything for me—but I want to be more generous than he is—I'm only sorry that I'm not staying on in Paris to show him that I can get along quite well without him—and that I'm as good as his Piccini,[69] even though I'm only a German. The biggest favor he has done for me was to lend me 15 louis d'or, which he gave me little by little at the time of the illness and death of my dear mother—is he perhaps worried about getting it back?—if he has any doubt, he really deserves a kick in the rear, because he is doubting my Honesty, which is the one thing that can really make me angry—he is also doubting my Talent; but I knew that already because he told me once to my face that he didn't think I was capable of writing a French opera. . . . But enough of all this—we'll talk more when I get home; at any rate, Mad.^me d'Epinai has a better heart; the room I live in belongs to her, not him; it's a kind of sickroom; whoever is ill in the house is quartered there; it offers nothing attractive, except the view, only bare walls, not even a chest of drawers, nothing—now you tell me whether or not I could have endured staying here any longer; I would have told you all this long ago, but I was afraid you wouldn't believe me—but now I can't be silent any longer—whether you believe me or not. . . . Monsieur Grimm has figured out that it will be best for me to leave in 8 days; *he is in that much of a hurry*—but I told him, I can't go right now—and the reasons why: . . . I still have to finish 6 Trios[70] —which will bring me good money—and I still have to get my money from Le Gros and Duc de Guines—and, finally, the Mannheim court will be moving to Munich at the end of the month, and I would like to get there at the same time so that I can personally present my sonatas to the Electress.[71] . . . I will also sell my 3 Concertos, the "Jeunehomme" and the "Litzau," as well as the one in B minor, in cash to the engraver who did my sonatas.[72] I'll do the same with my 6 difficult sonatas if I can; I

69. In the famous rivalry between Christoph Willibald Gluck and Niccolò Piccinni in Paris, Baron von Grimm was in the camp of the Piccinnists.

70. There is no trace of these trios.

71. Elisabeth Maria Aloysia Auguste, wife of Elector Karl Theodor. Mozart would dedicate six of his violin sonatas, K. 301–306 to her in Munich.

72. The three piano concertos are no. 9, K. 271; no. 8, K. 246; and no. 6, K. 238. The engraver is Jean-Georges Sieber of Paris.

won't get much, but it's better than nothing. One needs money on a trip. As far as my Sinfonies are concerned—most of them are not in the taste of the Parisians; if I have time I'll rearrange the violin Concertos—that is I'll shorten them—because in Germany the taste is for longer concerts, but, in fact, short and good quality is better. . . . I hope to get a quick answer to this letter from you; I won't leave here until I have it. I figured it out already: you'll get this letter on September 22, answer me immediately, the mail leaves on the 25th, that is on Friday, then I'll get your answer by October 3rd; and I can leave on the following 6th. Actually, there is no reason for me to be in such a rush, for I'm not just sitting around here doing nothing, with no work; in fact, I'm going to lock myself in and work in order to earn as much money as possible. . . .

I have one more request, which I hope you will not refuse me; in the event that the Weber family has not gone to Munich but has remained in Mannheim—I'm just assuming this as a possibility, although I wish and believe that it is not the case—but if they are still in Mannheim, may I be permitted the pleasure of traveling via Mannheim so I can visit them? It would be a detour, yes, but a small one, at least as far as I am concerned;—I don't really think that I'll need to make this detour—I will probably see them in Munich—by tomorrow I expect to have a letter telling me this for sure;—if, however, they are still in Mannheim, I'm convinced that you in your generosity would not deny me this pleasure. Dearest father! If the Archbishop really wants to hire a new female singer, I swear to god, there's none better than the Weber girl; . . . As soon as I am back in Salzbourg, I will plead the case of this dear friend of mine with all possible determination—but in the meantime I'm asking you to do all you can for her; you can do your son no greater favor. Now all my thinking is concentrated on the pleasure of soon embracing you—I beg you, get assurances for all the things the Archbishop promised—especially my request that I want to be at the Clavier; my greetings to all good friends, particularly Herr Bullinger; oh, what fun we are going to have together! I can see it all in my imagination—it's right before my eyes. Adieu. I kiss your hands 100 000 times and embrace my sister with all my heart; I remain in the hope that I will receive an answer right away so I can leave soon, your obedient son,

Wolfgang Amadè Mozart

🕮 *Mozart left Paris on September 26, 1778. In a letter from Nancy, his first stop, he admitted to his father that he would not bring home many new compositions. The Mozart scholar Alan Tyson has concluded, "The painful fact, which he attempted to conceal from his father in a variety of ways, seems to have been that he had written very little in Paris. . . . But the reason for his lack of productiveness remains a mystery. One possibility is that he became deeply depressed and withdrawn as a result of his mother's death, so that for a while he was virtually unable to compose" (Tyson, Mozart, 113).*

To his father, in Salzburg

Nancy, October 3, 1778

Mon Trés cher Pére!

I apologize for not informing you of my departure while I was still in Paris, however, this whole affair was so rushed beyond my own calculation, judgment, and willingness that I cannot begin to describe it to you.——At the very last moment I had wanted to have my luggage brought to the house of Count Sückingen rather than to the Bureau of the Diligence,[73] so I could spend a few more days in Paris—and upon my honor I would have done so—if I hadn't been thinking of you—for I didn't wish to cause you any anxiety—at any rate, we'll have more time to talk about these matters in Salzburg;—at present only this much: just imagine, Monsieur Grimm lied to me when he told me that I would be going with the Diligence and be in Strassburg in 5 days;—not until the last day did I find out that he had put me on a different coach service, one that travels at a walking pace, doesn't change horses, and takes 10 days;—well, you can imagine how angry I was;—but I expressed my anger only to my good friends, toward Monsieur Grimm I acted agreeable and cheerful;—when I got into the carriage, I heard the happy news that we would be on the road for 12 days.——So, here you can see the great wisdom of Herr Baron von Grimm!—to save money he sent me by this slow carriage and didn't think that it would cost me just as much because you have to spend more money in inns.——Well, it's all behind me now;—what annoyed me most in this whole affair is the fact that he didn't tell me straight out;—in other words, he saved money for himself, but not for me—because he paid for the transportation but

73. The express coach service.

not for the food—if I had stayed in Paris for another 8 to 10 days I would have been able to pay for the trip myself and make better arrangements.—

I was able to put up with this coach for 8 days; but then I couldn't stand it any longer—not because of the wearisome ride, actually the wagon had good springs, but for want of sleep. Departure time every morning was at 4 o'clock, so we had to get up at 3 in the morning; twice I had the honor of rising at 1 o'clock at night because the coach left at 2 o'clock; and you know, I cannot sleep in coaches—therefore, I just couldn't continue without the risk of getting sick.—Moreover, one of our travel companions was badly afflicted with the French disease[74]— and he made no secret of it—well, that alone was enough for me to want to take the postal coach. But then I found that wasn't necessary, because I was lucky enough to become friends with a gentleman with whom I got on very well; he is a German, a merchant who lives in Paris and deals in English goods.—We already talked a little before boarding the coach and from that moment on we always stayed together;—we didn't eat with the others but ate in our room, which we also shared for the night;—I am happy to have this man's company because he is well traveled and knows all about it;—he, too, found the coach ride very wearing, so we both left the coach and we'll travel tomorrow to Strassburg with a better conveyance, something not too expensive.—I hope to find a letter from you there and learn from it how you want me to proceed.—I hope you received all my letters; I have received all of yours in good order. Please forgive me for not writing much, because when I'm not in a town where I am well known, I'm never in good humor;—but I think if I were known here I would be glad to stay because the town is charming—handsome houses, wide streets, beautiful squares.—There is one more thing I want to ask you to do for me—and that is to put a large chest into my room, for I would like to have all my things close at hand;—and if I could have the small Clavier, the one from Fischetti and Rust, next to my writing desk, that would make me very happy, for I can work with it better than with the small one by Stein. I am not bringing many new compositions, because I didn't write much.—I don't have the 3 Quartetti and the flute concerto that I did for Monsieur De

---

74. Venereal disease.

Jean,[75] because he packed them in the wrong trunk when he went to Paris and so they are still in Mannheim;—but he promised to send me the music as soon as he gets back to Mannheim.—I will ask Wendling to send it all;—at any rate, I won't bring anything finished except my sonatas;[76] Le Gros bought my 2 overtures and the sinfonia concertante;[77] he thinks he alone has that music now, but that's not quite true, for I still have it fresh in my head and shall write it down again as soon as I get home;—The acting troupe from Munich has probably begun its tour in Salzburg by now?—How are they doing?—Are people attending the performances?—I suppose the "Fischermaiden," *la Pescatrice* by Piccini, or the "Peasant Girl at Court," *la Contadina in Corte* by Sacchine, are the first Singspiele on the program? And is Mad.[selle] Kaiser the prima donna?—She is the singer I wrote to you about from Munich—I don't actually know her—I only heard her sing;—at the time she had been onstage only for the third time and had learned the music only 3 weeks before.—Farewell for now;—I won't have a quiet hour until I can be together with all my loved ones again —

I embrace my dear sister with all my heart and kiss you 1000 times, and I remain your most obedient son,

Wolfgang Amadè Mozart

Mozart arrived in Strasbourg probably on October 14 and remained there for two weeks. In spite of his constant assurances that he wanted to fly into the arms of his father, in spite of Leopold's message that he was spending sleepless nights worrying about him on the road, Mozart seemed in no hurry to leave Strasbourg. He arranged for several concerts, one of which was attended very poorly. Before departing from Strasbourg, he visited with the two sons of the famous organ builder Andreas Silbermann and played on two of his organs. And then, to his father's utmost chagrin, Mozart was off to Mannheim.

75. The "3 Quartetti" are K. 285, 285a, 285b (Anh. 171); the "flute concerto" is probably K. 313.
76. The piano sonatas K. 301–306.
77. One of the "overtures" is probably the "Paris" Symphony; the "sinfonia concertante" is the lost concerto for wind instruments, K. 297b.

To his father, in Salzburg

Strasbourg, October 15, 1778

Monsieur mon trés cher Pére!

I received your 3 letters of Sept.^bre 17th, Sept.^bre 24th, and Oct.^bre 1st,[78] but it was impossible for me to answer you before now;—I hope you received my last letter, the one from Nancy all right;—I am glad with all my heart that you are both well, god be praised! I too am well, thank the lord, very well indeed. . . .

Dearest father!—I can assure you that if it weren't for the pleasure of embracing you soon, I would most certainly not come back to Salzburg!—for, apart from that desirable and truly beautiful sentiment, I am probably committing the biggest folly in the world;—and believe me, this is very much my own thinking and not anyone else's; . . . if this business of my departure had not come over me like a thunderstorm, if I had had time to reflect on the matter with a clear mind,—I would probably have asked you to be patient a little longer and let me stay in Paris; I can assure you I would have gained honor, fame, and money— and most certainly pulled you out of your debts;—but it's done now; and don't think that I feel sorry about it;—however, only you, dearest father, only you can sweeten the bitterness of Salzburg for me; and I know you will do that for me; I'm sure of it; still I must confess in all frankness that I would come back to Salzburg with an easier mind if I did not know that I am already engaged in service there;—it is the only unbearable thought I have!—Look at it—put yourself in my position;— at Salzburg I don't know who I am—I am everything and then again I'm nothing—I ask neither *too much* nor *too little*—but I want something—I need to be somebody—everywhere else I know what my duties are— whoever is a violinist remains a violinist, and whoever is a Clavierist, etc.—well, I'm sure all this can be worked out.—I hope it will all turn out for the best and to my satisfaction;—I rely totally on you.—

Things are in a pretty poor state around here—but still I will give a subscription concert tomorrow, that's Saturday, the 17th, I will perform *alone,* just for a few good friends, amateur musicians, and connoisseurs, so I won't incur any expenses—if I played with an orchestra it would

---

78. The three letters were forwarded to Mozart from Paris.

cost me, together with lighting, more than 3 louis d'or; and who knows whether we'll take in that much. . . .

Adieu for now,—I embrace my dear sister with all my heart, and you, my dearest and most beloved father, I kiss your hands in the pleasant hope of being able to embrace you myself soon; I remain your most obedient son,

Wolfgang Amadè Mozart

🔖 *Mozart had traveled to Mannheim by the diligence, the fastest conveyance available. He had hoped to find Aloysia still there, but she had moved with her family to Munich, where she had been engaged by the court theater for 600 gulden a year. Leopold, in his desperation to bring Wolfgang back to Salzburg, wrote two letters to him. The first, dated November 19, was full of Leopoldian thunder: "Mon trés cher Fils! I really don't know what to say anymore—I will either lose my mind or die of exhaustion. . . . Your whole intent is to ruin me so you can build your castles in the air." After giving Wolfgang a detailed account of the family debts, he pulled out the last stop by insinuating that Wolfgang was responsible for his mother's death: "I hope that, after your mother had to die in Paris already, you will not also burden your conscience by expediting the death of your father." The second letter, written on November 23, is a masterpiece of Leopoldian shrewdness: why did Wolfgang want to stay in Mannheim, he cleverly asked, when Aloysia was now in Munich and Munich was after all only a short distance from Salzburg? Besides, Salzburg was also so much closer to Italy than Mannheim was. Still, Wolfgang hesitated to come back to Papa, the archbishop, and Salzburg.*

To his father, in Salzburg

Mannheim, November 12, 1778

Mon Trés cher Pére!

I arrived here safely on the 6ᵗʰ and surprised all my good friends most pleasantly;—god be thanked and praised, I am back in my beloved Mannheim!—I can assure you, if you were here you would say the same; I am staying with Mad.ᵐᵉ Cannabich—who, together with her family as well as all my other good friends, was beside herself with joy when she saw me again;—we haven't yet finished talking about everything; she is giving me a complete report of all the events and changes that have occurred since I've been gone;—I haven't eaten at home once since I arrived here—everybody wants to see me; in one word: as I love Mannheim, Mannheim loves me.—

I don't know yet for sure, but it could well be that I'll get a position here after all!—I mean here, not in Munich; because I have the feeling that the Elector will be soon ready to reestablish his residence in Mannheim because he can't possibly endure for long the crude manners of those Bavarians!—You probably know that the Mannheim acting troupe is in Munich?—well, their two best actresses, Mad.^me Toscani and Mad.^me Urban, were greeted there with boos, in fact, there was such a row that the Elector himself leaned over his box and tried to shush the crowd—and then, when nobody paid attention, he sent down a messenger;—and Count Seau, when he told some officers not to make such a noise, because the Elector didn't like it, received as an answer:—they had paid their own good money to get in and no one could tell them what to do—but I'm foolish to tell you all this! you probably know it already from our friends there.

Now listen: I *may* be able to earn perhaps 40 louis d'or here! Of course, it would mean I'll have to stay here for 6 more weeks—2 months at the most;—The Seyler Acting Troupe is in town[79]—you probably know them by reputation;—Herr von Dallberg is the director;[80]—and he is determined to keep me here until I've composed a Duodrama[81] for him, and, in fact, it didn't take me too long to make up my mind,—for I've always wanted to write a play of this sort;—I can't remember whether I wrote to you about these dramas when I was here before?— At that time I went twice to see such a play, and I saw it with the greatest pleasure!—in fact, nothing had ever surprised me quite as much!—I had always thought that this sort of performance could not be effective on stage!—You probably know that there is no singing but only Recitation—and the Musique functions like an obbligato Recitative—now and then the words are recited with the Musique and then the effect is most magnificent.—What I saw was "Medea" by *Benda*[82]—he also did another play, "Ariadne auf Naxos"; both works are

79. "The Seyler Acting Troupe" was the most prominent theater group in Germany at that time.
80. Wolfgang Heribert Reichsfreiherr von Dalberg, director of the Mannheim National Theater.
81. "Duodrama," or "melodrama," is a stage play consisting of spoken text and background music. If only one actor is involved, the term "monodrama" is used. Mozart began composing a melodrama entitled *Semiramis* (K. Anh. no. 11), but he never completed it.
82. Georg Benda, Kapellmeister in Gotha, Thuringia.

truly superb;—you know that *Benda* has always been my favorite among Lutheran kapellmeisters, and I like those two works by him so much that I always keep them in my possession. Now, just imagine how delighted I was when I was requested to do something that I always wanted to do! You know what I think?—One should do most operatic recitatives in this manner—and only once in a while, *when the words can be easily expressed through music,* one should actually sing the recitatives.—

They are establishing an Accademie des Amateurs here, just like the one in Paris—Herr Fränzl will lead the violin section—so I have just begun to write a concerto for clavier and violin.[83]—My good friend Raaff was still in Mannheim when I arrived, but he left on the 8th.— He has been singing my praises and did everything he could for me here—I hope he'll do the same in Munich.—Do you know what this cursed scoundrel Seau[84] said about me here?—He said my opera buffa had been booed off the stage in Munich![85] Unluckily for him, he said it in a place where I am very well known!—but I'm annoyed about so much impudence because, after all, when people from here come to Munich they will hear just the opposite!—A whole contingent of Bavarians is here—Fräulein de Pauli is among them—I don't know her present name—but I already paid her a visit because she sent for me right away—Oh—what a difference there is between the people from the Palatinate and those Bavarians—what is it with that Bavarian language anyway!—it's so coarse!—and what manners they have!— . . .

Farewell in the meantime, my dearest and most beloved father; I kiss your hands 1000 times and embrace my dear sister with all my heart, and I remain your most obedient son

Wolfgang Amadè Mozart

Mozart could not convince his father that it would be good for him to stay in Mannheim for a while. In a sharp rebuke, Leopold thundered, "I don't want you to be appointed in Mannheim or anywhere else—I don't want to even hear the word appointed . . . and I don't want to hear about these 40 louis d'or that you

---

83. The concerto, K. Anh. 56, remained a fragment.
84. Count Joseph Seeau, director of the court theaters in Munich, seemed friendly and helpful to Mozart in 1777 in Munich but may well have intrigued against him all along.
85. Mozart's opera buffa *La finta giardiniera,* first performed in Munich in 1775.

*might be able to earn." Mozart remained committed to the idea of writing a mon-
odrama and tried to get a commission from Dalberg.*

To Wolfgang Heribert von Dalberg, in Mannheim

Mannheim, November 24, 1778

Monsieur Le Baron!

I called on you twice already but was not fortunate enough to find
you at home; yesterday, it appears, you were home, but I still was not
able to see you!—Therefore, I hope you will forgive me for troubling
you with these few lines,—for it is of great importance for me to explain
myself to you.—Herr Baron! You know me—I am not after selfish
interests, especially when I know that it is within my abilities to be of
service to a great lover and connoisseur of music such as you;—yet, I
am equally certain that you would not want me to suffer a loss here.—
So I take the liberty of giving you a final offer in this matter because I
cannot possibly remain here any longer, given these uncertainties.—

I am willing to commit myself to write a monodrama for the sum
of 25 louis d'or—and remain here for two more months—so I can fulfill all obligatory conditions, i.e., attend rehearsals, etc., but with the following stipulation: no matter how things work out, I shall be paid by
the end of January.—

It is understood, of course, that I would have free access to the theater;—this, Herr Baron, is pretty much all I can do!—If you consider
it well, you will see that I am acting quite unselfishly.—As far as your
own opera[86] is concerned, I can assure you that I would be happy to set
it to music;—but you will have to admit yourself that this kind of work
I could not possibly do for 25 louis d'or, for at its lowest estimate it
would require twice as much work as a Monodrama—however, what
would keep me from doing it more than anything else is the fact that,
as you told me yourself, Gluck and Schweizer are already working on it.
But even if you wanted to give me 50 louis d'or for it, I would still, as
an Honest Man, advise you against it. An opera without singers!—how
does one do that!—Yet, if in the meantime there should be any prospect
that it could be performed, I will not refuse to accept this task, if only

---

86. Dalberg had written a play titled *Cora* and was casting about for a composer; but he was already negotiating with Christoph Willibald Gluck and Anton Schweitzer about the same play.

to do you a favor;—but it would not be a small task, I swear it upon my honor.—Now I have given you my thoughts on the matter clearly and honestly—please let me know as soon as possible what your decision is—if I could know it already today, it would be all the better because I have heard that someone will be traveling all alone to Munich next Thursday and I would love to take advantage of this opportunity.—In the meantime, I have the honor of remaining respectfully yours,

Monsieur Le Baron!

Ce mecredi le 24 Nov.^bre 1778

Your most obedient servant,
Wolfgang Amadè Mozart

Neither Mozart's proposals to compose a monodrama nor his offer to write the music for Dalberg's play bore fruit. Finally, he ran out of options and excuses and, volens nolens, had to write to his father on December 3, "Next Wednesday, that is on the 9th, I will be leaving Mannheim."

To his father, in Salzburg

Mannheim, December 3, 1778

Monsieur mon trés cher Père!

I must ask your pardon for two things: first, that I haven't written to you for so long, and second, that I must be brief today.—The fact that I haven't answered you for a while is no one's fault but your own—it was on account of your first letter to Mannheim;—to tell you the truth, I could have never imagined that—but silence! I will say no more about it—it's all behind me now.[87] Next Wednesday, that is on the 9th, I will be leaving Mannheim—I couldn't leave any earlier, because I thought I would be here a couple of months, so I took on several pupils and, therefore, I want to complete my 12 lessons.[88] You can't even imagine what good and special friends I have here—this will all become evident in time.—And why must I be so brief?—because I have my hands full with work. I am at present writing the First Act of the melodrama I was

---

87. Mozart is reacting painfully to his father's insinuation (letter of November 19, 1778) that he was to blame for his mother's death.
88. Twelve lessons was the customary number a music student expected when hiring a teacher.

asked to compose for Herr von Gemmingen,[89] but I'm also doing it for my own enjoyment; and I'm doing it *for nothing;*—I will take it with me and finish it at home; you see, my desire to do this kind of Composition is that strong;—Herr von Gemmingen is the Poët, of course,—and the title of the Duodrama is "Semiramis."—I have also received your most recent letter of Nov.^bre 23rd—so I shall depart from here next Wednesday, and do you know who is offering me this opportunity?—the Imperial Abbot of Kaysersheim.[90] When a good friend of mine spoke to him about me,—he recognized my name instantly—and indicated that he would be pleased to have me as his traveling companion; he is, although a Priest and a Prelate, a rather amiable man; so I'll be traveling via Kaysersheim and not via Stuttgard—but that's fine with me, for it's important on such a trip to spare the purse, which has gotten very thin in the meantime.—Would you please answer me the following questions? How do the people of Salzburg like the actors from Munich?—Isn't there a girl singing in that troupe by the name of Kaiser?—

Does Herr Feiner play the English horn as well? If only we had clarinets in the orchestra!—You wouldn't believe what marvelous effects flutes, oboes, and clarinetti produce in a Sinfonie.—There's much I have to tell the Archbishop at my first audience with him and perhaps I'll make a few suggestions;—oh, our orchestra could be so much better and much more refined, if only the Archbishop wanted it so;—the main reason why it isn't any better is probably that they have to give too many performances.—I have nothing against chamber Musick,—only against big concerts.—By the way, you're not saying anything about my trunk, but it must have arrived by now.—if not, Herr von Grimm would bear the responsibility.—In the trunk you will find the aria I wrote for Mad.^selle Weber;[91] you can't imagine how great it sounds when it is performed with orchestra; one cannot see that just by looking at the score;—and, of course, it has to be sung by a singer such as the Weber girl;—I beg you, don't give the aria to anyone,—it would be the greatest unfairness you could do, for it was written solely for her and

89. Otto Freiherr von Gemmingen-Hornberg, a diplomat and writer, residing in Mannheim.
90. "The Imperial Abbot" is Coelestin II, Angelsprugger, and "Kaysersheim" is really Kaisheim, near Donauwörth, seat of an old Cistercian monastery.
91. "Non sò, d'onde viene," K. 294.

fits her like a garment that was tailored just for her.—Farewell for now, dearest, most beloved father;—I embrace my dear sister with all my heart—and please give all kinds of greetings to our good friend Bullinger; my compliments to Ceccarelli, Herr Fiala, his wife, Herr Feiner, and to all the people of Salzburg who do know a little what the world looks like outside of the Salzburg area.—Adieu, I kiss your hands a Thousand times and remain your most obedient son

Wolfgang Amadè Mozart

Mozart left Mannheim on December 9, traveling in the carriage of the abbot's sec-retary and wine steward. The party took the route via Heidelberg, Dinkelsbühl, and Nördlingen and arrived in Kaisheim on December 13. Mozart remained at the monastery as guest of the abbot until December 24 when the friendly clergyman continued his journey to Munich and invited Mozart, once again, to travel with him as his guest.

Mozart had thought of visiting his cousin, Maria Anna Thekla, in Augsburg on his way to Munich and Salzburg, but when Abbot Coelestin II invited him to join his traveling party all the way to Munich, Mozart, who was virtually without money, immediately accepted. His letter to his cousin is an apology, but it also recalls the fun, humor, and linguistic exuberance of his earlier letters to his Bäsle. *Why he wanted her to come to Munich is not clear, but it is generally assumed that it was in connection with his plans to marry Aloysia.*

To Maria Anna Thekla Mozart, in Augsburg

Kaisheim, December 23, 1778

Ma trés cher Cousine!

I am writing in greatest haste—and with deepest regret and sorrow, also with the stiff resolve to let you know that tomorrow I am leaving for Munich.—Dearest cozz, don't be a buzz—I would have loved to come to Augsburg, I assure you, but the Herr Imperial Prelate wouldn't let me leave, still I don't have a beef, because it would be against god's law and that of nature even more, and whoever doesn't think so is a wh-re, and that's what is in store galore.—Maybe I'll be able to hop over to Augsburg from Munich for a few days; but that's far from certain.— But if you are as glad to see me as I am to see you, then please come to Munich that splendiferous city—make sure that you get there before the New Year, so I can look at you from afar and from near—I will show you around town, if you don't mind, and if need be I'll clean your behind—the one thing, I'm sorry to say, I cannot offer you is a place to stay, for I won't lodge at an inn but at a—well, where?—I wonder who will take me in? But all jokinggg aside—it's precisely for this reason that I need you to come and stay—for you might have an important rôle to play;—so be sure to come even for a bit, otherwise we'll be in deep shit. I shall greet you high and nobly with pizazz and put my personal seal on your ass, I will kiss your hands and have such fun shooting off my rear-end gun, I shall Embrace you with a smack and wash you down front and back, I shall pay up all I owed you from the start and then let go a resounding fart, and perhaps even drop something hard—well, adieu, my Angel, my heart, I'm waiting for you with a smart, please send me right at this moment a little note of about 24 pages to Munich, *Poste restante*,[92] but don't tell me where in Munich you will be, so I won't find you and you can't find me;—

votre sincere Cousin
W. A.

P.S. Shit-dibitare, shit-dibitate,
the pastor of Rodempl,
he licked the ass of his kitchen maid,
to set a good example.

Vivat—vivat—

Mozart came to Munich to present his Violin Sonatas K. 301–306 to Electress Elisabeth Auguste and to give his aria "Popoli die Tessaglia—lo non chiedo, eterni Dei," K. 316, to Aloysia Weber. It appears that he had hoped to make the aria an engagement present for Aloysia. But Aloysia, according to Nissen, rejected him. "When he entered, she seemed no longer to know the man for whom she had once shed tears" (Nissen, 414). Mozart was totally devastated. His sorrowful admission to his father, "Today I can do nothing but weep," is probably a reaction to Aloysia's rejection, whereas Leopold, upon reading the letter, thought his son was filled with remorse and guilt about coming home. The flutist Johann Baptist Becke, a family friend, wrote to Leopold that it took him an hour to still Wolfgang's tears.

---

92. "Poste restante" is general delivery.

But Wolfgang must have soon gotten a hold of himself because, again according to Nissen, he sat down at the piano and sang in a loud voice: "Let the wench who doesn't want me kiss my ass" (Leck mir das Mensch im Arsch, das mich nicht will).

To his father, in Salzburg

Munich, December 29, 1778

Mon trés cher Pére!

I am writing this letter in the house of Herr Beckè—I arrived here safe and sound on the 25th, god be thanked and praised; but I was unable to write to you until now.—I'm saving my full report until I have the pleasure and good fortune of seeing you in person—for today I can do nothing but weep—I have too sensitive a heart.—At the moment I simply want to tell you that I received my sonatas the day before I left Kayserheim, I will therefore be able to present them to the Electress in person. . . .

I have by nature a poor handwriting, you know that, for I never quite learned how to write properly, but in all my life I have never written anything as poorly as today; I simply can't write—my heart is on the verge of tears all the time!—I hope you will write to me very soon and console me. Perhaps it would be best if you wrote to me Poste restante—then I can fetch the letter myself;—I am staying with the Weber family—perhaps it would even be better, indeed it would be best, if you sent your letters to our good friend Beckè.—I am going to write a Mass here[93]—this is just between you and me, it's a big secret; all my friends here are advising me to do it.—I cannot describe to you what wonderful friends Cannabich and Raff are! Now farewell, dearest, most beloved father! Please write soon, I kiss your hands a thousand times and I embrace my dear sister with all my heart and remain until death your—

A happy New Year!—I can't manage more than this today!

your most obedient son,
Wolfgang Amadè Mozt

---

93. There is no trace of this mass.

 Mozart is preparing himself mentally for his return to Salzburg. His cousin, *Maria Anna Thekla, who had come from Augsburg to be with him in Munich, followed his wishes and agreed to come for a visit to Salzburg.*

To his father, in Salzburg

Munich, January 8, 1779

Mon trés cher Pére!

I hope you received my last letter. I had wanted to send it privately with the driver of a coach, but I missed him and therefore sent the letter by mail. I have received all your letters safely, including the last one of Dec.[br] 13, which you had addressed to Herr Beckeè;—I let him read my letter from you, and he let me read his.—

I can assure you, my dearest father, that I'm looking forward to seeing *you* but not Salzburg, because I feel reassured by your last letter that you understand me better now than you did before!—There was never any other reason for my long hesitation to come home than the doubts I had in this regard; I felt a kind of sadness that I could no longer hide, so I opened up my heart to my friend Beckeèe. What other reason could I possibly have had?—As far as I know I have done nothing wrong that would make me worry about reproaches from you;—I have committed no wrong—for a wrong is in my opinion something unbecoming a Christian and an Honest man;—in one word, I'm quite in a serene mood, anticipating the most pleasant and agreeable days—but only in your and my dear sister's company.—

I swear by my honor that I can't stand Salzburg and its inhabitants; I mean the native Salzburgians; I find their language—their manners quite insufferable. . . . But to continue;—yesterday I went to see the Electress, together with my dear friend Cannabich; I presented my sonatas to her. Her living quarters are very much like what I would like to have some day—she lives like a private person, everything is comfortable and attractive, except for the view, which is totally uninspiring; we spent a good half hour in her company, and she was very gracious.— I made sure that she was told that I will be departing in just a few days so that I would get my present without delay.—Don't worry about Count Seau in this respect, I think he has nothing to do with this matter, and even if he did, he wouldn't dare say anything.—In short, you must believe me that I am burning with desire to embrace you and my sister—if only it were not in Salzburg; but as it is impossible to see you without coming to Salzburg, I will come there gladly.—

I must hurry now because the mail coach is about to leave.—My Bäasle is here—why?—to please me, her cousin?—That, of course, is the reason we told everyone!—however—well, we'll talk about it in Salzburg;—and because of it I wished she could come with me to Salzburg!—you will find something written by her own hand and nailed to page four of this letter;—she would like to come;—so if you would like for her to pay you a visit, please be so kind and write to your brother, letting him know that such a visit is all right with you. When you see and know her, you will undoubtedly have a positive impression of her[94] —everybody likes her.—Now farewell, dearest, most beloved father;— I kiss your hand 1000 times and I embrace my sister with all my heart and remain

forever your most obedient son,

W A Mozart

🖎 *On January 13 or 14, Mozart traveled in the company of the merchant Franz Xaver Gschwendtner to Salzburg. Whether his cousin was with him is not entirely clear; she was to have followed in a stagecoach on the 20th, but it is also possible that she traveled with him.*

🖎 *By the time Mozart arrived in Salzburg, Leopold had already drafted a petition to the archbishop ready to be signed by Mozart.*

To Prince Archbishop Hieronymus Count Colloredo, in Salzburg

Salzburg, January 1779

Your Princely Grace!
Most Worthy Prince of the Holy Roman Empire!
Most Gracious Ruler and Lord!

Your Princely Highness was most Gracious in taking me into his Highness's Exalted Service after the Decease of Cajetan Adlgasser. I therefore beg most humbly that it be decreed that his Graces high post of Court Organist be assigned to me. Toward such Favor, as for all other

94. Leopold had seen Maria Anna Thekla last when she was about eight years old.

High Favors and Kindnesses, I recommend myself in most profound submission,

> Your Princely Grace
> Most gracious Ruler
> and Lord's
> > most humble and most obedient
> > Wolfgang Amade Mozart

🔖 *The petition for the post of court organist was approved by Archbishop Colloredo on February 25, 1779, with the stipulation that Mozart, in addition to his court and chapel duties, would also compose new works. His annual salary was 450 gulden.*

After a journey of fifteen months, after the most painful losses and rejections, Mozart was now forced to accept an uninspiring job in a town he loathed. He concealed his unhappiness through the creation of some of his most mellifluous and sophisticated church music, such as the Missa in C major ("Coronation"), K. 317, and, sometime later, the Vesperae solennes de confessore in C major, K. 339, with its breathtaking "Laudate Dominum."

🔖 *It is not clear how long Maria Anna Thekla "Bäsle" stayed in Salzburg; it may have been a month or two; in fact, little is known about her visit with the Mozarts. But she was still, as this letter shows, Mozart's favorite playmate in the art of nonsense.*

To Maria Anna Thekla Mozart, in Augsburg

Dearest, best
most beautiful, most charming,
most enchanting,
little bass[96]
or
little Violoncello,
so enraged by a worthless
fellow.

Salsbourg, 10th of May
1709er[95]
blow into my rear.
—:—
nothing could be finer
bon appètit!

95. 1709 is, of course, the wrong year, but Mozart needed it for his rhyme: "1709er/[. . .] nothing could be finer" (1709ni/blass mir hint' aini).
96. Mozart's German for "little bass" is *bässchen*, which is a pun on "Bäsle."

Whether I, Joannes Chrisostomus Sigismundus Amadeus Wolfgangus Mozartus, will be able to calm, soothe, or soften your anger, which has increased your enchanting beauties (visibilia and invisibilia)[97] by the full height of a slipper heel, that is a question I am prepared to answer right off:—to soften means as much as carrying Someone softly in a soft chair—I am by nature soft and mild, and I also like to eat mild mustard, especially with roast beef. . . . Yes, my dear little violoncello! that's the way of the world I'm told, one has the purse, the other has the gold, and whoever has neither, has nothing, and nothing is as much as very little, and little is not much, therefore nothing is always less than little, and little is always more than not much, and much is always more than little, and—well, that's the way it is, was, and always will be. Now, why don't you come to an end with this letter, seal it, send it off, and be done with it—*feigele:*

> Your most humble servant with a spleen
> my ass is not from Wien.

Please turn page V.S.[98]

P.S. Has Böhm's acting troupe[99] left town yet—please tell, dearest, I beg you for Heaven's sake! ah!—They have probably reached the city of Ulm by now, don't you think? Oh, do set my mind at ease, I implore you by all that is sacred—the gods know how truly concerned I am.

Is the "Thüremichele"[100] still there in one piece?—
blow into my hole.
Do Herr Vogt and his wife get along anymore?—
or is there a big fight in store?
questions galore.

A Tender Ode![101] —
Your picture sweet, O Bäsle,
hovers before my eye

97. "visibilia and invisibilia" is part of the "Credo" of the Latin mass ("Credo in . . . factorem . . . visibilium omnium et invisibilium"). Mozart is using it here as a parody.
98. "V.S." is *Vertatur subito:* "turn immediately."
99. Johann Heinrich Böhm was director of "Böhm's acting troupe," a touring theater company.
100. "Thüremichele" is the figure of Saint Michael above the clock on the city tower of Augsburg.
101. Mozart's poem is an adaptation of the "Ode to Edone" by the German poet Friedrich Gottlieb Klopstock.

but each sad tear will tell me
that you are—nowhere nigh.
I see it in the setting sun,
I see it in the rising moon,
I see it and I weep and sigh
that you are—nowhere night.
In the flowers of the valley
which I have gathered for her,
in each of the myrtle branches
which I twist and twine for her,
I conjur up her image, I implore her to appear;
if only by some magic
I could bring Bäasle here.

        finis coronat opus, Baron von Pigstail.

From me and all of us here best regards to your progenitors—I mean the two who made the effort of producing you as well as to her who let it happen. Adieu—Adieu—Angel!

My father sends his Uncle-ish blessings and my sister sends you one thousand Cousine-ish kisses. And this here Cousin gives you something he is not supposed to give you.

        Adieu—Adieu—Angel.

I'll write more next post day and at that time I will write something quite Sensible and Important and so that's it for now, until next time. Adieu—Adieu—Angel!—

Idomeneo or
The Making of an Opera

Munich, 1780

IDOMENEO.
DRAMMA
PER
MUSICA
DA RAPPRESENTARSI
NEL TEATRO NUOVO DI
CORTE
PER COMANDO
DI S. A. S. E.
CARLO TEODORO
Come Palatino del Rheno, Duca dell'
alta, e bassa Baviera, e del Palatinato
Superiore, etc. etc. Archidapifero,
et Elettore, etc. etc.
NEL CARNOVALE
1781.

La Poesia è del Signor Abate Gianbattista Varesco
Capellano di Corte di S A. R. l'Arcivescovo, e Principe di Salisburgo.
La Musica e del Signor Maestro Wolfgango Amadeo Mozart Academico di Bologna, e di Verona, in
sin attual servizio di S A R. l'Arcivescovo, e Principe
di Salisburgo.
La Traduzione è del Signor Andrea Schachtner,
pure in attual servizio di S A R l'Arcivescovo, e
Principe di Salisburgo.

MONACO.
Appresso Francesco Giuseppe Thuille.

WHEN MOZART ARRIVED in Munich in early November 1780, he was twenty-four years of age, happy to be away from Salzburg, and eager to write a new opera. While still in Salzburg, he had received a commission from the Bavarian court at Munich to compose an opera seria for the carnival season of 1781. The request had come in the form of a contract for the length of time it would take to write and stage the opera, but the terms did not keep Mozart from nurturing the hope that this commission might lead to a lasting appointment in the Bavarian capital.

It is not known who at the Munich court had persuaded Elector Karl Theodor to give him the commission for the opera. Mozart's friends from the former Mannheim orchestra—Cannabich, Ramm, Ritter, the Wendling brothers, the singer Anton Raaff, who had all come to Munich with the elector—may well have had a hand in it. Nor is it known who selected Abbate Gianbattista Varesco to write the text; but the powers in Munich chose this native Italian, a well-educated court chaplain at Salzburg, and directed him to use as his model a seventy-year-old French *tragédie lyrique, Idomenée* (with a text by Antoine Danchet set to music by André Campra), and turn it into a libretto for *Idomeneo,* an opera seria. In Varesco's dramatization of the mythic story, Idomeneo, king of Crete, is returning from the Trojan War and nearly perishes in a terrible storm near his native island. To assuage the wrath of the gods, he makes a pledge to Neptune that he will sacrifice the first living thing that he meets on shore. The storm abates, the Cretans are saved, but the first living thing the king encounters on the island is Idamante, his son. Ultimately, Idamante accepts his fate to die for his father; but when Ilia, a captive Trojan princess, offers herself to be sacrificed in Idamante's place, Neptune relents and spares the noble pair. Through an oracle, he announces the end of the ordeal and proclaims Idamante and Ilia as the new rulers of Crete.

When Mozart arrived in Munich, he had Varesco's text and parts of the music with him in his travel bag. For ten weeks, he worked feverishly to shape Varesco's unwieldy baroque libretto into a cohesive, viable piece of musical theater. Since Varesco had remained in Salzburg, numerous letters had to be exchanged between composer and librettist to finalize the text and the music. Mozart's father served as an intermediary, in other words, Mozart wrote his suggestions to Leopold, who would discuss them with Varesco and then report back to Mozart. Leopold, it appears, had a distinct and fruitful role to play in the creation of this opera, one that must have reminded him poignantly of the times in Milan when his son still asked for his advice and relied on his helping hand.

The letters so exchanged between father and son in the winter of 1780–81 are among the most fascinating of Mozart's entire correspondence. Mozart reveals himself not only as the consummate musician, attending to the minutest details of both music and text, but also as a practical, hands-on dramatist, better acquainted with the possibilities and limitations of the stage than his Salzburg librettist. Over and over, Mozart requested shortening of texts and tightening of scenes. What Varesco had written was an old-fashioned opera seria with drawn-out recitatives and bravura arias; what Mozart wanted was a dynamic music drama. Instead of virtuoso exit arias, in which all action comes to a halt, he wanted a continuous flow of movement. Mozart never fully succeeded in overcoming the static and reflective nature of the piece, but he worked hard to bring new dimensions and dynamics into the old baroque genre. To give but one example: the first version of Idomeneo's great aria in act 2, scene 3, "Fuor del mar ho un mar in seno" (Escaped from the sea, I find a sea in my breast), was a traditional bravura aria of extreme virtuosity. When Mozart revised the aria because the tenor Anton Raaff found it too difficult, he not only shortened it but removed the virtuoso part, incorporating the aria into the dramatic action.[1] Reworking Varesco's text, Mozart had, wittingly or unwittingly, moved away from an antiquated form of music theater and created a new, more dynamic style of opera seria.

The greatest significance of Mozart's *Idomeneo* letters lies in their implicit dramaturgy of text and music; but their style and structure deserve attention as well. Brevity and hurriedness are the two most dominant aspects. "I'm writing in haste" is a remark we find throughout Mozart's correspondence, but it is never more in evidence than at this time in his life. The words seem to practically tumble out of him, as if he could not get his thoughts down on paper fast enough. Some of his sentences are short and compressed; others are long and overstuffed with ideas and suggestions. Of course, because Mozart knew he

1. Küster, *Mozart*, 123.

was writing to his father, who was used to deciphering his hurried prose, control of diction was not a major concern. As a consequence, the letters allow a rare glimpse into the composer's workshop, here, in particular, into his efforts to shape a text.

We also witness a new face of Mozart. The effects of the disastrous journey to Paris have worn off, as has the rejection by Aloysia Weber. Mozart knew that with *Idomeneo* he was creating a bold and brilliant work, and the letters show his pride and excitement. He loved his stay in Munich, but, as on so many previous occasions, he was not offered a permanent appointment. Perhaps it was for the better, because fate and the archbishop of Salzburg would take him into an even more promising direction: Vienna, the capital of Austria and one of the great music centers of Europe.

Mozart left Salzburg by stagecoach on November 5, 1780. His first letter from Munich, written in obvious haste, shows right away that the production of Idomeneo *was not going to be an easy task: the libretto was too long, the tenor Anton Raaff too old, and Vincenzo dal Prato, a castrato singing the part of* Idamante, *too inexperienced. In spite of all these problems, Mozart never lost his patience or concentration.*

To his father, in Salzburg

Munich, November 8, 1780

Mon trés cher Pére!

How happy and relieved I felt when I arrived here.—Happy because we met with no misfortune on the road, relieved because we could hardly wait to reach our destination, for the trip, although short, was quite uncomfortable.—I can assure you, none of us was able to sleep even one minute throughout the night,—the kind of carriage we had jolts your very soul out of your body!—and the seats!—hard as a rock!— from Wasserburg on I thought that I couldn't bring my rear end to Munich in one piece!—it was so sore—and I suspect fiery Red— between two stations I sat with my hands pressed against the seat holding my rear suspended in the air—but enough of that, it's over now!— but from now on, if I can help it, I will go on foot rather than ride in a postal coach.—Now about Munich: we arrived at 1 o'clock in the afternoon, and I went to call on Count Seeau[2] that very same evening and, as he was not at home, I left a message for him.—Next morning I went to visit him with Beckè,[3] who sends greetings to you, to the Fiala family, and all his friends in Salzburg;—Seeau has been cut down to size by the Mannheim musicians here—and as far as the libretto[4] is concerned, the Count thinks it is not necessary for Varesco to copy it once more and send it back—because it will be printed here—but *I* think he should put it all together neatly in one copy, and not to forget the *small notes,*[5] and then mail it to me with a synopsis of the plot as soon as possible. . . .

Now I have a request for the Abbate;[6]—I would like to have Ilia's aria in the second Act, second scene, altered a little so it will fit better with what I have in mind;—"se il Padre perdei in te lo ritrovo";[7] that verse couldn't be better—but now comes the thing that always seems so unnatural to me, N.B. in an aria—namely, speaking aside. In a dialogue this sort of thing is quite natural—for one can speak a few words aside very quickly—but in an aria—where words have to be repeated—it makes for a poor effect—and even if this were not the case, I should prefer an aria here—he can keep the beginning if he is happy with it because it is Charming—an aria that has a natural flow—which doesn't completely tie me to the words but rather allows an easy flow for my composition, indeed, we agreed to have an Aria Andantino here that will be sung in concert with 4 wind instruments, that is a flute, an oboe, a horn, and a bassoon.—Please, send me these changes as soon as you possibly can.

Now a real pain in the rear:—I have not, it is true, had the honor of meeting the hero, del Prato;[8] but judging from what people say, I think that even Ceccarelli might be better; they say he gets out of breath already in the middle of an Aria—and, N.B., he has never been onstage

2. Count Joseph Anton Seeau was still the manager or controller of operatic performances at the court of Munich.
3. Johann Baptist Becke, Mozart's flutist friend in the Munich court orchestra.
4. The text of *Idomeneo.*
5. I.e., stage directions.
6. "The Abbate" is the librettist Gianbattista Varesco.
7. "Though I lost my father / you are now my homeland."
8. Vincenzo dal Prato sang the role of Idamante in the opera.

before. And Raaff[9] stands around like a statue—so now just picture it for yourself what the scene in the first Act looks like.—

But here is something positive. Mad.[me] Dorothea Wendling is Arci-Contentißima[10] with her scene—she wanted to listen to it 3 times in a row. The Grand Master of the Teutonic Order[11] arrived here yesterday—they performed Esex[12] for him at the Court Theater—and a Magnificent Ballet. The entire theater was illuminated. The performance began with an overture by Cannabich that, since it is one of his latest pieces, I had never heard.—I am sure, if you had heard it—it would have pleased and touched you just as it did me!—and if you hadn't known it beforehand, I'm sure you would not have been able to guess that it was by Cannabich—why don't you come soon and hear—and admire—the Orchestra here? That's all I have for now. There will be a big concert this evening. Mara[13] is to sing 3 arias—is it snowing as much in Salzburg as it is here?—

Give my regards to Herr Schickaneder,[14] tell him I'm sorry I cannot send him the aria just now, I haven't been able to finish it yet.—I kiss your hands a thousand times and embrace my sister with all my heart and remain,

> Mon trés chér Pére,
> your most obedient son,
> Wolf. Amdè Mozart

🖎 *Mozart continually raised questions about the text and structure of* Idomeneo; *after consultation with Varesco, Leopold would answer these point by point. They did not always come to an agreement, but the debate on dramaturgy shows Mozart as a master of stage management and theater techniques.*

---

9. The tenor Anton Raaff, Mozart's friend from Mannheim and Paris, sang Idomeneo.

10. Dorothea Wendling, soprano and wife of the flutist Johann Baptist Wendling, sang the part of Ilia. *Arci-contentissima* means "highly satisfied."

11. The grandmaster of the Teutonic Order was Archduke Maximilian Francis, youngest son of Empress Maria Theresa.

12. "Esex" is *The Unhappy Favourite, a Tragedy on the Fate of the Earl Essex (Die Gunst der Fürsten)*, by John Banks, 1681.

13. "Mara" is Gertrud Elisabeth Mara-Schmehling, a famous soprano.

14. Emanuel Schikaneder, actor-manager and playwright, who performed with his troupe in Salzburg. He would later collaborate with Mozart on *Die Zauberflöte.*

To his father, in Salzburg

Munich, November 13, 1780

Mon trés cher Pére!

I am writing in greatest haste because I'm not yet dressed and am supposed to go to lunch at Count Seeau's. Cannabich, Quaglio,[15] and Le Grand, the ballet master, will be there as well to discuss some important details about the opera.

Yesterday I lunched with Cannabich at the house of the Countess Baumgarten, née Lerchenfeld.[16]—My friend is well regarded there, and so am I now—it is the best and most helpful family for me. I owe them my good fortune here and, God willing, things will continue in this way. She is the lady with a *F*oxtail sticking out of her *A*ss, and she has *V*-shaped chains dangling *O*n her ears, and a beautiful *R*ing, I saw *I*t myself, even if death should *T*ake me, *I*, unfortunate man, without a *N*ose.[17] sapient. pauca.[18]

Well, I must get dressed now—but quickly the most urgent: I want to say that the main purpose of this letter is to wish you, my dearest and best father, every conceivable happiness for your Name Day. I continue to recommend myself to your fatherly love and assure you of my Eternal obedience. . . . Yesterday Count Seeau presented me to his Highness, the Elector, who was very gracious to me. If you were to speak with Count Seeau these days, you would scarcely recognize him, that's how much the Mannheim musician have turned him around.

The 2nd Duetto is going to be omitted altogether—and it will be more to the advantage of the opera than to its disadvantage; for if you read the scene over again, you will see that if we put an Aria or Duetto in there the scene will become bland and uninspired—and very awkward for all the others onstage who just have to stand there; apart from that, it would make the noble struggle between Ilia and Idamante too long and thereby diminish its effect. . . .

I'm supposed to write a formal reply to Abbate Varesco on behalf and in the name of Count Seeau—but I don't have the time, and I was

15. Lorenzo Quaglio, a painter who did the stage scenes for *Idomeneo.*
16. Countess Josepha Paumgarten, who may have been helpful in securing Mozart's commission.
17. The sentence seems like a nonsense statement, but it is a coded message; the italicized capital letters spell FAVORITIN (favorite) in German, indicating the position of the countess at court.
18. "Bits of wisdom."

not born to be a secretary. Herr Quaglio came up with the same objections to scene VIII in the First Act, the one we raised from the very beginning, namely, that it is not fitting for the king to be all alone on the ship—if the Abbé thinks that it is reasonable to show him alone and abandoned by Everyone, exposed to the greatest dangers in this terrible storm, and *without the ship*, then he can keep the scene as is, but, N.B., it must be without the ship; he simply cannot be shown alone on the ship—if we keep the ship in the scene, then some generals or loyal companions must come ashore with him, but in that case the King must direct a few words to his companions, in particular, he must let them know he needs to be alone—that would be quite Natural, given the wretched situation he finds himself in. Apropòs, the Aria for Mad.^{me} Wendling—may I have it soon? Mara did not have the good fortune of receiving my approbation—she isn't doing enough with her voice so she could be compared to a Bastardina,[19]—(for she sings in that style)—yet she is doing too much with her voice to be able to touch your heart as the Weber girl can—or any other sensible singer.

Mon trés cher Pére,

I am your most obedient son

Wolf. Amd. Mozart

P.S. My regards to all good friends, male and female.

Apropòs: Count Seeau would like to have the opera translated in Salzburg because translations are not done very well here.[20] Only the arias need to be in verse.—I am supposed to write a Contract. Poet and translator would be paid at the same time. Let me have an answer soon. . . .

The opera will not be given until the 20th of January. Please be so kind as to send me the complete scores of the 2 Masses I brought along—also the Mass in B.[21] Count Seeau wants to speak to the Elector about them—and I should like to be known here in that style of composition as well.

---

19. "Bastardina" (also called Bastardella) is Lucrezia Agujari, the Italian soprano whom Mozart met in Italy and admired for her brilliant coloratura.

20. The request was for a translation of the libretto from Italian into German; the translation was done by the Salzburg court trumpeter Johann Andreas Schachtner, a friend of the Mozarts.

21. Probably the Missa in C ("Coronation"), K. 317, and the Missa solemnis in C, K. 337; the "Mass in B" is the Missa brevis in B-flat, K. 275.

To his father, in Salzburg

Munich, November 15, 1780

Mon trés cher Pére!

I have received your letter—or rather the whole parcel—in good order. Thank you so much for the letter of credit—so far I have not eaten at home once—and therefore have no expenses, save for hairdresser, barber, and laundress—and breakfast.

The Aria is excellent now;—however, there's yet another change; Raaf is responsible for this one, but he is right;—and even if he were not, his gray hair deserves some consideration. He came to me yesterday; I trotted out his First Aria for him and he was very pleased with it;—Well, now, the man is old, and in the aria "fuor del mar hò un maré in seno," etc., in the second Act, he is no longer able to show off his voice as he would like to; therefore, since he has no Aria in the third Act and cannot sing as much Cantabile as he would like to in his Aria in the first Act (because he has to concentrate on the expression of the words), he requested a pretty Aria after his last speech, "O Creta Fortunata! ò me Felice," to take the place of the quartetto. This would allow us to eliminate another unnecessary segment, and the third Act would be much more Effective.—Now—in the last scene of the 2nd Act, Idomeneo has an aria between the choruses or rather a kind of Cavatina; perhaps it'll be better to substitute for this a mere Recitativo with strong instrumental accompaniment, for in this scena, which will be the most exciting in the entire opera (because of its dramatic action and groups of people moving about, as we discussed it recently with Le Grand), there will be so much noise and Confusion onstage that an aria would not work well at that spot—besides, there'll be the thunderstorm coming up just then—and it can scarcely be expected to wait because Herr Raaf has to sing an aria.—Anyway, the Effect of a Recitative in between the choruses is decidedly better. Lisel Wendling has sung her two Arias half a dozen times already—she is very happy with both. I have it from a third party that the 2 Wendlings have praised their Arias very highly. And Raaf, well, he is my best and dearest friend.[22]

---

22. It is very uncharacteristic of Mozart to have such tender feelings toward a fellow musician as he shows here toward the tenor Anton Raaff. Raaff was sixty-six years old and past his prime, but Mozart does all he can to write some good arias for him. It is true that Mozart liked Raaff's cantabile, but there may well be a more personal reason why he is so accommodating: when they were in Paris together, Raaff was very

But as far as my molto amato Castrato del Prato is concerned, well, I'll have to teach him the whole opera. He is simply not able to come into an aria with a good strong tone; and then there's his uneven voice!—He has a contract for one year, and when that ends, which will be next September, Count Seeau will hire someone else. Maybe Ceccarelli could try his luck.—Serieusement!—

I almost forgot the best news. Last Sunday after the service, Count Seeau presented me *en passant* to his Highness, the Elector, who was very Gracious to me. He said: *I am pleased to see you again,* and when I said that I will make every effort to earn his Highness's approval, he tapped me on my shoulders and said: *O, I have not the slightest doubt that all will go very well.*—à Piano, piano, si và lontano.[23] . . .

> Adieu,
> your most obed. son
> Wolf Am. Mozart

Tell my sister not to be lazy but practice hard—people here are already looking forward to hearing her.—

I am living in Burggasse at M.ᵣ Fiat's, but you don't have to put the exact address on the envelope, because I am well known at the post office—and they know where I live.

In spite of his cold, which stayed with him through most of the rehearsals, Mozart's work on Idomeneo *moved along with speed and energy. Being away from Salzburg and doing what he liked most lifted his spirits. The letter also contains a wonderful example of Mozart's spontaneous writing style, recording right into his writing the unexpected arrival of a member of the opera cast: "Come in!—Oh, it's Herr Panzachi."*

To his father, in Salzburg

Munich, November 22, 1780

Mon trés cher Pére!

Here is, finally, the aria for Schickaneder that I had promised him long ago.[24] During my first week here I couldn't get it done, because of

---

sweet to Mozart's mother; he often visited her and to her great delight sang for her. Mozart may well have remembered Raaff's kindness.

23. "Whoever goes slow, goes farther."

24. Mozart had promised an aria for Carlo Gozzi's *Le due notti affanose,* which Schikaneder was putting on in Salzburg. The aria was apparently used successfully but was lost.

my other work, which is, after all, what brought me here; and then, the other day, Le Grand, the ballet master visited me—he is an insufferable chatterbox and bore—and with all his babble he made me miss the mail coach. I hope my sister is completely recovered—but now I have a cold, which is much the fashion here because of the bad weather we're having. I believe, I hope, that I've pretty much beaten my cold into retreat, certainly its two light brigades, rot and slime, have begun to slow down their attack. In your last letter you are saying repeatedly: Oh, my Poor Eyes—I don't wish to become blind with all this writing—it's half past seven at night and no spectacles! But why are you writing at night?—and why without spectacles?—I don't understand it. . . .

Dell Prato gave a recital in the Accademie the day before yesterday, it was a disgrace—I am willing to wager that this man will not get through the rehearsal, much less the opera—the whole fellow seems unsound to the core. Come in!—Oh, it's Herr Panzachi!—He has visited me already 3 times—and he just invited me out to a meal on Sunday. I hope it won't turn out to be something like our invitation for koffèe.—At any rate, he is asking very humbly whether instead of "Se la sà" he may not sing "se co là"—well, why not "ut re mi fa sol la?"[25]

I am happy when you write a lot—but don't write at night—and not at all without your spectacles.—But please forgive me for not writing much—every minute here is valuable— . . .

When the castrato[26] comes to me, I have to Sing his role with him because he has to learn his part like a child. He doesn't have a penny's worth of method. Next time I'll write more. . . .

Greetings to all good friends, male and female, also my compliment to Katherl Gylofsky's Ass, and to Pimperl you can give a pinch of Spanish snuff and some good wine sop, plus three smacks; don't you miss me?—1000 greetings from all—all—all—*Adieu*. I kiss your hands 1000 times and I kiss my sister from the heart, I hope she'll feel better soon. Adieu.

Your most obedient son
Wolfgang Amadè Mozart

25. Domenico de' Panzacchi sang the role of Arbace in *Idomeneo*. In spite of his ironic remark, Mozart changed Panzacchi's aria (no. 22) to "Se colà ne' fati è scritto."
26. "The castrato" is Vincenzo dal Prato.

This letter contains the clearest indication yet that Mozart hoped for an appointment at the Munich court. As so many times before, he mistook flattery for genuine interest. As for his relentless cold, his father offered good advice: keep warm, drink no wine, take a little black powder before going to bed and some hot footbaths. But nothing helped. Leopold also offered to take care of Wolfgang in case his cold got worse, but then he added insensitively, "If I had been with your Mother, I would like to believe, she would still be alive."

To his father, in Salzburg

Munich, November 24, 1780

Mon trés cher Pére!

I have received your package as well as your last letter from the 20th, all in good order—Herr Schachtner will get 10 Ducats for his translation—and I hope you received the Aria for Herr Schickaneder in the meantime. . . .

I also hope my sister is quite well again!—And I beg you, don't send me such sad letters anymore—because—right now I need a cheerful spirit, a clear head, and good inspiration for my work, none of which is possible when one is sad;—I know it and, by God, I feel it, how much you deserve some hours of Peace! but—am I the problem? I certainly don't wish it to be, and yet, unfortunately, I fear I am! but if I reach my goal—that is, if I get a good position here, then you must leave Salzburg at once. You will say: that will never happen—well, if it doesn't, it is not because I'm not doing my best.—

Do try to come up here soon to see me. . . . We can all stay together here at my place. I have a spacious alcove in my front room with two beds in it—that will be just charmant for you and me. As far as my sister is concerned, we have no choice but to put a stove into my second room—that's a matter of about 4 to 5 gulden; because one could heat the stove in my front room until it breaks, and keep the door open, and still the back room would not get warm enough—because it's so bitter cold in there. Please ask Abbate Varesco whether we could not stop after the chorus sings "Placido è il mar," etc., in the 2nd Act, after Elletra's first strophe—and the chorus has been repeated—or at least after her second strophe—it will otherwise be far too long! I hope to receive the Recitative and Aria for Raaf in the next mail.

My catarrh has kept me home for two days now—the good thing

about it is that I have so little appetite—because I would find it rather inconvenient to have to pay for all my meals if these rehearsals were to continue for a long time. . . .

I kiss your hands 1000 times and embrace my sister with all my heart—I hope she is in good health again, and I am Forever your

most obedient son
Wolfgang Amadè Mozart

The following letter has no address and no signature; it was sent through an acquaintance, and perhaps some pages were lost. Mozart's reference to Hamlet *makes the letter especially fascinating. First of all, it shows very succinctly and graphically how determined he was to shorten Varesco's lengthy text; second, it is interesting to know that Mozart was familiar with Shakespeare's play. He probably saw a performance in Salzburg just prior to his departure, because Schikaneder's company staged* Hamlet *there on October 13, 1780, in the German translation of Friedrich Ludwig Schröder.*

To his father, in Salzburg

Munich, November 29, 1780

Raff is not happy with his Aria that you just sent, and neither am I; . . . it's supposed to transmit a feeling of peace and contentment, but that isn't conveyed until the second part. . . . Also, don't you think that the speech of the subterranean voice is too long? Just think about it!— imagine yourself in the theater; the voice has to convey a feeling of terror—it should go through and through—one has to think it's real— how can you get such an effect if the speech is too long; for the longer it goes on, the more the audience will become aware that there's nothing real about it.—If the speech of the Ghost in "Hamlet" were not quite so long, it would be much more effective.—The speech of the subterranean voice can be easily shortened and it will thereby gain more than it will lose.

Now, for the march in the 2nd Act—the one you hear from afar, I need mutes for the trumpets and horns, which I cannot get here. Would you send me one of each with the next mail coach, so I can have them reproduced here?

To his father, in Salzburg

Munich, December 1, 1780

Mon trés chér Pére!

The rehearsal went exceptionally well;—we had only 6 violins present but a full complement of wind instruments; no audience was allowed in, except the sister of Count Seeau and young Count Sensheim.—We'll have a second rehearsal a week from today. At that time there'll be 12 violins for rehearsing the first Act, which will be copied out in the meantime, the 2nd Act will be rehearsed along with it the way we did the first Act the week before. I cannot tell you how delighted and surprised everybody was.—But I never expected anything else; I can tell you honestly that when I went to that rehearsal I was as calm as if I were going to some dinner party.—Count Sensheim said to me: *I can assure you that I expected quite a bit of you—but I truly never expected anything like this.*—The Cannabich house and the many people who go in and out there are indeed my truest friends.—When I went with Cannabich to his house after the rehearsal—we still had much to talk over with Count Seeau—Mad.^{me} Cannabich came out to greet me and embraced me with great exuberance because the rehearsal had gone so well; Ramm and Lang had been there already, singing my praises; this good woman—such a true friend—had gone through a thousand worries on my behalf, for she had to stay home because Rose was sick. Ramm said to me—and when you get to know him you will say: now, there's a true German for you—for he says what he thinks right to your face—he said to me: *I must honestly confess that no Musique has ever made such an impression on me; and I can assure you that I thought at least 50 times of your father, and the joy he will have when he hears this opera.*

Enough of this.—My cattarrh has gotten worse during the rehearsal—I guess one gets fired up when Honor and Reputation are at stake, no matter how cool you may be in the beginning.—I did everything you suggested—but it takes time; it's of course very inconvenient right now; Composing won't stop a cold—and compose I must. . . .

Farewell for now. I kiss your hands 1000 times and embrace my sister with all my heart, Forever your

most obedient son
Wolfgang Amadè Mozart

🕮 *Empress Maria Theresa, having ruled Austria, Bohemia, and Hungary since 1740, died in Vienna on November 29, 1780. She was succeeded by her eldest son, Joseph II, who had been her coregent. Mozart does not appear to have been terribly affected by the death of the empress; to the contrary, he makes light of it—in his own way. His concentration is clearly on* Idomeneo; *he continues to worry about the length of the opera and concerns himself with the minutest details of the text. Sometimes he would change a single word or even a vowel to get the best effect for the singer.*

To his father, in Salzburg

Munich, December 5, 1780

Mon trés cher Pére!

The death of the Empress won't affect my opera at all, since no theaters are being closed here and all performances are going on as usual—and the period of mourning won't be longer than 6 weeks—besides, my Opera will not be given before the 20ᵗʰ of January anyway.—Now a request: would you have my *black suit* thoroughly brushed, shaken out, and spruced up as much as possible and send it to me with the next mail coach?—Next week everybody will be in mourning dress—and as I am constantly on the move, one moment here, another moment there, I will have to *Weep* along with the rest of them. . . . With regard to Herr Raaff's *ultima aria,*[27] I wrote to you already that both Raaff and I would like to have something more touching, words with a sweeter expression;—the word *era* is rather forced—the beginning is fine—but "gelida maßa" is already too harsh again. In other words, far-fetched or unusual words are always inappropriate in an aria that is meant to please.—

I should like it also if the aria would exude a sense of Peace and Contentment, and if it had only *one part,* it would be just as good, indeed, I would prefer it.—I also wrote something about Panzachi in my letter—we have to make some allowances for that Honest old gentleman.—He would like to have his Recitative in the 3ʳᵈ Act expanded by a couple of lines—which would actually be very effective because of his Chiaro e scuro,[28] but also because he is really a good actor. . . .

27. Raaff's "ultima aria" ("Sazio è destino al fine") was replaced in the final version by "Torna la pace."
28. "Chiaro e scuro" is a term taken from art history and means "light and shadow"; here it refers to Arabace's wavering between hope and fear.

More next time.—Adieu—I kiss you hands 1000 times and embrace my sister with all my heart and remain Forever your

most obedient son
Wolfg. Amadè Mozart

On December 11, Leopold wrote to Mozart, "Let me suggest that in your work you think not only of the musical cognoscenti but also of those listeners who are unmusical. You know that there are 100 unmusical listeners for every 10 connoisseurs; so don't forget to bring in the so-called popular style, which tickles the long ears." Mozart's reply to his father has become somewhat of a classic.

To his father, in Salzburg

Munich, December 16, 1780

Mon trés cher Pére!

. . . As far as the so-called Popular style is concerned, don't worry about it; in my Opera you'll find Musick for every kind of listener—except for those with the long ears.[29]—

Apropós, how are we doing with the archbishop?—Next Monday it will be six weeks that I have been away from Salzburg; and you know, dearest father, that I am remaining in . . . .[30] only for your sake;—for god knows—if I had to worry only about myself, I would have, before I left, wiped my behind with the most recent contract they gave me, because, by my honor, it's not Salzburg, but the Prince and the high-and-mighty Nobility that is getting more insufferable every day. So, I would accept it with greatest pleasure if I were informed that my services are no longer needed; I would be sufficiently safeguarded through the patronage I am enjoying here for now and the future—except, of course, if there should be a death; but no one can guard against such things—but which would not necessarily hurt a person of talent who is single; but I'll do anything in the world to please you—although it would be easier for me if once in a while I could get away for a short time just to breathe freely.—You know how hard it was to get away this

---

29. I.e., asses. Mozart's German here reads, "ausgenommen für lange ohren nicht."
30. The points here are by Mozart; the word he omitted (because of censorship) was most likely "Salzburg."

time; without some important reason, one couldn't even think of it. It's enough to make you cry if you think about it,—therefore, let's not think about it.—

Adieu!—I kiss your hands 1000 times and embrace my sister with all my heart and remain Forever yours.

Please, come to Munich soon—
and hear my opera—
then tell me whether I am
wrong to be miserable when
I think of Salz . . . . !

Your most obedient son
Wolfgang Amadé Mozart

Mozart's original leave granted by the archbishop was for six weeks, and the six weeks were now up. Reflecting on it leads Mozart to one of his favorite subjects: I hate Salzburg. As it turned out, the archbishop did not insist that Mozart return home immediately after the premiere of Idomeneo; *in fact, he permitted Mozart to stay in Munich until the beginning of March 1781.*

To his father, in Salzburg

Munich, December 19, 1780

Mon trés cher Pére!

I have received the last aria for Raaff, who sends his regards, the 2 mutes for the trumpets, your letter dated the 15th, and a pair of under-stockings, all in good order.—The last rehearsal went very well, just like the first one;—the orchestra and everybody in the audience found themselves happily deceived in the assumption that the 2nd Act could not possibly be better than the first in expression and innovation; next Saturday we'll rehearse the 2nd Act again but that time in a more spacious room at court, something we had wished to do for a long time because Count Seeau's apartment is simply too small.—The Elector will be there *incognito* and listen from an adjoining room—Cannabich said to me, well, in that case, we'll have to bust our backs—at the last rehearsal he was completely soaked in sweat. . . .

Apropós, just the most urgent messages, for I'm in a hurry; I hope I'll receive at least the First Act complete with translation with the next mail coach.——The scene between father and son in the first Act——and the first scene in the second Act, the one between Idomeneo and Arabace,——they are both too long——the audience will most certainly be bored——especially since in the first Act both singers are terrible actors——and in the 2nd Act one of them is; besides, all that happens onstage is a narration of something the audience has already seen with its own eyes; the scenes are going to be printed as they are——

I only wish for the Abbate to indicate where to make the cuts——and they should be as drastic as possible——otherwise I'll have to make them myself——for these two scenes cannot stand as they are——I mean when set to music. . . . Please let me know at least a week ahead when you think you'll be coming to Munich so I can have a stove moved into my second room. Adieu.

What terrific handwriting! I kiss your hands 1000 times and embrace my sister with my heart, and remain your

most obed. son
Wolf. Amde. Mzt

mes Compliments à tous nos amis et amies,
next time more and more legible.

Mozart's constant efforts to shorten the libretto did not always find approval from Signor Varesco and his father. Here is what Leopold replied on December 22: "So you absolutely want to shorten the two recitatives. I had Varesco come to my house immediately because I just received your letter this evening at 5 o'clock and the mail coach will leave tomorrow. We kept reading and reading, but neither of us found any appropriate spot to cut. The text is translated from the French, and we have it just as it is written there."

Elector Karl Theodor probably meant well when he said, "Who would think that such great things can come out of such a small head," but his remark has certainly become one of the treasures of Mozart's anecdotal history. Also, Mozart's difficulties with Raaff concerning the quartet in the third act ("Andrò ramingo e solo") is not so much a struggle over singing technique as it is a generational problem. The quartet in question has individual parts (with individual asides), which was unprecedented in opera seria.

To his father, in Salzburg

Munich, December 27, 1780

Mon trés Cher Pére!

I have safely received the entire text for the opera—also Schachtner's letter, your note, and the pills.—As to the two scenes that ought to be shortened, it was not my suggestion but simply my consent—and the reason I fully agreed was that Raaff and del Prato are singing the recitative without any spirit or fire—they just drone it out monotonously;—they are the most Wretched actors ever to appear on a stage. The other day I had a dreadful row with Seeau on account of the clumsiness, unnaturalness, and near impossibility of omitting anything—it's quite enough if everything appears in print—something he was dead set against—but finally agreed to because I really got furious.—The last rehearsal was Magnificent.—It took place in a large room at the castle; the Elector was there—this time we rehearsed with full orchestra, that is with as many players as can be seated in the opera house. After the First Act the Elector shouted Bravo, and when I went up to him to kiss his hand, he said: *this opera is going to be charmante, it will bring you great honor.* Since he didn't know whether he could stay for the rest, we had to play the aria that is accompanied by wind instruments[31] and produce for him the thunderstorm that comes at the beginning of the second Act.—After that he once again gave me his friendliest approbation and said, laughing: *who should think that such great things can come out of such a small head. . . .*

I've had a lot of trouble with Raaff about the quartet.—The more I try to imagine how the quartet will sound onstage, the more I know it will be effective;—everybody who heard it with the piano accompaniment liked it.—The only one who thinks it will not be effective is Raaff; he told me privately: *non c'è da spianar la voce—it is too Tight*—as if in a quartetto one shouldn't speak the words more than sing them—but he doesn't understand such things.—so I only said to him, dearest friend!—if I knew of one single note that I could change in this quartetto, I would do it immediately. But, nothing in the entire opera pleases me as much as this quartet; and after you hear it all together, I think you'll change your mind.—I have made every effort to serve you well

---

31. Ilia's aria in act 2, "Se il padre perdei."

with your two arias—and I shall do the same with your third aria—and hope I'll be able to do it right again; but as far as Terzets and Quartets are concerned you have to leave things up to the Composer—at which point he said he was satisfied. . . .

Now I have to close because the mail coach will leave in just a minute.—I had to have my black suit turned, it just looked too shabby—now it looks fine. Adieu. . . . I embrace my sister from the heart and kiss your hands 1000 times and remain Forever your

most obedient son
Wolfg. Amd. Mozart

🖎 *The Elector was not the only one impressed by Mozart's innovative music in* Idomeneo. *Even in Salzburg people took notice. Leopold wrote, "All over town there is talk about how great your opera is." Mozart's reference to the ballet is of special interest. It was customary in an opera seria to have ballet performances between acts; these ballets were usually written by other, often local composers. In* Idomeneo, *Mozart wrote his own "divertissement" (a group of intermittent dances); it is about half an hour long and was probably performed after the first act.*

To his father, in Salzburg

Munich, December 30, 1780

Mon trés cher Pére!

Happy New Year! —forgive me for writing very little this time—I'm now up to my neck in work—I'm not quite finished with the third Act—and, as there won't be any extra ballets, I also have the honor of composing a divertissement that is suitable for the opera[32]—but I actually like it better this way, for the music will be from *one* composer. The third Act will turn out to be *at least* as good as the first two.—I think, in fact, it will be superior—so that one can say in all fairness: finis Coronat Opus.[33]—The Elector was so delighted at the last rehearsal that the next morning, as I told you already, he praised my opera at his

---

32. Mozart's divertissement includes a Chaconne, Passepied, Gavotte, and Passacaille and is recorded as K. 367 on a Philips CD, *Mozart: Theater and Ballet Music.* Unfortunately, in most modern performances of *Idomeneo,* these sprightly dances are omitted because including them would lengthen the opera by half an hour.
33. "The end crowns the work."

morning meeting—and then again in the evening at a reception at court.—I also know from a reliable source that on the evening after attending my rehearsal, he spoke to Everybody who came to see him of my music, saying something like this: *I was quite surprised—no Musick has ever had such an Effect on me—this Music is Magnifique.—*

The day before yesterday we had a rehearsal of recitatives at the Wendling house—we also rehearsed the quartet together—we went through it 6 times—now we have it down pat. The stumbling block was Del Prato;—that boy has no ability whatever;—his voice wouldn't be so bad if only he could get it out of his throat—besides, he has no intonation—no method—no feeling—his singing is on about the level of the best boys who audition for our chapel choir. . . .

Adieu, I kiss your hands 1000 times and embrace my sister with all my heart and I remain forever

your obedient son
Wolfgang Amadè Mozart

To his father, in Salzburg

Munich, January 3, 1781

Mon trés cher Pére!

My head and my hands are so full of the third Act that it's a won-der I'm not turning into a third Act myself.—This act alone has cost me more trouble than a whole opera—because there's almost no scene in it that isn't extremely interesting.—The accompaniment to the Subterranean Voice consists of only 5 instruments, namely 3 trombones and two French horns, which are placed at the exact location where the the voice is coming from.—The rest of the orchestra is silent at this point.—The dress rehearsal will be on the 20th for sure—and the first performance on the 22nd. . . .

No doubt, we will still have to make a number of adjustments in the 3rd Act once we put it onstage;—for instance, after Arabace's aria in scene VI, the stage directions read: *Idomeneo, Arabace, etc.;* but how can the latter reappear so quickly?—well, fortunately, he can stay away alto-gether—but to be safe I have written a somewhat longer introduction to the recitative of the High Priest.—After the chorus of mourners, the king and everybody will leave the stage—but in the following scene it says: *Idomeneo in ginochione nel tempio*[34]—and that's impossible—he must appear with his entire retinue—the scene calls clearly for a march—so I composed a very simple march with 2 violins, viola, bass, and two oboes, which will be played *à mezza voce*,[35] during which the king will step forward while the priests prepare everything for the sacrifice—then the king kneels down and begins his prayer. . . .

Adieu. I kiss your hands 1000 times and embrace my sister with all my heart and remain forever

> your most obedient son
> Wolfg. Amad. Mozart

To his father, in Salzburg

Munich, January 18, 1781

Mon trés cher Pére!

I have safely received your letter from the 11th and your last one from the 13th, courtesy of Herr Fiala,—please forgive me for sending you such a short note, but I have to run off to rehearsals right this minute, it's almost 10 o'clock—in the morning, of course.—Today will be the first rehearsal of recitatives in the theater—I've not been able to get a little ahead of the game with my writing, because I've been so busy with these confounded dances—Laus deo[36]—I am now all done with them.—So quickly the most urgent news: the rehearsal of the third Act went exceedingly well; they say it is much superior to the first 2 Acts.—However, the text is far too long and so is, consequently, the music, which I said all along; so, we must cut Idamante's aria, "Nò, la morte io non pavento"—which isn't quite right in that spot anyway—but those who heard it with the music are sighing in distress about the cut—and Raaff's last aria will have to be cut as well, which is generating even greater sighs—however—you have to make a virtue of necessity.—The speech of the oracle is still too long as well—I have already shortened it—Varesco doesn't need to know any of this; in print it will appear just as he wrote it. . . .

34. "Idomeneo kneels down in the temple."
35. "At half volume."
36. "God be praised!"

We won't be able to have the stove, it's too expensive.—I'll have another bed put into my alcove room, we'll just have to manage as best we can.

Don't forget my small watch; maybe we'll make a visit to Augsburg, in which case we could have its enamel repaired.—My other wish is for you to bring the operetta by Schachtner[37]—it might be good for some of the people who come to Cannabich's house to hear this sort of music.—Now I must be off to the rehearsal!—Adieu. I kiss your hands 1000 times and embrace my sister with all my heart, I remain

your most obed. son
W. A. Mzt

Leopold and Nannerl arrived in Munich on January 26, one day before the dress rehearsal of Idomeneo, *which was on the 27th, Mozart's twenty-fifth birthday. The premiere of* Idomeneo, rè di Creta *took place on January 29 in the new Electoral Opera House (today the Alte Residenztheater, also called the Cuvilliés Theater) under the baton of Christian Cannabich. With Mozart's father and sister in Munich, staying through the carnival season, there is no report by Mozart or anyone else on the success of* Idomeneo. *There were only two further performances that year: on February 3 and March 3. On March 7, Leopold, Nannerl, and Wolfgang traveled to Augsburg, where Wolfgang and Nannerl gave a concert for two and three pianos (K. 242 and 365); they stayed until March 10. While in Augsburg, Mozart received orders from Archbishop Colloredo to join him and his retinue in Vienna. Mozart, who had stretched his leave of absence from six weeks to four months, had no choice but to follow the order. He returned to Munich on March 10 or 11, and on March 12 he was on his way to Vienna.*

37. "The operetta by Schachtner" is Mozart's singspiel *Zaide*, K. 344, which he had begun in Salzburg; Johann Andreas Schachtner wrote the libretto.

PART THREE

MOZART IN VIENNA

1 7 8 1 – 1 7 9 1

Breaking with
the Archbishop

March 16–June 13, 1781

In January 1781, when Count Hieronymus Colloredo, prince archbishop of Salzburg, traveled to Vienna to visit his ailing father, he traveled in style. His entourage included administrators, clerks,
cooks, valets, footmen, and three musicians, who were summoned later. One of these musicians, the court organist
Wolfgang Amadé Mozart, had to be brought all the way
from Augsburg. When he arrived in Vienna on March 16, he was
assigned lodgings at the House of the Teutonic Order, near St. Stephen's
Cathedral, which served as headquarters for the archbishop and most of
his retinue.

Mozart's relationship with the archbishop had never been very cordial; here, in Vienna, their suspicion of each other surfaced almost
instantly. The archbishop regarded musicians, in the spirit of the time,
as members of his household staff, obliged to serve at the whim of their
master. Mozart, on the other hand, chose this moment not only to
question such attitudes and customs but to demand greater freedom as
a performer and more personal and social recognition as a composer.
He felt himself equal to any aristocrat in both a moral and an artistic
sense. "Perhaps I have more honor in me than many a count," he wrote
to his father on June 20, 1781; "it is the heart that enobles man, not his
position." After only three months in Vienna, he submitted his resignation to the archbishop and afterward wrote to his father, "I am no
longer so unfortunate as to be in Salzburg's services—today was that
happy day for me." The tense and highly emotional struggle between the
prince and his musician ended ingloriously: the archbishop's chief stew-

ard, Count Arco, dismissed the unruly musician with a "kick in the ass," as Mozart reported to his confounded father.

Mozart's letters from this three-month period in Vienna reflect the full range of this intense struggle, his seething anger at the archbishop, and his bitter disappointment about his father's lack of support. Since all of Leopold's and Nannerl's letters to Wolfgang are lost, Leopold's reactions to his son's daring steps in Vienna must be surmised from Wolfgang's replies. There can be no doubt: Leopold did not want Wolfgang to leave the archbishop's service, fearing a permanent separation between him and his son. As it turned out, his fears were well founded. When the break occurred, it was a break not only with the archbishop but with Leopold as well. The crack in the relationship between father and son that had first surfaced after the death of Maria Anna Mozart in Paris had now developed into an irreparable rift.

Mozart's letters to his father had never lacked tension or drama. His infatuation with Aloysia Weber, the death of his mother, the staging of *Idomeneo* in Munich—all these experiences found their way into Mozart's correspondence with all the ups and downs, anguish and excitement fully recorded. None of the previous episodes, however, had such a penetrating mental and physical impact on Mozart as his struggle with the archbishop. Never before had Mozart been driven "to the point of madness," never before had he been so emotionally depleted that he would "stagger about in the street like a drunkard," but also, mutatis mutandis, never before had he been so determined to take control of his life and future. Despite the archbishop's exhortations and his father's anxious pleas, Mozart remained in Vienna, which he thought to be a "Magnificent place—and for *my Métier* the best place in the world."

Mozart's writing style reflects the gradual clarification of purpose that he himself experienced. It seems that his resolve to stand up for himself had a positive effect on his language as well. Aside from two or three highly charged letters during this period, most of his writing is focused, well-organized, orderly in syntax and diction. Misspellings have almost disappeared. Also, Mozart had finally mastered the art of dealing with Leopold by slowly distancing himself through formulaic assurances, calling him the "best of all fathers," absolving him of all responsibilities, and calmly telling him that he would remain in Vienna and try to make it on his own. Mozart's tone is self-assured and conciliatory, his writing unhurried and firm; he had freed himself from

Salzburg, from the archbishop, and from his father. Probably for the first time in his life, he felt in command of himself, and his writing style shows it.

🐦 *Mozart's first letter from Vienna gives a half-humorous, half-chagrinned description of the table order in the archbishop's quarters. According to that order, musicians were of lower rank than valets. Such ranking was not unique to the household of the archbishop; rather, it was customary in the eighteenth century for court musicians to be treated as servants. Mozart knew it and had accepted it in Salzburg, but here in Vienna it is beginning to weigh on his pride.*

To his father, in Salzburg

Vienna, March 17, 1781

Mon trés cher amy![1]

Yesterday, on the 16th, I arrived here, god be praised and thanked, all alone in a mail coach;—Oh, I almost forgot to mention the time—it was at 9 o'clock in the Morning;—I had gone by mail coach until Unter-Haag—but by that time my ass and the various parts it is connected with had become so sore that I couldn't possibly endure it any longer—so I thought I would continue my trip with the ordinaire[2]— Herr Escherich, a government official, also had had enough of the mail coach and kept me company until Kemmelbach—in Kemmelbach I thought I would wait for the ordinaire, but the Herr Postmaster made it perfectly clear that he could under no circumstances allow me to take the ordinaire, because Kemmelbach was not a major postal station—so I had to go on per express coach—and arrived on Thursday, the 15th, dog-tired at 7 o'clock in the evening at St. Pölten—slept until 2 o'clock in the morning and then continued straight on to Vienna.—I am writing this—where?—in Mesmer's garden in the Landstrasse[3]—the old lady is not at home, but the former Fräulein Franzl, now Frau von Bosch, is here and she most sincerely wants me to send you and my sister 1000 greetings;—and let me tell you, upon my honor, I almost didn't

1. "My very dear friend!" It is the only time Mozart addressed his father so intimately.
2. A regular coach service but with fewer stops than the mail coach.
3. The suburban garden of Dr. Franz Anton Mesmer. The Mozarts had been friends with Dr. Mesmer since their stay in Vienna in 1767–68.

recognize her anymore, she's become so fat and heavy;—she has 3 children—2 young ladies and one young gentleman;—one girl, named Nannerl, is four years old but you'd swear she is 6—the young gentleman is 3—but you'd swear he is already 7—and the baby is three quarters of a year but could easily be taken for 2—they have all grown so big and strong.—Now about the Archbishop—I have a charming room in the same house in which the Archbishop is lodging—Brunetti and Ceccarelli[4] were put up in a different house—che distinzione![5]—my neighbor is Herr von Kleinmayern,[6] who showered me with all kinds of courtesies when I arrived—he is quite a Charming man—

We take our meals at 12 o'clock noon—unfortunately too early for me—seated at the table are the two gentlemanly valets who are the archbishop's body-and-soul attendants, the Herr Comptroller, Herr Zetti, the pastry chef, the 2 cooks, and then Ceccarelli, Brunetti, and—little me;—N.B. the two Messieurs valet are sitting at the head of the table—I at least have the honor of sitting above the cooks—so, I think to myself, well, it's like being back in Salzburg—there's a lot of crude and silly joking at the table; but not with me, for I don't say much and if I *must say something*, I do it always with great seriousness—and as soon as I am finished with my meal, I get up and leave.—No meals are served in the evening, instead we each get 3 ducats[7]—and wow, you can really go to town with all that.—The Herr Archbishop graciously covers himself with glory by showing off his people—but he steals from their income—and doesn't pay them for their service.—

We already did a concert yesterday at 4 o'clock[8]—present were at least 20 persons of the highest nobility—Ceccarelli had to sing at Balfi's, today we are to perform at Prince Gallizin's,[9] who was present at yesterday's concert as well; now I'll just have to wait and see whether I will get some gratuity; if I get nothing, I will go to the Archbishop and tell him straight out: if he won't allow me to earn something on my own, he will have to give me some extra pay so I won't have to live off my own money;—

4. Antonio Brunetti, a violinist, and Francesco Ceccarelli, a castrato, were the other two musicians who had been summoned by the archbishop.
5. "Quite a distinction!"
6. Franz Thaddäus von Kleinmayer(n), chairman of the archbishop's Court Council.
7. Three ducats are about 13 gulden, which is not as niggardly as Mozart makes it out to be.
8. It means that Mozart had to perform on the day of his arrival, after traveling all night.
9. Prince Dimitri Mikhailovich Galitzin, Russian ambassador at the Viennese court.

I must close now; I will take the letter to the post office and mail it on my way to Prince Gallizin's—I kiss your hand 1000 times and embrace my sister with all my heart and remain forever your most obedient son,

Wolfgang Amadè Mozart

P.S. Rossi the Buffo is here—
I have already visited the Fischer family,
I can't describe the joy they had in seeing me—
they all send their greetings—
I hear there are concerts in Salzburg?—
I'm losing out terribly!—*Adieu.*
My address is: At the Deutsche Haus,
Singerstrasse.

To his father, in Salzburg

Vienna, March 24, 1781

Mon Trés Cher Pére!

I received your letter from the 20th of this month and read therein with pleasure that you both got home safely and are doing well.[10]— please blame my poor ink and pen if you have to decipher each word of this letter rather than being able to just read it.—Basta;[11] I have no choice, what must be written, must be written. . . . What you are saying about the Archbishop—namely that it tickles his pride to have me around—is pretty much true; but of what use is it to me?—I cannot live on that.—and believe me, here he won't let my *light shine*—what distinction is he really giving me?—Herr von Kleinmayer and Benecke sit at a separate table together with the illustrious Count Arco;[12] now, if I were invited to sit at their table, *that* would be a distinction;—but there is no distinction in sitting with the valets who, *apart from occupying the top seats at the table,* light the chandeliers, open the doors, and then must stay in the anteroom *while I am allowed inside*—nor is there any distinction in sitting with the cooks. And when we are summoned somewhere to give

10. Leopold and Nannerl had just returned to Salzburg from Munich.
11. Enough said!
12. Count Karl Joseph Arco, chief steward of the archbishop.

a concert, Herr Angelbauer has to keep watch outside until the Salzburg musicians arrive, then he calls a lackey to accompany them inside, so they will be allowed in—this is what Brunetti told me in conversation—but I thought: just wait until I am invited—So when we were called to Prince Gallizin's the other day, Brunetti said to me in his courteous manner: tu, bisogna che sei qui sta sera alle sette, per andare insieme dal Prencipe gallizin. l'Angelbauer ci condurrà.—hò risposto: và bene—ma—se in caso mai non foßi qui alle sette in punto: ci andate pure; non serve aspettarmi—sò ben dovè stà, e ci verrò sicuro;[13]—So I went there alone, on purpose, because I am ashamed to go with them anywhere;—when I got upstairs, Herr Angelbauer stood there ready to tell the lackey to show me inside—but I paid no attention to either the Herr Valet or to the Herr Lackey, but I went straight through the rooms to the music room, for all the doors stood open;—and I went right up to the Prince and paid him my respects—and remained standing there conversing with him;—I had totally forgotten about my two companions, Ceccarelli and Brunetti; they were not to be seen anywhere;—well, they were standing in the rear of the orchestra leaning against a wall and didn't dare come forward.—When a gentleman or a lady addresses Ceccarelli, he always presents a smiling face—but if someone speaks to Brunetti, he blushes and gives short and bashful answers.— . . . This evening I'll be going with Herr von Kleinmayer to visit Court Councillor Braun, a good friend of his; everybody tells me that he is the greatest connoisseur of piano music; I have also eaten twice at the house of Countess Thun,[14] I'm there almost every day—she is the most charming and endearing lady I have ever met; and she thinks very highly of me—her husband is still a bit peculiar—but an honest and right-minded gentleman.—I have also had dinner at the house of Count Cobenzl,[15] which came about through Countess von Rumbeck,[16] his cousine; she is the sister of Cobenzl of the "Pagerie" and has been to Salzburg with her husband.

13. "You must be here at seven o'clock this evening, so we may go to Prince Gallizin's together. Angelbauer will take us there. I replied: That's fine. But if I'm not here at seven sharp, go on ahead. You need not wait for me. I know where he lives and will come there for sure."
14. Countess Maria Wilhelmine Thun-Hohenstein. The countess was a great admirer and supporter of Mozart in Vienna, especially in his early years there.
15. Count Johann Philipp von Cobenzl, vice chancellor for court and state in Vienna.
16. Countess Marie Karoline Thiennes de Rumbeke, Mozart's first piano student in Vienna.

My main goal right now is to meet the emperor[17] in some agreeable fashion, I am absolutely determined that he *should get to know me.*—I would be so happy if I could whip through my opera[18] for him and then play a fugue or two, for that's what he likes.—If I had only known that I'll be in Vienna during Lent, I would have written a short oratorio and performed it in a theater for my own benefit as is customary here.—It would have been easy to write beforehand because I know all the singers here;—how happy I would be to give a public Concert as they like to do here, but I know for sure I wouldn't get permission; just imagine the following: you know they have a Society here that organizes concerts for the benefit of the Widows of Musicians.[19]—anybody in music will give a gratis performance there—the orchestra is 180 members strong and no virtuoso with even the least sense of charity would decline to play when asked by the Society—for to play there puts you in favor with the emperor as well as the Public.—

Starzer[20] was asked to approach me for such a concert, and I agreed at once, but with the proviso that I would need to get permission from my prince—I had no doubt whatsoever that it would be granted, since this is a charitable function and I would receive no fee because, after all, it is for a good cause.—*He did not give his permission!*—The entire nobility was out of sorts with him—I feel badly about the whole thing, and for the following reason: I wouldn't have given a Concert, but because the emperor usually sits in his loge at the Proscenium, I should have extemporized by myself (and Countess Thun would have lent me her beautiful Stein Pianoforte), then I would have played a fugue, and afterward the variations "je suis lindor."[21] Every time I played this program in public, I always had the greatest applause—because the difference in the two pieces is so striking and it brings something for Everybody; but Pazienza!— . . .

28th March: I couldn't finish the letter, because Herr von Kleinmayer came to fetch me in his carriage for a Concert at Baron Braun's. So I can

17. Emperor Joseph II.
18. It is generally assumed that Mozart is referring to *Idomeneo,* but given that the emperor had an interest in the German singspiel, Mozart might have been thinking of his singspiel *Zaide.*
19. The Wiener Tonkünstler-Sozietät, founded in 1771 to support widows and orphans of musicians, was modeled after a similar society in London.
20. Joseph Starzer, a violionist and composer, was probably a founding member of the widows' society.
21. Twelve Variations for Piano ("Je suis Lindor"), K. 354, on a theme by Antoine-Laurent Baudron from Beaumarchais's *Le Barbier de Séville.*

tell you now that the archbishop *did* give his permission for me to play at the Widows' Concert. Starzer had gone to the concert at Gallizin's, and he and the entire nobility worked on the archbishop until he gave his permission. *I am so glad.*—Since I've come here I've eaten only 4 times at my own place;—it's just too early for me—besides, the food is terrible.—I eat there only when the weather is really bad, as today for Example—

Write me some news from Salzburg; I'm being pestered with questions all the time—these gentlemen here are definitely more curious about news from Salzburg than I am.

Your most obedient son
Wolfg. Amadè Mozart

🐦 *After arriving in Vienna—it was Mozart's fourth visit but his first without his father—Mozart felt instantly that Vienna was a good place for him. He knew the Viennese were a music-loving public, and he thought he could find wealthy patrons to support him. Once this conviction was lodged in his mind, it did not really matter much what the archbishop said or did not say, or what his father advised him to do. Mozart had found a court and a city that seemed promising, and he was determined to stay.*

To his father, in Salzburg

Vienna, April 4, 1781

Mon trés cher Pére!

I must be brief today, but on Sunday Brunetti will be leaving for Salzburg, and I'll be able to give him a longer letter for you.—You wish to know how things are with us here in Vienna—but I hope you really mean what's happening to me, because I do not count the other two as part of me.[22]—

I already told you the other day that the archbishop is a big obstacle for me here, for I lost at least 100 ducats because of him, which I could have earned by giving a Concert in the Theater—the ladies had already offered of their *own accord* to distribute tickets for me.—I can

---

22. Brunetti and Ceccarelli.

say in all honesty that I was most delighted with the Viennese public yesterday.—I played at the Widows' Concert in the Kärntnerthor Theater;[23] I had to start over again because there was no end to the applause. Just think what I could earn if I were able to give a concert for my own benefit, now that the Public knows me?—But that arch-oaf of ours won't give me permission—he just doesn't want his people to have any kind of profit, only losses. But he cannot do that to me; for even if I have only 2 pupils here, I'll be doing better than in Salzburg— and I don't need his lodging and food either. Now listen to this: Brunetti was telling us at table today that Arco gave him a message from the archbishop that he *should inform the rest of us* that we will be receiving money for our coach fares and should be leaving by Sunday;—but whoever wanted to stay on, *O holy Wisdom!*—could stay, but would have to live at his own expense, because food and lodging will no longer be provided by the archbishop.—Brunetti, qui ne demande pas mieux,[24] licked his 10 fingers in anticipation; Ceccarelli, *who would love to stay,* but isn't known well enough and doesn't know his way around as well as I do, will try to find something, but if he can't, he will, in God's name, go back. There is no lodging or table in all of Vienna where he wouldn't have to pay.—When they asked me what I had decided to do—I answered: *I will ignore for the time being that I'm supposed to leave*—*because unless Count Arco tells me personally I don't believe it*—*and to him*—*well, I'll give my answer to him when he asks me.*—*Take that and stuff it!* Benecke, who was there, grinned.—Oh, I'm so eager to make a fool of the archbishop, I would do it with the greatest of glee—and with the greatest *Politesse,* for he wouldn't be able to escape me here. Enough of this, I will write you more soon—let me just assure you that if I don't find myself on *firm* ground here and can't figure out a good advantage for myself—I will certainly not stay. But if I can find an advantage, why shouldn't I profit from it?—In the meantime you'll be drawing 2 salaries and don't have to feed me.—I can assure you that if I stay here I shall soon be able to send you some money.—I really mean what I say: if things don't work out, I shall be back.—Adieu for now! Next time more, much more. I

---

23. Mozart probably played the "Je suis Lindor" Variations, K. 354; in addition, either his "Paris" Symphony, K. 297, or his Symphony no. 34 in C, K. 338, was performed.
24. "Who does not ask for anything better."

kiss your hands 1000 times and embrace my sister with all my heart, I hope she has answered Mad.^{selle} Hepp.—Adieu. Forever, your

most obedient son
Wolfg. Amadè Mozart

My greetings to
all—all—all

P.S. I can assure you that this here is a Magnificent place—and for *my Métier* the best place in the world.—Anyone will tell you that.—I like it here and am taking full advantage of everything as best I can. Believe me, it is my full intention to make as much money as I possibly can; for, after your health, it's the best thing you can have in life. Think no more about my former follies, I have long regretted them from the bottom of my heart—one learns by one's mistakes—and right now my head is filled with so many other things.

Adieu—next time more and all of the news.

To his father, in Salzburg

Vienna, April 8, 1781

Mon trés cher Pére!

I had started a more detailed and longer letter—but I wrote too much about Brunetti; and I was afraid he would open it out of sheer curiosity because Ceccarelli is with me.—I shall send you that letter with the next post and will be more specific than I possibly can be now—you probably received my other letter in the meantime.—I already wrote to you about the applause in the Theater, but let me add that what delighted me most of all, and surprised me, was—the astonishing Silentium—and the shouts of Bravo in the middle of my playing. In Vienna, where you have so many good Clavier players, that is certainly a great honor.—

Today we had—I'm writing this at 11 o'clock at night—a concert. 3 pieces of mine were performed; New pieces, of course: a Rondeau for a concerto for Brunetti, a Sonata with violin accompaniment for myself;—I composed it between 11 and 12 o'clock last night—but in order to get it done in time I wrote out only the violin part for Brunetti and kept my own part in my head; and, finally, a Rondeau for Ceccarelli—

VUE DE LA VILLE CAPITALE DE SALZBOURG AVEC LA FORTERESSE.
Dédié à l'Illustre Chapitre de *l'Eglise Metropolitaine de Salzbourg.*

1. View of Salzburg in an engraving by Anton Amon after a painting by Franz von Naumann, 1791 (© Internationale Stiftung Mozarteum Salzburg)

2. Mozart's earliest surviving letter, a postscript to his mother from the town of Wörgl, December 14, 1769 (The Pierpont Morgan Library, MA 836. Photo: The Pierpont Morgan Library/Art Resource, NY)

3. Mozart in Verona at age fourteen in a
painting by Saverio dalla Rosa, January
1770 (Private collection, Paris)

4. Mozart's father, Leopold Mozart, in a painting
attributed to Pietro Antonio Lorenzoni, c. 1765
(© Internationale Stiftung Mozarteum Salzburg)

5. Mozart's mother, Maria Anna Mozart, née Pertl, in a painting attributed to Pietro Antonio Lorenzoni, c. 1775 (© Internationale Stiftung Mozarteum Salzburg)

6. Mozart's sister, Maria Anna Mozart ("Nannerl"), as a
child in a painting attributed to Pietro Antonio Lorenzoni,
1763 (© Internationale Stiftung Mozarteum Salzburg)

CAV. AMADEO WOLFGANGO MOZART ACCAD. FILARMON: DI BOLOG: E·DI VERONA

7. Mozart wearing the insignia of the Golden Spur, in an anonymous painting, 1777 (Civico Museo Bibliografico Musicale, Bologna/Art Resource, NY)

8. Mozart's cousin, Maria
Anna Thekla Mozart
("Bäsle"), in an anonymous
pencil drawing, 1778
(© Internationale Stiftung
Mozarteum Salzburg)

9. Postscript written by Mozart to his father from Mannheim, November 8, 1777 (© Internationale Stiftung Mozarteum Salzburg)

10. Mozart's sister-in-law Aloysia Weber, later Lange, shown in the role of Zémir, from André Grétry's opera *Zémir et Azor*, in a painting by J. B. von Lampi, 1784 (Private Collection)

11. The Mozart family, showing Nannerl and Wolfgang
at the keyboard, Leopold holding a violin, and Mozart's
late mother in the oval portrait, in a painting by Johann
Nepomuk della Croce, winter 1780–81 (© Internationale
Stiftung Mozarteum Salzburg)

OPPOSITE 12. St. Stephen's Cathedral in Vienna, in an engraving by
Carl Schütz, 1792 (Österreichische Nationalbibliothek)

ABOVE 13. Count Hieronymus Joseph Colloredo, Prince-Archbishop
of Salzburg, in an anonymous painting (© Internationale Stiftung
Mozarteum Salzburg)

14. Mozart's wife, Constanze Mozart, née Weber,
in an anonymous lithograph after a 1782 painting
by Joseph Lange, before 1828 (© Internationale
Stiftung Mozarteum Salzburg)

15. Portrait of Mozart, unfinished
painting by his brother-in-law Joseph
Lange, Vienna, 1789 (© Internationale
Stiftung Mozarteum Salzburg)

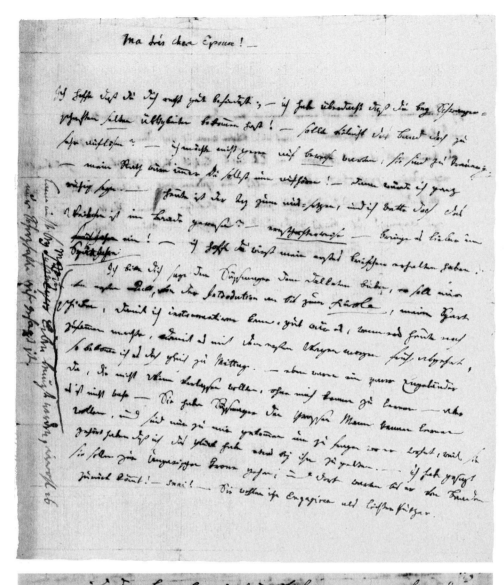

16. First page and signature lines from a letter by Mozart to his wife, Vienna, July 2, 1791 (The Pierpont Morgan Library, HMS 152, Dannie and Hattie Heineman Collection. Photo: the Pierpont Morgan Library/Art Resource, NY)

which he had to Repeat.[25]—Now I am requesting a letter from you as soon as possible with some fatherly, by which I mean friendly, advice about the following: we were told that we'll be going back to Salzburg in two weeks;—however, it is possible for me to stay on here not only without incurring a loss but with some *profit* to myself.—I have in mind, therefore, to request the archbishop to permit me to stay here longer.— Dearest father, I love you very much, you can see that from the fact that on account of you I am denying myself all wishes and desires—For if it weren't for you, I swear by my honor, I would not hesitate for a moment to quit my service, give a major Concert here, take on 4 pupils, and do well enough to earn at least one Thousand Thalers a year.—I can assure you that it is at times hard for me to put my own fortune aside—I am still young, as you keep telling me, and, of course, it's the truth, but if you waste your young years in such a miserly place doing nothing, then it is sad enough and a loss besides. That's where I need your fatherly and well-meaning advice—but quickly—because I have to make a decision—by the way, you can have complete confidence in me in everything—I am now much more level-headed—farewell, I kiss your hands 1000 times and embrace my sister with all my heart. I remain Forever

your most obed.
W. A. Mozart

To his father, in Salzburg

Vienna, April 11, 1781

Mon trés cher Pére!

Te Deum Laudamus,[26] that rude and filthy Brunetti is finally gone; he is a disgrace to his master, to himself, and to the whole orchestra— that's what Ceccarelli and I are saying;—the messages you got from Vienna are all lies, except that Ceccarelli will sing at the opera in Venice

---

25. The "Rondeau . . . for Brunetti" is the Rondo for Violin and Orchestra in C major, K. 373; "A sonata with violin" is the Violin Sonata in G major, K. 379; the "Rondeau for Ceccarelli" is the Recitative and Aria "A questo seno deh vieni," K. 374. The three pieces were performed at a concert given by the archbishop for his father, Prince Rudolph Joseph Colloredo, on April 8, 1781. Since Mozart had few compositions on hand, he had to write new ones in a hurry; in spite of the brevity of time, all three works are considered excellent compositions.
26. "God, we praise Thee!"

during the coming carnival season;—Heavenly Thunder, a Thousand Devils and no End!—I do hope this is not a curse, because if it is I'll have to go to confession all over again, although I'm just coming back from one; tomorrow, that's on Thursday before Easter,[27] the Archbishop, himself, in his own Exalted Persona, will give communion to the entire court. . . .

Now briefly: a week from next Sunday, that's on the 22nd, Ceccarelli and I are supposed to return to Salzburg.—When I think that I am to leave Vienna without bringing home *at least* 1000 gulden, I feel a pain in my heart. So I'm supposed to kick away One Thousand gulden because of a small-minded prince who harasses me every day for a lousy 4 hundred gulden?—because that's what I would certainly be earning if I gave a Concert here.—When we had our first big concert here, at the House of the Teutonic Order, the archbishop sent 4 ducats to each of the three of us; and for the last concert, for which I wrote a new Rondeau for Brunetti, a new sonata for myself, and a new Rondeau for Ceccarelli, I received nothing at all.—But what's driving me to despair is the fact that on the same evening when we had our stinky concert here, I had also been invited to the Countess Thun—but wasn't permitted to go; and who was there?—*the emperor!* Adamberger[28] and Madame Weigl[29] were there, and they Each got 50 ducats![30]—what an opportunity!—

I can't send a message to the emperor and tell him if he wants to hear me, to be quick about it, because I'll be leaving in just a few days—one simply has to be ready for such opportunities;—I can't stay here, and I won't, unless there's a chance to give a Concert—of course, I would be better off here than at home, even if I had only 2 pupils;—however—if you have 1000 or 1200 gulden in your pocket, you can afford to be a bit more choosy, and also, ultimately, get a better salary.—but he doesn't permit it, this misanthrope.[31]—I have no choice but to call him that because that's what he is, and all the nobles here say the same thing. But enough of this. I hope to learn by the next post whether I am supposed to continue burying my young years as well as my talent in Salzburg—or whether I have permission to make my for-

27. Maundy Thursday.
28. Johann Valentin Adamberger, a well-known Viennese tenor.
29. Anna Maria Weigl, the prima donna of the German National Theater in Vienna.
30. About 225 gulden, a substantial sum.
31. The German here is *Menschenfeind*.

tune as long as I am capable of doing so—or whether I am to wait until it is too late.—of course, I can't do it in a fortnight or in 3 weeks, as little as I can do it in 1000 years in Salzburg. Still, it's better to wait with a thousand gulden a year than with four hundred. And that's what I can do here—if I want to!—All I have to do is give the word that I want to stay—I'm not even counting my compositions—and furthermore: Vienna and—Salzburg? When Bono[32] dies, Salieri[33] will become Kapell-meister—then Starzer will get Salieri's position and Starzer's posi-tion?—well, no one has been mentioned yet. Basta; I leave it all up to you, dearest Father!—

Have I visited Bonno?—that's where we rehearsed my Sinfonie the 2nd time.[34]—I forgot to tell you the other day that the Sinfonie was Magnifique, it was a complete Success—we had 40 violins—the wind instruments had been doubled—10 violas—10 contrabasses, 8 violon-cellos, and 6 bassoons.— . . .

Farewell, remember that all your son is trying to do is to *establish him-self*—because—four hundred gulden he can get anywhere.—Adieu, I kiss your hands 1000 times and I embrace my dear sister with all my heart and remain Forever your

most obedient son W. A. Mzt

To his father, in Salzburg

Vienna, April 18, 1781

Mon trés cher Pére!

I can't write much this time either, because it's almost 6 o'clock and I have to give this letter to Zetti in just a moment.—I've just come back from Herr, Frau, and Fräulein von Auerhammer,[35] where I ate lunch and all of us drank a toast to your health.—In regard to that lengthy letter of yours, I can't say anything, except that you are both right and wrong;—although the points in which you are right very much out-weigh those in which you aren't—therefore—I will return home for sure and with the greatest of joy; because I am truly convinced that you

---

32. Giuseppe Bonno, court Kapellmeister in Vienna.
33. Antonio Salieri, who became, as Mozart predicted, Bonno's successor.
34. Presumably the symphony performed at the widows' concert, either K. 297 or K. 338.
35. Johann Michael von Auernhammer, his wife, Elisabeth, and his daughter, Josepha Barbara. The last became one of Mozart's star pupils.

would never stand in my way if I want to make my fortune. But until now I have not received any word about the date of my departure. I certainly won't travel on Sunday, because as I said from the beginning I will not take the mail coach again.—I have decided to take the ordinaire— if Ceccarelli wants to come with me, it will be all the more pleasant, but in that case we might as well take the express coach.—the whole difference (people find it laughable) is just a few gulden—because I would be traveling day and night, and therefore wouldn't need much money for food.— . . .

There's nothing to be done with Schachtner's operette right now.[36] The reason is—well, it's the same reason that I mentioned to you many times.—Stephanie the Younger will provide me with a new piece,[37] and, as he says, a good piece; if I should no longer be here, he'll forward it to me.—also, I couldn't disagree with his assessment.[38] I told him that the work, with the exception of the long dialogues (which can easily be altered) is really very good; but it's not suitable for Vienna; here they prefer comedies.—Now be well and I'll be Forever

your most obedient son
W. A. Mzt

To his father, in Salzburg

Vienna, April 28, 1781

Mon trés cher Pére!

You are expecting me with great joy, my dearest father!—Well, that's about the only thing that can make me decide to leave Vienna— I'm writing all this in plain German[39] *because the whole world may and should know that the Archbishop of Salzburg has only you to thank that yesterday he, and I mean he personally, did not lose me forever;*—yesterday we had a grand concert here—probably the last one;—the concert went very well and, in spite of all the obstacles his archbishopric Grace threw in my way, I had a

---

36. The unfinished singspiel *Zaide*.
37. Gottlieb Stephanie, a librettist, whom Mozart met in 1773; the "new piece" is the text for the singspiel *Die Entführung aus dem Serail*.
38. The "assessment" was of Schachtner's libretto for *Zaide*, which Mozart had given to Stephanie to read.
39. Leopold and Wolfgang often used a coded language in their correspondence so as to fool the archbishop's censors. At this point, however, Wolfgang threw caution to the wind and deliberately used plain language (ich schreibe das alles nun in der Natürlichen teutschen sprache), almost as if to provoke the archbishop.

better performance than Brunetti. Ceccarelli will tell you all about it.—
Just to make the arrangements proved to be very annoying—at any rate,
it's easier to talk than to write about it; but if this sort of thing should
happen again, and I hope it won't—I can tell you for sure that I won't
be able to muster enough patience anymore, and I'm sure you'll forgive
me for it—and one thing I beg of you, dearest father, you must give me
permission to return to Vienna during next Lent at the end of the
Carnival season—and this depends on you alone, not on the archbishop—because if he doesn't give me permission I'll go anyway, and it
won't be my misfortune, certainly not! Oh, if he could only read this! I
would not mind at all.—but you must give me your promise in your
next letter, for I shall return to Salzburg only under that condition;—
but it must be a *definite promise,* so I can give the ladies here my word—
Stefanie will give me a German opera to compose—I am eagerly expecting your reply about all this.— . . .

Now I must close because I'm expected at the Countess Schön-
born's—Yesterday, after the concert, the ladies kept me at the piano for
an entire hour—I think I would still be sitting there if I hadn't made a
secret getaway.—I thought I had played enough *for free*—

Adieu—I kiss your hands 1000 times and embrace my sister with all
my heart, and I remain Forever

your obed. son,
W. A. Mozart

Mozart had played with the idea of leaving the services of the archbishop as far back
as his journey to Mannheim in 1777; however, his father had always pulled him
back to Salzburg. Now, after weeks of indecision, Mozart found the right moment
to literally leap into freedom. It was a daring step, for he had no basic support in
Vienna, but Mozart was willing to take his chances. His report to his father about
his confrontation with the archbishop is brilliant with joy and intensity.

To his father, in Salzburg

Vienna, May 9, 1781

Mon trés cher Pére!

I am still boiling with bitterness!—and I'm sure that you, my best
and dearest father, feel just like me—my patience has been tried and

tried again—finally it burst. I am no longer so unfortunate as to be in Salzburg's services—today was that happy day for me; listen!

Twice before,—this—oh, I'm at a loss for words what to call him—has thrown the greatest insults and *impertinences* into my face, which I did not want to tell you, in order to spare your feelings, and the only reason why I did not avenge myself on the spot was that I always had you, my dearest father, before my eyes.—He called me a knave and a slovenly fellow, told me I should get out of here—and I—I endured it all—but I felt that not only my honor was attacked but yours as well—but as you would have it so, I remained silent.—But now listen to this: a week ago his footman came to me unexpectedly and told me that I had to move out of my lodgings instantly.—All the others had been told what day they had to move, only I had not been informed. So I quickly gathered my belongings into my trunk—and old Mad.^me Weber[40] was kind enough to offer me her home—where I now have a pretty room and am among helpful people who lend a hand with things one might need in a hurry, the sort of thing one just doesn't have when one lives alone.

I had decided to take the ordinaire on Wednesday, that's today, the 9th;—but I couldn't collect the money that is due me within such a short time; so I had to postpone my departure until Saturday.—When I came to the archbishop's quarters this morning, the valets told me that the Archbishop wanted me to take a package to Salzburg for him—I asked whether there was any hurry about it, they said Yes, it was of great Importance.—In that case I am sorry that I have to forgo the Privilege of serving his Highness because I can't leave before Saturday for all the reasons mentioned above.—I had to get out of my room, I now have to live at my own expenses—so it is quite Natural that I cannot travel until I have the means to do so—I'm sure no one will want me to bear a loss.—Kleinmayer, Moll, Benecke, and the two valets all said that I was quite right.—When I entered his room—N.B., first I must mention that Schlaucher advised me that I should give as an excuse that the ordinaire was already full—that would be a more convincing reason in his judgment;—anyway, when I entered his room, it began like this:—Arch: Well, young fellow, when are you off?[41]—I: I had wanted to leave

40. Maria Cäcilia Weber, the mother of Aloysia. The Webers had moved first to Munich and then from there to Vienna, following Aloysia and her career as a singer.
41. Actually the archbishop addressed Mozart not with "you" but with the third person "he" (*Erz.:* Nun, wann geht er den Bursch?).

tonight, but the seats were all taken. At that moment he burst into one unstoppable tirade: I was the most worthless fellow he knew, no one has served him as poorly as I have—he would advise me to leave today or else he will write to Salzburg to stop my pay—I couldn't get a word in, his words came out like a blaze of fire. I listened to it all patiently— although he lied right into my face that I was drawing 500 gulden— called me a scoundrel, a lousy rogue, a cretin!—oh, I don't want to write you all the things he said—finally, as my blood began to boil, I said— so Your Highness is not satisfied with my service?—what, are you threatening me? You cretin, oh, such a cretin!—there is the door, right over there, see it?, I don't want to have anything to do with such miserable scum anymore.—At last, I said—and I don't want to have anything to do with you anymore either—so then get out!—*and I:* (as I was leaving)—I hope this decision is final;—I'll give it to you in writing, tomorrow.—Now, dearest father, tell me whether I didn't say all these things rather too late than too early?—Listen: my Honor is worth more to me than anything else, and I know, the same is true of you.

Don't worry about me;—I am so sure of doing the right thing that I would have quit even if there had been less of a reason—but since I did have a good reason, in fact, this is the third time—I can no longer think of it as a special accomplishment; O Contraire,[42] I had been a coward twice—I couldn't possibly be a coward a third time.—

As long as the archbishop remains here, I shall not give a concert. If you fear that I have damaged my reputation with the nobility here and perhaps with the emperor, you are very mistaken—the archbishop is hated here, and most of all by the emperor—the thing that really soured the archbishop is that the emperor did not invite him to Laxenburg.[43] I'll be sending you a little money by the next post to convince you that I am not starving here.

Apart from all this, I beg you to be cheerful—because my good fortune is just beginning now, and I hope that my happiness will also be yours.—Write to me in a coded message that you are pleased about it all, and, truly, you have reason to be pleased—but publicly you can give me a good scolding, so no one will blame you for anything—if, however, the archbishop should nevertheless give you the slightest grief, then

42. Mozart means *au contraire* (to the contrary).
43. Laxenburg is an imperial country estate south of Vienna.

you come immediately with my sister to Vienna and stay with me—I can assure you, upon my honor, that there is enough to live on, for all three of us,—although it would be preferable if you could wait one more year;—don't write any more letters to me at the Deutsche Haus, or include one in any package—I don't want to have anything to do with Salzburg anymore—I hate the Archbishop to the point of madness.

Adieu—I kiss your hands 1000 times and embrace my dear sister
with all my heart, and I remain Forever your obed. son.
Write on your letter
to be delivered at
Peter's Place, in the Eye of God, 3rd floor.[44]
Please let me know how pleased
you are, it's the only thing
missing in my present state of
happiness. *Adieu.*

W. A. Mozart

🕮 *On May 12, Mozart wrote two letters to his father; one contains his famous out-burst: "I didn't know I was a valet" (Ich wuste nicht daß ich kammerdiener wäre), the other contains the message to his father that he should "pretend to be angry." Mozart sent the first letter by mail because he did not care whether the censors would read it, but the second letter he sent with a friend who happened to be trav-eling to Salzburg.*

To his father, in Salzburg

Vienna, May 12, 1781

Mon trés cher Pére!
You know from my last letter that I have asked the prince for my discharge.—because he himself ordered me to. In 2 previous audiences he had said to me already: *get out of here if you don't want to serve me properly;* he will, of course, deny it, but that won't change the fact that it is as

---

44. This highly romantic address, "Auf dem Peter, im Aug=Gottes, im 2ten Stock," was the address of the Weber family in Vienna; Wolfgang rented a room from Mrs. Weber, originally intending to stay there only until his departure for Salzburg, perhaps for a week. Leopold, of course, would be greatly alarmed that Wolfgang was back with the Webers.

true as there is a god in Heaven.—Can it be any wonder that finally, after I had been driven completely mad with words like knave, scoundrel, rascal, slovenly fellow, and other such edifying expressions out of the mouth of a prince, I took his *get out of here* quite literally?—The very next day I handed Count Arco a petition to give to His Grace; I also returned the travel money consisting of 15 gulden and 40 kreuzer for the Diligence, and 2 ducats for food.—He did not accept either; and he insisted that I could not resign without first obtaining your consent.— That's your duty, he said;—I assured him in return that I knew my duty toward my father as well as he and perhaps Better—and I should be very sorry if I had to learn it first from him.—All right then, he said, if he is satisfied, you can request your discharge, if not—you can request it anyway.—Now, there's a real Distinction for you!—All these lofty remarks the Archbishop had uttered during the three audiences I had with him, especially the last one, and all the subsequent things this splendid servant of god dished out, had such a terrific effect on my body that in the evening I had to leave the opera in the middle of the first Act and go home so I could lie down.—I felt quite hot and fever- ish—my body was trembling all over—and I staggered about in the street like a drunkard.—I stayed home the following day, that was yes- terday—and stayed in bed all morning because I had taken some tamarind water.[45]

In addition, the Herr Count was so kind as to write many lovely things about me to his father, which you probably have had to swallow already.—The report undoubtedly contains a number of fabulous items—after all, if you want to write a Comedy and desire applause, you have to exaggerate a bit rather than stick to the facts—and, you must keep in mind, these gentlemen wish to show how eager they are to please their master.—

I only want to put down here, without getting too worked up because I value my health and life more—and I'm sorry that I am being forced to do it at all—I want to put down the main accusation that has been leveled against my service:—I didn't know I was a valet. And that's what did me in.—I was expected to waste a couple of hours every morning in the antechamber—true, I had been told more than once

---

45. A form of wine made from *Tamarindus indica*, a tree native to India; "tamarind water" was also used as a laxative.

that I should make myself more visible—but I could never get it into my head that this was part of my duties and, therefore, I appeared on time only when the Archbishop sent for me.—

Now I will confide to you briefly my unalterable resolution, but so that the whole wide world may hear it;—if I should be able to earn 2000 gulden from the Archbishop of Salzburg and only 1000 from somewhere else—I would prefer to go somewhere else;—for in place of the extra 1000 gulden, I would rather enjoy health and peace of mind.— So I hope that you in your fatherly love, which you have shown me in such plentiful measure from my childhood on and for which I cannot ever thank you enough, but least of all in Salzburg, if you want to keep your son well and happy, please don't write to me about this affair but rather bury it in deepest oblivion—because one single word about it would be enough to put me Once Again, and even you—you might as well admit it—even you—into a state of bitter rage.

Now farewell and be happy that you don't have a coward as a son. I kiss your hands 1000 time and embrace my sister with all my heart and remain Forever your

most obedient son
Wolfgang Amadè Mozart

To his father, in Salzburg

Vienna, May 12, 1781

Mon trés cher Pére!

In the letter you received by mail, I spoke to you as if we were in the presence of the archbishop.—But now I'm talking just with you, my dearest father;—I don't even want to say anything about all the injustices I have received from the archbishop from the beginning of his reign, about the incessant scoldings, the lies and insults he said right to my face, and of my indisputable right to leave his services; for all these things are perfectly clear. I only want to talk about the things that would have persuaded me to leave him—even if he had not offended me. I am enjoying here the finest and most useful contacts in the world—I am a favored and well-respected guest in the noblest families, I'm shown all sorts of honors—and get paid on top of it—and I should languish in Salzburg for a mere 400 gulden?[46]—with no significant income, no

---

46. Mozart keeps saying that his salary at Salzburg was 400 gulden, whereas the archbishop maintains it is 500; actually it was 450 gulden per year.

encouragement—languish and not be able to help you, when I can truly be of use to you from here? What would be the Point of it all?—it would always remain the same, I would have to suffer abuse until I die, or leave again.—I don't need to tell you all this, you know it yourself. Just let me add this: all of Vienna knows my story by now—and all the Nobles agree that I should not be duped any longer.

Dearest father; they will come and talk to you sweetly, but—they are snakes and vipers—all lowly creatures are like that; disgustingly arrogant and proud, but then—they crawl—how revolting. The 2 valets are aware of the whole shitty business; Schlaucher said to somebody: *I can't blame Mozart entirely—in fact, he is quite right—he*[47] *should have tried to do that to me—he treats him like a beggar boy, I heard it all myself—it's really infamous.* The archbishop is aware of his own injustice—and didn't he have numerous opportunities to recognize that he is in the wrong? has that improved his behavior?—No!—so let's be done with it.—If I hadn't worried that you might be adversely affected by it all, I would have changed things long ago.—But what can he actually do to you?—nothing;—and as long as you know that I am doing all right, you can easily do without the archbishop's Blessings;—he can't take your salary away—after all, you are doing your duty.—and I can Guarantee you that I'll be doing just fine—otherwise I wouldn't have taken such a step—although I must confess that after being insulted like that—I— would have left him even if I had to go begging; for who would allow himself to be pushed around like that, especially if one has a chance to better oneself. If you are worried—then pretend to be angry with me,—scold me in your letter, just as long as you and I understand how things really stand.—but don't let them win you over with flattering words.—Be on your guard!—Adieu—

I kiss your hands 1000 times and embrace my dear sister with all my heart—I will be sending off the Portrait,[48] the Ribbons, the thin wool blanket,—Adieu, I am Forever your

most obedient son
Wolfgang Amadè Mozart

47. The archbishop.
48. A painting of Mozart's mother by the painter Rosa Hagenauer-Barducci, wife of Johann Baptist Hagenauer, who had taken it to Vienna. Leopold had asked Wolfgang to bring the portrait back to Salzburg. The "Ribbons" are a present for Mozart's sister, Nannerl.

To his father, in Salzburg

Vienna, May 16, 1781

Mon trés cher Pére!

I cannot explain it in any other way than that you wrote down all those things I just had to read as a first surprised reaction because, after all, you were expecting me to come home with such certainty.—But in the meantime you were able to reflect on the matter more thoroughly, and as a man of honor you now feel the insults more acutely—and now you know and understand that what has been in your own thoughts for some time—no longer needs to happen because it has happened already;—in Salzburg it is much harder to break away,—for there he is Lord and Master, but here—he is only a *fool*, just what I am in his eyes. And then—you can certainly believe me, I know you and I also know the goodness in my heart for you.—Even if the archbishop had given me a couple of hundred gulden more, and I—I had remained with him, it would be the same old story all over again.

Believe me, my dearest father, I need all my Manly strength to write to you what common sense bids me to write—God knows how difficult it is for me to leave you;—but even if I had to go begging I would never want to serve such a Master again—what I experienced I won't forget for the rest of my life—and—I beg you, I beg you by all you hold dear in the world, strengthen me in my Resolution rather than try to dissuade me from it, for it makes me miserable and uncreative;—it's My Wish and hope to gain Honor, Fame, and Money, and I have reason to believe that I can be of better help to you in Vienna than in Salzburg.—The road to Prague is less closed to me from here than if I were in Salzburg.[49] What you're saying about the Weber family, I can assure you it's not what you think—I know I was a fool about Frau Lange,[50] that is true, but that's the way it is when you are in love!—I really loved her, and even now she is not indifferent to me—it's lucky for me that her husband is a jealous Fool and won't let her go anywhere, so I see her very rarely.—Trust me when I say that old Mad.^me Weber is

49. Mozart may be thinking of Prague because he met Josepha Duschek, a singer from Prague, and her husband in 1777 in Salzburg.
50. Aloysia Weber had married the actor Joseph Lange and lived in Vienna, where she was engaged by the German Opera at the Burgtheater.

a very helpful woman and that I cannot return her helpfulness proportionately, because I just don't have the time.

Now I am longing for a letter from you, my Dearest, most beloved father—cheer up your son, for only the thought of displeasing you can make him unhappy amid all of his promising prospects. Adieu—farewell a thousand times, I am Forever yours—and kiss your hands 1000 times as your

most obedient son
W. A. Mzt

🙞 *Mozart's letter of May 19 allows a point-by-point reconstruction of Leopold's angry reaction to his son's decision to leave Salzburg and the services of the archbishop.*

To his father, in Salzburg

Vienna, May 19, 1781

Mon trés cher Pére!

I don't know what to write first, my dearest father, because I have not recovered from my Bewilderment and, in fact, will not be able to do so ever if you continue to think and write as you just did;—I must confess that there was not a single sign in your letter by which I can recognize my father!—a father perhaps, but not the Best, the most loving father who would be concerned for his honor and the honor of his children—in other words, not my father; but perhaps it was just a dream—and now you are awake—and no longer in need of a reply from me to your arguments, and you are truly convinced that I—*now more than Ever*—cannot go back on my decision.—Still I must reply to some of your points because my honor and my character have been most painfully assaulted in several of your passages.—You say you can never approve of the fact that I resigned from my Salzburg services here in Vienna;—I think that if one has a desire to do so, although I didn't really have such a desire at first, otherwise I would have done it on a previous occasion, it is best to do it in a place where people are favorably disposed to you and where you have the best prospects in the world.—It is, of course, understandable that you cannot give your approval in the presence of the archbishop, but toward me you cannot but think that my decision was Good.—You are also saying that I can save my honor only by abandoning my resolve.—How can you even think of such a contradiction?—You didn't consider when you wrote this down that through such a renunciation I would become the most despicable fellow in the world. All of Vienna knows that I have left the archbishop—and why!—they know that my honor was insulted—and, indeed, insulted three times—and now I should make a public show of the opposite?—turn myself into a lowly liar and the archbishop into an Honorable prince?—the former can be done by no one, least of all by me, and the latter—can be done only by God, that is, if he chooses to enlighten him.—I have never shown you any love?—and should finally show it? now?—can you really say such things?—

I don't want to sacrifice my pleasures for you?—What kinds of pleasures am I having here?—Do you mean those painful efforts I am making to put something in my purse?—you seem to be thinking that I am swimming in amusement and entertainment.—Oh, how you are deceiving yourself!—True, for the time being I have only as much as I need—But now the subscription for my 6 sonatas[51] is under way, and I'll get some money from that.—and plans for the opera[52] are proceeding on course—also, during the Advent Season I'll give a Concert; and from there on things will get better and better—for in the winter season one can really earn a pretty good penny around here.—If it can be called a pleasure to get a prince off your back who doesn't pay but works you to death, then, it's true, that is a pleasure for me.—Even if I had to think and work from early Morning till Night, I would gladly do it, only so I wouldn't have to live by the grace of such a—I don't even want to call him by name.—I've been forced into taking this step—and cannot deviate a hair's breadth from my decision—impossible—all I can say to you is that I am sorry only on your account, dearest father, that I've been forced into this—and that I wished the Archbishop had handled it with more common sense, only so I could spend the rest of my

---

51. Mozart's "6 sonatas," which he circulated for subscription, are the Sonatas for Piano and Violin, K. 296, K. 376–380; printed at the end of November 1781 by Artaria & Co., they were his first compositions published in Vienna.
52. *Die Entführung aus dem Serail.*

life with you—for to please you, my dearest father, I would sacrifice my happiness, my health, and my life—but my honor—that is to me—and it must be to you, too—above everything.—Let Count Arco read this letter, let all of Salzburg read it.—After these insults—after these threefold insults, even if the Archbishop personally would offer me 1200 gulden, I would not accept it.—I am no slovenly fellow, no knave—and if it weren't for you I would not have waited around for him to say *get out of here* to me for a third time. . . .

Dearest, most beloved father, ask me anything you want, only not to return to the archbishop—the thought alone makes me shake with anger—Adieu—I kiss your hands 1000 times and embrace my sister with all my heart and I am Forever your

most obedient son
Wolfgang Amadè Mozart

After many emotional outcries, including his distress at his father's siding with the archbishop, Mozart offers a clear and rational account as to why he felt that Vienna was so much better for him than Salzburg. He was right: Salzburg was a small, provincial town in terms of music. The archbishop was a man of the enlightenment and progressive in many ways, but he did not champion the arts.

To his father, in Salzburg

Vienna, May 26, 1781

Mon trés cher Pére!

You are quite right, just as I am right as well, my dearest father!—I know and I am aware of all my faults; but—is it not possible for someone to improve?—may he not have improved already?—No matter how much I turn this matter over in my mind, I always come to the conclusion that I can help myself and you, dearest father, as well as my dear sister best in every way if I remain in Vienna. It seems as if good fortune is waiting to embrace me here.—It is as if I *must* stay.—In fact, I already had this feeling when I left Munich.—I was so looking forward to Vienna and didn't know why.—If you're willing to have a little patience, I will soon show you how useful Vienna can be for all of us.—Believe me, I have changed completely—I now recognize that, apart from my health, nothing is more Important than money; I'm certainly not a miser—for it would be very difficult for me to become a miser, still, people here think I'm more inclined toward penny-pinching than toward wasting money—and that's always good for a start.—As far as pupils are concerned, I can have as many as I want; but I don't want that many—I want to be better paid than other musicians—so I can afford to have fewer pupils. One has to stand up for oneself right in the beginning, otherwise one has lost out forever and has to trot along with the rest of them. The subscription is going quite well,—and there is no reason why I should go slow with the opera[53]—Count Rosenberg,[54] whom I visited twice already, has received me most courteously and has heard my opera at Countess Thun's together with van Suiten[55] and Herr von Sonnenfels.[56]—And since Stephani[57] is my very good friend, all is well.— Believe me, I don't enjoy leisure, I love to work.—In Salzburg, yes, it's true, I had to make an effort, and I could almost not get myself to work, but why?—because my spirits were down; you have to admit yourself that in Salzburg—at least for me—there isn't a penny's worth of stimulation; there are many with whom *I don't wish to associate;*—and most of the others, well, they do not think that I am good enough for them; not exactly an inspiration for my talent!—When I play, or when one of my Compositions is performed, it is as if the audience consisted of nothing but tables and chairs.—If at least they had a theater that was worth something; it provides my entire entertainment here. In Munich, it's true, I put myself in a bad light in your eyes, much against my own will, but you're right, I was too preoccupied with entertainment—but I swear to you, by my honor, that before my opera was finished I never went to the theater and never went anywhere, except to the Cannabichs.—and it's also true, I had to work the hardest and most intense at the last minute; not because I had been lazy or negligent, but rather because I had gone for two weeks without writing a Note, it was simply *impossible* for me to write—of course, I was writing but not on

53. It seems that Leopold had written to Wolfgang to slow down his plans for *Die Entführung.*
54. Count Franz Xaver Wolf Orsini-Rosenberg, chief chamberlain at the Viennese court and director of the court theaters.
55. Baron Gottfried van Swieten, formerly a diplomat and now director of the court library. It was at his house that Mozart deepened his knowledge of Johann Sebastian Bach and George Frideric Handel.
56. Joseph von Sonnenfels was professor at the University of Vienna and a leading figure of the Enlightenment in Austria.
57. Johann Gottlieb Stephanie, the librettist of Mozart's new opera, *Die Entführung.*

paper.—Much time was lost by that, but I don't regret it;—and the fact that I was a bit too jolly afterward was just Youthful foolishness; I thought to myself, well, where are you going from here?—to Salzburg!—so then, let's have a good time right now!—It's true, in Salzburg I long for a 100 different forms of entertainment, but here—not a single one—for just to be in Vienna is entertainment enough. Have faith in me, I am not a fool anymore—and that I should be a godless, ungrateful son? You probably believe that even less.—Just have confidence in my head and in the goodness of my heart—you will not regret it.—

Where, pray, would I have had an opportunity to get to love money?—I've had far too little so far in my possession.—I remember when I had 20 ducats once, I thought I was rich.—Necessity alone teaches one the value of money.—

Farewell, my dearest, most beloved father!—it is my duty now to make good and replace through care and work all the things that you feel were lost by this affair.—I will do just that and do it with a joyful heart!—*Adieu.* I kiss your hands 1000 times and embrace my dear sister with all my heart and remain Forever

your most obedient son
Wolfgang Amadè Mozart

P.S. As soon as someone from the archbishop's staff goes to Salzburg, I'll send the Portrait along—hò fatto fare la sopra scritta d'un altro espreßamente, perchè non si può sapere.[58]

To his father, in Salzburg

Vienna, between May 26 and June 2, 1781

Mon trés cher Pére!

Day before yesterday Count Arco sent a message saying I should come to see him at 12 o'clock noon; he would be expecting me.—He had sent similar messages to me before, Schlaucher did too, but because I hate conversations where almost every word listened to is a lie—I never showed up.—I would have done the same this time if he hadn't added to his message that he had received a letter from you.—So I went to see him at the appropriate time.—It would be impossible for me to

---

58. "I got someone else to write the address because you can never be too careful."

write down the entire conversation, which went calmly and without irritation because that's what I had requested right in the beginning.—In short, he put everything before me in the friendliest manner; one could have sworn that he spoke from the heart.—He, on the other hand, could surely not swear that what I had to say came from the heart.—With all possible calm, courtesy, and the most endearing manner in the world I countered his rhetoric with the actual truth—and he—was unable to say one word against it. In the end, I wanted to hand him my memorandum and the travel money, both of which I had brought along.—But he assured me that he felt too sad about the whole thing to want to get mixed up in it; I should just give the memorandum to one of the valets—and he would take back the money only when everything was finally settled.—The Archbishop is running me down before all the world and is not bright enough to understand that this will bring him no honor; because around here I'm esteemed more highly than he is;—they think of him as an arrogant and conceited priest[59]—who feels superior to everybody around here—whereas I am thought of as an amiable person. It is true, I can get very proud when I notice that someone wants to treat me with contempt and en bagatelle.—And that's how the Archbishop indeed treats me—but—with some kind words—he could have won me over.—That's what I told the count; I also said: the Archbishop isn't even worthy of the high opinion you have of him.— And at the end I said: of what use would it be if I went back to Salzburg now—in a few months I would, even without any insults, request my discharge anyway, for I can't—and I won't—stay in his service for this kind of pay. But why not?—because, I said, because I could never be happy and content in a place where my pay is such that all the time I'd have to wonder, oh, if only I were here! or there!—but if I get paid well enough that I don't need to think about other places, then I can be content. And if the Archbishop pays me such a salary, I'll be prepared to leave for home today.—

How glad I am that the Archbishop did not take me at my word. For it'll be undoubtedly your fortune as well as mine if I stay here. You shall see! Now farewell, most beloved, dearest father! All will be well!— I'm not writing this in a dream—after all, my own well-being is at stake.

59. Mozart uses the word *Pfaff*, a highly disparaging term for "priest."

Adieu. I kiss your hands 1000 times and embrace my dear sister with all
my heart and remain Forever
P.S. My regards   your most obedient son
—to all good *friends.*   Wolfgang Amadé Mozart

To his father, in Salzburg

Vienna, June 2, 1781

Mon Trés Cher Pére!

You know from my last letter that I spoke with Count Arco myself;
God be praised and thanked, it went well.—don't worry about anything, you have nothing to fear from the archbishop;—Count Arco did
not say one word that I should really think this matter over *lest it could
bring you harm*—and when he told me that you had written to him and
complained about me bitterly, I immediately interrupted him by saying:
*and don't you think that I heard from him too?—he wrote to me in such a way that I
thought I should lose my mind over all the things he said—but still, I can turn the matter this way or that—I just can't,* Etc.—He told me then: believe me, you
allow yourself to be dazzled too easily;—a person's fame is of short
duration here—in the beginning one is given a lot of accolades, and one
earns good money, that's true—but for how long?—after a few Months
the Viennese will want something new;[60]—You are quite right, Herr
Count, I said, but do you really think I will remain in Vienna?—Not at
all; I know where I want to go.—the fact that this incident occurred
here, in Vienna, is the fault of the Archbishop, not mine.—if he knew
how to treat people of talent, this thing wouldn't have happened.—
Herr Count, I am the most good-natured fellow in the world—just as
long as I am treated decently;—Yes, he said, the Archbishop thinks you
are a thoroughly Conceited person. I believe it, I said, because that's how
I behave toward him; I treat people the way they treat me;—when I see
that Someone is contemptuous of me and puts me down, I can be as
proud as a Baboon.—

Among other things he asked me whether I realized that he, too,
had to swallow some harsh words now and then?—I shrugged my
shoulders and replied: I'm sure you have your reasons for putting up
with it, just as I have mine for not putting up with it.—The rest you

---

60. These words by Count Arco would prove prophetic for Mozart.

know from my last letter.—Dearest, most beloved father, don't have any doubts; this is all for my best and consequently also for your best.—To be sure, the Viennese are people who like to shoot you down,—*but only in the Theater.*—My kind of music is far too popular for me not to be able to make a living. This here is a true Clavier land! and èven if we agree that things change, it wouldn't happen for a number of years, not now.— In the meantime one can gain a reputation and money,—and, after all, there are other places in the world—and who knows what other opportunity may come along?—I will send you *something* with Herr von Zetti, I've talked to him already—this time you'll have to be content with a small sum—I cannot send more than 30 ducats.[61] Had I foreseen these events, I would have accepted all the pupils who wanted to be taught by me—but at that time I thought I would be leaving within a week; and now they are all in the countryside.—The Portrait will follow; if Zetti can't take it, it will come to you by mail coach. Now farewell, best and dearest father. I kiss your hands 1000 times and embrace my dear sister with all my heart and remain Forever your

most obedient son
Wolfgang Amadè Mozart

If Leopold still had any hope of persuading his son to reconsider his petition for discharge (which, in fact, Mozart never received formally), a new confrontation between Count Arco and Mozart put all such hopes to rest. The break between Mozart and Salzburg becomes final with the famous "kick in the ass." The letter shows that Mozart is adamant about the occurrence that finally decided his fate.

To his father, in Salzburg

Vienna, June 9, 1781

Mon trés cher Pére!

Now Count Arco has really done it!—so that's the way to persuade people, draw them closer to you: by refusing to accept a petition because you were born dumb, by not informing your master because you lack the courage to do so and because you love being a pedantic

---

61. Leopold was probably pressing Wolfgang to help him pay off the debts he had incurred during his travels to Mannheim and Paris. Mozart never sent the money.

bureaucrat; for all these reasons you keep a fellow dangling for four weeks and, finally, as this fellow is forced to hand in his petition himself, instead of *at least* granting him access, you throw him out the door and give him a kick in his Behind.—And that's the Count who, according to your last letter, has only my interest at heart,—and that's the court I'm supposed to serve—where a person who wants to submit something in writing, instead of being helped with his petition, is given this kind of treatment? . . . I wrote three Memoranda, submitted them 5 times, and each time they were refused.—I kept them in a safe place, and whoever wants to read them can do so and convince himself that they contain nothing offensive whatsoever.—Finally, when Herr von Kleinmayer returned the Memorandum to me in the evening, for that's his job, and the Archbishop's departure was set for the next day, I was beside myself with anger—I couldn't let him leave like this, for I knew from Arco (at least that's what he told me) that the archbishop was not aware of my Memorandum, so I thought the Archb. could really be angry with me for being here for so long and then wait until the last minute to submit such a petition.—

I therefore drafted a new Memorandum in which I conveyed to him that I had had a Memorandum ready to submit to him for the last 4 weeks, but since I had been put off all this time, I didn't really know why, I was now compelled to hand him the Memorandum myself and, as it were, at the last minute.—Well, with the help of this memorandum I got my discharge from service in the best manner of the world;— for who knows whether it wasn't done by order of the Archbishop?— If so, Herr von Kleinmayer, if he wishes to be still counted as an Honest man, and the Archbishop's servants were witness to the fact that his command was carried out.—now I don't need to send another petition, the whole matter has come to a close. I really don't want to say anymore about the entire affair; and even if the Archb. would now offer me a salary of 1200 gulden, I wouldn't stay after this kind of treatment.—And how easy it would have been to persuade me! But with a little dignity, not with arrogance and rudeness. I sent Count Arco a message saying that *I had nothing to discuss with him;* because of the way he had yelled at me the first time and had treated me like a rogue—which he has no right to do;—and—by god! as I told you already, I wouldn't have gone to see him the last time either if he hadn't given me to understand that he had a letter from you.—Well, it was the last time.—What business is it of his if I want to have my discharge?—if he really thinks well of me, then let him come forth and persuade me with reasons—or let the matter be as it is; but not throw words such as lout and knave at you and then throw you out the door with a kick in the ass; but I keep forgetting that maybe it all happened on highest Princely orders.

Let me be brief in answering your letter; for I'm so tired of the whole thing that I really don't want to hear about it anymore. Considering the *causes* of my quitting, which you know all too well, no father would think of being angry with his son about something like that, rather the opposite, I mean *if he hadn't quit.*—You had even less reason because *you knew it was my desire to leave even without such a cause.*—so—you cannot possibly be serious.—I assume you have to act like this on account of the court.—I beg you, my dearest father, don't crawl too much.—The archbishop cannot really harm you,—if he did!—I almost wished he would—it would really be something—a new scandal that would totally finish him with the emperor.—For the emperor not only can't stand him, he hates him. If you were to come to Vienna after this kind of treatment by the archbishop and tell your story to the emperor, you would receive from him—at least the same salary you were making before—for in such matters the emperor behaves very admirably.[62]— But that you are Comparing me to Mad.^me Lang[63] has caused me much bewilderment and depressed me all day.—This girl lived off her parents when she didn't have any income of her own—but by the time when she was able to show some gratitude to her parents—NB: her father died Before she had yet earned a penny—she left her poor mother, took off with an actor, married him—and her Mother doesn't get— a penny—from her.[64] Good god!—heaven knows that my only goal is to be of help to you and all of us; do I have to tell you a hundred times that I can be more Useful to you here than in Salzburg.—I beg you, my dearest, most beloved father, don't write this kind of letter to me anymore, I beseech you, because they are of no use, except to fog up my brain and disquiet my heart and spirit.—and I, who am now constant-

---

62. Mozart's claims and assumptions of Joseph II's attitude toward the archbishop of Salzburg are based on hearsay and rumors; they do not seem to have had any basis in fact.

63. Aloysia Lange, née Weber.

64. Joseph Lange, Aloysia's husband, writes in his autobiography that he gave Mrs. Weber an allowance of 700 gulden a year. Mozart's information comes obviously from Mrs. Weber herself, who is playing on his sympathies.

ly called upon to Compose, need a clear head and a peaceful spirit. The emperor is not in town, Count Rosenberg is not in town; but the latter has commissioned Schröder,[65] the celebrated Actor, to look for a good libretto and to give it to me so I can write the music for it. Herr von Zetti was ordered to leave unexpectedly early so that I will have to send the Portrait, the ribbons for my sister, and *the other thing we talked about,* [66] by mail coach a week from tomorrow.

Farewell for now, dearest, most beloved father!—I kiss your hands 1000 times and embrace my dear sister with all my heart and I remain Forever your most obedient son

Wolfgang Amadè Mozart

To his father, in Salzburg

Vienna, June 13, 1781

Mon Trés Cher Pére!

Best of all fathers! how gladly would I continue to sacrifice my best years for you in a place where the pay is so poor;—if only that would be all the evil there is; but poor pay and being subjected to mockery, contempt, and torment—that is truly too much.—For the Archbishop's concert here I composed a Sonata for myself, and a Rondeau each for Brunetti and Ceccarelli, played twice at Each concert and last time, after the program was over, I played for a whole hour variations on a theme given to me by the Archbishop, and I earned so much applause that the Archbishop, if he had the least bit of Humanity in his heart, should have felt great joy; but instead of showing me at least his satisfaction or some kindness—or even nothing at all—he treats me like a street urchin—tells me to my face I should clear out, he could get a hundred others who would serve him better than I;—and why?— because I couldn't leave on *precisely the day* that he had thought best. I had to leave my lodgings, had to live off my own money, and was not at liberty to choose the day of departure that is best for my purse; all this when I wasn't even needed in Salzburg and the whole difference in departure time consisted of two days.— . . .

65. Friedrich Ludwig Schröder, a well-known Shakespearean actor, who at this time played at the Burgtheater in Vienna.
66. The 30 ducats Mozart had promised his father.

It is as if they wanted to get rid of me on purpose; well, if they don't want me, after all, it's my wish as well;—Count Arco could have accepted my petition, or he could have gotten me an audience, or he could have advised me to forward my petition to the archbishop, or he could have persuaded me to leave things as they are and reflect on them, enfin, he could have suggested any number of things—No—he throws me out the door and gives me a kick in the behind.—Well, that means in straightforward German that Salzburg no longer exists for me; except to find a good opportunity to administer to the Herr Count a kick in the ass in return, even if it should happen on a public street. . . .

You need not worry about the salvation of my soul, dearest father!— I know I am still a young man, capable of errors, but it were to be wished—and that's my consolation—that others had erred as little as I.—You may well be believing things about me that are not true;—my main fault is that I *give the appearance* of not always behaving the way I should—and it's not true that I bragged about eating meat on every fast day; what I said was that it was not a big concern of mine, and that I didn't think it was a sin, because I take fasting to mean abstaining, eating less than usual.—I go to Mass every Sunday and holiday and, if I can, on work days as well. . . . Be assured that I am holding fast to my Religion—and if I should Ever have the misfortune of getting on the wrong side of the track, which god may prevent, I shall absolve you, my dearest father, of all responsibility.—I alone would be the villain—to you I owe all the good that has come to me for my earthly and spiritual welfare and salvation.

Now I must close or I will miss the mail coach. I kiss your hands 1000 times and embrace my dear sister with all my heart and remain Forever your most obedient son

Wolfgang Amadè Mozart

The drama about Mozart's discharge had ended. Mozart had won his freedom and remained in Vienna as a freelance pianist and composer. As it turned out, the struggle with the archbishop had been only act 1 in a continuing drama of liberation from Salzburg, specifically Wolfgang's liberation from Leopold Mozart. Act 2 was about to begin, and the new star in the play was Constanze Weber.

Mozart and Constanze

I<small>N THE SUMMER</small> of 1781, two female protagonists, Constanze and Konstanze, vied for Mozart's attention. The Constanze with a *C* was a lively, attractive nineteen-year-old, the younger sister of Mozart's erstwhile beloved Aloysia. Constanze lived with her mother in Vienna at "The Eye of God, 3ʳᵈ floor." The Konstanze with a *K* happened to be the heroine of Mozart's new opera, a German singspiel titled *Die Entführung aus dem Serail* (The Abduction from the Seraglio). A model of virtue and nobility, she would make her debut at the Burgtheater in Vienna on July 16, 1782. It is difficult to say which of the two women received more of Mozart's love and attention between the summers of 1781 and 1782, and in the course of the year, he began to confuse not only the spelling of their names but even, at times, their respective roles in his life. In the end, he rescued Constanze from the tyranny of her mother, just as Belmonte, the hero of his singspiel, rescued Konstanze from Turkish captivity. No wonder that Mozart and his friends spoke with amusement of not one but two abductions occurring in Vienna in the summer of 1782: *The Abduction from the Seraglio* at the Burgtheater and the abduction of Constanze Weber from "The Eye of God, 3ʳᵈ floor."

Mozart had come to Vienna with two things in mind, or perhaps more accurately, two subconscious intentions: he wished to gain his independence from the archbishop of Salzburg, and he wished to establish himself as the premier composer in the German-speaking lands. He succeeded in both endeavors, breaking with the archbishop and taking a giant step toward ultimate recognition by composing *Die Entführung aus dem Serail*.

Die Entführung is sung in German and belongs to the German tradition of the singspiel, the musical play in which, contrary to Italian-style opera, the dialogue is not sung but spoken. The German singspiel tradition had just received a boost by the founding of a German National Theater in Vienna. When the librettist Stephanie the Younger approached Mozart with a German text and suggested that he set it to music for the new German theater, Mozart was enthusiastic and ready. The subject of the play, the rescue of virtuous women from a fate worse than death, was not new for Mozart; he had already begun to compose a similar German-language drama, Zaide, when his work was interrupted by the Idomeneo commission. A plot featuring virtuous Christian women in Turkish captivity and magnanimous Turkish potentates who would unexpectedly set their captives free was popular fare in European theaters at the time. And for Mozart, Die Entführung was a continuation of his earlier project under a different title. Zaide remained a fragment, but Die Entführung became a huge success, in fact, it became Mozart's most popular theater piece during his lifetime. However, it was not only the themes of human virtue, tolerance, and forgiveness that brought the Viennese in droves to the Burgtheater, it was also Mozart's new and rich singspiel music, his orchestration, his "Turkish" effects (cymbals, triangles, piccolos), and, not least, his creation of Osmin, the grumpy overseer of Pasha Selim's estates. Inspired by the powerful voice of Johann Ludwig Fischer, a Viennese basso profundo, Mozart created one of the great comic characters in German theater and a challenging singing role for a bass. "My opera was given yesterday with big applause for the third time," he wrote to his father on July 27, 1782; "in spite of the terrible summer heat, the theater was packed." Then he added wistfully, "it really feels good to hear this kind of applause."

Die Entführung was not the only significant work to emanate from Mozart's first year in Vienna. We have, in addition, his six Piano and Violin Sonatas, K. 296 and K. 376–380, the Serenade for Winds in E-flat, K. 375, the Symphony no. 35 ("Haffner"), K. 385, and the Fantasy and Fugue in C major, K. 394. Even the Rondo for Piano and Orchestra, K. 382, written as a new finale for his Piano Concerto in D major, K. 175, may be mentioned here. Critics have called it a poor substitute for the more "learned" original allegro, but Mozart himself was very fond of the sprightly little rondo and called it "a gem." The Viennese loved it too. Whenever he performed his D-major Concerto, which he did often, he invariably had to repeat the new finale. With its energetic, humorous, and convivial spirit, Mozart had apparently struck a chord with the Viennese. There is no question, however, that *Die Entführung* is the great achievement of Mozart's early Viennese period. Critics, musicians, poets—Johann Wolfgang Goethe among them—understood that Mozart had redefined the German singspiel, that he had made it richer in music and given it more depth by mixing comedy and pathos. His own letters ring with pride and enthusiasm about his work, about the changes he wrought in Stephanie's text, about the right nunaces in expressing his characters' emotions, about the overall balance of text and music. Only his encounter with the fugues of Bach and Handel at the home of Baron van Swieten was as rich a source of discovery and enjoyment for him as was his own marvelous creativity.

The letters of 1781–82 are, as we find so often in Mozart's correspondence, a mixture of personal woes and professional news. Yet some of the details Mozart shares with his father about his compositions are exceptional if not amazing. Although he mockingly calls his enthusiastic reports a lot of "chatter," the fact remains that Mozart allowed another rare and precious glance into his workshop and his work in progress. He would never be so frank and open about his work again. Leopold, angered by his son's break with Salzburg and his renewed association with the Weber family, showed his hurt by remaining cool toward Mozart's growing success in Vienna. Mozart, deeply disappointed by his father's lack of support, fell more and more silent about the details of his work. But he stayed on course: Mozart and Konstanze premiered in July 1782; Mozart and Constanze were married in August of the same year.

📖 *As Mozart was trying to establish himself as a professional musician in Vienna, he found that opportunities for freelancing were not as plentiful as he had imagined. At this point, he had to survive on the income from only one student.*

To his father, in Salzburg

Vienna, June 16, 1781

Mon Trés cher Pére!

Tomorrow the Portrait and the Ribbons for my sister will go under sail. I don't know whether the Ribbons will be to her taste—but I can assure her that here they are the latest fashion: if she wants more of them, or perhaps some plain, unpainted ones, she should let me know; anyway, if there is anything else she thinks would be nice to have from Vienna, all she has to do is write to me. . . .

Now I can finally write something about Vienna again; until now I always had to fill my letters with that shitty business.[1]—God be praised that it is over.—The present season is the worst for anyone who wants to earn any kind of money; you certainly know all about that; the most distinguished families are away in the countryside, all I can do right now is to prepare ahead for the winter season when there will be less time for composing.—As soon as the Sonatas are finished,[2] I shall look for a small Italian Cantata and set it to music;[3] I will present it in a theater during Advent; for my benefit, of course. I have a little trick up my sleeve; doing it this way I can perform it twice and also get paid twice because when I give it the second time I'll also play something on the pianoforte.—At the moment I have only one pupil, Countess Rumbeck, the cousin of Kobenzl. Of course, I could have more students if I would lower my fee.—but if you do you immediately lose your reputation—my fee is 6 ducats for 12 lessons; and even then I make it clear to them that I am doing it as a favor.—I would rather have only 3 pupils who pay me well than 6 who pay poorly.—The income from this one pupil is just enough for me *to get by*; it's enough for the time being.—I am writing this only so you don't think that I am being selfish when I'm sending you only 30 ducats. Believe me, I would not hesitate to send you whatever I have, if only I had anything!—but it will come in time; however, one cannot let people know how one really stands.

Now a word about the theater. I believe I wrote to you not so long ago that Count Rosenberg, before leaving, asked Schröder to find a libretto for me; well, it has been found and Stephani the Younger, who is manager of the Opera, has it in his hands. . . . I'm not at all worried about the success of an opera as long as the libretto is good.—Do you really think I would write an Opera Comique as if it were an opera Seria?—There shouldn't be anything frivolous in an opera Seria, but much that is learned and rational, just as there shouldn't be anything

1. I.e., the affair with the archbishop.
2. Sonatas for Piano and Violin, K. 296, 376-380.
3. Nothing is known about such a piece.

serious in an opera Buffa, but all the more things that are frivolous and funny.

I can't help it if people also want some comic Musick in an opera Seria;—but here they do differentiate quite well in such matters.

At any rate, it's my perception that Hanswurst[4] has not yet been eradicated in Musick; and in this regard the French are right.— . . .

Adieu for now, farewell; I kiss your hands 1000 times and embrace my sister with all my heart and remain Forever your

most obedient son
W. A. Mzt.

To his father, in Salzburg

Vienna, June 20, 1781

Mon trés cher Pére!

I have received your package safely and hope you got the Portrait and the Ribbons in the meantime.—I don't know why you didn't pack everything together into one trunk or chest; sending things piecemeal means you have to pay for each small item separately, but putting it all together wouldn't cost all that much.—I can well believe that those petty court bureaucrats look at you with disdain; but why even bother to acknowledge such Worthless Rabble; the more hostile they act toward you, the more contemptuous and haughty you must behave toward them. And as far as Arco is concerned, all I need to do is consult my own mind and heart; I don't need a lady or personage of rank to tell me what's right or wrong, and not to do too much or too little;—it is the heart that enobles man; and though I am not a count, I have probably more Honor in me than many a count; and whether I am dealing with a lackey or a count, if he insults me, he is a scoundrel.—I shall make it clear to him from the beginning how badly and miserably he has handled this matter;—but in the end I may have to make sure in writing that he understands he can still expect a kick in the ass and a couple of slaps in his face from me.—When someone insults me, I have to avenge myself; if I don't do more to him than he did to me, then it will only be retaliation and not punishment; in fact, I would be putting myself

4. Hanswurst (Jack Sausage) is the German-Austrian version of Jack Pudding or Harlequin, i.e., a funny, bawdy character in a comedy. The German literary critic Johann Christoph Gottsched was trying to eradicate Hanswurst from the German stage, but he still flourished in Vienna.

on the same level with him, and I am too proud to compare myself to such an oaf.

From now on I shall write to you but once a week, unless something urgent comes up because I am terribly busy at the moment. I will close now because I still have to complete some variations for my pupil. I kiss your hands 1000 times and embrace my sister with all my heart and I remain Forever[5]

To his father, in Salzburg

Vienna, June 27, 1781

Mon trés cher Pére!

. . . I spend almost every day after lunch at the house of Herr von Auerhammer.—The young lady of the house is hideously ugly![6]—her playing, however, is enchanting, even though she lacks that true, delicate touch, that singing quality in the Cantabile; she plucks everything apart.—She let me in on a plan that she keeps a secret, namely that she wants to study hard for 2 or 3 more years and then go to Paris and make piano playing her profession.—She says: *I am not beautiful,* o contraire, I am ugly; and I don't want to marry some petty clerk in the chancellery with a salary of 300 or 400 gulden;[7] and I don't have a chance of getting anyone else; so I'd rather stay single and make a living off my talent. And she is right; she asked me to help her realize her plan;—but she doesn't want to tell anyone before the time is right. I will send you the Opera as soon as possible;[8] Countess Thun still has it, and she is at her country estate right now.—Please have the Sonata à quatre mains in B and the 2 Concertos for 2 Pianos[9] copied out and sent to me as soon as possible.—I would also like to have my Masses.[10]

Gluck[11] has suffered a stroke, and they say his condition is not very good.—Tell me, is it true that Beckè was almost bitten to death by a dog in Munich?—I must close now because I am invited to lunch at the

5. In the autograph, the signature is cut off.
6. Mozart's pupil Josepha Auernhammer. Mozart consistently misspells her name.
7. In the end, that is precisely what Josepha Auernhammer did: she married a city clerk.
8. *Idomeneo.*
9. Piano Sonata for Four Hands in B-flat major, K. 358. The two concertos are K. 365 and K. 242; the latter, the Triple Concerto ("Lodron"), was arranged as a double concerto by Mozart himself.
10. Probably K. 275, 317, and 337.
11. Christoph Willibald Gluck.

Auerhammers. Adieu. I kiss your hands 1000 times and embrace my sister with all my heart and remain Forever your

most obedient son
Wolfg. Amadé Mozart

Madame Bernaskoni[12] is here; she is
getting a salary of 500 ducats
because she sings all her arias
a fraction higher than anyone else.
It's true art because she manages to keep in tune.
Now she said she would sing
a ¼ tone higher still,
but she wants twice the money. *adieu.*

In spite of Mozart's criticism of her playing, "she plucks everything apart," and in spite of his uncharitable description of her physical appearance, Mozart recognized the pianistic talents of Josepha Auernhammer and asked his father to send him pieces for four hands so that he, Mozart, could perform with her. He also dedicated the six Sonatas for Piano and Violin, K. 296 and 376–380, to her; they are known as the "Auernhammer" sonatas.

Mozart had always been fond of his sister. In earlier years his letters to Nannerl were full of verbal fun and bathroom humor. Here, in his first letter to Nannerl from Vienna, he makes a noticeable effort to be sweet, thoughtful, and civilized—to show that he has grown up.

To his sister, in Salzburg

Vienna, July 4, 1781

Ma très chère Soeur!

I am so glad that the Ribbons were to your liking; as far as the price of both the painted and the unpainted Ribbons is concerned, let me find out; I don't know it offhand, because Frau von Auerhammer, who was kind enough to get them for me, would not let me pay for them and

12. Antonia Bernasconi had sung in Mozart's first opera, *Mitridate.*

instead asked me to send you her best regards—even though she doesn't know you personally; she wants you to know that she would be very happy to do a Favor for you anytime; I have already given her your kind regards in return. Dearest Sister! I already wrote to our dear father the other day that—if there is anything you would like to have from Vienna, whatever it may be, I would be very happy to be of service; I'm repeating now my offer with the added message that I would be very hurt if I found out that you had asked someone else in Vienna to send you something. I am thoroughly pleased that you are well; I am, God be Praised and Thanked, healthy and happy as well.—My sole entertainment here is the Theater; I so wished you could come here and see a tragedy! I don't know of any other theater where the various types of plays are done so *superbly*; each individual role—even the smallest, least important one is done well and has an understudy. Now I would like to know how things stand with you and and a certain good friend?[13] Please write me about it! Or do I no longer have your confidence in such matters? In any case, please write to me more often, only, of course, if you have nothing better to do; I would love to get some news once in a while, and you are, after all, the living chronicle of Salzburg because you record everything that happens, so why don't you write it down twice just as a favor to me—but you must not get angry if at times I have to let you wait a bit for an answer.

As regards new compositions for the Clavier, let me tell you that 4 sonatas are ready to be engraved; the sonatas in C and B are among them, new are only the other two. Then I have written 3 arias with variations,[14] which I could send you, of course; but it's not worth the trouble now, I'd rather wait until I have more things to send. I guess the Shooting Fest will soon be held again?[15] I beg you all *solemniter* to drink a toast to this loyal marksman here. And when it's my turn again to be Master of the Shoot, let me know in time and I will have a target paint-

---

13. Nannerl's friend and suitor was Franz Armand d'Ippold. Leopold was against a marriage because the suitor was not acceptable to him.

14. The Violin Sonatas in C major, K. 296, and in B-flat major, K. 378; the new sonatas are in F major, K. 376, and in G major, K. 379. The three set of variations are 8 Variations (for piano) on "Dieu d'amour," K. 352; 12 Variations (for piano and violin) on "La Bergère Célimène," K. 359; 6 Variations (for piano and violin) on "Hélas, j'ai perdu mon amant," K. 360.

15. Air gun competition (Bölzelschießen).

ed. Now fare well, dearest, most beloved sister, and be assured that I will always be

>your
>true friend and sincere brother
>Wolfgang Amadè Mozart

🐦 *In July 1781, Mozart visited Count Johann Philipp Cobenzl, court vice-chancellor and chancellor of state, at his country estate in the Vienna Woods. Mozart stayed several days and must have been deeply touched by the garden, the pond, and the count's famous grotto, for he does something he does rarely: talk about the natural beauty of his surroundings. The estate still exists and is known today as the Cobenzl.*

To his father, in Salzburg

Reisenberg, July 13, 1781

Mon trés cher Pére!

I can't write much, because Count Kobenzl is about to drive into town, and if I want this letter to be posted right away, I have to send it along with him.—The place I am writing from is called the Reisenberg; it's an hour from Vienna.—I had been here once before and spent the night; but this time I'll be staying several days.—The little house is not much;[16] but the surroundings!—the woods—where he had a grotto built that looks as if it had been done by Nature herself—all of it is Magnificent and so agreeable. I have received your last letter. I've been thinking about moving out of the Weber household for some time now; and I assure you, it will happen. . . . But I won't move until I have found a good, inexpensive, and well-situated place. Even then I'll have to tell the good woman some sort of lie because—I really have no reason for moving.—Herr von Moll[17] has, I don't know why, a vicious tongue, which really surprised me about him;—he said to me that he was hoping I would truly think this thing over and return to Salzburg forthwith because it would be hard for me to find anything here as convenient as in Salzburg;—I was staying on here, he said, mostly for the sake of

---

16. Starting in 1781, the "little house" on the Cobenzl estate was replaced by a castle.
17. Ludwig Gottfried Moll, an official in the service of the archbishop, had spread rumors about Mozart and Constanze in Salzburg.

women. Fräulein von Auerhammer told me all this. But he is getting unexpected responses everywhere;—I can pretty much guess why he's saying these things; he is a strong supporter of Koželuch;[18]—Oh! how simpleminded!— . . .

I must close, the count is about to leave; farewell; I kiss your hands 1000 times and embrace my dear sister with all my heart; I am Forever your

most obedient son
Wolfgang Amadè Mozart

Mozart had barely won his battle with the archbishop when he faced a new crisis: the gossip about him and Constanze Weber. Mozart had been renting a room in the Weber household since the beginning of May, and by now tongues were wagging. The gossip had spread all the way to Salzburg, and Leopold immediately suspected intrigues by the "Weber women," i.e., Constanze and her mother.

To his father, in Salzburg

Vienna, July 25, 1781

Mon trés cher Pére!

Let me say once again that I've had it in mind for some time now to move to another place, but only because people are gossiping—and I'm sorry that I am compelled to do it because of all this foolish chatter, which contains not a single word of truth. I would dearly like to know what kind of joy certain people derive from spreading groundless rumors all day long;—just because I am living with them, people assume I'm marrying the daughter; no one said anything about us being in love, they conveniently skipped that part; their logic is: I take a room in this house, *I get married.*—If I've ever thought about *not* getting married, it's definitely now!—The last thing I wish for is a rich wife, but even if I could make my fortune by marriage right now, I could not oblige, because I have too many other things on my mind.—God has not given me my Talent so that I should hitch it to a woman and waste my Young life in idleness.—I am just beginning to live; am I to bring bitterness into my life through my own doing? I have nothing against

18. Leopold Koželuch was a pianist (later also a music publisher) in Vienna.

the state of matrimony, but at the moment it would be a disaster for me.—Well, there's no other way, even though there is no truth to the matter, I must avoid even the appearance of it;—although the appearance of it is based on nothing more than the fact that I am living there—and people who do not come into the house can't even tell whether I see her as much as I see any other of God's creatures; for the Weber girls[19] rarely go out—and when they do they never go anywhere but the theater, and I never join them, because I'm usually not home by the time the theater starts.—Once or twice we went to the Prater amusement park, but the mother was with us; and as I happened to be at home at that time, I could not refuse their request that I come along—and at that time I hadn't heard any such foolish talk either. I must add here, too, that they let me pay only *my share*.—and since the mother has also heard the gossip,—she also knows it from me—I have to say that she, too, doesn't want us to go out anymore; indeed, she advised me to move somewhere else in order to avoid further annoyance; she says she wouldn't want to be an unwitting cause of my misfortune.—That's really the only reason why I had it in mind for some time now—ever since this gossip arose—to move out—but if the truth be told, I have no real reason to move, only the wagging tongues are providing the reason. If it were not for the gossip, I would probably not move; although I can easily get an even nicer room, I can probably not get the same comfort, nor the same friendly help.—I am not saying that I am unsociable with the mademoiselle in the house, I mean the one I'm supposed to be married to already, I'm not saying I never speak to her—but I am not in love with her.—Yes, I joke around with her and have fun whenever time allows, and that's only in the evening when I'm taking supper at home—because in the morning I stay in my room and write and in the afternoon I am rarely at home and—that's all. If I had to marry every lady with whom I've been joking around, I would easily have collected 200 wives by now.— . . .

Now farewell, dearest and best father!—Believe and trust your son, who has the warmest feelings toward all right-minded people;—so why should he not have the same feelings toward his dear father and sis-

19. In addition to Constanze, two other unmarried Weber daughters were still living with their mother: Josepha, twenty-three, and Sophie, eighteen.

ter?—believe him and trust him more than certain other people—who have nothing better to do than to speak negatively of Honest people.— Adieu for now—I kiss your hands 1000 times and remain Forever your

most obedient son

Wolfgang Amadè Mozart

To his father, in Salzburg

Vienna, August 1, 1781

Mon trés cher Pére!

I picked up the sonatas for four hands right away because Frau von Schmidl lives right across from the Auge Gottes.[20] Should Mad.^{me} Duschek have arrived in Salzburg already, please give her my most cordial regards and ask her whether a gentleman had called on her before she left Prague and brought her a letter from me;—if not, I shall write to him at once so he can forward the letter to Salzburg;—it's Roßi from Munich; he had asked me to help him with a letter of recommendation—he took several very good letters from here with him to Prague.— If my letter contained only his recommendation, I would certainly leave the matter to his convenience, but I also included a request for Mad.^{me} Duscheck to help me with my subscription[21] for the 6 sonatas.—I was especially glad to do this favor for Roßi because he wrote the text for the Cantate I want to offer during Advent for my benefit.

Well, the day before yesterday Stephani the Younger brought me a libretto with the intent that I set it music. I must tell you frankly that, unpleasant as he can be at times to other people, about which I really know nothing, he is a good friend to me.—The libretto is good. The subject is Turkish and the play is entitled: *Bellmont* und *Konstanze* oder *die verführung aus dem Serail.* [22] I am going to write the overture, the first-act chorus, and the final chorus in the style of Turkish Musick. Mad.^{selle} Cavalieri, Mad.^{selle} Teyber, Monsieur Fischer, Monsieur Adamberger,

---

20. Frau von Schmidl, a neighbor, apparently brought the sonatas from Salzburg.

21. Subscriptions were coming into vogue at Mozart's time; they allowed interested participants to acquire copies of a composition (or book) for a prepublication price.

22. The correct title of the libretto is *Belmonte und Constanze, oder Die Entführung aus dem Serail* (Belmonte and Constanze, or The Abduction from the Seraglio). Mozart, however, wrote *verführung* (seduction), instead of *Entführung* (abduction). The error is probably unintentional.

Monsieur Dauer, and Monsieur Walter *will be the singers*.[23] I am so excited about working on this libretto that I have already finished the first aria for Cavalieri and one for Adamberger as well as the trio that will conclude the First Act. Time is short, that's true; the performance is to take place in mid-September;—yet—the circumstances associated with its first performance and, generally speaking, all the other prospects have lifted my spirits so high that I'm now hurrying to my desk with greatest eagerness and remain seated there with the greatest joy in my heart.

The Grand Duke of Russia will be visiting here; and that's why Stephanie asked me whether it was possible to compose the opera in so short a time. Because the Emperor and Count Rosenberg will return to Vienna shortly and the question will come up whether anything new is in the works.—Stephanie will then be able to say with great satisfaction that Umlauf[24] will finish his opera (which he's been working on for a while) and that I am composing a new one specifically for the occasion.—And he will surely count it to my credit that I have undertaken to write the opera just for this purpose in such a short time.—Nobody knows anything about this, except Adamberger and Fischer; Stephanie asked us to keep it quiet because Count Rosenberg has not yet returned, and news of this could lead to a thousand rumors.—Stephanie does not wish to appear too friendly with me, but rather wants to give the impression that he is doing it because Count Rosenberg wants it that way; indeed, it is a fact that Rosenberg had told him before his departure to talk to me about a libretto.

I can't think of anything else to write to you at the moment—I have no other news; the room I'm supposed to be moving into is ready for me;—I'm now going out to rent a piano because unless I get a piano into that room, I can't live there, especially now when I have a lot to write and not a minute to waste.—As it is, I will have to do without a lot of comfort in my new lodgings,—especially regarding meals. When I was very busy with my writing, they would wait with the meal as long as I wanted them to, and I could go on writing *without having to get dressed* and then simply walk through the next door to eat, whether it was at

---

23. The singers mentioned by Mozart are Caterina Cavalieri (Konstanze), Therese Teyber (Blondchen), Johann Ignaz Ludwig Fischer (Osmin), Johann Valentin Adamberger (Belmonte), Johann Ernst Dauer (Pedrillo), and Johann Ignaz Walter (Bassa Selim, a speaking role).
24. Ignaz Umlauf, a Viennese composer of singspiele.

noon or in the evening.—Now, if I don't want to spend money to have my meals brought up to my room, I'll be losing at least an hour just getting dressed, something I usually didn't do until the afternoon, and, in addition, I have to go out—certainly in the evening.—You know that I often write until I feel hungry—and all the good friends where I could go for supper eat at 8 o'clock or half past 8 at the latest.—At the Webers' we never went to table before 10 o'clock in the evening.—Well, adieu for now, I must close and go look for a piano.—Farewell, I kiss your hands 1000 times and embrace my sister with all my heart and remain Forever your

most obedient son
Wolf. Amadè Mozart

P.S. Greetings to all of Salzburg.

To his father, in Salzburg

Vienna, August 8, 1781

Mon trés cher Pére!

I have to write in a hurry because I just finished the Janissary chorus,[25] and it's already past 12 o'clock noon and I promised to drive out to Mingendorf, near Laxenburg, with the Auerhammers and Mad.*selle* Cavalieri; it's where the summer camp is.[26]—Adamberger, Cavalieri, and Fischer are all very happy with their arias.—

Yesterday I had lunch with Countess Thun, and tomorrow I'll be eating there again.—I played for her all the finished pieces.—She said at the end that she would confidently wager her life that what I have done so far will certainly be a success.—but I don't accept *praise or criticism from anyone* in this matter—not until people have heard everything as a *whole*; right now I am simply following *my own feelings*—but you can tell how much she must have been impressed to say something like this.— . . .

---

25. "Janissaries" (Yeni Cheri) were elite troops in the service of the sultan. Here, in act 1, scene 6, they address to their master the rousing chorus: "Singt dem großen Bassa Lieder" (Sing songs to the great Pasha).

26. "Mingendorf" is Münchendorf, a small town south of Laxenburg, where the emperor had his summer retreat.

Farewell for now, I kiss your hands 1000 times and embrace my dear sister with all my heart and remain Forever your

most obedient son
W. A. Mzt

Greetings to the Duschecks.
I hope to see them here. *Adieu.*

🔖 *The letter shows that Mozart had not lost his great narrative talent of earlier years; his description of the "Rat's Nest" and his characterization of Mademoiselle Auernhammer are vivid, visual, and humorous. He also continued to be a target for idle tongues. This time, however, he wanted to be ahead of the game and report to his father before the rumors spread to Salzburg.*

To his father, in Salzburg

Vienna, August 22, 1781

Mon trés cher Pére!

I cannot tell you anything about the address of my new living quarters, because I don't have any yet; but I am negotiating with two lodgings about the rent, and I'm sure I'll take one of the two because I can't stay here any longer; I need to move by next month.—It looks as if Herr von Auerhammer wrote to you—and told you that I had a room already! It's true, I really had found one, but what a place it was! fit for rats and mice but not for humans.—Even at midday, 12 noon, you couldn't see the stairs without a lantern, the room itself was like a closet; to get to it you had to go through the kitchen, and in the door of the room there was a tiny window; they assured me they would put up a little curtain, but they also requested that as soon as I was dressed I should open the curtain again, otherwise they couldn't see a thing in the kitchen or in the next room.—Frau Auerhammer called the place a Rat's Nest; in one word, it was frightful.—What a Splendid apartment it would have been for someone like me who has all sorts of distinguished people visiting him.— . . .

They are by and large good and decent people but nothing more;— they have enough sense to realize how useful I am for their daughter, who, as everybody who heard her play before I came to their house agrees, has changed entirely.—I won't even try to describe the mother;

it's enough if I tell you that at table it is hard to keep from laughing;
basta! you know Frau Adlgasser; well, this piece of humanity is even
worse, for she is stupid, malicious, and slanders people. Now about the
daughter. If a painter wished to portray the devil as lifelike as possible,
he would have to seek out her face;—she is heavy like a peasant wench,
sweats to make you sick, and walks around dressed so scantily that one
can read the message plainly: *I beg you all, look right here!* True, there's plenty to see, enough to strike you blind; but—if one is so unfortunate as
to let one's eyes wander in that direction, one is punished for the rest of
the day—Weinstein[27] might be the only cure!—it's all so horrid, filthy,
and revolting!—Pfui Teufel![28] Well, I already wrote you how she plays
the piano.—and I have told you why she asked me to help her.—Well,
I enjoy doing favors for people, but I don't want to be taken advantage
of.—She is not satisfied with the 2 hours I spend with her every day;
she wants me to sit there all day.—and she is playing up to me! even
more than that; she is in love with me, *sérieusement*—at first I thought it
was a joke, but now I know it for sure;—when I first noticed it—
because she took some liberties—for instance, she reproached me tenderly when I was a bit later than usual, or if I couldn't stay very long,
and more such things;—so, I was compelled, in order to keep her from
making a fool of herself, to tell her the truth tactfully;—but that didn't
work; she only became more smitten with me than ever; I finally adopted a behavior of distant politeness toward her, except when she came
with her stupid talk, at which point I would get rude—with the effect
that she took my hand and said: *dear Mozart, don't be so angry—you may say
what you please, I love you all the same.*—The whole town is full of talk that
we are going to be married. People are wondering why I would take
someone with a face like hers. She told me that whenever people say
such things to her, she just laughs in response; but I also know from
somebody that she had answered yes and had added that we're planning
to go traveling together.—That really got me mad.—So, the other day,
I gave her a piece of my mind—straight out; I told her not to abuse my
kindness.—Now I no longer go there every day, but only every other
day, so this thing will gradually die. She is nothing more than a lovesick fool. Before she even knew me, she said in a theater where she had

27. A substance (tartar emetic) that was used to induce vomiting.
28. *Pfui Teufel* is an expression of extreme disgust; here it might be translated as "shame on her."

heard me play: he is coming to see me tomorrow, and I shall play his variations for him with the very same style and *gusto.*——For that very reason I didn't go to see her, because it was a boastful remark and——she had lied,——I knew nothing about seeing her the next day.——Well, adieu, my paper is full. The first Act of the opera is done. I kiss your hands 1000 times and embrace my dear sister with all my heart and remain Forever your

obed. son
W. A. Mozart

🕮 *In the fall of 1781, Mozart was working hard on his new opera. Although excited and full of ideas, he was also discouraged by all the gossiping and, most of all, his father's lack of support. Thus, only five months after he had written that Vienna was "for my Métier the best place in the world," he was thinking of returning to Paris.*

To his father, in Salzburg

Vienna, September 5, 1781

Mon trés cher Pére!

I am writing to you right now from my *New Room, auf dem Graben,* No. 1175, 4ᵗʰ floor.[29]——From the way you reacted to my last letter, I can see (and I am very sorry about it) that you put more credibility in the gossip and scribblings of others than in me—as if I were an arch-scoundrel or a dummy or both—and that, in fact, you have no confidence in me at all. But I can assure you that this doesn't really bother me—let the people write until their eyes pop out of their heads—and you may applaud them as much as you please,—it will not change me by a hair's breadth, rather I shall remain the same Honest fellow that I've always been.——And I swear that if *you* hadn't insisted that I move to different lodgings, I would'nt have done it.——The whole thing appears to me as if somebody were exchanging his own comfortable traveling carriage for a mail coach.——But not another word on this matter—it's of

---

29. "Auf dem Graben, No. 1175" (no. 17 today), Mozart's new apartment, was within walking distance of the Webers.

no use anyway—because the strange stories that somebody, God only knows who, has put into your head, outweigh all my reasoning.—I only ask you this: when you write to me about something that you find wrong in my behavior or you believe that I could do better in some things—and I reply to you with my own thoughts on the matter,—I always regard it as a matter just between father and son, in other words, something confidential, and not as something that everybody needs to know—therefore, I beg you, just leave things be and don't involve other people, for, by god, I don't want to give anyone else even the smallest account of what I do and what I don't do, even if it were the emperor himself.—Just have some trust in me, for I deserve it.—I have worries and troubles enough just to manage my daily living here; to also have to read unpleasant letters is not a good thing for me.—From the first day I came here I had to live entirely from my *own* resources, from whatever I was able to earn by my own effort;—the others always got their salaries extra—Ceccarelli earned more than I did—but he also managed to spend every penny of it; if I had done the same, I wouldn't have been able to quit my service.—You, my dearest father, have not yet received any money from me, but it's not my fault, it's because of the poor season here at present.—Have patience!—I, too, have to be patient.—I swear by god, I won't forget you!—At the time of my affair with the Archbishop, I asked you to send me some clothes.—I didn't have anything with me, except my black suit;—but the mourning was over, and the weather got warm—still, my clothes didn't come;—so I had to have some made—I couldn't walk around Vienna like a tramp; particularly under these circumstances;—my shirts were pitiful to look at—no servant around here would wear shirts of such coarse linen as I did—and that's certainly the most objectionable thing in a man's appearance;—so there were expenses;—and I had only one pupil, and she was away for 3 weeks—again a considerable loss;—and one can't lower oneself completely, that's a matter of principle here, for one would be ruined forever—whoever is the most *aggressive* gets the preferred treatment.—I see from all your letters that you believe I do nothing but amuse myself;—well, you are very much mistaken;—indeed, I can say truthfully that I enjoy no pleasures here—none at all—save the single one that I am not in Salzburg.—In the winter I hope that everything will go much better—and then, my dearest father, I shall certainly think of you.—If I can see that things are going well, I'll continue my stay here, if not, I have in mind to go straight to Paris.—Please tell me what you think about this.

Farewell for now. I kiss your hands 1000 times and embrace my dear sister with all my heart and remain Forever

your most obedient son
W. A. Mzt

P.S. My greetings to the Duschecks.—Please send me when you can *the aria which I wrote for Madame Baumgarten, the Rondeau I did for Madame Duscheck*—and the one for Ceccarelli.[30]—*Adieu.*

To his father, in Salzburg

Vienna, after September 19 and before September 26, 1781

Mon trés cher Pére!

Forgive me if this time you'll have to pay a little extra for the letter;—I wanted to give you at least some idèe of the First act, so you can conclude what the rest of the opera will be like;—and it couldn't be done with fewer examples.[31] I hope that your dizzy spells will disappear;—also, you gave me quite a scare about my sister because the news of her illness came so unexpectedly;[32] I do hope she is feeling better now.—I kiss her 1000 times and kiss your hands 100 times and remain Forever your

most obedient son
W. A. Mzt.

📧 *On the reverse side of the above letter is the text of Konstanze's aria "Ach, ich liebte" (Ah, I loved), from act 1, scene 7, of* Die Entführung. *The aria is written in Constanze Weber's hand.*

---

30. The aria for Countess Paumgarten is "Misera, dove son!," K. 369; the rondo for Madame Duschek is "Ah, lo previdi," K. 272; the rondo for Ceccarelli is "A questo seno deh vieni," K. 374.
31. Mozart did not send the entire first act, but the first fourteen measures of the overture, Belmonte's first aria, "Hier soll ich dich denn sehen", (So here, then, I am to see you), and parts of Osmin's aria, "Solche hergelauf'ne Laffen" (Such vagabonds, I hate them).
32. In a letter to his sister (September 19, 1781), Mozart talked about Nannerl's frequent illnesses and gave her one single advice on how to cure them: get married!

aria, Costanza

Ah, I loved,
was truly happy,
never Knew the pain of love;
swore true faith
to my beloved,
gave to him my loving heart.
But how quickly joy has vanished,
Separation was my fearful lot;
and my eyes with tears are brimming,
sorrow now rests in my breast.[33]

📖 *Constanze Weber's handwriting on the reverse side of Mozart's note is intriguing proof that they were seeing each other. The question is, did Mozart want to give his father a signal, or did Constanze write it because she was identifying with Konstanze?*

To his father, in Salzburg

Vienna, after September 19 and before September 26, 1781

I am sending you a little Praegusto[34] of the opera because there's nothing New or Important to write at the moment.—The characters are:

Bassa Selim—Herr Jautz	*An Actor,* has nothing to sing
Konstanze, Belmont's beloved	Mad.^{me} Cavalieri
Blonde, Konstanze's maid	Mad.^{lle} Teiber
Belmont	Herr Adamberger
Pedrillo, Belmont's servant and overseer of Bassa Selim's gardens	Herr Dauer
Osmin, steward of Bassa Selim's country house	
A rude fellow	Herr Fischer, *Bass*

33. "Ach, ich liebte/war so glücklig,/kannte nicht der liebe schmerz:/schwur ihm treue/dem geliebten,/gab dahin mein ganzes Herz,/ *doch im Hui* schwand meine freude/Trennung war mein banges loos;/und nun schwimmt mein Aug' in Thränen/kummer ruht in meinem schoos."
34. Preview.

Please send the concertos soon.

🖎 *Mozart called the letter of September 26 "a lot of chatter," but it is a letter of great-*
est significance. First of all, it shows how much Mozart involved himself in the
shaping of an opera text. Second, it contains some of his most significant statements
about composition and musical aesthetics. In describing the compositional structure
of Osmin's first aria, "Solche hergelauf'ne Laffen" (Such vagabonds, I hate them),
he is describing the limitations and balance that he feels music must impose on the
expression of human emotions. Music is to remain calm, orderly, harmonious in
all situations. The language of the letter is convoluted and unwieldy, but its content
is clear: Mozart's "chatter" contains the very essence of what would later be known
as Viennese classicism.

To his father, in Salzburg

Vienna, September 26, 1781

Mon trés cher Pére!

Forgive me for having made you pay more postage the other day!—
however, I didn't have anything important to tell you—so I thought it
would please you if I would give you a bit of an Idée about the opera.—
The original text began with a monologue,[35] but I asked Herr Stephani
to make a little arietta out of it,[36]—and create a Duett instead of the
two[37] prattling with each other after Osmin's little song.[38]—Since we gave
the part of Osmin to Herr Fischer—who has an outstanding bass
voice,—although the Archbishop said to me that he sang too low for a
bass and I assured him that he would sing higher next time—we had to
take advantage of such a man, especially since he is a great favorite with
the public here. In the original text Osmin has only this one little song
to sing, and apart from that he has nothing, except the Trio and the
finale. Well, I gave him an aria in the First Act and will give him one in
the 2nd Act as well.—I described to Stephani exactly what I needed for
the aria;—in fact, I had finished most of the Music already before

---

35. The original text was a play by Christoph Friedrich Bretzner of Leipzig, entitled *Belmonte und Konstanze,*
oder Die Entführung aus dem Serail. Stephanie the Younger based his libretto on Bretzner's play.
36. An arietta is a short, simple aria. Here Mozart is referring to Belmonte's first aria, "Hier soll ich dich
denn sehen?" (So here, then, I am to see you?).
37. Belmonte and Osmin.
38. "Wer ein Liebchen hat gefunden" (If you have found yourself a sweetheart).

Stephani even knew anything about the change.—I have sent you only the beginning and the end of the aria, I think it will prove to be very effective—for Osmin's anger will be rendered comical by the use of Turkish Music.—In composing the aria I made Fischer's beautiful deep tones really glisten, in spite of that Salzburger Midas,[39]—The passage *Therefore, by the beard of the Prophet,* etc.,[40] is, to be sure, in the same tempo, but with quick notes—and as his anger increases more and more, the allegro assai—which comes just when one thinks the aria is over—will produce an excellent Effect because it is in a different tempo and in a different key. A person who gets into such a violent rage transgresses every order, moderation, and limit; he no longer knows himself.—In the same way the Music must no longer know itself—but because passions, violent or not, must never be expressed to the point of disgust, and Music must never offend the ear, even in most horrendous situations, but must always be pleasing, in other words always remain Music, I have not chosen a tone foreign to f, the key of the aria, but one that is friendly to it, not however its nearest relative in D minor, but the more remote A minor.—Now about Bellmont's aria in A Major. "Oh how anxious, oh how passionate!"[41] do you know how I expressed it?—even expressing the loving, throbbing heart?—with two violins playing in octaves.— This is the favorite aria of everyone who has heard it—it's mine too.— And it was written entirely for Adamberger's voice; one can see the trembling—faltering—one can see his heaving breast—which is expressed by a crescendo—one can hear the whispering and the sighing—which is expressed by the first violins with mutes and one flute playing unisono.—

The Janissary Chorus has everything you can desire from a Janissary Chorus, it's short and lively—written entirely for the Viennese.—I sacrificed Konstanze's aria a bit to the agile throat of Mad.^selle Cavalieri— "Separation was my fearful lot;/and my eyes with tears are brimming."[42]—I tried to be as expressive as an Italian Bravura aria will permit.—The *hui*—I changed to *quickly;* so it now reads: *but how quickly joy has vanished,*" etc.[43] I really don't know what our German poets are think-

39. Midas is a mythological king, who had the power of turning everything he touched into gold. Mozart is making a sarcastic remark about the archbishop of Salzburg.
40. "Drum beim Barte des Propheten."
41. "O wie ängstlich, o wie feurig!"
42. "Trennung war mein banges loos, und nun schwimmt mein aug in Thränen."
43. "Doch wie schnell schwand meine freude."

ing of;—if they don't understand anything about theater, particularly opera—at least they shouldn't make people talk as if they were looking at a bunch of pigs—hui Sau![44]

Now for the Terzett! I mean the one at the end of the First Act.— Pedrillo has passed off his master as an architect so that he can have an opportunity to see Konstanze in the garden. Bassa Selim has taken him into his services.—Osmin, who is the overseer and doesn't know anything about this—he is also rude and boorish and an arch-enemy of all foreigners—won't let them come into the garden. The first part is very short—and because the text lent itself to it, the three-voice piece I wrote came out pretty well; then comes a pianissimo in the major key that has to go very fast—but at the end it will become very noisy—and that's really what you need for the end of an act—the noisier, the better;—the shorter, the better—so the audience won't cool off in its applause.—

I sent you only 14 measures of the overture,—which is fairly short— and alternates between forte and piano; each forte produces some Turkish music and keeps modulating in this manner throughout—I venture to say you cannot fall asleep while it plays, even if you haven't slept all night.—But now I have a real problem—I finished the First Act 3 weeks ago;—one aria in the 2nd Act and the drinking duet, per li Sig.n vieneri,[45] which is a sort of Turkish tattoo, is also completed;—but I can't do anything else right now, because the whole story is being reworked—and it is done at my insistence. I had planned a charming quintet or finale at the beginning of the third Act—but now I would rather have it at the end of the 2nd Act; but in order to make that work, we have to really change things around, even come up with a whole new story line—and Stephani has more work right now than he can handle; so I'll have to be patient a bit;—everyone is down on Stephani—it's possible that to me, too, he is only nice to my face—but he is doing the libretto for me—and he is doing it the way I want it—exactly—and, by god, I can't ask for anything more!—Well now, what a lot of chatter about my opera; but it's good to do that once in a while.—Please send me the March I mentioned the other day.—Gylofsky tells me that Herr Daubrawaick will soon come this way.—Fräulein von Auerhammer and

44. "Hui Sau!" is an expression for herding pigs, e.g., "Get a move on, pigs!"
45. "For the Viennese gents."

I are still eagerly awaiting the 2 double Concertos—I hope we shall not be waiting in vain like the Jews for their Messiah.—Adieu for now—farewell, I kiss your hands 1000 times and I embrace my sister, whose health I hope has been improving, with all my heart and remain Forever

your most obedient son
W. A. Mozart

🐚 *"In an opera the Poesie must always be the obedient daughter of Music," is one of the most frequently quoted statements from Mozart's correspondence. Again, Mozart was almost embarrassed about discussing issues of such weight and called it "silly stuff." It is important to keep in mind, however, that Mozart did not claim absolute musical superiority in the relationship of words and music; rather, he argued that music is the primary element in such a relationship. Some of the arias in* Die Entführung, *especially those of Osmin and Belmonte, are perfect examples of the creative symbiosis between words and music that he had in mind.*

To his father, in Salzburg

Vienna, October 13, 1781

Mon trés cher Pére!

I thank you, as does Fräulein von Auerhammer, for sending the Concertos.—Monsieur Marchal brought young Herr von Mayern to my place yesterday morning, and in the afternoon I drove out to fetch my things.[46]—Monsieur Marchal hopes to become a tutor at the house of Count Jean Esterhatzy.[47] Count Kobenzel gave him a written recommendation for the count;—he said to me: J'ai donnè une lettre à Monsieur votre protegè.[48]—Then, when he saw Marchal again later, he said to him: d'abord que J'aurai de reponse, Je le dirai à M.ʳ Mozart votre protecteur.[49]—

Now to the text of the opera.—As far as Stephani's work is concerned, you are quite right, indeed.—Yet, the Poesie is totally in tune with the character of this stupid, coarse, and malicious Osmin.—and I

---

46. The "things" Mozart is referring to are probably musical scores and other matters brought by Monsieur Marchal, who is not otherwise identified, from Salzburg.
47. Count Johann Nepomuk Esterházy was a music lover and master of a Freemasonic lodge in Vienna.
48. "I gave a letter to the gentleman, your protégé."
49. "As soon as I have an answer, I will let your protector, Monsieur Mozart, know."

am well aware that the kind of verse used here is not the best—but it agrees so completely with the musical ideas that had been wandering around my head, even before I had seen the text, so I couldn't help liking it;—and I'm willing to bet that when it is performed, nothing will be found inadequate. As far as the Poesie of the original play is concerned, I cannot say anything against it either. Belmont's aria, "Oh, how anxious," etc., could almost not have been written any better for the music.—Konstanze's aria is not bad either, especially the first part, except for the *hui* and "sorrow now rests in my breast,"[50]—for you cannot say sorrow "rests."—I don't know, but it seems to me—that in an opera the Poesie must always be the obedient daughter of the Music.— Why are Italian comic operas so popular everywhere?—in spite of their wretched texts!—even in Paris—where I saw it myself;—because the Music reigns supreme—which makes one forget everything else.—and an opera that is well designed must, therefore, please all the more; where words are written expressly for the Music and not merely to suit some miserable rhyme here and there; god knows, they contribute nothing, no matter what they offer, to the success of a theatrical performance, but they can certainly do a lot of harm; I'm talking about creating words— or entire strophes—which ruin the composer's entire concept.—Verses are probably the most indispensable element for music—but rhymes— created solely for the sake of rhyming—are the most detrimental.— Those gentlemen who work in such a pedantic fashion will always go under, together with their music.—

It is so much better if a good composer, who understands something about the stage and can make a suggestion here and there, is able to team up with an intelligent Poet and create a true Phoenix.—In such a case one need not worry about the applause even of the ignorant!— The Poets seem to me almost like trumpeters with their professional tricks!—if we composers always just follow our rules, which were quite useful in years past when one didn't know any better, we would come up with a kind of music that is just as useless as their librettos.—

Now, it seem to me that I have been chattering enough silly stuff; so let me inquire quickly about things closest to my heart, I mean your health, my dearest father!—in my last letter I recommended for your

---

50. "Kummer ruht in meinem schoos"; the verb *ruht* (rests), which Mozart objects to here, did remain in the text; instead of removing the word, he chose to show the restlessness in his music.

dizzy spells two kinds of remedies that, if you are not familiar with them, may have sounded not quite right to you.—But I had been assured that they will show good results and the pleasure of knowing that you might get well added a certain credence and certainty to these assurances so that I could not refrain from suggesting this medicine to you, together with my sincere wish that perhaps you won't need it anymore—but if you do need it, I hope it will help you recover completely.—And I hope that my sister, too, will get better day by day.—I kiss your hands 1000 times my most beloved, dearest father, and I remain your most obedient son.

W. A. Mozart

The following letter is Mozart's last to his cousin, Maria Anna Thekla, in Augsburg. His wish that their correspondence would start up again did not come true. Obviously, the cousin had warned him of the rumors circulating about him and Constanze Weber; they had spread even to Augsburg. Mozart's reply is warm and friendly but devoid of any extravagant language that was so characteristic of his earlier letters to Bäsle.

To Maria Anna Thekla Mozart, in Augsburg

Vienna, October 23, 1781

Ma très chère Cousine!

I've been eagerly awaiting a letter from you, dearest cousin, for quite some time now;—and I wondered what you would say in it! Well, you said just what I had imagined you would say.—If I had allowed 3 months to go by, I would not have written anymore—even if an executioner, with his sword drawn, had stood right behind me;—because I wouldn't have known: how, when, where, why, and what?—so there was no choice, I had to wait for your letter.—

In the meantime, as you probably know, a number of significant changes have occurred in my life that have given me a lot to think about but also caused me annoyance, vexation, worry, and a troubled mind, all of which can serve as an excuse for my long silence.—As for all the other things, let me say that the gossip that people like to circulate here about me is in part true and in part—false; I can't say anything more about it at the moment; but, let me add for your peace of mind that I do nothing—without a reason—and in fact—without a well-founded reason.—If you had shown me more friendship and trust and had turned directly to me rather than to others—I mean!—but quiet!—if you had turned directly to me, you would probably know more than everyone else—and, if it were possible, more than I know myself!— However—Oh, I must not forget—dearest and best cousin, would you please be so kind and take the enclosed letter to Herr Stein;[51]—and ask him to give me an immediate answer—or at least give you a message that you can write to me.—because I hope, dear Bäsle, that our Correspondence is really just beginning now!—I only worry that the letters will be too expensive for you!—If you should honor me with a reply, as I hope you will, please be so kind and address your letter just as you did with your last one—that is, *auf dem Peter, im auge Gottes, im 2ten Stock*; I don't actually live there anymore, but this address is so well known at the post office that if a letter is addressed to me at my new lodging, it gets delayed by one or two days.—Farewell for now, dearest and best cousin! and keep me in your friendship, which is so dear to me; you can always be sure of mine; I remain Forever

> Ma trés chere Cousine,
> your sincere cousin and friend,
> Wolfgang Amadè Mozart

To his father, in Salzburg

Vienna, November 3, 1781

Mon trés cher Pére!

Forgive me for not having acknowledged at last post day the receipt of the cadenzas,[52] for which I thank you most sincerely now.—It happened to be my Name Day[53]—so in the morning I did my Prayers and then, just as I was about to write to you, a whole bunch of well-wishers invaded my room—then at 12 noon I took a carriage out to Leopoldstadt to visit Baroness Waldstädten[54]—where I spent the rest of my Name Day. At night, at 11 o'clock, I was treated to a serenade of 2 clarinets, 2 horns, and 2 bassoons—which as it so happens was my own

---

51. Mozart's letter contained an order for a piano from Andreas Stein in Augsburg for Count Czernin zu Chudeniz.
52. Probably the cadenzas for the Double Piano Concerto, K. 365.
53. Mozart's name day was October 31.
54. Baroness Martha Elisabeth von Waldstätten. The baroness, an excellent pianist, became one of Mozart's friends and patrons.

composition.[55]—I had composed it for St. Theresia's Day—for the sister of Frau von Hickl, or the sister-in-law of the court painter Herr von Hickel, at whose house it was actually performed for the first time.— The 6 gentlemen who performed it are poor devils who, however, played quite well together, particularly the first clarinetist and the two horn players.—The main reason why I had written the serenade was to give Herr von Strack,[56] who visits there daily, a chance to hear something that I had composed; for that very reason I had put a little extra care into the composition;—and indeed, it was very much applauded.— During St. Theresia's night it was performed at three different locations—they had no sooner finished playing in one place than they were asked to play it somewhere else—and for money, too. At any rate, these night musicians had asked for the doors to be opened and, after positioning themselves in the courtyard, they surprised me, just as I was getting undressed, most agreeably with the opening chord of E-flat. . . .

It would all be just perfect if my opera were finished now; for Umlauf cannot produce his opera right now, because Mad.[me] Weiss and Mad.[selle] Schindler are not well. I'm about to go and see Stephani because he sent word, at last, that he has something ready for me.—

There's nothing new to tell you—after all, small things cannot possibly interest you, and big things you probably know just as quickly as we know them in Vienna.—That there is a Dauphin now[57]—is certainly a small thing—at least for the time being—until he grows to be a big thing.[58] I am writing this only so that the Duc d'Artois will not have the honor of being the only one to come up with a Bon Mot; he said once to the queen, when she was complaining during her pregnancy that the Dauphin was making things difficult for her: il me donne des grands Coups de pied au ventre—to which the Duc replied: o Madame, laißéz le venir dehors, qu'il me donnera des grands coups de pied au cul.[59]—

On the day this news arrived in Vienna, all theaters and spectacles were free—and now it's three—so I must hurry off to Stephani—oth-

---

55. Serenade for Winds in E-flat, K. 375.
56. Johann Kilian Strack, Emperor Joseph's personal valet.
57. Marie Antoinette, the queen of France and daughter of Maria Theresa, had given birth to Louis-Joseph-Xavier-François on October 22, 1781.
58. Mozart uses the word *großheit* (bigness); he must have created it because the word does not exist in German.
59. "He is giving me kicks in the stomach" . . . "Oh, Madame, let him come out so that he can give me some kicks in the rear."

erwise I'll miss him—and have to wait even longer.—I hope you'll get better every day, I wish the same for my dear sister, whom I embrace with all my heart.—Farewell, I kiss your hands 1000 times and remain Forever your

most obedient son
W. A. Mozart

📧 *Mozart was obviously very pleased that he was treated to a little night music on his name day, especially since it was his own composition. Writing this to Leopold was a subtle way of showing his father that somebody in Vienna appreciated him and his music.*

To his father, in Salzburg

Vienna, November 24, 1781

Mon trés cher Pére!

I happened to be playing in a concert at the Auernhammers yesterday when Ceccarelli delivered your letter; as he did not find me at home, he left it with the Webers, who then sent it over to me. Countess Thun was at the concert—I had invited her—and Baron van Suiten, Baron Godenus, the wealthy converted Jew Wetzlar,[60] Count Firmian, and Herr von Daubrawaick with his son.—We played the Concerto à Due, and a Sonata for two that I had composed specifically for the occasion and that was very well received.[61] I will send you the sonata with Herr von Daubrawaick, who told me that he is proud to have it traveling in his suitcase; actually it was the son who said that, a Salzburger, nota bene. His father said to me, just before leaving, in a loud voice: I am proud to be your Landsman—you bring much honor to Salzburg.—I hope the times will change so that you will come back;—and then we certainly won't let you go again.—I said in reply: My fatherland will always have the first claim on me.— . . .

The Bigwig, the Grand Duke, has arrived.[62] Tomorrow they are going to give Alceste in Italian at Schönbrunn Castle;[63] there will also

---

60. Karl Abraham Wetzlar von Plankenstern; his son Raimund would be Mozart's landlord a year later.
61. Probably the Sonata in D major for Two Pianos, K. 448.
62. Grand Duke Paul Petrovich of Russia, later Czar Paul I, who was assassinated in 1801.
63. *Alceste* by Christoph Willibald Gluck was performed on December 3 at Schönbrunn, the summer residence of the Habsburgs.

be a free public ball.—I have been looking around for some popular Russian songs, so I could play variations on them.

My sonatas were published at last;[64] I will send them to you at the next best opportunity.

No doubt Ceccarelli will want to give a concert with me. But I don't think I want to do one with him, because I don't really like sharing this sort of thing.—All I can do is let him sing in my concert that I'm planning for the Lenten season, and—then play gratis for him in his concert.—

I must close, for I have an appointment with Frau von Trattner.[65] I'll write to my dear sister, whom I kiss with all my heart, in the next few days; and I kiss your hands, dearest and best father, 100,000 times and remain Forever your

most obedient son
W. A. Mozart

After many denials and evasive answers, Mozart finally came out with the news that he wanted to get married—to Constanze Weber. He knew how his father felt about the "Weber women," so his letter is carefully staged with prologue, theatrical high point, and epilogue. The letter, a testimony to Mozart's dramatic talent, left the intended audience, Leopold and Nannerl, unimpressed.

To his father, in Salzburg

Vienna, December 15, 1781

Mon trés cher Pére!

Just this moment I received your letter of the 12th—Herr von Daubrawaick is bringing you this letter, along with the watch, the Munich opera, the 6 engraved sonatas, the sonata for two pianos,[66] and the cadenzas.—As to the Princess of Würtenberg and my hopes to be appointed as her teacher, well, that's all decided now. The emperor killed it for me, for the only one who counts in his eyes is Salieri.[67] Archduke Maximilian had suggested *Me* to her;—she told him that if

---

64. The six Sonatas for Violin and Piano, K. 296 and K. 376–380, published by Artaria & Co.
65. Maria Theresia von Trattner became one of Mozart's pupils.
66. *Idomeneo;* K. 296, 376-380; and K. 448.
67. Antonio Salieri, court composer and conductor of the court orchestra.

she could have had her choice, she would have never taken anyone but me; but the emperor had suggested Salieri to her—because of her singing. She said she was very sorry about it all; what you wrote about the House of Würtenberg in relation to you, that is information I might possibly find useful some day.—

Dearest father, you are asking me to give you an explanation of the words I wrote to you at the end of my last letter![68] Oh, how happy I would have been to open my heart to you long ago; but the fear of reproaches you might have made to me, namely *that I was thinking of such a things at the wrong time,* kept me from telling you—although there can never be a wrong time for thinking.—It has become my endeavor in the meantime to secure a small but *sure* income—which, together with what opportunity might provide, will allow me to live here reasonably well—and then—well, get married!—you are taken aback by this thought?—I beg you, dearest and best father, listen to me!—I have had to reveal my inner concerns to you, now you must permit me to reveal my reasons for them as well, my, indeed, well-founded reasons. The voice of nature speaks in me as loud as in any man, louder perhaps than in some big, robust brute of a fellow. It's impossible for me to live as most young men live nowadays.—First of all, I have too much Religion in me, second, I have too much love for my neighbor and too great a sense of decency that I could seduce an innocent girl, and third, I have too great a horror and disgust, dread and fear of diseases, in fact, I like my health too much to play around with whores; I swear that I never had anything to do with a woman of that sort;—if it had happened, I would not have kept it from you, for to err is Natural for a human being, and to err *once* would only show a moment of weakness,—although I dare not say that I could have kept it to just one time if I had erred once in such a matter. And for the life of me, this is the honest truth. No matter how strong such a drive is in me, it is not strong enough to tempt me. As my personal disposition is more inclined toward a quiet and domestic life than toward noise and excitement—and as I never had to attend to any of my daily needs, such as linen, clothes, etc., from my very youth—I cannot think of anything more essential to me than a wife.—I can assure you that I often spend money needlessly because I don't take care of my

---

68. Mozart had written, "I therefore was unable to fulfill all your wishes in the manner you had expected of me." He was alluding to his marriage plans, and Leopold picked up on it immediately.

things;—I am completely convinced that I can manage better with a wife, even with just the income I have now.—And think of all the unnecessary expenses that can be avoided?—of course, other expenses take their place, but one is aware of them, one can plan ahead, in one word: one can lead an orderly life.—In my eyes, an unmarried person lives only half a life,—at any rate, that's what my eyes are telling me, I can't help it.—I have thought about it and reflected on it time and time again—but I always come back to the same conclusion.

Well now, and who is the object of my love?—Don't be upset by that either, I beg you,—surely not one of the Webers?—Yes, one of the Webers—but not Josepha—not Sophie—it is Constanza, the Middle one.—Never have I seen, in any family, such differences in temperament.—The oldest is a lazy, coarse, deceitful person, not to be trusted.—Mad.^me Lange is a false, malicious person, and a Coquette.—The Youngest—well, she is too young to be anything in particular;—she is not much more than a good-natured, but all too frivolous, young thing! May god protect her from evil.—The Middle one, however, I mean my good, dear Konstanze,[69] she is the Martyr of the family, and probably because of it the most kindhearted, the most skilled, in one word, the best of them all.—She takes care of everything in the household—but still she can't do anything right in the opinion of the others. Oh, dearest father, I could fill pages with my description of all the stormy scenes that have happened in that house on account of the two of us; if you really want to know, I'll tell you everything in my next letter. But before I leave you alone with my chatter, I must make you better acquainted with the character of my beloved Konstanze;—she is not ugly, but also not really beautiful;—her whole beauty consists of two little black eyes and a graceful figure. She has no great wit but enough common sense to fulfill her duties as a wife and mother. She is not extravagant in her appearance, rumors to that effect are totally false;—to the contrary, she is in the habit of dressing very simply—because what little her mother has been able to do for her children, she has done for the other two girls, never anything for her.—It's perfectly true that she would like to dress attractively and cleanly but not necessarily in the latest fashion.— And most of the things a woman needs, she can make herself; indeed,

---

69. Mozart varied his spelling of Constanze; at first he wrote it with a *C*, later increasingly with a *K*.

she does her own hair every day;—she knows all about householding and has the kindest heart in the world—I love her and she loves me with all her heart—now tell me whether I could wish for a better wife?—

I must tell you also that I was not in love with her at the time I resigned my service—my love for her was born through her tender care and helpfulness when I lived at their house.—

So, as I said, I wish for nothing more than to have a small but secure income, for which I have, thank god, some tangible hopes; after that I shall never stop entreating you that I may rescue this poor girl—and me along with her—and, if I may say so, make us all happy—for surely you are happy when I am happy?—and half of my *secure* income will be for you to enjoy, my dearest father!—Now I have opened my heart to you and explained the words in my letter.—But now I am asking you to explain some words from your last letter to me: "you probably will not believe that I know *of a proposal that was made to you* and to which *you did not respond*, at the time I found out about it";—I don't understand one word of this. I know of no proposal.—Please take pity on your son! I kiss your hands 1000 times and remain Forever yours,

your most obedient son
W. A. Mozart

For all of Mozart's explanations and assurances about the Weber women and the goings-on in the Weber household, Leopold remained skeptical. And although Constanze seems to have shown courage and character in this domestic drama, Leopold was not convinced of her sincerity either. When he found out that Mozart had been made to sign a marriage contract, he felt that Constanze's mother and her guardian should be put in irons for having coerced his son into marriage.

To his father, in Salzburg

Vienna, December 22, 1781

Mon trés cher Pére!

I am still full of gall and fury about the shameful lies of that arch-scoundrel Winter[70]—yet I feel calm and unperturbed because they don't

---

70. Peter von Winter, violinist, composer, and, later, Kapellmeister. He was in Vienna in 1781, studying with Salieri, and evidently reported to Leopold Mozart all the rumors concerning Wolfgang and Constanze that were floating around.

really touch me—and I am happy and content to have such a worthy, dearest and very best father!—But I never expected anything else given your sound judgment and your love and affection for me.—You will have received by now my most recent letter containing my declaration of love and my intentions for the future,—and you will have seen from it that I shall not be so foolish, in my 26th year of life, as to marry without some assurance of a secure income.—you will have seen, too, that my reasons for getting married as soon as possible are well founded and that, after describing my girl to you, you can also see that she will be a very suitable wife for me.—For as I have described her to you, that's how she is—not one whit better or worse.—As far as the Marriage contract is concerned, I will make an honest confession to you, convinced that you will forgive me for taking this step because I know that if you had been in my situation you would have acted the same.—The only thing I'm asking your forgiveness for is that I haven't informed you about this earlier—I already apologized about it in my last letter and wrote you the reason why I had hesitated to tell you. I hope, therefore, you'll forgive me, especially since no one has suffered more in this matter than I have—and even if you had not brought up the subject in your last letter, I would have written and told you everything anyway, for, by god, I couldn't have kept it to myself any longer—no, not any longer.—

But let me talk now about the Marriage contract, or rather the written assurances of my honorable intentions concerning the girl; you do know, don't you, that they have a guardian because—unfortunately for the family and also for me and my Konstanze—the father is no longer living—and this guardian, who doesn't even know me, must have gotten an earful about me by such servile and loudmouthed gentlemen as Herr Winter:—that one must beware of me—that I had no secure income— that I was too intimate with her—that I might jilt her—and that the girl would be done for in the end, etc.; all this stuff wafted like a bad odor into the guardian's nose—because Constanze's mother, who knows me and my honest behavior, allowed all this to be said without saying anything that would put it right.—Yet, my entire association with them consisted in my—living there—and afterward in my visiting there every day.—No one ever saw me with her outside the house.—But this guardian filled the mother's ears with stories about me for so long until she finally told me about it and asked that I have a talk with him myself, because he was supposed to come by the house in a few days.—He came—I spoke with him—the result was (because I did not explain things as clearly as he had wished) that he told the mother to forbid all association between me and her daughter until I had settled the matter with him in writing.—The mother told him: his entire association with her consists in coming to my house and—I can't forbid him my house—he is too good a friend for that—a friend to whom I am obliged in many ways.—I am satisfied and I trust him—you must work out an agreement with him yourself.—So then he forbade me to have anything to do with the girl until I acknowledged my relationship in writing. So what other recourse did I have?—to give him a written contract or—never to see the girl again—but if you love honorably and truly, can you forsake the one you love?—could not the mother, could not my beloved herself, come up with the ugliest interpretation of my conduct?—Such was my situation! So, I drew up a document in which I stated *that I obligated myself to marry Mad.^selle Constance Weber within the time of 3 years; if it should prove impossible for me to do so owing to a change of mind, she would be entitled to receive from me 300 gulden a year.*— Nothing in the world was easier for me to write—because I knew I would never have to pay these 300 gulden—for I shall never forsake her—and even if I should be so unfortunate as to undergo a change of mind—I should be glad that I can liberate myself for a mere 300 gulden—and Konstanze, as I know her, would be too proud to let herself be bought off.—

But what did this heavenly girl do as soon as her guardian had left?—She demanded that her mother give her the document—then said to me—*dear Mozart! I don't need any written assurances from you; I believe what you say;*—and she tore up the writ.—This gesture endeared my dear Konstanze to me even more.—and because she tore up the contract and the guardian gave his Parole d'honneur to keep this matter to himself, my mind, dearest father, was somewhat put at ease when I thought about you.—For I am not worried about obtaining your consent to get married when the time comes, for the only thing the girl lacks is money—and I know how reasonable you are in such matters. So will you forgive me?—I do hope so!—in fact, I don't doubt it all.— . . .

Just one more word about *Winter*—he said once to me among other things: you are a fool if you want to get married;—you are making enough money, indeed, you can afford it: keep a mistress!—What should keep you from doing it?—that little bit of Religion?—Now, believe what you will. *Adieu.* I kiss your hands 1000 times and embrace my sister with all my heart and remain Forever your

most obedient son
W. A. Mzt

The address of the Baroness is:

Madame La Baronne de Waldstaetten
nèe de Scheffer à
Leopoldstadt N.° 360. *Vienne.*

On December 24, 1781, Mozart and Muzio Clementi, the eminent composer and pianist, who happened to be in Vienna, were invited to engage in a piano contest sponsored by Emperor Joseph II. Maria Feodorovna, wife of Grand Duke Paul of Russia, supplied some of the contest material: a handwritten sonata by Giovanni Paisiello to be played at sight. There is no clear indication as to who won the contest, but rumor has it that Joseph II had laid a wager with the grand duchess that Mozart would excell. And he did.

To his father, in Salzburg

Vienna, January 16, 1782

Mon trés cher Pére!

I thank you so much for your kind and affectionate letter!—if I were to answer all your questions in detail, I would have to fill the pages of a whole book;—since that is impossible, I will restrict my answers to your most important questions. The guardian's name is Herr von Thorwarth—he is Inspector of theater properties—in one word, everything that has to do with the theater has to go through his hands.—The 50 ducats the emperor sent me[71] were channeled through him;—he is also the one I talked to concerning my concert in the theater because he is in charge of most of these matters—and he is well regarded by Count Rosenberg and Baron Kienmayr.[72] I must confess that I thought he would inform you about this whole affair without even saying a word to me, but instead he publicized it all over Vienna, although he had

---

71. A present from Joseph II for Mozart's participation in the piano contest with Clementi.
72. Count Orsini-Rosenberg was director of the court theaters and Baron Johann Michael Kienmayr his deputy.

given me his word of honor that he wouldn't, and that really made me take back the good opinion I once had of him.— . . . But it's all over now;—and love has to come to my defense;—but Herr von Thorwarth did wrong;—not quite so much that he and Mad.ᵐᵉ Weber should be put in chains, be forced to sweep streets, and carry a placard around their neck inscribed with the words: *Seducers of Youth.*[73] That, too, is exaggerated;—even if what you say were true, namely that they intentionally opened all doors to me and allowed me the run of the house, thus giving me all the opportunities, etc., etc., even then such a punishment would go too far;—at any rate, I don't need to tell you that it wasn't like that—I am hurt enough by your insinuation that you think your son would frequent a place where such things were going on.—Let me just say that you should believe exactly the opposite—but enough of this!—

Now about *Clementi.*[74]—He is a very solid Cembalo player.—but that is all.—he has great facility in his right hand.—his best passages are Thirds.—apart from that he doesn't have a penny's worth of taste or feeling—he is a mere Mechanicus.

The emperor declared, after we had paid each other quite enough compliments, that *He* should go first. He said *La santa chiesa Catholica,* for he is a Roman.—He began with a prelude and then played a Sonata;[75]— after that the emperor said to me: allons, fire away!—I also began with a prelude and then played variations.[76] Then the Grand Duchess handed us sonatas by Paesello[77] that were poorly written out in his own hand; from these I had to play the allegro and he the Andante and Rondò. Then we had to choose a theme from the sonatas and develop it on 2 pianos.—The strange thing is that I had borrowed the pianoforte of the Countess Thun, but I could use it only when I played alone. That's how the emperor wanted it.—and N.B., the other piano was out of tune and 3 of its keys stuck.—*it doesn't matter,* said the emperor.—Well, I am giving this a very positive interpretation, namely that the emperor already knows my pianistic skills and expertise of music, and he wanted to hear what the foreigner could do.

73. These were all suggestions by Leopold.
74. Muzio Clementi, a native of Rome, made his living in London as pianist and conductor.
75. Clementi's Sonata in B-flat, op. 24.
76. It is not known which variations Mozart played.
77. Giovanni Paisiello, who had been Maria Feodorovna's music teacher in St. Petersburg. The piano sonatas she offered for the contest were probably dedicated to her by Paisiello.

Besides, I know from a good source that he was very pleased with me. The emperor was very gracious toward me and talked with me privately about all sorts of things.—he even spoke to me about my marriage.—who knows—perhaps—what do you think?—one can always hope.—

More in my next letter.—Farewell; I kiss your hands 1000 times and embrace my dear sister with all my heart and remain your

most obedient son
W. A. Mozart

To his father, in Salzburg

Vienna, January 30, 1782

Mon trés cher Pére!—

I am writing to you in haste, in fact, at half past 10 o'clock at night. I had intended to wait with my letter until Saturday, but I have an urgent request to make and hope you won't mind that I must be very brief today.—Will you please send me the libretto of Idomenèe with your next letter?—with or without the German translation.—

I lent a copy to Countess Thun—but she has moved and can't find it—it may well be lost.—Fräulein Auerhammer has the other copy—she has been looking but hasn't found it yet.—perhaps she'll find it—but—if she doesn't—just now when I really need it, I'll be in an awkward spot;—so, to be on the safe side, I'm asking you to send it to me right away no matter what the cost,—for I need it to properly prepare my concert, which will take place on the 3rd Sunday in Lent.[78] So please send it off immediately.—

I'll be sending my sonatas with the next mail coach.

My opera has not gone to sleep;[79]—but it has been delayed because of Gluck's big operas[80] and because of all the changes we made in the libretto; it is to be staged right after Easter.—

I must close now—just one more thing, for without saying it I wouldn't be able to sleep well.—Don't suspect my dear Konstanze of

---

78. Mozart gave a concert on March 3, 1782, in which he played parts of *Idomeneo* arranged for piano; he also played his Piano Concerto in D major, K. 175, with a new finale, the Rondo in D major, K. 382, and free improvisations.
79. *Die Entführung aus dem Serail.*
80. Performed were three of Gluck's operas: *Iphigenie in Tauris, Alceste,* and *Orfeo.*

having such conniving thoughts—you must believe me that I could not possibly love her if she were a schemer. She and I—both of us—became aware of her mother's plans already some time ago—but she is deceiving herself—because—it's her wish to have us, after we are married, in her house, for she has an apartment to let—but nothing will come of it,—for I would never want to do that, and my Konstanze even less.—O Contraire—it's her intention to visit her mother very rarely, and I'll do my best to see to it that it won't happen at all.—We know her too well!—Dearest and best father,—I wish for nothing more than that we should see each other very soon, so you will have a chance to see her and—love her—for I do know you love those who have a good heart;—now farewell, dearest, most beloved father!—I kiss your hands 1000 times and remain Forever your

most obedient son
W. A. Mozart

I embrace my dear sister with all my heart.—
And I will not forget the variations.[81]

To his sister, in Salzburg

Vienna, February 13, 1782

Ma trés chére soeur!

Thank you so much for sending me the libretto, for which I so eagerly waited!—I hope that when you get this letter, our dear, beloved father is already back with you.[82]—Just because I don't always answer your letters, you must not conclude that I don't welcome your letters!—The honor of receiving a letter from you, dear sister, will always be a special pleasure for me. If my business, so important for my livelihood, would allow me more time, god knows, I would answer you at once!—Have I really never ever sent you a reply?—well, then!—it can't be forgetfulness—it can't be negligence either—therefore, it must be some other problem: yes, it's the sheer impossibility of it!—After all, don't I write sparingly even to my father?—that's bad enough, you might say!—but for heaven's sake—you both know what Vienna is like!—isn't a person who does not have a penny of reliable income busy enough with

---

81. Probably K. 352, 359, and 360.
82. Leopold Mozart had gone to Munich for the carnival season.

just thinking and working day and night in such a place?—our father, after he has finished his duties at church, and you, after you are done with your handful of pupils, you can both do what you wish for the rest of the day, you can write letters filled with entire litanies.—But I can't.— I wrote my daily schedule to my father already the other day, but let me repeat it to you: at 6 o'clock in the morning I'm already done with my hair; at 7 I'm fully dressed;—then I compose until 9 o'clock; from 9 to 1 o'clock I give lessons.—Then I Eat, unless I'm invited by someone who doesn't eat lunch until 2 or 3 o'clock as, for instance, today and tomorrow at the Countess Zizi[83] and Countess Thun.—I cannot get back to work before 5 or 6 o'clock—and quite often I can't get back at all, because I have to be at a performance; if I can, I write until 9 o'clock. After that I go and visit my dear Konstanze;—however, our pleasure of seeing each other is often ruined by the galling remarks of her mother—something I'll explain to my father in my next letter—but this is the reason why I want to liberate and rescue her as soon as possible.— I get home around half past 10 or at 11 o'clock at night;—it all depends on her mother's darts or my ability to endure them.—Since I can't depend on being able to compose in the evening, because of the concerts that are taking place but also because of the uncertainty whether I might be summoned somewhere, it has become my habit to compose a little before going to bed, especially when I get home a bit earlier.— Often enough I go on writing until 1 o'clock—and then, of course, up again at 6 o'clock.—

My dearest sister!—if you believe that I could ever forget my dearest, best father and you—then—but quiet! god knows what's in my thoughts, and that gives me enough peace of mind;—may god punish me if I can ever forget you!—Adieu—I remain Forever

your sincere brother
W. A. Mozart

P.S. If my dearest and best father has already returned to Salzburg, I kiss his hands 1000 times.

83. Countess Anna Maria Zichy, Mozart's fourth piano student.

To his father, in Salzburg

Vienna, March 23, 1782

Mon trés cher Pére!

I am so sorry that I found out only yesterday that Herr Leitgeb's[84] son was traveling by mail coach to Salzburg; I would have had a great opportunity to send you a lot of things without cost.—But it was impossible to have the Variations copied within two days.—Therefore, I could give him only 2 copies of my Sonatas;—at the same time I'm sending you my *most recent* composition[85]—which I wrote for my concerto in D and which is making quite some noise around here.—Please guard it like a *gem*—don't give it to anyone—not even to Marchand and his sister[86]—I wrote it *specially* for myself—and no one may play it, except my dear sister. . . . Just this moment my dear Konstanze came up to me with the question whether it might be all right to send my sister a little souvenir?—but she also wants me to apologize ahead of time— she says she is a poor girl and doesn't have much;—but it's the thought that counts and she hopes my sister will understand that.—The little cross doesn't have much value, but it's the fashion in Vienna;—and the little heart with the arrow in the middle is a little like my sister's *Heart and Arrow*—and will probably please her more. Farewell for now. I kiss your hands 1000 times and embrace my sister with all my heart and remain Forever yours.

🐦 *Mozart was easily deceived by smooth-talking courtiers. Here in Vienna it was Herr von Strack, the emperor's personal valet, who pretended to be helpful to Mozart when, apparently, the opposite was the case.*

To his father, in Salzburg

Vienna, April 10, 1782

Mon trés cher Pére!

I see from your letter from the 2ⁿᵈ of this month that you received

---

84. Joseph Leutgeb, formerly a horn player in the court orchestra of Salzburg, had moved to Vienna in 1777. Mozart wrote the Horn Quintet, K. 407, and the Horn Concerto, K. 412, for him.
85. Mozart's new rondo, K. 382.
86. Heinrich Marchand, age twelve, and Margarethe Marchand, fourteen, were music students from Munich living with Leopold. Heinrich became a noted violinist and Margarethe an opera singer.

safely everything I sent you; I am so glad that you like the ribbons for your watch and the snuffbox, and that my sister likes the two bonnets.—I didn't buy the snuffbox or the ribbons, I received both as a gift from Count Zapara.—I gave the compliments from both of you to my dear Konstanze—she kisses your hands with gratitude, dear father, and embraces my sister with all her heart and with the desire to become her friend.—She was so happy when I told her that my sister liked the 2 bonnets; that had been her greatest wish.—Your postscript regarding her mother is correct only in that she likes to drink and, to be sure, more—than a woman should. But I've never seen her drunk, it would be a lie if I said so.—Her daughters drink only water—and although the mother almost forces wine upon them, she doesn't succeed in getting them to touch it; they often quarrel about it—can you imagine a mother wrangling with her children about such a thing?—

What you are writing about the rumors going around that I will be taken into the service of the emperor—well, the reason that I haven't written anything to you about it is that—I myself know nothing.— One thing is certain: the whole town is full of this talk and a good number of people have already congratulated me;—and I can readily believe that there has been some talk about this matter in the emperor's presence and that he may even be giving it some thought,—but so far I haven't heard a word.—It's interesting that matters have proceeded to the point that the emperor is thinking about something of this sort when, I, in fact,—haven't taken one step to further such a move!—It's true, I've been to see Herr von Strack, who is a good friend of mine, just to make myself visible and because I like his company, but I didn't see him often, so I would not become a nuisance or make him think I had certain intentions.—If he speaks as an Honest Man, he will have to say that I never mentioned one word that could have made him think I wanted to stay here, let alone to enter the emperor's service. We spoke of nothing but Musique.—It must be that he spoke so favorably of me to the emperor from his very own feelings, without anyone's pressuring him.—But as this whole thing has proceeded so far without my involvement, it should come to a conclusion the same way;—because if they know you are eager, they immediately pay you less as a result, for the emperor is a skinflint anyway.—If the emperor wants me, let him pay—the Honor alone of being in the emperor's service is not enough for me;—if the emperor offers me 1000 gulden, and some count offers me 2000—I'll send my compliments to the emperor and go to the count—but, of course, it would have to be a sure thing.—

Apropòs; I wanted to ask you, when you return the Rondeau to me, please include the 6 fugues by Händel, and the Toccatas and fugues by Eberlin. Every Sunday at 12 noon I go to visit Baron von Suiten—and there we play nothing but Händl and Bach.—I am just putting together a collection of Bach fugues—that is Sebastian as well as Emanuel and Friedeman Bach.[87] I am also collecting Händel's and I am missing only the 6 fugues I mentioned.[88] I should like the Baron also to hear Eberlin's fugues.—You probably know already that the English Bach died?[89] What a loss to the world of music!—Farewell for now; I kiss your hands 1000 times and embrace my dear sister with all my heart, and remain Forever your

most obedient son
W. A. Mozart

P. S. I would like to ask you to send me, when you get a chance—the sooner, the better—my concerto in C, written for the Countess Litsow.[90]

Mozart credits Constanze with stimulating him to write his Fantasy and Fugue in C major, K. 394. Some biographers have expressed surprise that Constanze had such an "austere" taste in music; others think that Mozart deliberately exaggerated Constanze's influence in order to create a good impression on Leopold and Nannerl. Of greatest fascination and wonderment, however, is Mozart's nonchalant description of how he composed the work: writing down the fugal part while composing the prelude in his head.

To his sister, in Salzburg

Vienna, April 20, 1782

Most beloved sister!—

My dear Konstanze has finally plucked up her courage and followed the dictates of her heart—that is to write you, my dear sister, a letter.—

---

87. Carl Philipp Emanuel Bach, J. S. Bach's second son, and Wilhelm Friedemann Bach, J. S. Bach's eldest son.
88. The collection of fugues by G. F. Handel was found among Mozart's music after his death.
89. Johann Christian Bach, J. S. Bach's youngest son, died on January 1, 1782. Mozart had met him in London in 1764 and again briefly in St. Germain in 1778.
90. Mozart's Piano Concerto in C major, K. 246.

If you should honor her—which I dearly wished you would so I could read her pleasure of receiving a letter from you on the forehead of this good creature—if you wish to honor her with a reply, please enclose it in a letter to me.—I am saying this as a precaution, for you must know that her mother and sisters do not know that she wrote to you.—I am including here a prelude and fugue for three parts;[91]—indeed, this is the very reason why I didn't answer you right away because—I couldn't get finished any sooner, writing down all these wearisome little notes.—Also, the whole thing is written down incorrectly—the Praeludio actually should be first, followed by the fugue. The reason for the mixup is this: I had already composed the fugue and was writing it down while I worked out the prelude in my head.—I only hope that you'll be able to read it (I wrote it so small) and, of course,—that you'll like it.—I'll be sending you something better for the piano some other time.—The reason that this particular fugue came into being has to do with my dear Konstanze.—Baron van Suiten, whom I visit every Sunday, let me take works by Händel and Bach home with me, after playing them for him at his house.—When Konstanze heard these fugues, she fell completely in love with them—now she wants to hear nothing but fugues, particularly, in this kind of composition, Händl and Bach.—So she asked me, because she had heard me play some fugues from my head recently, whether I had written any of them down?—when I said no—she really scolded me, saying that I didn't want to compose the most artistic and beautiful things in music; and she did not relent until I composed a fugue for her, so that's how this one came to be.—I have purposely written Andante Maestoso on top of it so that it won't be played too fast—for if a fugue is not played slowly one cannot hear the entering theme clearly enough and it loses its effect.—I will compose 5 more just as soon as I have the time and opportunity,[92] and then present them to Baron van Suiten, who has great treasures of good music—excellent in quality, although small in quantity;—and that's the reason I'm asking you to keep your promise and not show it to anyone;—learn it by heart and then play it.—For a fugue cannot be so easily copied if you just

91. Fantasy and Fugue in C major, K. 394.
92. K. Anh. 33 and K. Anh. 40 seem to be the only evidence of Mozart's plan to compose five fugues for Baron van Swieten. However, he did arrange three-part fugues and four-part fugues by Johann Sebastian Bach.

hear it.—If Papa has not yet had the Eberlin fugues copied, tell him that's fine with me;—I obtained them myself by chance and saw to my regret (for I had not remembered them well) that they are not that good and certainly do not deserve to be placed on a level with Händl and Bach. With due respect for his 4-part piece, his piano fugues are nothing but drawn-out little versetts.[93] Farewell for now; I'm so happy you like the two bonnets. I kiss you 1000 times and remain your

sincere brother
W. A. Mozart

I kiss Papa's hands.—I did not receive a letter today.

Mozart's only surviving letter to Constanze before their marriage was occasioned by a lovers' quarrel. Constanze seems to have committed an indiscretion at a party that probably took place at the house of Baroness von Waldstätten. What is interesting, perhaps even surprising, is the moralizing tone of Mozart's letter. He now seems to be taking a position his father had frequently taken toward him.

To Constanze Weber, in Vienna

Vienna, April 29, 1782

Dearest, most beloved friend!—

Surely you will still allow me to address you in this manner?—and surely you don't hate me so much that I cannot be your friend anymore and you—no longer mine?—and—even if you don't wish to be my friend any longer, you can't really forbid me to think kindly of you, my friend, now that I have become so used to it.—Please consider carefully what you said to me today.—You have, regardless of all my pleas, turned me away 3 times and told me straight to my face that you wish to have nothing to do with me anymore.—I am not as careless as you in giving up the object of my love and I am not as emotional, unthinking, and unreasonable to simply accept your refusal.—I love you too much to take such a step.—So I call on you once more to think and reflect about the cause of this unfortunate incident, namely the fact that

---

93. "Versetts" are brief organ pieces.

I voiced my disapproval that you had been so impudent and inconsiderate as to tell your sisters—Nota bene, in my presence—that you allowed some Chapeaux[94] to measure the calves of your legs. No woman intent upon her honor does that sort of thing.—I do understand the *maxime* that when you are with others, do as others do—but one has to think about certain related matters—whether it is a gathering of good friends and acquaintances?—whether I am a child or a young woman of *marriageable* age—but especially, whether I am already engaged to be married?—Important, too, is whether the people present are of my social standing or of a lower class—or, which is of particular importance, whether there are people present of superior rank?—If it's true that the Baroness permitted the same thing to be done to her, well, that's something entirely different because she is a woman past her prime who cannot possibly excite anybody anymore—besides, she is known to be a connoisseur of the Et caetera.—I do not wish, my dearest friend, that you would Ever want to live a life like that, even if you don't wish to become my wife.—If you cannot possibly resist playing along with the others, although the *playing along* does not look good in a man and even less in a woman, you should have, in god's name, taken the ribbon and measured your calves *yourself*; that's what I saw *honorable women* do in similar situations, you should not have had it done by some chapeau; I—I—would never have done that to you *with others around*—I would have handed you the ribbon—I could never have imagined that a stranger would be allowed to do it—someone about whom I know nothing and don't care for.—But it's over now—and a mere acknowledgment of this unwise exhibition would have been enough to make everything all right and—if you don't take it amiss, dearest friend—would still make it all right.—You can see from this how much I love you.—*I don't flare up like you;*—I think—I reflect—and I feel—*If you, too, can feel*—*if you allow your feelings to come forth*—then I know for sure that on this very day I can say to myself confidently: Konstanze is the virtuous, Honorable—sensible and truly beloved of that Trustworthy and well-meaning

Mozart

---

94. *Chapeau* means "hat" in French, but in eighteenth-century courtly parlance it also meant "male escort" or "paramour." The measuring of ladies' calves was often part of an adult game of forfeit.

In a previous letter, Mozart had tried to impress Leopold and Nannerl with Constanze's musical taste; now he is advertising her domestic virtues. Although very busy finishing Die Entführung and preparing for his first summer concert in the park, he took time out to write about Constanze's skills in decorating dresses. His attempts to produce friendly relations between Constanze and his family are touching but fruitless.

To his father, in Salzburg

Vienna, May 8, 1782

Mon trés cher Pére!

I have received your last letter from April 30 in good order, and yesterday the letter of my sister arrived with the enclosure for my dear Konstanze, which I handed to her immediately.—She was so touched by it, and she will take the liberty of writing to her soon again. In the meantime, as I cannot possibly write to my sister today, I must ask you a question from Konstanze, which is whether *fringes* are being worn in Salzburg?—whether my sister is wearing them?—whether she can make them herself?—Konstanze has just trimmed 2 Picquèe dresses with them;—it's the big fashion here;—and because she knows how to do it, she wanted to do some for my sister, all she needs to know is the colors my sister prefers, because these fringes come in all different colors: white, black, green, blue, puce, etc. Of course, a dress in satin or gros de turc silk must be trimmed with silk fringes—and Konstanze has one like that;—but a simple dress of Saxonian picqèe—with cotton fringes, which if you don't touch them can hardly be distinguished from silk; it also looks very pretty and in addition has the advantage that the fringes and the dress are washable.—

Please let me know how you liked the Salieri opera in Munich.[95]— I am quite certain you saw it; if not, you probably know how well it was received.—

I went to see Count Daun twice, but was unable to find him home; but I got the Musique that he brought with him.—He is at home only in the morning, and at that time I not only don't leave the house but don't even get dressed, because I'm so pressed for time with my writ-

---

95. Antonio Salieri's opera *Semiramide* had its premiere in Munich in January 1782.

ing.—I'll try again next Sunday;—maybe, in addition to the variations, he'll be able to take the Munich opera back with him.—

Yesterday I was at Countess Thun's and pranced through my 2nd act,[96] which gave her no less pleasure than the first act.—I had Raaff's aria copied recently and gave it to *Fischer,* who had Raaff's permission.[97] You wrote to me some time ago that you would like to have the Robinig music;[98] but who has it?—I don't.—I thought Eck had returned it to you.—I requested it from you in my letter when I asked you for the serenades in F and B.[99]

Please send me as soon as you can the scena I composed for Countess Baumgarten.[100]—They are now arranging concerts every Sunday throughout the summer in the Augarten.[101] A certain Martin had organized amateur concerts during this past winter; they took place in the Mehlgrube[102] every Friday.—I am sure you know that Vienna has a great number of amateur musicians, both men and women, and they are all very good.—But these concerts had not been organized well—at least as far as I was concerned.—But now this Martin has obtained a permit under a charter from the emperor, along with the emperor's assurances of his approbation, to arrange 12 Concerts in the Augarten and 4 grand evening serenades in the most beautiful squares in the City.—The subscription price for all these summer events is 2 ducats. I think you'll agree that we'll get enough subscribers;—all the more because I am involved and associated with the events.—Let's assume we'll get only 100 subscribers, that means each of us would have 300 gulden profit, even if our expenses run to 200 gulden, which, however, is too high a figure.—Baron van Suiten and Countess Thun are actively participating.—the Ochestra is made up of Amateurs—except for the bassoon players, the trumpeters and drummers.—

Clementi, I hear, will be leaving tomorrow;—have you seen his sonatas?—

96. Act 2 of *Die Entführung.* Mozart's description of his playing is wonderfully concrete and energetic; he does not say *vorgespielt* (played through) but *vorgeritten* (pranced through).
97. The aria is "Se al labbro mio non credi," K. 295, written for Anton Raaff.
98. Divertimento no. 17 in D, K. 334.
99. Divertimentos no. 10 in F major, K. 247, and no. 15 in B-flat, K. 287.
100. "Misero, dove son!," K. 369.
101. The Augarten is a public garden in the Leopoldstadt suburb of Vienna. Joseph II had decreed that the park, which belonged to the imperial family, be opened to the public.
102. The Mehlgrube (Flour store) was an old building at the Neue Markt in Vienna; one of its halls had been converted to an auditorium. Today it is the site of the Ambassador Hotel.

Please be patient a little longer with poor Leitgeb;[103] if you knew his circumstances and could see how he has to muddle through, I'm sure you would feel sorry for him. I shall have a talk with him, and I know for sure he'll pay you back, little by little.—Farewell for now, I kiss your hands 1000 times and remain Forever your

most obedient son
W. A. Mzt

To his father, in Salzburg

Vienna, May 25, 1781[104]

Mon trés cher Pére!

I have to steal a minute to write to you because I didn't want you to have to wait so long for a letter.—Tomorrow is our first concert in the Augarten.—At half past 8 o'clock Martin is coming to fetch me in his carriage;—then we'll have to make 6 more visits; at 11 o'clock I'll have to be done with it because I am expected at the house of Countess Rombeck.—Afterward I'm having lunch with Countess Thun;—N.B. in her garden; in the evening will be a rehearsal for the concert.—We'll be performing a symphony by van Suiten and one by me.[105] An amateur singer, Mad.^selle Berger, is going to sing.—A boy—by the name of Türk—will play a violin concerto—and Fräulein von Auerhammer and I will play the Duett Concerto in E-flat.[106]

Mozart's brief note to his father contains the following postscript by Constanze. It is printed here in English and German to give the reader an idea of Constanze's writing style and orthography, if only to show how much Mozart's own writing and spelling had improved over the years.

"Your dear son has jusst been summonned to the countessa Thun and hasn't had time to finnish his ledder to his deare father, for which he's verry sorrie, he has given me Comision to let you know this, becaus today is poste day and he don't

---

103. The horn player Joseph Leutgeb, formerly of Salzburg, owed Leopold money that he had borrowed in 1773.
104. Mozart's error; the actual date is May 25, 1782.
105. Baron van Swieten's symphony is not known; Mozart's symphony was probably the Symphony no. 34 in C major, K. 338 (composed in 1780).
106. Concerto for Two Pianos in E-flat major, K. 365.

wish you to be without a ledder from him; the neckst time he will write more to his deare father. please forgive that it is me writing, it is not so nice as what your son would have writ. I remein your true servent and friende, Constanza Weber." (so öben ist ihr lieber sohn zur graffin thun gerufen worden, und hat also die zeit nicht seinem lieben Vatter dan briff zu eintigen, daß ihm ser leit ist er hat mir die Comesion gegeben ihnen es zu wisen zu machen, weil nun heit der posttag ist damit sie nicht ohne briff von ihm sein daß nöchtemal würt er seinem lieben Vatter schon daß mehere schreiben, bitte also um Verzeiun daß ich schreibe, daß, was ihnen nicht so angenem ist, als daß was ihnen ihr herr sonn geschrieben hette; ich bin ihre ware dinerin und freindin,

Constanza Weber).

✒ Mozart's *singspiel* Die Entführung aus dem Serail *premiered on July 16, 1782, and brought in "1200 gulden in 2 days"; Mozart, however, received only an agreed-upon sum of 100 imperial ducats, or 426.40 gulden. The opera was barely launched when Leopold prevailed upon his son to write a symphony in honor of the ennoblement of Sigmund Haffner the Younger, burgomaster of Salzburg. In 1776, Mozart had already composed a serenade for the Haffner family, K. 249 and 250, occasioned by a wedding. However, the present request came at a very busy time for Mozart, and he sounds a bit exasperated in his response. To please his father he wrote the symphony, the "Haffner" Symphony, K. 385, in a hurry. Today it is one of his best-known symphonies.*

To his father, in Salzburg

Vienna, July 20, 1782

Mon trés cher Pére!

I hope you received my letter in which I gave you an account of the good reception of my opera.[107]—Yesterday it was given for the 2nd time;—can you imagine that yesterday there was an even stronger cabal against it than on the first night?—throughout the first act people were hissing—but they couldn't silence the loud shouts of *Bravo* during the arias.—So my greatest hope was the trio at the end,[108] but as luck would

---

107. The letter Mozart is referring to is lost. He had told his father that *Die Entführung* had premiered at the Burgtheater on July 16 with great success.
108. The trio is "Marsch, marsch, marsch!," the final number of act. 1.

have it Fischer was off—which threw Dauer (Pedrillo) off too—and Adamberger alone couldn't pull it together; so the effect of the trio was lost, and this time there was *no repeat.*—I was beside myself with anger and so was Adamberger—and I told them immediately that I would not allow another performance until we had a brief rehearsal for the singers.—In the 2nd act the two Duets were repeated just as in the first night and so was the Rondeau by Belmont *When the tears of joy are flowing.*[109] The theater was perhaps even more crowded than the first night.— The day before you couldn't get a reserved seat anymore, be it in the parterre or on the 3rd circle; and the boxes were all sold out as well. In 2 days the opera brought in 1200 gulden.

What I am sending you here is the original score and two copies of the libretto.

You'll find a lot of passages crossed out; it is because I knew that the score gets copied here right away—so I let my imagination run free—and made some changes and cuts here and there just before I had it copied.—what you see now, that's the way it was performed.—here and there the trumpets and drums, flutes, clarinets, and the Turkish music are missing—because I couldn't get music paper with enough lines;—those parts are written on separate sheets of paper—the copyist probably lost them because he couldn't find them. Unfortunately, the first act fell into the mud when it was taken somewhere (I don't know anymore where); that's why it is so full of dirt.—

At the moment I'm extremely busy.—A week from Sunday I have to be done with arranging my opera for wind instruments—otherwise someone else will do it before me—and collect the profits instead of me; and now you want me to write a new Symphony! how can I do that!—you don't know how difficult it is to arrange an opera for winds—you have to suit the character of each wind instrument, yet not lose the original effect.—Well, that's the way it is, I'll just have to work at night, I cannot do it any other way—but I will make this sacrifice for you, dearest father.—I'll be sending you something for sure every post day—and I'll write as fast as I possibly can—and produce—as much as haste will allow me—quality work.

Just this moment I got a message from Count Zitchi asking me to drive to Laxenburg with him so he can introduce me to Prince Kau-

---

109. "Wenn der freude thränen fliessen," act 2, scene 9.

nitz.[110]—I must close now and get dressed;—if I have no plans to go out, I usually remain en Negligèe.

And just this minute the copyist is sending me the remaining parts of the music.

adieu. I kiss your hands 1000 times and embrace my sister with all my heart and remain Forever your

most obedient son
W. A. Mozart

P.S. My dear Konstanze
sends greetings to you both.

To his father, in Salzburg

Vienna, July 27, 1782

Mon trés cher Pére!

You may not want to believe your eyes when you see that I'm send-ing you only the First Allegro;[111]—but there simply wasn't enough time to do more—I had to compose a Night Musique in a great hurry,[112] but one for winds, otherwise I could have used it for you as well.—On Wednesday, the 31st, I'll be sending you the 2 minuets, the Andante, and the last movement;—if I can do it, I'll be sending you also a March— if not, you'll have to take the one from the Hafner Serenade,[113] which is *very* little known.

I composed the new symphony in D because I know you prefer that key.—My opera was given yesterday for the third time with big applause in honor of all the Nannerls in the world,[114]—and in spite of the terrible summer heat the theater was packed.—It was supposed to

110. Prince Wenzel Anton Kaunitz-Rietberg was the imperial chancellor of state.
111. The first movement of the "Haffner" Symphony, K. 385.
112. Serenade in C minor, K. 388, which Mozart also composed in a great hurry for Prince Alois Joseph Liechtenstein.
113. "Haffner" Serenade K. 249.
114. This performance of *Die Entführung* was on July 26, Saint Anne's Day.

be given again next Friday, but I objected to it because I don't want it to be whipped to death.—I can say this much: people are quite crazy about the opera.—It really feels good to have this kind of applause.— I do hope you have received by now the original score of the opera. Dearest and best of all fathers!—I must implore you, implore you for all you hold dear in the world: please give me your consent so that I can marry my dear Konstanze.—Don't think it is only for the sake of getting married—if it were for that reason alone, I'd be glad to wait a little longer.—However, I feel that it is absolutely necessary on account of my honor as well as that of my girl, but also on account of my health and peace of mind.—My heart is in turmoil, my head confused—how can one think and work intelligently under such circumstances?—and where does it all come from?—most people believe we are married already—her mother gets upset about such talk—and the poor girl is being tormented to death—and so am I.—All this can be remedied quite easily.—Believe me, one can live in this expensive Vienna just as easily as anywhere else, it all depends on how well you economize and manage your affairs.—Such thinking is never found among young people in love.—But whoever gets the kind of wife I am getting can be fortunate indeed.—We shall be living quietly and withdrawn—and yet we'll be happy.—And don't worry—for even if I should be taken sick today, which god may prevent, I would wager that the leading nobles here would provide me with good protection, and all the more for being married. I can say it in all confidence—I know what Prince Kaunitz said about me to the emperor and Archduke Maximilian.—I am waiting eagerly for your consent, my beloved father—I feel sure you will give it to me—my honor and my peace of mind depend on it.—Don't wait too long for the pleasure of embracing your son and his wife. I kiss your hands 1000 times and remain Forever your

obed. son
W. A. Mozart

To his father, in Salzburg

Vienna, July 31, 1782

Mon trés cher Pére!

You can see that my intentions are good; but what you can't do, you can't do!—I don't want to scribble down just anything,—therefore, I cannot send you the complete symphony before next post day.—I could have sent you the last part already, but I prefer to wait until I have it all together, it will all cost the same.—what I have sent you before has already cost me 3 gulden.—

Today I received your letter of July 26, but I could never have imagined such an indifferent, cold reply to the message I sent you about the good reception of my opera.—I thought, to judge from my own feelings, you could hardly wait to open the pacquet, eager to lay your eyes on your son's work, which is not only pleasing the Viennese audiences but creating such a sensation that they don't want to see or hear anything else, and the theater is packed full at each performance.—Yesterday the opera was given for the 4th time and will be given again this Friday.—But—*you* didn't have sufficient time—and the whole world says that because of my boasting and criticisms the Profeßori of music and many others have become my enemies![115]—what world do you mean?—probably the world of Salzburg; because anyone here—can see and hear plenty to the contrary;—and this is my answer to all that.—You probably received my last letter in the meantime;—I am not really in doubt that you will send me your consent for my marriage in your next letter;—you can't possibly have anything against it—and I don't think you actually do!—your letters tell me that!—After all, she is an Honest, decent girl from respectable parents,—and I am able to *provide* for her—we love each other—and we want each other;—everything you have written to me and could possibly still write—is not much more than *well-intentioned advice!*—which no matter how beautiful and well-meaning it may be is no longer fitting for a man who has already gone this far with his girl.—So there's nothing gained by postponement.—It's much better that one put one's house in order—and conduct oneself as an Honest fellow!—that's what god will always reward.—I don't want to do anything for which I'll have to reproach myself later.—

Farewell for now, I kiss your hands 1000 times and remain Forever your

most obedient son
W. A. Mozart

115. This sentence appears to be an indirect quotation from Leopold's letter of July 26, which, like all of his letters of this period, is lost.

It appears that Constanze had left her mother and was staying at the house of Baroness Waldstätten

To Baroness Martha Elisabeth von Waldstätten, in Vienna

Vienna, before August 4, 1782[116]

Most Highly Esteemed Baroness!

Mad.^{me} Weber's maidservant brought me my music, and I had to give her a written receipt for it.—The maid told me something in confidence that, although I didn't think such a thing was possible, because it would be a disgrace for the whole family, I nevertheless now think might just be true, given the stupidity of Mad.^{me} Weber, and therefore it worries me after all.—Sophie[117] apparently came to the maid in tears—and when she asked what's the matter, Sophie said: tell Mozart confidentially that he should see to it that Constanz will return home because—my mother is determined to have her fetched by the police!— Is it possible that the police here can just walk into anybody's house?— Maybe it's only a trick to get her to come home.—If such an action is legal here, I would know of no better way to avert it than to marry Constance tomorrow morning—even today if it could be arranged.— Because I wouldn't wish to expose my beloved to such a disgrace—and once she is my wife they cannot do that anymore.—One more thing: Thorwath has been requested to come to the Webers today.—I am asking Your Grace for Your kind advice—and a friendly hand to help us poor creatures. I will be at home as always.—I kiss your hands 1000 times and I am your most

> deeply appreciative servant
> W. A. Mozart

In the greatest of haste: Constance knows *nothing* of this.
Did Herr von Thorwath come to the house of Your Grace?
Do you think it is necessary that the two of us see him after lunch?—

Mozart and Constanze were married on August 4, 1782, in St. Stephen's Cathedral. Leopold's consent arrived after the wedding ceremony. Two weeks before, in prepa-

---

116. The letter is undated.
117. Constanze's youngest sister.

ration for his married life, Mozart had moved to a larger apartment with a won-
derfully adventurous address, "To the Red Saber, at the High Bridge" (Zum Roten
Säbel, an der Hohen Brücke). It was the same house in which he and his family
had stayed in 1768, when Mozart was twelve and still the apple of his father's eye.

To his father, in Salzburg

Vienna, August 7, 1782

Mon trés cher Pére!

You are very much mistaken about your son if you think him capable of a dishonest deed.——

My dear Konstanze, now, thank god, my wedded wife, has long known my situation and what I can expect from you.——However, her friendship and love for me are so great that she gladly——and with the greatest joy sacrificed her entire future for me——and my destiny.——I kiss your hand and thank you with all the tenderness a son can feel for his father for the consent and fatherly blessing you have given me so cordially.——I knew I could depend on you!——For you know that I myself could see it all only too well——I mean all the things that could be said against such a step——but also that I couldn't act differently without blemishing my conscience and my honor——consequently, I knew I could count on your consent!——What happened was that I waited for 2 days in vain for your letter, but the marriage ceremony had already been set for a day that was thought to be absolutely sure; so I let myself——sure of your consent and consoled by that——be wedded to my beloved in god's name.——The following day I received your 2 letters at once.——And now it's over!——I beg your pardon only for my all too hasty trust in your fatherly love——but in this, my honest confession, you have yet another proof of my love for truth and my hatred of lies.——Next post day my dear wife will ask for the fatherly blessing of her dear, beloved Papa-in-law, and a continuation of her Most Valued friendship with her beloved sister-in-law.——No one attended the wedding ceremony, except for her mother and her youngest sister.——Herr von Thorwart was present as her guardian and witness——Herr von Zetto, district councillor, was there as a witness for the bride, and Gilowsky[118] was my best man.——When we

---

118. Franz Xaver Wenzel Gilowsky von Urazowa, a surgeon in Vienna and a childhood friend of Mozart's.

were joined together, my wife and I began to cry—everybody was touched by that, even the priest;—they all wept when they saw how deeply moved we were in our hearts.—Our wedding feast consisted of a supper given for us by Baroness von Waldstädten—which indeed was more princely than baronial.—Now my dear Konstanze is looking forward a hundredfold to traveling to Salzburg!—and I wager—I wager—you'll rejoice in my happiness once you get to know her!—what else could there possibly happen if in your eyes, just as in mine, a right-thinking, honest, virtuous, and amiable wife remains a blessing for her husband.—

I am enclosing a brief march![119]—I only hope it will get to you in time—and that it is to your taste.—The first Allegro must be played with great fire—and the last one—as fast as possible.—My opera was given again yesterday—at Gluck's[120] request.—Gluck has given me many compliments about it. Tomorrow I will lunch with him.—You can see how I have to rush. Adieu. My dear wife and I kiss your hands 1000 times, and both of us embrace our dear sister with all our hearts and I remain Forever, your

most obed. son
W. A. Mozart

119. The March in D major, K. 408, nr. 2, which was still missing for the "Haffner" Symphony, K. 385; it came too late for the ceremony.
120. Christoph Willibald Gluck, one of the most celebrated composers of the time, was now living in Vienna.

Success, at Last!

In the second week of February 1785, Leopold Mozart undertook a journey to Vienna. He had at last given in to Wolfgang's pleas to visit him and Constanze, and he wanted to introduce his gifted violin student, Heinrich Marchand, to the music world of Vienna. After four days of heavy snow and icy roads, the travelers reached the Mozarts' new apartment in Große Schulerstraße on February 11 at one o'clock in the afternoon. It had been a strenuous trip, but if Leopold, now sixty-six, was weary from the journey, he was given little time to rest. At six o'clock that same evening, his son was giving a concert at the Mehlgrube (a converted flour market), his first subscription concert of the Lenten season. Mozart was the conductor and featured pianist that evening, and he introduced a new piano concerto that he had completed just the night before. Leopold was overwhelmed. "The concert was incomparable, the orchestra superb," he reported to Nannerl, "in addition to the synfonies, a singer from the Italian Theater sang 2 arias; and then *came a new splendid clavier concert by Wolfgang*, which was still being copied when we arrived, and your brother did not even have time to run through the Rondeau once more, because he had to supervise the copying." The concerto, which Mozart had finished in such a hurry, would be known to posterity as the Piano Concerto no. 20 in D minor, K. 466, one of the most moving and exquisite concertos ever written for piano.

The following day, Joseph Haydn came to Große Schulerstraße for an evening of chamber music. Mozart and some of his guests played his own new string quartets, the B-flat major, the A major, and the C major; it is said that he himself played the viola, Leopold one of the violin parts, and the two Barons von Tinti violin and cello. Haydn, the guest of honor, said to Leopold, "I say to you before God and as an honest man, your son is the greatest composer whom I know in person and by reputation: he has taste and, what is more, he has the most thorough knowledge of composition." Six months later, Mozart dedicated the three quartets, together with three others, to Joseph Haydn, who had profoundly inspired him in this difficult genre; the group of six is known today as the "Haydn" Quartets.

On February 13, the third day of Leopold's visit, it was back to the Mehlgrube for another subscription concert. The hall was filled to capacity, and the emperor was in attendance. Again, Leopold described the event: *"Your brother played a magnificent concerto that he had composed for Mademoiselle Paradis in Paris.* I was sitting in the back, only two boxes away from the beautiful Princess of Württemberg, and had the pleasure of hearing the interplay of all the instruments so clearly that tears of joy came into my eyes. When your brother left the stage, the emperor waved his hat to him and shouted *bravo Mozart."*

For Leopold, these days in Vienna, indeed the entire ten weeks of his visit, must have been a revelation. Not that he had been unaware of Wolfgang's successes: he knew that *Die Entführung* was highly acclaimed and popular, and he had seen Wolfgang's busy performance schedule as well as his list of subscribers, which included many of Vienna's most prominent families. But he was surely not prepared for the adulation that was lavished on his son by the Viennese. And Wolfgang? He must have been in seventh heaven. To have his father come to Vienna and hear himself lauded as the greatest living composer, and to have the emperor shout "Bravo Mozart" in his father's presence, must have been an experience both exhilarating and deeply satisfying. Mozart knew he had become Vienna's most popular musician, and this knowledge spurred him on to even greater productivity. Over the course of the year, he wrote two more piano concertos (nos. 21 and 22), a piano quartet, a piano and violin sonata, and the Fantasy in C minor; in addition, he gave at least twenty performances. The following year, 1786, Mozart's work schedule was even more intense: three piano concertos (nos. 23, 24, 25), a horn concerto (no. 4), two quartets, three trios, a symphony (no. 38, the "Prague"), and—an Italian opera. Mozart had at long last found an exciting text for a new opera buffa: Beaumarchais's *Le Mariage de Figaro.* Also, he had connected with the best librettist in Vienna, the brilliant new court poet of the Italian Theater, Lorenzo da Ponte. The collaboration of Mozart and da Ponte proved to be most felicitous, generating three of the greatest masterpieces for the operatic stage: *Le nozze di Figaro, Don Giovanni,* and *Cosi fan tutte.*

Le nozze di Figaro premiered at the Burgtheater on May 1, 1786. The composer had worked at a furious pace. "As fast as I wrote the words," da Ponte recalled in his *Memoirs,* "Mozart set them to music. In six weeks everything was in order." Then came the fights, the delays: Joseph II had forbidden the French play in Austria because he considered it a dangerous attack on the privileged and ruling classes of Europe. Indeed, he had judged correctly, for Beaumarchais's play would help prepare the way for the French Revolution. But the version of the play by da Ponte and Mozart was meant to be funny and sentimental, not political. Where Beaumarchais had created social types, da Ponte and Mozart were bringing individuals to the stage; where Beaumarchais had shown a world of inequality, da Ponte and Mozart showed that all classes were subject to human misjudgments and the dictates of eros. Not that Mozart's opera was totally devoid of political content—Figaro's angry cavatina "Se vuol ballare, signor Contino" (If you want to dance, my dear little Count) certainly has a strong political flavor. But still, the motor of his comedy was sex not politics, and what made it all so moving, true, and eternally young was Mozart's music, the delicate shadings with which he imbued his characters: the sweet confusion of the young, lovesick Cherubino, the tender dignity of the countess, the foolishness of the count and of Figaro. Mozart's music told a rich and funny—and yes, also political—story, but beyond its function in the drama, the music had become, like Shakespeare's dramatic language, a thing of beauty in itself.

To persuade the emperor and his censors that *Figaro* was just a comedy, an opera buffa, took time—and some diplomatic effort by da Ponte. But there were also cabals, behind-the-scenes activities of courtiers and musicians intent on undermining Mozart's ever-growing stature. In a letter to Nannerl about her brother, Leopold described them as a "tremendously strong clique against him." In the end, Mozart and da Ponte prevailed, and their opera was finally staged in Vienna.

Whereas we have considerable information about Mozart's work on *Idomeneo* and *Die Entführung,* we know little about his work on *Figaro.* For one thing, Mozart simply was too busy to write lengthy letters to his father; for another, whatever letters he wrote were lost. What we know about Mozart's life in 1785 and 1786 we know primarily from Leopold's letters to Nannerl, who by then had married and lived a half day's drive from Salzburg. The following letter, dated November 3, 1785, typifies the sketchy information Leopold had of his son during this period; "A few days ago I ran into the newspaper editor, who said to me: it's quite astonishing how many things your son is publishing; in the musical news I read nothing but the name of Mozart. . . . I couldn't reply to him with anything, because I know nothing; I haven't had a letter from him in six weeks. The man said also something about a new opera. Basta! I'm sure we'll hear about it!"

Mozart, so it seems, no longer wrote to his father to consult with him on matters of music; he had outgrown him and, for that matter, all of his contemporaries. Mozart had entered into a realm of artistic perfection attained by only a very few. As Goethe observes in his *Conversations with Eckermann*, "I cannot help thinking that the daemons, to tease and fool us humans, have placed before us single individuals who are so alluring that everyone strives after them, yet so far beyond us that nobody can reach them. Thus they set Raphael before us with whom thought and act were equally perfect, . . . thus Mozart as someone unattainable in music, and thus Shakespeare in poetry."

🎵 *Unhappy with Joseph II, the Viennese court, and the German princes in general, Mozart thinks of returning to Paris, which is ironic in view of his claim a few years earlier that he could not stand the French. The truth is that Mozart had felt unappreciated in Paris, just as he now felt unappreciated in Vienna.*

To his father, in Salzburg

Vienna, August 17, 1782

Mon trés chèr Pére!

I forgot to mention in my last letter that my wife and I went to the service at the Church of the Theatines on Purtiunkula Day;—even if we had not had an urge to worship, we would have been obliged to go because of the certificate without which we could not have been mar-

---

1. "Purtiunkula Day," celebrated on August 2, is a day for the granting of indulgence dating back to Saint Francis.

ried.[2]—We had already attended holy mass there several times before we were married and had gone to confession and communion together—and I found that I had never prayed so fervently and never confessed and took communion so earnestly as when I was by her side;—and she felt the same way;—in one word, we are made for each other—and god who orders all things and therefore also arranged our union will not forsake us. We both thank you most obediently for your fatherly blessings.—I hope in the meantime you have received the letter my Wife wrote to you.—

My thoughts about *Gluck* are the same as the ones you expressed in your letter, dearest father.[3]—And I will tell you something else.—These Viennese gentlemen, by whom I mean mainly the emperor, had better not think that I am on this earth alone for the sake of Vienna.—There is no monarch in the world I'd rather serve than the emperor—but I shall not go begging for a post here.—I believe I'm capable of bringing Honor to any Court.—And if Germany, my beloved fatherland, of which I am Proud, as you know, will not have me, then, in god's name, let France or England become richer by another talented German—to the disgrace of the German Nation.—You know that it is the Germans who have always excelled in almost all the arts—but where would they find their fortune, and where their fame?—certainly not in Germany!—even *Gluck!*—was it Germany that made him a great man?—unfortunately not!—Countess Thun,—Count Zitschy, Baron van Suiten—even Prince Kaunitz, they are all very unhappy with the emperor for not placing greater value on people of talent—and allowing them to leave his realm.—Prince Kaunitz said recently to Archduke Maximilian, when they were talking about me, *such people come into this world only once in a 100 years, and they should not be driven out of Germany—especially when one is fortunate enough to have them right here in the Capital.*—You would not believe how kind and courteous Prince Kaunitz was to me when I visited him recently.—At the end of my visit he said to me: *I am much obliged to you, my dear Mozart, for taking the trouble of coming to see me.* Etc., and you would hardly believe how much Countess Thun, Baron van Suiten, and other impor-

---

2. "The certificate" is a "certificate of confession," required of couples who wished to be married in the Catholic Church.
3. What Leopold and Wolfgang thought about Gluck is not known, but they certainly hoped that Wolfgang would succeed Gluck as court composer in Vienna.

tant people are trying to keep me here—however—I cannot wait around indefinitely—and I don't *want* to wait for an act of mercy—for it is my sense that, even though he *is* the emperor, I don't want to be dependent on his favor.—My idea is to go to Paris for the next Lenten season; of course not without some preparation.—I have already written to Le Gros[4] about this matter and am now waiting for a reply. I have mentioned it here and there—especially to *people of influence*—just in passing;—you know very well that one can drop a casual word in conversation once in a while, which is more effective than pompous pronouncements.—If I could be affiliated with the Concert Spirituel and the Concert des amateurs—and I would surely attract some pupils;—but also, since I have a wife now, I am able to attend to my pupils with greater ease and concentration.—and then there is always my Composing, etc.,—especially opera, to which I am drawn most of all.—I began, a little while ago, to practice my French—and I have already taken 3 English lessons.—In about 3 months I hope to be able to read and understand English texts quite well.—Farewell for now. My wife and I kiss your hands 1000 times and remain Forever

your most obedient son
W. A. Mozart

To his father, in Salzburg

Vienna, August 24, 1782

Mon trés cher Pére!

You never suggested anything but what I myself had wished all along—and, indeed, still wish for;[5]—but I also must tell you truthfully that my wife and I are waiting every day to get some *definite* news about the arrival of the Russian Visitors,[6] so we can go ahead with our planned trip or delay it; and because we know nothing for sure at this moment, I can't write you anything for sure.—Some say the Russians will arrive on September 7th—others say they are not coming at all;—if the latter were the case, we would be in Salzburg at the beginning of

---

4. Joseph Legros, director of the Concert Spirtuel; he was the first to perform Mozart's "Paris" Symphony, K. 297.
5. Probably a reference to a proposed trip to Salzburg.
6. Grand Duke Paul Petrovich and his wife, Maria Feodorovna, were visiting Vienna for the second time within a year.

October;—if, however, they are coming indeed, then it would not only be very Necessary for me to be here, as my good friends tell me, but my absence would be a real Triumph for my enemies and consequently quite damaging to me!—If I were to become music master to the Princess of Würtenberg,[7] a leave for visiting my father could easily be arranged;—at any rate, if the trip will have to be postponed, no one will be more sorry than my wife and I—because we can hardly wait for the moment when we will be able to embrace our dearest and best father as well as our dearest sister.

With regard to France and England, you are perfectly right!—It's a step I can always take—it's better if I hold out here a bit longer—besides, things can change in the meantime in those countries as well.—

Last Tuesday, after a pause of two weeks, thank heaven!—my opera was performed again with the greatest of applause.[8]—

I'm delighted to hear that the Sinphonie is to your taste.[9]—à propòs—you don't even know (or do you?) where I am living at present; where do you think?—in the Same house where we were lodging 14 years ago—at the High Bridge in the Grünwald House—which is now called the Groshaubtische House, N.° 387.[10] Stephani the Younger came back yesterday; I saw him today.—Elisabetha Wendling has arrived as well. Now you must forgive me for closing so soon, but I spent too much time chatting with Herr von Strack.—In my heart I wish the Russian nobility weren't coming, so that I would soon have the pleasure of kissing your hands.—

My wife weeps tears of joy whenever she thinks of our trip to Salzburg; farewell!—we kiss your hands 1000 times and embrace our dear sister with all our hearts and remain your

most obedient children
W. A. Mozart,
Man and wife
are one life.

7. Elisabeth Wilhelmine Louise von Württemberg was the niece of the emperor; Mozart still had hopes of becoming her music teacher, but they were not fulfilled.
8. *Die Entführung.*
9. The "Haffner" Symphony, K. 385.
10. Now 19 Wipplingerstraße, in Vienna's first district.

To his father, in Salzburg

Vienna, September 11, 1782

Mon Trés cher Pére!

I am much obliged to you for the tongues you sent—I gave two of them to the Baronness and kept the other 2 for myself, and tomorrow we'll have a feast;—please tell me how you would like me to pay for them.—If you can also get me a few Schwarzenreuther,[11] you'll really be giving me great pleasure.—The Jewess *Escules*[12] was probably a pretty effective instrument in breaking up the friendship between the emperor and the Russian court—she *was taken to Berlin yesterday* so she can give the king there the pleasure of her company;—she is truly a swine of the first order—because she was the one and only cause of Günther's misfortune;[13]—if you can call 2 months of house arrest in a comfortable room with all your books, your fortepiano, etc., a misfortune; the same goes for losing your old position but getting a another one somewhere else with a salary of 1200 gulden; he left for *Hermannstadt* yesterday.— Still—an affair like this is always hurtful to an Honest man, and nothing in the world can make up for it.—But you can see from all this that he did not commit such a major crime.—His whole crime is— Etourderie—carelessness—in other words—lack of discretion— which, of course, is a major flaw in a Privy Councillor. . . . Just imagine how strange and unexpected the whole affair was for me and how deeply I was affected because Stephani, Adamberger, and I were having supper with him one evening and the very next day he was under arrest.—Now I must close, for the mail coach might dash off without my letter. My dear wife and I kiss your hands 1000 times and embrace our dear sister with all our heart and remain Forever your

most obedient children
Konstanze and Mozart

My wife is now
entering her
91st year.[14]

11. "Schwarzenreuther" is a kind of trout found in Austrian and Bavarian lakes.
12. Eleonore Eskeles, daughter of the chief rabbi of Bohemia and Moravia, was accused of spying for the king of Prussia but was later (after the death of Joseph II) exonerated.
13. Johann Valentin Günther, privy councillor in the cabinet of Joseph II; he was accused of giving secret information to Eleonore Eskeles, with whom he had an illicit affair.
14. Mozart means, of course, 19th year.

To Baroness von Waldstätten, in Vienna

Vienna, September 28, 1782

Most Esteemed Baroness!

When Your Ladyship graciously invited me yesterday to dinner for tomorrow, Sunday, I did not remember at the time that I had already accepted an engagement for dinner at the Augarten a week ago.—My friend Martin, who thinks he owes me for various things, wants *absolument* to treat me to a Dinèe.—So yesterday I thought I could still change things around to suit my wishes, but Herr Martin has already ordered the dinner and made all the arrangements; consequently all his expenses would be for naught.—So I hope Your Grace will find the inspiration to make a new accommodation so we can bring our complementation and veneration, say, next Tuesday, together with some purification to keep us from vexation if Fräulein von Auerhammer makes a presentation.[15]—But joking aside; the concerto I played at the theater? Well, I would not want to sell it for under 6 ducats;[16] but I would throw in the cost of copying it.—As for the beautiful red jacket that is tickling my heart so mercilessly, please let me know *where it can be bought and how expensive it is,* for I completely forgot to check how much it was; my attention was totally drawn to its beauty and not to its price.—I simply must have such a jacket so it will be worth my effort to get those buttons, which I can't get out of my mind.—I saw them some time ago in the Brandau Button Shop opposite the Milano at the Kohlmarkt[17] when I bought some other buttons for a suit. They are made of mother-of-pearl with several white stones around the edge and a beautiful yellow stone in the middle.—I would like to have all things that are good, genuine, and beautiful!—I wonder why it is that those who cannot afford it would like to spend all they have for this sort of thing and those who could afford it, don't?—Well, I think it's high time that I come to an end with my scribbling here—*J kiß your hands, and hoping to see you in good health the Tuesday j am*

your most humble servant[18]

Mozart.

15. Josepha von Auernhammer, Mozart's former student, had been living with the baroness after her father's death.
16. Piano Concerto no. 5 in D, K. 175.
17. Café Milani at the Kohlmarkt in Vienna.
18. Mozart was taking English lessons and probably wanted to show off his newly acquired skill; the English is printed here as he wrote it.

Constanze, my other half, kisses
your Grace's hands 1000 times,
she also gives a little kiss to the
Auerhammer girl, but I'm not
supposed to know about it,
for otherwise I'll get the creeps.

Mozart must have been in a good mood when he wrote these two letters to Baroness von Waldstätten. Their verbal spirit and imagination are a bit reminiscent of the Bäsle-Briefe, although within the limits of respectability.

To Baroness von Waldstätten, in Vienna

Vienna, October 2, 1782

Dearest, Best, and Most Beautiful,
Golden-, Silver-, Sugar-coated
Worthiest and Most Esteemed
Gracious Lady
Baroness!

I have the Honor of sending Your Grace the Rondeau we talked about,[19] together with the 2 volumes of Comedies and a small collection of tales.[20] I committed a capital blunder yesterday!—I had the nagging feeling that there was something else I wanted to tell you—but my dumb brain couldn't come up with it! What I had wanted to say was thank you, Your Grace, for going to such trouble right away because of that beautiful jacket—and also for Your Grace's kindness to promise me such a coat!—it had slipped my mind, which is something not so unusual for me.—I sometimes regret that I didn't study architecture instead of music; for I have heard it said that the best architects are those whose buildings never collapse.[21]—Let me say to you that I am both a happy and unhappy man!—unhappy ever since I saw Your Grace at the ball with that exquisite coiffure!—so—gone was my peace of

19. Mozart's new finale for his Piano Concerto no. 5, K. 175.
20. It is not known which comedies or tales Mozart is referring to here.
21. Mozart is making a pun on the word *einfallen*, which in German has two meanings: "to collapse" (to fall down) and "to be struck" (hit) by an idea.

mind!—nothing but sighs and groans!—the remaining time at the ball I wasn't dancing—I was jumping—and when the supper came—I didn't eat my food—I wolfed it down—and during the night, instead of slumbering softly and peacefully—I slept like a dormouse and snored like a bear!—and, without taking too much credit for my insights, I would almost be willing to wager that Your Grace had a similar experience—à proportion, of course!—You are smiling?—you are blushing?—oh yes—I am such a happy man!—My fortune is made!—But woe! Who is tapping me on my shoulder?—And who is peering into my writing?—auweh, auweh, auweh![22]—it's my Wife!—Well, in God's name, she is here, and she is all mine, and I must keep her! What's to be done?—I must give her a little praise—and pretend that it is true!—. . .

My wife, who is an angel of a woman, and I, a model of a husband, kiss Your Grace's hands 1000 times and we shall always be your

faithful vassals,

Mozart magnus, corpore parvus

et

Constantia, omnium uxorum

pulcherrima et prudentißima.[23]

To his father, in Salzburg

Vienna, October 19, 1782

Mon trés cher Pére!

I must again write in a hurry; I don't quite understand it, but I used to receive a letter from you every Friday after lunch;—now, no matter when I send off my letters, I never get yours until Saturday evening.— I am very sorry that you are having such troubles with my opera.[24]— Yes, I've heard about England's victories,[25]—you probably know that I am a dyed-in-the-wool Englishman—and I've heard the news with great delight!

22. "Woe, woe, woe!"
23. Mozart the Great with a small body and Constanze, who is the most beautiful and clever of all women.
24. Mozart had asked his father to have *Die Entführung* copied in Salzburg. A copy of the opera had been requested by the Prussian court.
25. Leopold presumably had asked Mozart whether he had heard of Lord Richard Howe's victory over the French at Gibraltar and Sir Edward Hughes's victory at Trincomalee.

The Russian Court left today. My opera was performed for them not so long ago; on that occasion I thought it advisable to resume my place at the clavier and do my conducting from there, partly to wake up the orchestra, which had fallen into a slight slumber, partly (as I happen to be in Vienna anyway) to show myself to the royal guests as the father of my child.——

Dearest father;——I must confess that I can hardly wait to see you and kiss your hands——and, following such inclination I had wanted to be in Salzburg for your Name Day on November 15; however——the most profitable season is just about to begin here.——The upper classes are just returning from the countryside and will be resuming their music lessons.——concerts will soon start again,——besides, I would have to be back in Vienna by the beginning of December anyway; how hard it would be for me and my wife to leave you so soon;——we would much rather stay longer so we can enjoy the company of our dear father and our dear sister!——Now it depends on you whether you'd like to have us come for a longer or a shorter period of time?——We thought of maybe spending the spring with you. If I even just mention Salzburg to my dear wife, she is beside herself with joy!——The Barber of Salzburg—— not the one from Seville——paid me a visit;[26] he brought me your, my sister's, and Katherl's greetings.——

Farewell for now, the two of us kiss your hands 1000 times, we embrace our dear sister with all our hearts and remain Forever your

most obedient children

M. C.[27] et W. A. Mozart.

The exact reasons why Mozart thought of himself as a "dyed-in-the-wool Englishman" (ein ErzEngelländer) are not known. It may have something to do with his favorable reception in London in 1764–65 and the fairness with which he was treated as a child performer and composer. The Honorable Daines Barrington, for instance, who tested his musical skills, not only concluded that the eight-year-old Mozart was a genuine wunderkind but reported his findings in his "Account of a very remarkable young Musician" to the Royal Society of London. Since there were

26. Mozart is referring to his childhood friend Wenzel Andreas Gilowsky, a surgeon in Vienna.
27. "M. C." stands for Maria Constanze.

always some intrigues against Mozart in Vienna, he must have remembered the English and their sense of fairness with great nostalgia.

To his father, in Salzburg

Vienna, November 20, 1782

Mon Trés cher Pére!

I can see now, alas, that I will have to postpone the pleasure of embracing you until the spring; my pupils *absolument* won't let me go— and, in fact, right now the weather is too cold for my wife;—everyone is urging me not to take the risk;—not until the spring; but as far as I am concerned spring already comes in *March*—or beginning of *April* at the latest; of course, I'm calculating from our own point of view, but we'll be able to travel because my wife does not expect her confinement until the month of June.—So, today I'm going to unpack our trunks again; I had left everything packed until I received word from you;—if you had insisted that we come—whoosh—we would have been gone— and not told anybody—just to show you that the delay was not on our account—. . . The emperor had another attack of fever—I fear—he will not live much longer—I so wish to be wrong.—. . .

I must close now; my wife and I kiss your hands 1000 times and embrace our dear sister with all our hearts and remain Forever your

most obedient children
W. et C. Mozart

To his father, in Salzburg

Vienna, December 21, 1782

Mon trés cher Pére!

Great as my longing to receive a letter from you after 3 weeks of absolute silence was, my consternation at the content of your letter was just as great;—in short, we were both in the same worrisome predica-ment![28]—I want you to know that I replied to your last letter on Decem.^bre 4th: consequently I expected an answer within a week—but

---

28. Apparently two letters were lost in the mail, one from Leopold to Wolfgang and one from Wolfgang to Leopold.

nothing came;—all right, I thought, perhaps you hadn't had time to write;—and, because your letter contained a hint of something—pleasant for us, we almost thought you might be coming for a visit.—. . .

My wife and I are quite well, god be thanked and praised. Is it true that the archbishop will come to Vienna right after New Year's?—Countess Litzow[29] has been here for 3 weeks, but I found out only yesterday;—Prince Gallizin mentioned it to me.—He has engaged me for all of his concerts; his carriage picks me up each time and brings me home afterward, and when I am at his place, I am treated with the greatest courtesy. On the 10th my opera was performed again with great applause, it was the 14th performance; the theater was as full as the first time—or rather—as always.—Count Rosenberg talked to me at Gallizin's and suggested that I compose an Italian opera;—I am already trying to get the latest libretti for opere buffe from Italy so I can make a choice, but I haven't received any yet. I have myself written to Ignaz Hagenauer for that reason;[30]—also, at Easter a number of Italian singers are coming to town.—Please send me the address of Lugiati in Verona.—I want to try him as as well.

A new opera or rather comedy was produced recently with ariettas by Umlauff, titled *Which is the best Nation?*—What a wretched piece; I was asked to set it to music, but I turned it down with the comment that whoever will compose this piece without changing the text will risk a storm of boos;—and if it hadn't been for the fact that Umlauff participated, it would have been booed off the stage for sure; as it was, people were only hissing.—No wonder, for one couldn't have endured the play even with the best of music; but to make things worse, in this case the Musique was so miserable as well that I'm not sure who will win the Prize of Wretchedness: the Poet or the Composer.—To its disgrace it was given a 2nd time, but I believe this will the Punctum Satis.[31]—

Now I must close otherwise I'll miss the mail coach. My dear wife and I kiss your hands 1000 times and embrace our dear sister with all our heart and remain Forever

your most obedient children
W. et C. Mozart

---

29. Countess Antonia Lützow, a niece of Archbishop Colloredo.
30. Ignaz Joachim Hagenauer, son of the Mozarts' former landlord in Salzburg, lived as a merchant in Trieste.
31. "This will be the end."

🖎 *The "subscription concerts" Mozart is referring to in the following letters are his earliest Viennese piano concertos, K. 413–415. He composed them between the second half of 1782 and early 1783. His description of the three concertos is a superb characterization of his own early Viennese style: music in the middle, i.e., a sound sophisticated enough to engage the expert and pleasing enough to be enjoyed by the common listener. The language in which Mozart conveys these fundamental truths about his art is of utter simplicity: "the middle thing—the truth in all things, is no longer known and appreciated" (das mittelding—das wahre in allen sachen kennt und schätzt man izt nimmer).*

To his father, in Salzburg

Vienna, December 28, 1782

Mon trés cher Pére!

I must write to you in greatest haste because it's already half past 5 and I have asked some people over for 6 o'clock to play a little Musique;—I'm so busy these days that at times I don't know whether I'm coming or going anymore;—the entire morning, until 2 o'clock, is taken up with music lessons;—then we eat;—and after lunch I have to grant my poor stomach a short hour of digestion; only the evening is left for composing—and not even that's a sure thing, because I am often asked to take part in a concert.—I still have 2 concertos to write to complete my subscription concerts.[32]—These concertos are a happy medium between what's too difficult and too easy—they are Brilliant—pleasing to the ear—Natural without becoming vacuous;—there are passages here and there that only connoisseurs can fully appreciate—yet the common listener will find them satisfying as well, although without knowing why. I am distributing tickets—for 6 ducats in cash.—I am also about to complete a piano version of my opera,[33] which is going to be engraved; in addition, I'm working on a quite difficult assignment, namely an Ode to Gibraltar by Denis.[34] It's a commission by a Hungarian Lady who wants to keep this a secret and present it to Denis as a tribute.—The ode is sublime, beautiful, anything you want—but—

32. The three piano concertos Mozart offered for subscription are K. 413–415.
33. *Die Entführung.* Mozart never completed his piano score of the opera, partly because other such versions appeared on the market.
34. Mozart's setting of the "Ode to Gibraltar" by Johann Michael Denis was never finished. The ode celebrates the victory of Admiral Richard Howe over the French.

it's too exaggerated and bombastic for my fastidious ears—but what is one to do!—the middle thing—the truth in all things, is no longer known and appreciated—to earn applause one has to compose things that are so simpleminded that a coachman can sing them after hearing them just once, or so complicated—that they please precisely because no sensible person can understand them;—but that's not really what I wanted to talk to you about; what I wanted to say is that I'd be really interested in writing a book—a brief Criticism of Music with Examples—but, *N.B.*, not under my name.—I am including here a letter from the Baroness Waldstätten, who is worried that this 2ⁿᵈ letter of hers might not find its way to you either;—it appears that you did not receive her previous letter since you haven't made any mention of it.— I asked you about this in my letter that was also lost.—Adieu for now; more next time. My sweet little wife and I kiss your hands 1000 times and embrace our dear sister with all our heart and remain Forever your

most obed. children

W. et C. Mzt

Mozart's "moral commitment" involved his promise to write a mass for Constanze upon their marriage. He worked on the mass during the years 1782 and 1783 but could not finish it. It was performed for the first time as the Mass in C minor in St. Peter's at Salzburg during Wolfgang and Constanze's visit. The missing parts were supplied from earlier masses.

To his father, in Salzburg

Vienna, January 4, 1783

Mon trés cher Pére!

I cannot possibly write much at the moment, because we've just come back from Baroness Waldstätten, and I have to change from head to toe, for I am invited to a private concert at the residence of Herr Court Councillor Spiellmann.[35]—We both thank you for your New Year's wishes and acknowledge freely that we are as dumb as oxen because we completely forgot our own duty of sending wishes to you— so we are sending you our wishes belatedly and won't even send them as

---

35. Anton Freiherr von Spielmann, court councillor and well-known music connoisseur in Vienna.

New Year's Wishes but just as the everyday wishes we always have for you—and we'll leave it at that.—About my moral commitment, yes, that's quite correct;—the word flowed from my pen not entirely without my intention—I made the promise firmly in my heart and I hope to keep it.—When I made it, my wife was still single—but the promise was easy to make because I was determined to marry her as soon as she was well again.—Time and circumstances prevented our trip as you know;—but as proof of my promise I have the score of half a mass that is lying here waiting to be finished.

Today I got a new pupil, Countess Balfi the older;[36] she is the daughter of the archbishop's sister;—so please keep it to yourself for a while since I don't know for sure whether they like this to be known.— It doesn't matter much whether you send me the Sinfonie of the Haffner Musique, which I wrote in Vienna, in the original score or copied out, because I'll have to have several copies made here anyway for my concert.—I also would like to have the following Sinfonies:[37]

and I would like to have them as quickly as possible.—Then I'd like to have the pieces with counterpoint by Eberlin; they are bound in small blue paper and

Porco
Sau
●
Sus[38]
Chochon

36. Countess Josepha Gabriela Pálffy.
37. The four symphonies, in the order of their listing, are K. 204, 201, 182, and 183.
38. Mozart inadvertently made a big ink blot in the middle of the page; the Italian *porco*, the German *Sau*, the French *cochon*, and the Latin *sus* all mean the same thing: pig!

there are also some pieces by Haydn[39] that I would like to have for Baron van Suiten, at whose house I am every Sunday from 12 until 2 o'clock. Tell me, are there any interesting fugues in Haydn's last mass and vespers, or perhaps in both?—If so, you would oblige me if you could have them copied for me by and by.

I must close now; . . . adieu, we kiss your hands 1000 times and embrace our dear sister with our hearts and remain Forever your

obed. children
W. et C. Mozart

N.B. The 3 concertos are being published; the price will be 4 ducats.[40]

To his father, in Salzburg

Vienna, January 22, 1783

Mon trés cher Pére!

Don't worry about the three concertos being too expensive;—I believe I should earn at least one ducat for each concerto—and I can't imagine that anyone could get it copied for one ducat!—besides no one can copy them secretly, because I'm not giving them out of my hands until I have a certain number of subscribers;—they have been advertised already for the 3rd time in the Vienna Diarium—and as of the 20th of this month I'm selling subscription tickets at my house—for 4 ducats in cash—and during the Month of April the concertos can be picked up at my house in exchange for the tickets.—I will soon send the cadenzas and introductions to my dear sister—I haven't yet changed the introductions for the Rondeau, because when I perform the concerto I always play what occurs to me at the moment.—Please, send the Sinfonies I requested as soon as possible;—I really need them!—And one more favor because my wife won't give me any peace about it—you know, of course, that we are in the middle of the carnival season and that there's a lot of dancing here just as there is in Salzburg and Munich.—and I would like to go dressed up, but please don't say a

---

39. Michael Haydn.
40. Mozart's three early Viennese piano concertos K. 413-415 were eventually published by Artaria & Co. in Vienna.

word to anyone, as a Harlequin—because around here there are so many—indeed nothing but—asses at the Redoute;[41]—therefore, I would like to ask you to send me your Harlequin costume—but it would have to be very soon—we are not going to the ball until we have the masks, although everything is already in full swing.—We actually prefer house balls.—Last week I gave one in our apartment.—Of course, each of the gentlemen had to make a contribution of 2 gulden.—We started at 6 o'clock in the evening and ended at 7;—what, only one hour?—No, No!—we ended at 7 o'clock in the morning;—but you can't understand how we could have enough space?—Oh yes! It just occurs to me that I forgot to tell you that we moved from our lodgings a month and a half ago—we are still at the Hohe Brücke—but a few doors away;—we now live in the Kleine Herbertsteinische Haus, Nr. 412, 4th floor;[42] in an apartment belonging to Herr von Wetzlar, a wealthy Jew.[43] There I have a room that is 1000 paces long and 1 pace wide[44]—one bedroom—an anteroom—and a very nice large kitchen;—there are also 2 beautiful spacious rooms adjacent to our apartment that are still unoccupied—and these were the rooms we used for our house ball.—Baron Wetzlar and his wife were at the ball—also Baroness Waldstätten—Herr von Edelbach—and Gilowsky, that old gasbag—Stephanie the Younger et uxor[45]—Adamberger and wife—Herr Lange and Frau Lange[46]—etc., etc.,— it's impossible to list them *all*—Now I must close because I still want to write to the Wendlings in Mannheim about my concertos.

Please remind that ever-ready opera composer Gatti[47] that I asked him for some opera libretti;—I wish I already had them now;—Adieu for now—We kiss your hands 1000 times and embrace our dear sister with all our hearts and remain Forever your

most obedient children
W. et C. Mozart

---

41. A masked ball.
42. This was Mozart's fourth move since he arrival in Vienna a year and a half earlier.
43. Raimund Wetzlar von Plankenstern, son of Karl Abraham Wetzlar; father and son were often helpful to Mozart.
44. "1000 paces long and one pace wide" was a favorite joke in the Mozart family.
45. "With his wife."
46. Frau Lange is Aloysia.
47. Abbate Luigi Gatti, court composer at Salzburg, who was about to be appointed Kapellmeister of the Salzburg court orchestra. Mozart's description of him as "ever-ready" was probably ironic.

🐚 *Mozart is highly critical of Viennese opera life; he makes no secret of his disdain. And why not? His own singspiel,* Die Entführung, *was a tremendous success, and he was probably right in his assessment of the competition.*

To his father, in Salzburg

Vienna, February 5, 1783

Mon Trés cher Pére!

I received your most recent letter safely and hope that in the meantime you also got my last letter, with the request to send me your Harlequin costume;—let me repeat my request with the added plea that you please be so kind to send it very soon;—also the sinfonies, especially the *last one*[48]—please send everything as soon as possible; my concert will take place on the 3rd Sunday in Lent, in other words, on March 23rd—and I will have to have a number of copies made.—

So I thought, if you haven't had it copied yet, you might send it back to me in the original score, just the way I sent it to you; and please include the Menuetts.—

Has Ceccarelli left Salzburg?—or had he not been given a part in Gatti's Cantata? I'm saying this because you don't mention him among the squabblers or bickerers!—

Yesterday my opera was performed for the 17th time with the usual applause as well as a full theater.—

Next Friday, that is the day after tomorrow, a New Opera will be performed, the Musique, a Galimathias,[49] is from a young local composer, a pupil of Wagenseil, with the name of Gallus Cantans, in arbore sedens, gigirigi faciens.[50]—It will probably not be well received;—but perhaps it will fare better than its predecessor, an old opera by Gasman, "La Notte Crittica," translated into German as "Die unruhige Nacht,"[51] which barely survived 3 performances; and before that we had the abominable opera by Umlauf that I mentioned to you before; that one didn't

---

48. He probably means the last one he composed, i.e., the "Haffner" Symphony, K. 385.
49. "Galimathias" is a kind of musical medley.
50. The composer of the new opera was Johann Mederitsch, nicknamed Gallus. His opera, *Rose, oder Pflicht und Liebe im Streit* (Rose, or the Quarrel between Duty and Love), text by Gottlieb Stephanie, was performed on February 9. Mozart was obviously not impressed and therefore wrote in Latin, "The singing Gallus is sitting in a tree and crows gigirigi."
51. *The Unquiet Night* (text by Carlo Goldoni) by Florian Leopold Gassmann.

even make three performances.—It's as if they were determined to kill the German opera, which in any event is coming to an end, before its time.—and it's the Germans who are doing it—pfui Teufel![52]—

I asked you in my last letter to remind Gatti as often as you can about the Italian libretti; and I am asking you once again;—but I also have to tell you what I really think:—I don't believe that the Italian opera will endure for long—and I—will stay with the Germans.—Even though it's more difficult for me, I prefer it.—Every nation has its own opera—why shouldn't we Germans have one as well?—is the German language not as singable as French and English?—is it not more singable than Russian?—Well now;—I'm going to write a German opera just for *myself*;—I have chosen a comedy by Goldoni—"Il servitore di Due Padroni"—and the first Act is already translated—Baron Binder is the translator.[53] But I'll keep it to myself until it's all done;—now tell me, what do you think about it?—Don't you think that I'll be able to make something of it?—Anyway—I must stop now; Fischer is here with me—the bass singer—he asked me to write to Le Gròs in Paris on his behalf;—he will be going to Paris during the coming Lenten Season;—they are committing an act of Folly here by letting a man go who can never be replaced.—My wife and I kiss your hands 1000 times and embrace our dear sister with all our heart and remain Forever your

most obedient children
W. et C. Mozart

🎵 *Mozart had composed the "Haffner" Symphony in such a hurry that he could not remember exactly what he had written. When he got the original score back from his father, he himself was "truly surprised" at its excellent quality.*

To his father, in Salzburg

Vienna, February 15, 1783

Mon Trés cher Pére!

I thank you with all my heart for the Musique you sent!—I am so sorry that I cannot make use of the Musique for Thamos.[54]—The play,

---

52. "Shame on them!"
53. Johann Nepomuk Friedrich Freiherr Binder von Krieglstein. Mozart never carried out his plan to set Goldoni's play to music.
54. Mozart's incidental music for Baron Tobias Philipp von Gebler's drama *Thamos, König in Ägypten*, K. 345.

which failed here, is now among the works rejected and will simply not be performed anymore.—It might be given again just on account of its music—but it is not very likely— and that's too bad!—I am including here the 3 cadenzas for the Concerto in D for my sister—and the 2 introductions to the Concerto in E-flat.[55] Please send me right away the little book that contains the oboe concerto I wrote for Ramm or rather for Ferlendi.[56]—Prince Esterhazi's oboist has offered me 3 ducats for it;—he'll pay me 6 if I'll write him a New one.—Should you have left for Munich already, then, Heavens, there's nothing to be done;—the only other possibility would have been to ask Ramm himself—but he isn't available either.—I would have liked to sit in a corner in Strasburg—but No—I don't think I would have had a quiet night.[57] The New Hafner Sinfonie has truly surprised me—I didn't remember anything about it;—I'm sure it is very effective.—Some of us will probably get together during the last days of the carnival season and perform a small Pantomime, but please, not a word to anyone. Also, I am glad to say that I finally got together with Chevalier Hipolity;[58]—he had not been able to find me until just now.—What a charming man.—He's been to see me once and will come back soon with an aria so I can hear him sing.—I must close now, for I am expected at the theater. My little wife and I kiss your hands 1000 times and embrace our dear sister with all our heart and remain your

most obedient children
W. A. Mozart

It is not known to whom Mozart owed money at this point; nor is it known whether Baroness von Waldstätten or perhaps Herr von Trattner helped him out. One thing, however, is clear: the letter gives the first indication that Mozart got himself not only into financial straits but also into a well-known vicious circle—borrowing money to cover debts.

---

55. K. 175 and 271.
56. Probably the original score of the Oboe Concerto, K. 314.
57. Mozart may be referring here to *Die Entführung*, which was just then being performed in Strasbourg.
58. The identity of Chevalier Hipolity has not been established.

To Baroness von Waldstätten, in Vienna

Vienna, February 15, 1783

Most highly Esteemed Baroness!

I got myself into a fine predicament!

Herr von Trattner[59] and I talked about getting an extension for 2 weeks;—as every merchant is willing to accommodate you in such matters, except perhaps the most unhelpful individual in the world, I was quite relaxed about it and thought, if I couldn't get the money together myself, I would be able to borrow the sum!—Now Herr von Trattner sends me word that the man in question is *absolument* not willing to wait any longer, and if I don't pay between today and tomorrow, he will *sue* me for the amount.—Just think, Your Grace, what unpleasantness this would mean for me!—I'm unable to pay it right now, not even half of it!—If I had known that the Subscription of my concerts would go so slowly, I would have taken the loan for a longer period!—I beg Your Grace, for Heaven's sake, help me not to forfeit my honor and good name!—My poor little wife is a bit indisposed; therefore, I cannot leave her alone, otherwise I would have come to ask Your Grace in person. We kiss Your Grace's hands 1000 times and remain both

Your Grace's
most obedient children
W. A. and C. Mozart

🖎 *On March 3 (Carnival Monday), Mozart and friends put on a pantomime during a masked ball at the Hofburg in Vienna. The group presented popular figures from the commedia dell'arte. Mozart was not only the guiding spirit of the event but also contributed the music (K. 446). Not surprisingly, he chose for himself the role of Harlequin.*

To his father, in Salzburg

Vienna, March 12, 1783

Mon trés cher Pére!

I do hope you didn't worry about my silence but rather somehow understood the reason for it, which quite simply was that I didn't know

---

59. Johann Thomas von Trattner, a merchant and publisher, who seems to have advised Mozart in financial matters; his wife was a pupil of Mozart's.

how long you would be in Munich and consequently I didn't know where to write to; therefore, I waited until now, when I'm almost certain that my letter will reach you in Salzburg.—My sister-in-law Madame Lange had her concert yesterday in the theater in which I, too, played a concerto.—The theater was very full; and I was greeted again so warmly by the Viennese public that it was truly gratifying.—I had already left the stage, but they didn't stop clapping—I had to repeat the Rondeau;—the applause was like a regular cloudburst.—It's a good omen for my own concert that will be coming up on March 23rd.—They also played my Sinfonie, the one I did for the Concert Spirituel. And my sister-in-law sang the aria *Non sò d'onde viene;*—Gluck was in a box next to the Langes—my wife was with them;—well, he couldn't find enough words of praise for both the sinfonie and the aria, and he invited all four of us to dine with him next Sunday.— . . .

On Carnival Monday we performed our Masquerade at the Redoute.—It consisted of a Pantomime that we did during the half hour of intermission.—My sister-in-law played Colombine, I was Harlequin, my brother-in-law Piero, *Merk,* an old dancing master, played Pantalon, and a Painter (by the name of Graßi) played the Dottore.—

The idea for the Pantomime and the Musick for it both came from me.—Merk, the dancing master, was kind enough to coach us, and I can tell you, we played quite charmingly.—I'm enclosing the announcement that was distributed to all the masques by someone dressed up as a limping postman.—The verses, some simple rhymed couplets, could have been better; but they were not my creation;—Müller, the actor, had scribbled them down in a hurry.—

I must close now because I must be off to a concert at Count Esterhazy's.—Farewell in the meantime—please don't forget about the Musique.—My wife and I kiss your hands 1000 times and embrace our dear sister with all our heart, I am Forever

your obedient son
W. A. et C. Mozart

In the space of three weeks, Mozart participated in three private concerts: one for Madame Lange (Aloysia), one for himself, and one for Therese Teyber, a Viennese soprano. Each of these "academies" had long, rich, and varied programs, and that gave Mozart an opportunity to introduce a good number of his own compositions. It marks the beginning of a sharp rise of his popularity in Vienna.

To his father, in Salzburg

Vienna, March 29, 1783

Mon trés cher Pére!

It's probably not necessary to tell you much about the success of my concert; you may well have heard it already. It's enough to say that the theater couldn't have been fuller, and all the loges were occupied.——But what pleased me most was that His Majesty, the Emperor, was there as well; and how delighted he was and how vociferously he applauded me;——he is in the habit of sending money to the box office before he comes to the theater, if it hadn't been for that I would have good reason to assume that he would have sent me more because his satisfaction was beyond all bounds.——He sent 25 ducats.——We did the following pieces: (1) the New Hafner Simphonie; (2) Mad.^me Lange sang the aria *se il padre perdei*, from my Munich opera, accompanied by four instruments; (3) the third of my Subscription Concertos; (4) Adamberger sang the scena I wrote for Countess Baumgarten; (5) the little concertante Simphonie from my most recent Final Musique; (6) I played the Concerto in D, which is so favored here; I sent you the Rondeau with variations from it; (7) Mad.^selle Täuber sang the szena *Parto m'affretto*, from my last Milano opera; (8) I played a short fugue because the emperor was present and did some variations on an aria from an opera called "The Philosophers"——which I had to repeat; then I did variations on the aria "unser dummer Pöbel meint," etc., from the Pilgrim of Mecka; (9) Mad.^me Lange sang the New Rondeau I composed; (10) the last movement of the first Simphonie.[60]

Tomorrow Mad.^selle Täuber will have a concert, where I will play as well. And next Thursday Herr von Daubrawaick and Gilowsky will be going to Salzburg and bring you the Munich opera, 2 copies of my sonatas, some variations for my sister, and the money I owe you for having the opera copied.——I received your packet with all the Musique safely;——and I thank you;——please don't forget the *Lauda sion*,[61] and the other

---

60. (1) "Haffner" Symphony, K. 385; (2) Ilia's aria in act 2 of *Idomeneo*; (3) Piano Concerto in C, K. 415; (4) "Misera, dove son!," K. 369; (5) Serenade in D, K. 320; (6) K. 175 with the new rondo, K. 382; (7) Aria no. 16 from *Lucio Silla*; (8) Six Variations on "Salve tu, Domine," from Paisiello's opera *Il filosofi immaginari*, K. 398; Ten Variations of "Unser dummer Pöbel meint," K. 455, from Gluck's opera *Pilgrimme von Mecka*; (9) "Mia speranza adorata," K. 416; (10) The finale of the "Haffner" Symphony was played separately at the end of the program.
61. A composition by Michael Haydn.

thing we'd like to have, dearest father, is some of your own best church music;—we love to converse with all possible Masters—old and modern;—so please let us have something from *you* as soon as possible.—

I must close now.

My wife and I kiss your hands 1000 times and embrace our dear sister with all our heart and remain Forever your

most obedient children
W. A. Mozart

To his father, in Salzburg

Vienna, April 12, 1783

Mon trés cher Pére!

This morning I got your letter from the 8th and was happy to learn that you received everything I sent along with Herr von Daubrawaick.—It's too bad that the mail coach won't leave again until a week from today and, therefore, I can't send you the two copies of my sonatas and all the other things any sooner.—

I will take this opportunity to send you the variations to the voice part of the aria *non sò d'onde viene,* etc.—Next time you have occasion to send me a parcel, please let the Rondeau for alto voice ride along, the one I wrote for the castrato who came to Salzburg with the Italian troupe,[62] and the Rondeau I did for Ceccarelli in *Vienna.* When the weather gets a bit warmer, please search in the attic under the roof for some of your own church music and send it to me as well; you don't need to be embarrassed.—Baron van Suiten and Starzer know as well as you and I that musical taste is changing all the time—and *unfortunately*—even church music is affected by these changes; it shouldn't be that way—but it's the reason why the true church music is to be found—in attics—almost eaten up by worms.—When I come to Salzburg with my wife in the month of July, as I expect, I'd like to talk to you more on this subject.—When Herr von Daubrawaick left for Salzburg from here, my wife could hardly be restrained, she wanted *absolument* to jump into a carriage with me and follow him. . . .

You will have read in my last letter that I was asked to play in yet another concert, namely in the academie of Mad.[selle] Teyber.—The

---

62. Alto Recitative and Aria, "Ombra felice," K. 255.

emperor was there, too.—I played my first concerto, the one I performed in my own concert.[63]—They wanted me to repeat the Rondeau—so I sat down again—but rather than just repeat the Rondeau, I asked to have the conductor's podium removed and played it alone.—I wish you could have heard how this little surprise delighted the audience—they didn't just applaud but shouted Bravo and Bravißimo!—The emperor stayed and listened until I had finished playing—and when I left the clavier, he left his loge.—He stayed just to hear me. . . .

Farewell in the meantime. My dear little wife and I kiss your hands 1000 times and embrace our dear sister with all our heart and remain Forever your

most obedient children
W. Et C. Mozart

To Jean-Georges Sieber, Paris[64]

Vienna, April 26, 1783

Monsieur!

I have been in Vienna for two years now;—you are probably acquainted with my Sonatas for Pianoforte and violin accompaniment that were engraved here by Artaria and Compagnie.[65] Since I am not altogether happy with these engravings, and even if I were, I would like to share, once more, some of my work with a Landsmann in Paris; therefore, I wish to bring to your attention that I have 3 piano concertos ready to be engraved; they can be played with full orchestra, that is with oboes and horn—or simply à quatro.[66] Artaria has agreed to engrave them, but you, my friend, have first choice.—To spare us long negotiations, I will tell you the lowest price right off;—you give me 30 Louis d'or[67] for them, and we have a deal.—I am furthermore composing 6 quartets for 2 violins, viola, and bass[68]—if you would wish to engrave these quartets as well, I'll be happy to let you have them.—But I can't

---

63. K. 175.

64. Jean-Georges Sieber, a native German, was a music publisher in Paris and had published Mozart's Sonatas for Piano and Violin, K. 301–306, in 1778.

65. K. 296 and 376-380.

66. K. 413–415. The concertos were published in 1785 by Artaria as Oeuvre IV.

67. 330 gulden.

68. The six "Haydn" Quartets, which would be published by Artaria as Mozart's op. X.

give them to you at a bargain price—indeed, I could not sell them for under 50 Louis d'or. So, if you were inclined and able to do business with me, please let me have your reply, and I shall communicate an addreß in Paris to you where you can pick up my compositions and, at the same time, make your payment.[69]—In the meantime I remain your

devoted servant
Wolfgang Amadè Mozart

🖎 *A charming little note from an outing to the Prater on a pleasant day in May. The Prater is Vienna's big city park with picnic areas, restaurants, and carousels; it is famous today for its giant Ferris wheel. Mozart and Constanze were obviously enjoying a rare moment of peace and happiness.*

To his father, in Salzburg

Vienna, at the Prater, May 3, 1783

Mon trés cher Pére!

I just can't make up my mind to go back to the city so early—the weather is so beautiful—and it's so pleasant to be in the Prater today.— We had a little something to eat here in the park, and now we'll stay until 8 or nine o'clock in the evening.—The only company I have is my pregnant little wife—*and her only company*—consists of her little husband, who isn't pregnant but fat and happy.— . . . I just didn't want to miss out on this beautiful weather, especially for the sake of my dear wife—after all, a little walking is good for her.—I only wanted to tell you today that we are both well, god be praised, and we received your last letter all right.—Farewell.

We kiss your hands 1000 times and embrace our dear sister with all our heart and are Forever your

obedient children
W. A. and C. Mozart

🖎 *Lorenzo da Ponte (original name: Emanuele Conegliano), a native of Venice, was appointed by Joseph II as the "poet" for the Italian Stage in Vienna. Mozart met da*

---

69. The publisher Sieber did not seem to be interested.

Ponte at the home of Baron Raimund von Plankenstern Wetzlar; he liked him and wished to work with him but was skeptical at first about his reliability. As it turned out, da Ponte was the most brilliant text writer Mozart ever had.

To his father, in Salzburg

Vienna, May 7, 1783

Mon très cher Père!

Here is another brief letter!—I had wanted to wait with my writing to you until next Saturday since I will have to go to a concert today, but there's something urgent I have to tell, so I'll have to steal a minute or two to write just a few lines.—The Musique I requested has not yet come; I don't quite understand why.—The Italian opera company has now started up again; and it's very popular. The buffo[70] is especially good; his name is Benuci.[71]—I have gone through at least 100—probably more—libretti—but—I found almost nothing acceptable;—at the very least a lot of changes would have to be made here and there;—and if a writer would want to invest his time in this kind of effort, it would probably be easier to write something altogether New.—and New—is always better.—

We have a certain Abate da Ponte here as a text poet;—he has an incredible number of revisions to do at the theater—he also has to do *per obligo* a whole New libretto for Salieri—which he won't be able to finish for 2 months.—He promised to write me something New after that;—but who knows whether he will keep his word—or even wants to!—You know, these Italian gentlemen, they are very nice to your face!—enough, we know all about them!—and if he is in league with Salieri, I'll never get a text from him—and I would love to show here what I can really do with an Italian opera.—So I thought perhaps *Varesco*, provided he isn't angry with me because of the Munich opera[72]—could write me a New libretto for 7 characters.—Basta; you probably know best whether this could be arranged or not;—he could start putting

---

70. The comic character in an opera buffa-e.g., Leporello in Mozart's *Don Giovanni*.
71. Francesco Benucci, a *basso buffo* from Venice who he came to Vienna in 1781.
72. *Idomeneo.* Mozart had insisted on so many changes in his collaboration with Varesco that their relationship had grown a bit tense.

down some ideas, and when I come to Salzburg we could work them out together.—The most essential ingredient is this: it has to be, on the whole, very *Comical*; and, if possible, include 2 *equally good female roles;*— one would have to be a Seria, the other a Mezzo Carattere—but *in quality*—both roles would have to be absolutely equal.—the third female character can be entirely buffa, and so could the male parts.—If you think Varesco is amenable to all this, then please talk to him about it, and soon;—but you *must* not let him know that I will be coming to Salzburg in July—otherwise he won't get going on it;—in fact, I should like it very much if I could have some of the text while I'm still here in Vienna.—He would most certainly get 400 or 500 gulden for his work—for it is the custom here that the Poet always gets the income of the third performance.

Now I must close, for I'm not fully dressed yet. Farewell in the meantime;—my wife and I kiss your hands 1000 times, and we embrace our dear sister with all our heart and are Forever your

most obedient children
W. A. Mozart

To his father, in Salzburg

Vienna, May 21, 1783

Mon trés cher Pére!

. . . It just occurred to me that I have moved twice recently and haven't kept you informed.—Baron Wetzlar had to accommodate a lady in his house—so, as a kindness to him, we moved before our lease was up to a rather uninspiring place at the Kohlmarkt.—He, however, did not let us pay any rent for the 3 months we were living there and, in addition, paid the expenses of our move.

In the meantime we were looking around for a nicer place to live— and we found one at the Juden Platz,[73] where we are living now.—Baron Wetzlar paid for everything while we were living at the Kohlmarkt.— So then, our new lodging is *Auf dem Juden Platz im Burgischen Haus, N.º 244, im ersten Stock.*—Now we wish for nothing more than to be fortunate

---

73. The "Juden Platz" (Jewish Square) had been the center of the Viennese Jewish community since the Middle Ages. It included a Jewish hospital, a school, a synagogue, and the house of the rabbi. The name Judenplatz was first documented in 1437.

enough to embrace you both very soon.—But can that be in Salzburg?—I think not, unfortunately!—For some time now certain thoughts have been running through my head—but as you, dearest father, never mentioned any such thoughts, I banished them from my mind.—But Herr von Edelbach and Baron Wetzlar both agree with my suspicion, and that is, whether the archbishop will have me arrested when I come back to Salzburg or at least—oh, well, Basta!—the thing I worry about most is the fact that I don't have an official discharge;— maybe they did it on purpose—so they can arrest me later.—Enough of it, you know best how to judge the situation;—and if you have a contrary opinion, we'll come without fail.—If, however, you agree with me—we'll have to choose a third location—maybe Munich.—I think a priest is capable of anything; apropós, did you hear of the notorious quarrel between the archbishop and Count Daun?[74]—and that the archbishop received an infamous letter from the Chapter at Passau?[75]— Please keep after Varesco with regard to the libretto.—The main thing is, it has to be comical; for I know the taste of the Viennese.—Farewell in the meantime; my wife and I kiss your hands 1000 times and embrace our dear sister with all our heart and are Forever your

most obedient children
W. Et C. Mozart

To his father, in Salzburg

Vienna, June 7, 1783

Mon trés cher Pére!

God be praised and thanked, I have now completely recovered!— But my illness left me with a cold as a souvenir; isn't that wonderful!— I received the letter of my dear sister in good order; but the Name Day of my wife is neither in May nor in March but on the 16th of Februario—and you won't find it in a calendar.—Nevertheless, my wife thanks you most cordially for your well-intentioned wishes; they are always welcome, even without a Name Day.—She would have liked to write to my sister herself, but one can't hold it against her if she is a bit

---

74. Count Karl Joseph von Daun was the head of the Salzburg cathedral and its clerics.
75. The "Chapter at Passau" is the membership of the clerics (Domkapitel) in the cathedral of Passau. The "infamous letter" apparently concerned the election of the bishop of Passau, which Archbishop Colloredo had wanted to influence.

inactive in her present condition or, as we say in good German, a bit lazy.—According to the midwife the baby should have come on the 4th of this month—but I don't think it will happen before the 15th or 16th.—If you ask her, she'll say: the sooner, the better! so she and I can enjoy the happiness of embracing you and my sister in Salzburg that much earlier.—As I didn't think it would get serious so quickly, I kept postponing what I meant to do all along, namely go down on my knees, fold my hands, and ask you, my dearest father, in all humility, to be the child's godfather!—As there is still time, I am asking you now.—And confident that you will not refuse me I have made arrangements, after the midwife had conducted her visual examination, that someone will hold the child over the font in your name, be it generis masculini or feminini!—We'll call it either Leopold or Leopoldine.—Now I need to say a word to my sister about the Clementi sonatas.—Anyone who plays them can hear or feel that as compositions they aren't very much.—There are no remarkable or striking passages, except the sixth and the octaves;—and even with those I am asking my sister not to spend *too much time*, so she will not ruin her quiet and steady touch, and lose the natural lightness, flexibility, and flowing rapidity of her hand;—after all, what's the good of it in the end?—she's supposed to do the sixth and the octaves with the greatest speed possible, which is something no one can do, not even Clementi himself; all she will produce is some atrocious chopping and hacking but nothing else in the world!—Clementi is a Ciarlattano[76] like all Italians.—He writes Presto and even Prestißimo and alla Breve on his sonatas—and plays them Allegro in 4/4 time;—I know, I heard him play;—what he does well are his passages in thirds;—but he really sweated over those day and night in London;—apart from that he has nothing to offer—nothing whatever—he has not the slightest expression or taste—and even less feeling.— . . .

No news yet from Varesco?—Please don't forget the matter;—we could work on the text so beautifully together while I'm visiting in Salzburg, if only we could have some sort of plan for a libretto in the meantime.—

76. A "charlatan" or "quack."

Now I wish you farewell; my wife and I kiss your hands 1000 times and embrace our dear sister with all our heart and are Forever your

most obedient children
W. et C. Mozart

Wolfgang and Constanze's first child, Raimund Leopold Mozart, was born on June 17, 1783. In spite of Mozart's rather dramatic plea to Leopold to become the child's godfather, he changed his mind at the last minute and named the boy Raimund after his landlord, Raimund Wetzlar. According to Nissen, Mozart composed the minuet and trio of the String Quartet in D minor, K. 421, in the night of the child's birth, a remarkable feat of emotional detachment.

To his father, in Salzburg

Vienna, June 18, 1783

Mon trés cher Pére!

Congratulations! You are a Grandpapa!—Yesterday morning, the 17th, at half past six, my dear wife was safely delivered of a fine, sturdy boy, round as a butterball;—the birth pangs began at half past 1 o'clock at night—consequently there was no rest or sleep for either of us that night anymore;—at 4 oclock I sent for my mother-in-law—then I sent for the midwife;—at 6 oclock she was put in the chair[77]—and at half past 6 it was all over.—My mother-in-law is now making up for all the bad things she did to her daughter when she was still *single*—she is going to stay with her all day.—

My dear wife, who kisses your hands and embraces her dear sister with all her heart, is as well as can be expected under the circumstances;—as she is taking good care of herself, I hope to God she will make a good recovery from her childbed.—

I am somewhat worried about her getting milk fever,[78]—because her breasts are so very swollen!—And now, against my wishes and yet not altogether against my will, they brought in a wet nurse for the child!—It has always been my firm resolve that my wife should not breast-feed her child herself, whether she was able to or not!—On the other hand, I didn't want my child to be nursed by a stranger!—rather I wanted to

77. A so-called birthing chair, which at that time was used for delivery.
78. "Milk fever," or puerperal fever, was erroneously attributed to the accumulation of milk in the breasts.

raise him with water, just as my sister and I were raised.[79]—However, the midwife, my mother-in-law, and most of the people here persuaded me not to insist on that, because most of the children here die if they are given water, for people here don't know how to handle this thing properly—well, that made me—give up my idea—for—I wouldn't want to be blamed for anything later on.—

Now about the question of godfather!—Here is what happened.—I sent immediately to Baron Wetzlar, who is a good and true friend to me, with the good news of the safe delivery of my wife;—he came straightaway himself—and offered himself as godfather—I couldn't refuse him—and so I thought to myself, well, I can still call the boy Leopold——and just as I was thinking it—the Baron said with the greatest delight—Ah, well, now you have a little Raymund—and he kissed the child—so what was I to do—well, I had the boy baptized Raymund Leopold.—But I confess to you honestly that if you had not given me your opinion on the matter in an earlier letter, I would have been in an embarrassing situation—and I might well have refused Baron Wetzlar's offer after all;—but your letter gave me the comfort and assurance that you wouldn't be unhappy no matter what I did!—and, after all, one of the boy's names is Leopold.—

I must close now—I and my dear wife kiss your hands 1000 times, and we embrace our dear sister 1000 times and we are Forever your

most obedient children
W. A. C. Mozart

To his father, in Salzburg

Vienna, June 21, 1783

Mon trés cher Pére!

I must be brief today and give you only the most urgent news; I simply have too much to do. A New Italian opera is being produced in which, for the first time, two German singers are participating: my sister-in-law Mad.me Lange, and the tenor Adamberger; and I've been requested to compose 2 arias for Mad.me Lange and a Rondeau for Adamberger.—I hope you have received my recent letter of jubilation.

---

79. Wolfgang and Nannerl were raised not on water but on gruel (made of oats and barley); Mozart seems to have remembered it as plain water.

Thank god, my wife has weathered the two most critical days, yesterday and the day before yesterday; she is quite well considering her condition;—we hope that things will continue this way.—The baby is also quite lively and healthy, he has a tremendous amount of things to do such as drinking, sleeping, crying, p . . . , sh . . . and spitting up, etc.

He kisses the hands of his Grandpapa and his aunt. A quick word about Varesco.—I think his plan is quite good.[80]—I'll have to speak with Count Rosenberg right away to make sure that there will be a remuneration for the Poet;—but I find it somewhat insulting that Varesco has doubts whether the opera will be received well.—There's one thing I can assure him of and that is: his libretto will certainly not be received well if the Musique isn't any good.—It's the Musique that is the main thing in an opera;—so if he wishes to be successful and expect a good reward, he has to let me alter things and recast the text as much and as often as I want to; we cannot just follow his ideas, for he has not the slightest experience and knowledge of the stage.—You may even intimate to him that it doesn't really matter whether he wants to do the opera or not.—I know the story now;—consequently anyone can write it for me just as well as he can; besides, I am expecting 4 of the newest and best opera libretti from Italy today; there must be one I can use.—At any rate, there's still time.—Now I must close; My wife and I kiss the hands of our best father 1000 times, and we embrace our dear sister with all our heart and remain Forever your

most obedient children
W. A. et C. Mozart

To his father, in Salzburg

Vienna, July 2, 1783

Mon trés cher Pére!

Last post day my mind was filled with so many things that I simply forgot to write to you. Mad.^me Lange was here trying out her 2 arias;[81] we also discussed how we could outshine our enemies, for I have plen-

---

80. Varesco had sent an outline of *L'oca del Cairo* (The Goose of Cairo). Mozart began work on the *dramma giocoso* immediately but completed only parts of the first act. *L'oca del Cairo*, K. 422, with its rather uninspired text remained a fragment.

81. The two arias Mozart wrote for Aloysia Lange are "Vorrei spiegarvi, oh Dio," K. 418, and "No, no, che non sei capace," K. 419.

ty of them, and Mad.^{me} Lange, too, has had enough of Storaci, the *New Singer.* [82]—I didn't remember that it was post day until I was alone again, and by the time I thought about it, it was too late.—The opera "Il curioso indiscreto" by Anfoßi,[83] in which Lange and Adamberger appeared, was given Monday, the day before yesterday, for the first time;—it was a complete failure, except for the 2 arias I had contributed;—in fact, my 2nd one, a bravura aria, had to be repeated.—Now I must tell you that my enemies were malicious enough to start a rumor beforehand, saying that *Mozart wants to improve on the opera by Anfoßi.*—I heard the rumor myself.—So I sent a message to Count Rosenberg to the effect that I won't give my aria to anyone unless the following text will be printed in the libretto in both German and Italian.

NOTICE

The two arias on pages 36 and 102 were set to music by Signor Maestro Mozart to please Signora Lange, because the arias of Signor Maestro Anfossi had not been written for the qualities of her voice, but for someone else. It is important to make this notification so that honor may be accorded to whom it is due without harming the reputation and name of the well-known Neapolitan.

The text was printed into the booklet—and I let them have the arias that brought me and my sister-in-law the greatest honor;—my enemies were quite confounded!—Now I have to tell you of a trick Herr Salieri played that, however, did more harm to poor Adamberger than to me.—I think I told you already that I composed a Rondeau for Adamberger as well.[84]—At a short rehearsal earlier, when the Rondeau hadn't even been copied yet, Salieri motioned Adamberger aside and said to him that Count Rosenberg would not particularly like it if he added an extra aria and, therefore, as a good friend, he would advise him not to do it.—Adamberger—furious at Rosenberg—and *overcome by Pride at the absolutely wrong time*—did not know how to properly revenge himself but said stupidly—*All right then*—*to prove that Adamberger has already*

---

82. Ann Selina (Nancy) Storace, an English soprano who came to Vienna in 1783 with her brother Stephen, became the first Susanna in Mozart's *Le nozze di Figaro*.
83. *Il curioso indiscreto*, by Pasquale Anfossi.
84. Mozart's "Rondeau" for Adamberger was "Per pietà non ricercate," K. 420.

made his reputation in Vienna and doesn't need to make a name for himself through music that was specially written for him, he will indeed just sing what's in the opera and never again introduce a new aria.—And what was the result of it?—He was a complete failure, as had to be expected!—Now he is sorry, but it's too late.—If he would ask me now to give him the Rondeau, I wouldn't give it to him anymore.—I can use it very well in one of my own operas.— The worst part of it is that his *wife's* and *my own* prediction came true, namely that Count Rosenberg and the management *knew nothing about it;* it had all been a trick by Salieri.—

My wife is quite well again, god be praised, except for a slight cold.—We both, together with our two-week-old Raimund, kiss your hands and embrace our dear sister with all our heart and are Forever your

most obedient children
W. A. C. Mozart

𐦢 *Interpolation of arias into someone else's opera was not an uncommon practice in the eighteenth century. What makes Mozart's report here especially interesting is that it is the first time he specifically refers to Salieri as an intrigant. How far Salieri or any other of Mozart's "enemies" went in his intrigues is not at all clear, but Mozart seemed to think that cabals against him were going on most of the time.*

To his father, in Salzburg

Vienna, July 5, 1783

Mon tres cher Pére!

We both thank you for the prayer you sent to god for my wife's safe delivery.—Little Raymund looks so much like me that people mention it right away;—he is the spitting image of me, which totally delights my dear wife because that's what she always wanted.—Next Tuesday he'll be 3 weeks old, and it's unbelievable how much he has grown. As far as the opera is concerned,[85] you gave me advice that I had already given to myself.—But as I prefer to work slowly and deliberately, I don't think I'm wrong by starting on it as early as possible. An Italian Poet recent-ly brought me a libretto that I may well use if he is willing to whittle it

---

85. Probably *L'oca del Cairo,* K. 422.

down to suit my wishes.[86]—I have no doubt that we'll be able to travel in the month of September;—and you can probably imagine that the two of us wish for nothing more than to embrace the two of you. The only problem is—and I don't want to keep my thoughts from you but must tell you frankly—that many people here are making me so nervous about it that I find it hard to describe;—*you know what I mean;* and no matter what I bring up against their arguments, they always insist: *just wait, you'll see, you will not get out of there anymore;—you don't know what this evil—malicious prince is capable of!—You don't know what kind of tricks they have up their sleeves in this kind of business.—Take our advice—meet your father at some third place.*—You see, this is the true reason why my wife and I have been so uneasy, and still are, about our trip.—I often think to myself, come on now, it can't be that way! But then my mind tells me right away, oh yes, it could be that way and it wouldn't be the first injustice these people have committed.—Basta!—No one can quiet my mind in this matter but you, my dearest father!— . . .

Farewell in the meantime—take care of your health—we both kiss your hands and embrace our dear sister with all our heart and remain Forever your

> most obedienty children
> W. C. Mozart.

P.S. Don't forget to keep prodding Varesco; who knows whether I'll like the opera of the Italian Poet here?

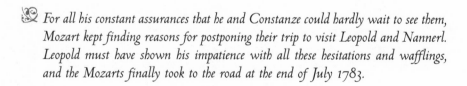 *For all his constant assurances that he and Constanze could hardly wait to see them, Mozart kept finding reasons for postponing their trip to visit Leopold and Nannerl. Leopold must have shown his impatience with all these hesitations and wafflings, and the Mozarts finally took to the road at the end of July 1783.*

---

86. The "Italian Poet" is most likely Lorenzo da Ponte. The libretto in question is probably that of *Lo sposo deluso* (The Disappointed Bridegroom), subtitled "La rivalità di tre donne per un solo amante" (The Rivalry of Three Women and One Lover). Mozart began this opera buffa but only finished the overture, an opening quartet, a trio, and two arias (K. 430).

To his father, in Salzburg

Vienna, July 12, 1783

Mon trés cher Pére!

I received your letter from the 8ᵗʰ of this month safely and saw to my great delight that you are both well, god be praised and thanked.

If you choose to call me a fool for something I consider a real threat, I can't prevent you from doing so;—anyone can call anything by a wrong name if that's what one wants to do;—but is it right?—that's another question.—Have I ever given you the impression that I have no desire or eagerness to see you?—certainly not!—what is true is that I have no desire to see Salzburg or the archbishop;—so, pray, tell me who would be the one who gets fooled if we met at a third place? *the archbishop and not you.*—I hope it's not necessary for me to tell you that I care little about Salzburg and nothing at all about the archbishop, and that I shit on both of them;—indeed, it would never enter my head to make a special trip to Salzburg were it not for you and my sister living there.—So, my whole worry was based on the well-meant concerns of my good friends, who are not entirely without common sense;—and I didn't think it was so unreasonable to inquire about your thoughts on the matter and then follow your advice;—the concern of my friends was simply that he would have me arrested since I don't have a discharge from his services.—But now you have put my mind completely at ease— and we shall come in August—surely in September at the latest.— . . .

Farewell for now. My wife and I kiss your hands 1000 times and embrace our dear sister with all our heart and remain your

most obedient children
W. A. C. Mozart

When Mozart and Constanze departed for Salzburg, little Raimund was placed in foster care in Vienna. He died there on August 21, 1783, of intestinal cramps before his parents could return from Salzburg.

Mozart and Constanze arrived in Salzburg on July 29, Nannerl's birthday was on the 30th, Wolfgang's poetic toast to his sister (Glücks-Wunsch, Beim Punsch!) is dated July 31. The poem is not preserved in Mozart's own hand but in that of Nannerl's son, Leopold Freiherr von Berchtold zu Sonnenburg. Mozart and Constanze remained in Salzburg (without any of the feared reprisals by the arch-

bishop) for three months and began their return trip on October 27, 1783. On that day Nannerl noted with utmost brevity in her diary, "At half past 9 o'clock my brother and sister-in-law departed."

To his sister, in Salzburg

Salzburg, July 31, 1783

With a Toast of this Brew,
I bring best wishes to You!
Today I went shopping, you did not know why,—
I will say only this, I did it on the sly
To find a little something to delight my sister dear,—
And I would spare no effort looking far and looking near.—
I do not know for certain whether punch is to your taste,
But, please, do not say—No!—it would be such a waste;
I know you love the English, and that's what I had thought,
For if you liked Parisians, it's ribbons I'd have brought,
Perhaps some pretty flowers, perfume with fragrance sweet,
But you are no Coquette, I say, so that's not what you need;
What you need is a drink, my dear, punch of the strongest brew,
So prosit, and enjoy the day! That is my wish for you.

Salzburg, July 31, 1783

W. A. Mozart
poeta laureatus of the
Shooting Club.

"Naturalness" in music and performance is a frequent subject in Mozart's letters; but never before had he spoken of it in such graphic and amusing language as in a message to his father from Linz, Austria, his first letter after the visit in Salzburg.

To his father, in Salzburg

Linz, October 31, 1783

We arrived here safely yesterday morning at 9 o'clock.—We spent the first night at Vögelbruck;[87]—on the following morning we reached Lambach[88]—just in time for me to accompany the Angus Dei on the organ during the mass.—The prelate was most delighted to see me again—and he told me an anecdote about himself and you in Salzburg.[89]—We stayed all day, and I played the organ and a clavichord.—Then I was told that an opera would be performed at Ebersperg in the house of Prefect Steurer, whose wife is the sister of Frau von Barisani; in other words, nearly all of Linz would be gathered there;—so I decided to join the party, and we drove out there.—Right after we arrived the young Count Thun, the brother of Count Thun in Vienna,[90] came up to me and informed me that his father had been expecting our visit for 2 weeks and I should drive to his house directly because he wanted us to stay with him.—I said I could easily find an inn—but when we came to the city gate of Linz the next day, a servant was waiting for us to take us to Count Thun the Elder,[91] where, in fact, we are staying at this moment.—It is hard to describe the wealth of courtesies that are being showered upon us in this house.—On Tuesday, that's November 4th, I will give a concert at the theater here.—and as I didn't bring one single Simphonie with me, I'll have to write a New one in a hurry, for it has to be finished by that time.[92]—I must close now, for I have to start work at once.—My wife and I kiss your hands, and we apologize for having inconvenienced you with our visit for such a long time; and we thank you once again for all the kindnesses we received.—Farewell for now.—Give our greetings to Gretl and Heinrich (of whom I have spoken here quite a bit) and to Hanni;[93]—and please

87. Vöcklabruck in Austria.
88. A monastery in which the Mozarts stayed in 1769 and 1773 on their way to Vienna.
89. The prelate's name was Amandus Schickmayr; he and Leopold Mozart had been students together at the University of Salzburg.
90. Count Franz Joseph Thun, husband of Countess Wilhelmine Thun, Mozart's friend and supporter in Vienna.
91. Count Johann Joseph Anton Thun.
92. The new symphony, written in a "hurry," is the no. 36 in C major ("Linz"), K. 425.
93. Margarethe Marchand, her brother Heinrich Marchand, and Johanna Brochard were all pupils of Leopold and stayed at his house in Salzburg.

tell Gretl from me, she should not strike such coy poses when she sings in performance; kisses and flatteries are not always appropriate.—Only dumb asses fall for such tricks.—I myself would prefer a simple peasant lad who is not ashamed to shit and piss right in front of me to such insincere cajoling, which is so thick that you can grasp it with your hands. Now Adieu.—We kiss our dear sister with all our heart.—I am Forever your most grateful son,

W. A. Mozart

Mozart had become very popular as a pianist in Vienna. He therefore dropped his two opera projects L'oca del Cairo *(Varesco) and* Lo sposo deluso *(Da Ponte) and concentrated on writing and performing piano concertos in the hope of helping his strained financial situation. In 1784, i.e., in the space of one year, he composed six piano concertos: no. 14 in E-flat, K. 449; no. 15 in B-flat, K. 450; no. 16 in D, K. 451; no. 17 in G, K. 453; no. 18 in B-flat, K. 456; and no. 19 in F, K. 459. Mozart was the toast of music-loving Vienna.*

To his father, in Salzburg

Vienna, February 10, 1784

Mon Trés cher Pére!—

It was such a stupidity of Artaria![94]—He thought that they would not take the Packet at the post office, and instead of returning it to me right away, he kept it until the next mail coach, without telling me one word.— . . .

I wrote you about Varesco and the opera in my last letter.—At the moment I can't even think about going ahead with it.—I am currently engaged in some compositions that will bring me money *now*,—*not later.*—The opera—well, I can always count on it for some income—but—if you take enough time—it will turn out even better. Herr Varesco's poetry betrays too much hurriedness!—I hope in time he will realize that himself. That's why I wish to see the opera *in its entirety*—he should make an outline of the whole plot—we can always do some basic revisions—but, truly, there's no need to rush this thing!—If you could hear the parts of the opera I have done already,

94. The Viennese music publisher.

I'm positive you'd wish what I wish, namely that is should not be thrown away on some inferior text!—and that can happen so easily!—and it happens quite often.—The Musique I have completed is resting comfortably in the meantime.—Of all the operas that are likely to be performed by the time this one is finished, none of them will have a single idea resembling any of mine; I can guarantee that!—Now I have to close because I must get back to work;—my whole morning is spent on giving lessons, so I have only the evening left for my favorite activity: Composing! . . .

Adieu for now, my wife and I kiss your hands 1000 times and embrace our dear sister with all our heart and remain Forever your

most obedient children

W. et C. Mozart

To his father, in Salzburg

Vienna, March 3, 1784

Mon trés cher Pére!—

I have received your letter of Feb. 24th safely;—it's better you send your letters through the mail—for instance, I received this letter of yours on Monday, if you had sent it through Peisser's office,[95] I wouldn't have gotten it until Tuesday or even Wednesday.—I haven't seen the concertos yet, but I shall ask Artaria about it right away;[96]—you must forgive me for writing very little these days, but I have no time whatsoever; I will be giving 3 subscription concerts in Trattner Hall during the last 3 Wednesdays in Lent, beginning with the 17th of this month; I have 100 subscribers already, and by the 17th I will easily get another 30.—The price for all 3 concerts is 6 gulden.—then I'll probably be giving 2 concerts at the theater this year—so you can well imagine that I will always have to offer something New—and therefore I have no choice but to write—the mornings are dedicated to my students—and almost every evening I have to perform.—Below is a list of concerts at which I am *definitely* scheduled to perform:— . . .

95. Franz Xaver Peisser, a banker and friend of the Mozart family; his office sometimes handled mail between Leopold and Wolfgang.
96. The Piano Concertos K. 413–415, which were being published by Artaria.

Thursday, Feb.ʳ 26ᵗʰ, at Gallizin's.
Monday, March 1ˢᵗ, at Joh. Esterhazy's.
Thursday, 4ᵗʰ, at Gallizin's.
Friday, 5ᵗʰ, at Esterhazy's.
Monday, 8ᵗʰ, at Esterhazy's.
Thursday, 11ᵗʰ, at Gallizin's.
Friday, 12ᵗʰ, at Esterhazy's.
Monday, 15ᵗʰ, at Esterhazy's.
Wednesday, 17ᵗʰ, My first *Private* concert.
Thursday, 18ᵗʰ, at Gallizin's.
Friday, 19ᵗʰ, at Esterhazy's.
Saturday, 20ᵗʰ, at Richter's.
Sunday, 21ˢᵗ, my First concert in the *Theater.*
Monday, 22ⁿᵈ, at Esterhazy's.
Wednesday, 24ᵗʰ, my 2ⁿᵈ Private concert.
Thursday, 25ᵗʰ, at Gallizin's.
Friday, 26ᵗʰ, at Esterhazy's.
Saturday, 27ᵗʰ, at Richter's.
Monday, 29ᵗʰ, at Esterhazy's.
Wednesday, 31ˢᵗ, my 3ʳᵈ *Private* concert.
Thursday, April 1ˢᵗ, my 2ⁿᵈ concert in the Theater.
Saturday, 3ʳᵈ, at Richter's.

Don't you think I have plenty to do?—I don't think I can get out of practice this way.—

Adieu.—We both kiss your hands and embrace our dear sister with all our heart and are Forever your

most obedient children
W. A. Mozart

The list of subscribers that Mozart sent to his father contains 174 names and is a veritable Who's Who of musical Vienna in the 1780s; the individuals are all identified in the Bauer/Deutsch edition, 6:167–77.

To his father, in Salzburg

Vienna, March 20, 1784

[...] Here you have the list of all my subscribers;—I have 30 sub-scribers more than Richter and Fischer put together.[97] The first concert on the 17th of this month went very well—the hall was filled to the brim;—and the New Concerto that I performed won extraordinary applause;[98] wherever I go now, I hear people speak in praise of that concert.—My first theater concert was supposed to take place tomorrow—but Prince Louis Lichtenstein[99] is putting on an opera at his palace—and has not only abducted the cream of the nobility but stolen the Best musicians from the orchestra.—So I postponed my concert to April 1st and announced the change in a printed pamphlet.—I must close now because I have to be off to a concert at Count Zitchi's.—Please be patient with me until after Lent is over. We both kiss your hands and embrace our dear sister with all our heart and are Forever your

most obedient children
W. A. Mozart

I received your most recent letter safely.

To his father, in Salzburg

Vienna, April 10, 1784

Mon trés cher Pére!

I beg you not to be angry with me for not having written for such a long time;—surely you know how busy I am these days!—I have gained much honor for myself with my 3 subscription concerts.—The concert I gave at the Theater was very successful as well.—I composed two grand Concertos[100] and then a quintet that was extraordinarily well received;—I myself think it's the best I've written in my entire life.—It is written *for 1 oboe, 1 Clarinetto, 1 Corno, 1 fagotto,* and the *Piano forte;*[101]—I

---

97. Georg Friedrich Richter was a popular Dutch pianist; "Fischer" is either Johann Ludwig Fischer, the bass singer, or John Abraham Fisher, an English violinist who was then concertizing in Vienna.
98. Piano Concerto no. 14 in E-flat, K. 449.
99. Prince Alois Liechtenstein.
100. Piano Concertos no. 15 in B-flat, K. 450, and no. 16 in D, K. 451.
101. Quintet for Piano and Winds in E-flat, K. 452. Mozart probably felt he needed to tell his father the instrumentation of the new quintet because such a combination of instruments was rare and may never have been used in a quintet before.

so wished you could have heard it!—and how beautifully they played it!—To tell you the truth, I've been feeling somewhat tired lately—from so much performing;—and it's not the least of my credits that my listeners *never* are.— . . . One more thing; since Hafeneder passed away, Herr von Ployer[102] has been charged with finding a new violinist.—I confidentially recommended to him a certain *Menzl*,[103]—a handsome, young, and skilled musician.—I asked him not to reveal my name, otherwise it might not work.—He is now awaiting a decision.—He would probably get 400 gulden—and a new *suit*—I already scolded Menzl about the suit—it's so beggarly.—Should something come of it, I'll ask Menzl to take a letter from me to you, and some Musique as well;—you'll find him a very Pleasant Violinist who is also a good sight-reader;—no one in *Vienna* has played my quartets à prima vista as well as he has;—besides, he is the best fellow in the whole world, who will be delighted to make some Musique with you whenever you like—I even asked him to be in the orchestra here when I did my concerts.—Now I must close; my wife and I kiss your hands 1000 times and embrace our dear sister with all our heart and remain Forever your

obed. children
Mozart

🐚 *This brief note is of interest because it contains some rare praise by Mozart for two fellow musicians. The violin sonata he wrote for Regina Strinasacchi had to be done so quickly that he had time only to write out the violin part; he played his pianoforte part from a sketch. Mozart must have had a lot self-assurance to do that in a performance attended by the emperor.*

To his father, in Salzburg

Vienna, April 24, 1784

We have the famous Strinasacchi from Mantua here right now;[104] she is a very good violinist, has excellent taste and a lot of feeling in her

---

102. Gottfried Ignaz von Ployer, Salzburg court agent in Vienna and father of Mozart's gifted pupil Barbara von Ployer.
103. Zeno Franz Menzel did not get the post in Salzburg but later became violinist in the Vienna court orchestra.
104. A well-known violinist and guitarist from Ostiglia, near Mantua.

playing.—I'm composing a Sonata for her[105] at this moment that we'll be performing together Thursday in her concert at the Theater. Also, some quartets by a certain Pleyel[106] have just been published; he is a pupil of Joseph Haydn. If you don't know them, try to get a hold of them; you'll find them worth your while. They are very well composed and most pleasant to listen to; you'll hear at once who his Teacher was. It would be a good and fortunate day for music, if someday Pleyel were able to be the new Haydn for us!

To his father, in Salzburg

Vienna, April 28, 1784

Mon trés cher Pére!

I must write in a hurry!—Herr Richter, the pianist, is going on a tour that will take him back to Holland, his native country.—I have given him a letter of introduction to the Countess Thun at Linz.—He also wishes to visit Salzbourg, so I gave him a 4-line note for you, my dearest father.—I'm letting you know that he will be there shortly after you receive this letter.—He plays well as far as execution is concerned,—however—as you will hear—his playing is too coarse—too belabored—without any taste and feeling.—Apart from that he is the best fellow in the world—and not a bit conceited.—When I played for him, his eyes were totally fixed on my fingers—then he burst out: Good God!—how hard I have to work, until I sweat, and—still I get no applause—and you, my friend, your playing is so playful.—Yes, *I said*, but I too had to work hard so that I don't now have to work so hard *anymore*—afin[107]—he is a man who will always be counted among the good clavier players and—he is a good and honest person—I hope that the Archbishop will want to hear him—because he is a Clavierist—en depit de Moi[108]—although I'm rather happy about the "depit" part of it.—As to Menzl the violinist, it's all going according to plan.—He will probably set sail on Sunday;—and in this way you'll get some Musique

---

105. Sonata for Piano and Violin in B-flat, K. 454.
106. Ignaz Joseph Pleyel, a pupil of Vanhal and Joseph Haydn, who settled in Paris, became a music dealer, and founded the "Pleyel" piano factory.
107. I.e., *enfin* (in one word).
108. I.e., *en dépit de moi* (in spite of me).

from me. And now farewell.—we both kiss your hands and embrace our dear sister with all our heart and are Forever your obed. children

W. C. Mozart

To his father, in Salzburg

Vienna, May 26, 1784

Mon très cher Pére!—

Your last letter brought me the good news that you received my letter and the Musique safely.—I thank my sister for her letter, and as soon as time allows I will write to her for sure.—In the meantime please tell her that Herr Richter either was mistaken about the key of the concerto or I couldn't read her writing correctly.—The concerto Herr Richter praised so highly is the one in B-flat;[109]—it's the one I did first, and he already praised it here.—I find it impossible to choose between the two Concertos—I think they are both concertos that make you sweat.—But as far as difficulty is concerned, the B-flat has the advantage over the D major.[110] I am actually quite curious to know which among the 3 concertos, the B-flat, the D, and the G,[111] you and my sister like best;—the concerto in E-flat[112] is not part of this group—it's a concerto of a special kind, written for a small rather than a big orchestra; so we are speaking only of the 3 grand concertos.—I am so interested to know whether your judgment is in accord with the *general* opinion here and also with *mine*; of course, it would be best if one could hear all three of them with full instrumentation and well executed.—I will be patient about getting them back—as long as they don't fall into somebody else's hands.—I could have had 24 ducats for one of them today;—but I find that it is to my advantage to keep them for my own performances for a couple of years and then have them engraved and published.— . . .

Well, I must close.—My wife thanks you both for your good wishes on account of her pregnancy and confinement later on; it will prob-

---

109. Piano Concerto no. 15 in B-flat, K. 450.
110. Piano Concerto no. 16 in D, K. 451.
111. Piano Concerto no. 17 in G, K. 453.
112. Piano Concerto no. 14 in E-flat, K. 449.

ably be in the first days in October.[113]—We both kiss your hands and embrace our dear sister with all our heart and are Forever your

most obedient children
W. et C. Mozart

P.S. . . . Please send me the *buckles*[114] with the next mail coach—I'm burning with desire to see them.

📧 *The letter of June 9, 1784, is the penultimate extant letter from Mozart to his father. Between this date and Leopold's death on May 28, 1787, at least twenty-five letters from Mozart to his father were lost, including all the correspondence referring to Leopold's trip to Vienna, which took place between the beginning of February and the end of April 1785. The only letter surviving from this three-year period is Mozart's famous last letter to his father from April 4, 1787.*

To his father, in Salzburg

Vienna, June 9, 1784

Mon trés cher Pére!

You have undoubtedly received my last letter; I have received the buckles and your letter from the 1ˢᵗ of this month.—The buckles are very beautiful but much too big;—I'll try to make good use of them somehow.—Next Friday the Court will go to Laxenbourg for 2 maybe even 3 months.—Last week I went to Baaden[115] with his Excellency, Count Thun, to visit his father, who had come there from Linz for a cure; on the way back we traveled by way of Laxenbourg and visited Herr Leeman, who is now Commander of the Castle.—His daughter wasn't home, but he and his wife were absolutely delighted to see me again. They both send their regards.—

June 12ᵗʰ. I had some visitors and because of it couldn't finish this letter;—in the meantime I also received your letter of the 8ᵗʰ. My wife is returning the greetings of my sister and will send off a pretty apron

---

113. The Mozarts' second child, Carl Thomas, was born on September 21, 1784.
114. Prince Joseph Wenzeslaus Fürstenberg of Donaueschingen had bought copies of Mozart's three piano concertos K. 413-415, which Leopold had sent to the court of Donaueschingen, Germany; the prince sent to Salzburg, as a gift for Wolfgang, a pair of buckles decorated with precious stones.
115. Baden is a spa about twenty-five kilometers south of Vienna.

for her with the next mail coach;—she wants to make it herself because it'll be less expensive that way and much prettier.—Please tell my sister that there mustn't be any Adagios in the concertos, only Andantes. It is absolutely correct that there is something missing in the C major solo passage in the Andante of the Concerto in D.—I shall send it to her as soon as possible along with the cadenzas. Tomorrow Herr Ployer, the court agent, will be hosting a concert at Döbling, out in the country; Fräulein Babette will play her New Concerto in G;[116]—I will play in the Quintet[117]—and together we'll perform my grand sonata for 2 Claviers.[118] I shall fetch Paesello[119] with my carriage, for I want him to hear my compositions as well as my pupil;—if Maestro Sarti[120] did not have to leave today, he too would have joined us.—Sarti is an honest and kind man! I played quite a bit for him and even wrote some Variations on an Aria of his, which pleased him greatly.— . . .

Now I must close; my wife and I kiss your hands 1000 times and embrace our dear sister with all our heart, and we are Forever your obed. children

W. et C. Mozart

🖎 *Maria Anna (Nannerl) Mozart was married on August 23, 1784, to Johann Baptist von Berchtold zu Sonnenburg, magistrate at St. Gilgen. This small town, which was a six-hour carriage ride from Salzburg, was the birthplace of Maria Anna Mozart, Wolfgang's and Nannerl's mother. In fact, Nannerl moved into the same house in which her mother had spent her childhood. Nannerl was thirty-three; her husband, who had been widowed twice and had five children, was forty-seven. Leopold Mozart attended the wedding in St. Gilgen with three of his pupils— Margarethe and Heinrich Marchand and Johanna Brochard.*

---

116. Barbara von Ployer was one of Mozart's most gifted pupils. The G-major concerto, K. 453, was the second one Mozart had written for her; the other one was no. 14, K. 449.

117. I.e., the piano part of the quintet.

118. Sonata for Two Pianos in D major, K. 448.

119. Giovanni Paisiello, who had stopped in Vienna on his way from St. Petersburg to Italy.

120. Giuseppe Sarti, composer and conductor, who was traveling from Italy to Russia to assume the post relinquished by Paisiello as director of the court orchestra at St. Petersburg. To Mozart's delight, the two Italian musicians crossed paths in Vienna.

To his sister, in Salzburg

Vienna, August 18, 1784

Ma trés chere sœur!

Potz Saperment![121]—It's high time for me to write to you if I want my letter to still reach you as a virgin!—A few days later and—it's gone!—

My wife and I wish you all the happiness and joy in your change of status and only regret with all our heart that we cannot have the pleasure of being present at your wedding; but it is our definite hope that we shall embrace you as Frau von Sonnenburg together with your husband next spring in Salzburg as well as in St. Gilgen. What we regret more than anything is that our dear father is now so completely alone!—Of course, you live not too far away, and he can easily drive out to see you—but, unfortunately, now he is tied down with that cursed choir service!—If I were in my father's place, I would do the following: as a man who has been in service for so long, I would petition the Archbishop to allow me to retire—and after getting my pension, I would move to my daughter in St. Gilgen and live there a quiet life.— Should the Archbishop refuse my request, I would ask for my discharge and move to Vienna to live with my son.—and that's what I chiefly wanted to ask you: please try hard to persuade him to do this. I made the same suggestions in a letter to him today.—And now let me send you 1000 good wishes from Vienna to Salzburg, especially the wish that the two of you may live as happily together as—the two of us here.— So take the following bit of advice, which comes from the Poetic corner of my brain! Here it goes:

Wedlock will teach you things galore
that seemed a mystery before;
now you won't wonder anymore
what knowledge Eve had to obtain
before she could give birth to Cain.
Marital duties are quite light,
and if you do them with delight
you need not have the least bit fright.

---

121. *Potz Saperment!* is a mild and friendly oath, similar to "Holy smoke!" or "Good gracious!"

But all things have at least two faces
and though a marriage offers graces,
it also brings you worries by and by.
So, if your husband shows you cool reserve,
which you feel you do not deserve,
but he, with knitted brow, thinks he's right:
just tell yourself, well, it's his way,
and say: yes, Master, thy will be done by day—
but my will shall be done at night.

Your faithful brother
W. A. Mozart

Privy Councillor Anton Klein, who was professor of philosophy and aesthetics in Mannheim, had written a play, Kaiser Rudolf von Habsburg, *and sent it to Mozart in the hope that he would set it to music. Mozart, however, busy with his opera* Le nozze di Figaro, *was hesitant to take on such a task; in fact, he never even began work on it. What is interesting and perhaps unexpected in his letter to Professor Klein is his "outpouring of the heart" on the subject of a German national theater.*

To Anton Klein, in Mannheim

Vienna, May 21, 1785

Most Highly Esteemed Herr Privy Councillor!
　　I must admit I was quite wrong in not informing you immediately of the safe arrival of your letter and the accompanying packet;—it is, however, not true that I received 2 additional letters from you in the meantime;—the first one would have awakened me from my slumber, and I would have answered you right away, just as I am doing now.— What happened was that last mail day I received your 2 letters at the same time.—I admitted my mistake already of not answering you right away;—but as far as the Opera is concerned, I would not have been able to tell you any more at that time than I can tell you now.—Dear Herr Privy Councillor—!—I have so much to do at this moment that I can hardly find a minute for myself.—As a man of insight and experience, you know better than I that this sort of thing has to be read with the greatest attention and thoughtfulness—and not just once—but sev-

eral times.—And up to now I did not have the time to read it even once—without interruption.—All I can say at this time is that I should not like to part with it yet.—So please, let me have the play a little longer. . . .

At this point I cannot give you any news about the future of the German Opera; things are rather quiet in this area, except for the renovations that are carried out at the Kärntnerthor Theater intended for a German stage.—The opening is supposed to be in the beginning of October; but I, for my part, have no great hope that it will go well.— Judging from what's happened so far, it seems to me that they are more intent on destroying the German Opera, which indeed has temporarily fallen on bad times, than on revitalizing—and maintaining it.—My sister-in-law, Mad.ᵐᵉ Lange, is the only singer permitted to join the German opera,—Cavallieri, Adamberger, Teüber, all of them Germans of whom Germany can be proud, are obliged to stay with the Italian theater—and will be made to compete against singers from their own country! . . . If we had only one director with a sense of patriotism— everything would acquire a different face!—But it also might mean that the *National Theater*, which began to sprout so handsomely, would actually bear some fruit; and it would certainly be an everlasting embarrassment for Germany if we Germans had the audacity to act as Germans—think as Germans—speak in German, and perhaps even Sing in German!!!—

Please forgive me, dearest Herr Privy Councillor, if I have gone too far in expressing my true sentiments!—Wholly convinced that I am speaking to a *true German*, I have allowed my tongue free rein, which is so rarely possible these days that one might well get drunk after such an outpouring of the heart, but without the risk of damaging one's health.—I remain, most Esteemed Herr Privy Councillor, in

deepest respect

Your most obedient servant
W. A. Mozart

Thomas Attwood was in Vienna on a scholarship sponsored by the Prince of Wales. He was Mozart's student in composition and music theory. Here is a one-sentence note for him from Mozart, written in English.

A Note to Thomas Attwood

Vienna, after August 23, 1785

This after noon I am not at home, therefore I pray to come to morrow at three & a half.

Mozart.

Mozart's dedication of six of his string quartets to Joseph Haydn, which begins like a traditional Italian fairy tale, "Un padre, avendo risolto," is a gracious gesture of thanks toward Haydn, who inspired his quartet music. The dedication was printed in Italian on the first page of the first edition of the quartets, published by Artaria in 1785 in Vienna.

To Joseph Haydn

Vienna, September 1, 1785

To my dear friend Haydn

A father, having decided to send his children out into the wide world, felt that he should entrust them to the protection and guidance of a famous Man who by good fortune also was his best Friend.—Here they are, distinguished Man and dearest Friend, my six children.—They are, to be truthful, the fruit of long and laborious efforts; however, the hope given to me by various Friends that my efforts will be at least somewhat rewarded encourages and flatters me to think that this offspring will be of comfort to me someday. You yourself, dearest friend, told me of your approbation of them during your last Visit here in our Capital. This acceptance gives me the courage to commend them to you and makes me hope that they would not be completely unworthy of your favor. May it please you to welcome them kindly and to be for them a Father, Guide, and Friend! From this moment on I hand over to you all my rights in them, begging you, however, to consider with indulgence their flaws, which a Father's uncritical eye may have overlooked, and in spite of them continue your generous Friendship toward one who so greatly appreciates it, while I remain, Dearest Friend, with all my heart, your most Sincere Friend,

W. A. Mozart

📧 *Although Mozart had a good income as a pianist, he and Constanze seemed to be in debt most of the time. More and more, the composer is beginning to reach out to friends, patrons, and publishers with requests for money. Here it is Franz Anton Hoffmeister, a Viennese composer and music publisher, whom Mozart asks for a small loan. Hoffmeister, who among other works published Mozart's G-minor Piano Quartet, K. 478, wrote on the envelope of the following note, "2 ducats."*

To Franz Anton Hoffmeister, in Vienna

Vienna, November 20, 1785

My dearest Hoffmeister!—

I turn to you in my hour of need, begging you to help me out with some money, which I need urgently at this moment.—Furthermore, I am asking you to give it your best effort in helping me with the matters we talked about.—

Forgive me for bothering you so often, but since you know me and therefore also know that I am very interested in the welfare of your business, I am quite convinced that you won't take my obtrusiveness amiss but rather want to be helpful to me just as I want to be helpful to you.

Mzt

📧 *On December 14, 1784, Mozart had become a Freemason in the Viennese lodge Beneficence (Zur Wohltätigkeit). Whether he had any specific reasons for joining the Freemasons is not known, but he was most likely attracted to their enlightened ideas and ideals, such as equality, tolerance, and the possibility of human improvement. In addition, many of his aristocratic and musical friends, who considered themselves liberals, were Freemasons; they may have encouraged Mozart to become a member. He joined on the level of "apprentice" but was quickly promoted to "journeyman" and, sometime before 1786, became "master." Count Paar was the grandmaster of a newly founded lodge, New Crowned Hope (Zur neugekrönten Hoffnung), which had been formed from three older lodges. The ceremony Mozart refers to in his letter was the first meeting of this new lodge on January 14, 1786, where two of Mozart's masonic choruses, K. 483 and 484, were performed.*

To Count Wenzel Paar, in Vienna

Vienna, January 14, 1786?

Dear Brother.[122]

It is now an hour since I arrived home—with terrible headaches and stomach cramps; I was hoping to get better—but when I noticed, to my dismay, that the contrary was true, I also realized that it was not possible for me to attend our first ceremony today; I therefore beg of you, dear Brother, to excuse me and give my apologies to everybody present.—Nobody loses more by my absence than I do.—

I remain Forever your trusted Brother
Mozart

On February 19, 1786, Mozart attended a masked ball disguised as an Indian philosopher and distributed pamphlets with riddles and sayings that he himself had written in the style of the Iranian philosopher Zoroaster. The sixth-century philosopher (Nietzsche's Zarathustra) is probably also the model for Mozart's Sarastro in Die Zauberflöte. *Mozart had sent a copy of the pamphlet to his father, who wrote on March 24, 1786, to his daughter in St. Gilgen, "The enclosure I'm sending you came from your brother. I solved the first 7 riddles right away just by reading them; but the 8th is hard. These fragments are good and true; I suppose they are for moral edification. . . . Please let me have the pamphlet back."*

PAMPHLET

"One can possess me without seeing me."
"One can carry me without feeling me."
"One can give me away without possessing me."
S. h. n. o. r.[123]

(1) Talk much—talk badly; but the latter will follow of itself; all eyes and ears will be directed toward you. (4) I prefer an open vice to a doubtful virtue; at least I know what to expect. (5) A hypocrite who is trying to imitate nature can do so only with watercolors. (10) It is not suitable for everybody to be modest; but it is appropriate for great men. (11) If you are poor but clever, arm yourself with patience, and work

---

122. I.e., brother of the lodge.
123. The jumbled letters spell "horns" (in German it is "D. e. e. h. i. n. ö. r. r.," i.e., *Die Hörner*).

hard. If you do not become rich, you will at least remain clever.—If you are an ass but rich, use your advantage, be lazy; if you do not become poor, you will at least remain an ass. (12) One can give praise to a woman in the surest and tenderest way by telling her unkind things about her rival. How many men are not women in this respect? (14) If you are a poor blockhead—become a C — — c.[124] If you are a rich blockhead, become a landlord. If you are an aristocratic but a poor blockhead, become whatever you can so you may gain your bread. But if you are a rich, aristocratic blockhead, become whatever you want to but not—I implore you—a man of reason.

Mozart's letter to his father, which accompanied the pamphlet, is lost. The fragment of the "Zoroastran Riddles" printed above was published in a newspaper (Oberdeutsche Staatszeitung, March 23, 1786) and thereby survived. Mozart, so it appears, had not only reached an apex of his musical career and popularity but also become a philosopher.

Sebastian Winter had been in the service of the Mozarts when they undertook their long journey to Paris and London from 1763 to 1766. He was now at the court of Prince Joseph Maria Benedikt von Fürstenberg in Donaueschingen, a small principality in the southwest of Germany. Winter had written to Mozart about acquiring some of his compositions for the orchestra of his prince, and Mozart had sent a catalog of themes, from which the prince had selected three piano concertos and and three symphonies.

To Sebastian Winter, in Donaueschingen

Vienna, September 30, 1786

Dearest friend!—

The music you requested will be sent off to you tomorrow by mail coach,—you'll find at the end of the letter a list of the expenses for the Copying of the music.—It is not unusual that some of my compositions find their way abroad—but those pieces go out into the world with my knowledge—and I have sent you a catalog of themes[125] only

124. "C — — c" is probably "cleric" (in German, "K — — r," i.e., *Kleriker*).
125. On August 8, 1786, Mozart had sent the opening themes of four symphonies (K. 425, 385, 319, and 338), five piano concertos (K. 453, 456, 451, 459, and 488), one sonata for piano and violin (K. 481), one trio (K. 496), and one quartet (K. 478) to Sebastian Winter.

because it is entirely possible that these works have not come to your attention. However, the compositions that I hold back for my own use, or for the use of a small circle of music lovers and connoisseurs (who promised *not* to share them with anyone), cannot possibly be known abroad, because they haven't been made public even here;—and so it is with the 3 Concertos that I have the honor of sending to His Highness; because of that I found it necessary to charge a small honorarium of 6 ducats for Each of the Concertos in addition to the cost of the Copying; even so I would like to request that His Highness not let these particular Concertos out of his hands.—The Concerto in A includes two clarinetti.[126]—If you should not have two clarinettists at your court, a good copyist could transpose these parts into the appropriate keys in which the first part is played by a violin and the second part by a viola. . . .

Well now, dearest friend!—Companion of my Youth!—Naturally, I've been to "Ricken"[127] many times throughout these years, and since I have never had the pleasure of seeing you there, it would be my greatest wish that you would come to visit me in Vienna or that I visit you in Donaueschingen.—forgive me, but I would almost prefer the latter!—for besides having the pleasure of embracing you, I would also have the high privilige of paying my respects to your most gracious prince and thereby be reminded most vividly of all the kindnesses I received at your court in my Younger Years,[128] something I shall not forget as long as I live.—

In the hope of receiving an answer soon, and in the flattering expectation of perhaps seeing you once more in this world, I remain Forever
your most devoted friend and servant
Wolfgang Amadè Mozart

---

126. Piano Concerto no. 23 in A major, K. 488.
127. "Ricken" is most likely the "Kingdom of Rücken," a fantasy land the seven-year-old Mozart made up on his journey to London.
128. In 1766, on their return trip from Paris to Salzburg, the Mozart family spent about ten days at the court of Donaueschingen, where Nannerl and Wolfgang played for Prince Joseph Wenzeslaus von Fürstenberg almost every day of their stay.

NOTA.

The 3 Concertos without the piano Parts.

109 sheets @ 8 kreuzer:_____ 14 gulden   32 kreuzer

The 3 piano Parts

33½ sheets @ 10 kreuzer: _____ 5   35

Honorarium for the 3 Concertos

18 ducats @ 4 gulden, 30 kr. _____ 81   —

The 3 Sinfonies

116½ sheets @ 8 kr. _____ 15   32

Customs and Postage _____ 3   —

Summa: 119 gulden   39 kreuzer

Mozart calculated his honorarium for three piano concertos as 81 gulden, a sum so small that it is hard to imagine nowadays. Yet he was buoyed by the fact that a German prince had requested music from him. (Prince Fürstenberg sent Mozart 143 ½ gulden.) Tucked into this little music sale is Mozart's most endearing remembrance of a fantasy land that he created and to which he and Nannerl would escape once in a while as they were traveling through the world as children.

Final Journeys

January 8, 1787–December 5, 1791

WHEN MOZART TRAVELED to Prague, the Bohemian capital, in January 1787 to conduct a performance of *Le nozze di Figaro* at the National Theater,[1] he was received with great warmth and applause by the Prague operagoers and was offered a contract for a new opera by Pasquale Bondini, the National Theater's director. Bondini's commission resulted in what music critics have called Mozart's greatest opera, *Don Giovanni.* When Mozart returned to Prague in the fall of that same year for the opera's premiere, the applause of his Prague audiences reached a level of unprecedented enthusiasm and celebration. It caused Lorenzo da Ponte, Mozart's librettist, to remark that the audiences of Prague had a special love and understanding for the music of Mozart. Not until four years later would Mozart have another such triumph, albeit in a less glamorous setting. On September 30, 1791, *Die Zauberflöte,* his grand opera in German, premiered at the Theater auf der Wieden, a ramshackle wooden building on the outskirts of Vienna. The opera was an instant success, and its fast-growing popularity buoyed Mozart's spirit in the final days of his life.

In between these highpoints lay four years of disappointments: Mozart's fruitless efforts to secure a permanent post (which made him seriously think of moving to England), the lack of a positive response to his subscription efforts, and, perhaps the greatest disappointment of

---

1. Founded in 1782 by Count Franz Anton von Nostitz (Nostiz), the theater was first named the Nostiz National Theater. In the nineteenth century it was usually referred to as Ständetheater or Stavoské (Theater of the Estates). Since 1976 it has been called the Tyl Theater.

them all, the rejection by his new sovereign, Leopold II of Austria. Emperor Joseph II, who died in February 1790, had not been a generous patron for Mozart, but he had liked Mozart and given him a modicum of support. But Leopold II, the former grand duke of Tuscany who succeeded Joseph II, completely ignored Mozart. He shut him out of court festivities in Vienna, and when he journeyed to Frankfurt to be crowned emperor of the German realm, he traveled with an entourage of 104 carriages, hundreds of horsemen, and a dozen musicians; but Mozart was not invited.

There were other, more personal, challenges: Mozart's father died in May of 1787. Although Leopold Mozart was a difficult man, cranky and unfulfilled, he had been his son's guide, mentor, and confidant in his earlier years, and Mozart genuinely loved and admired him. Also, Constanze's health was becoming increasingly precarious; she needed medical attention and costly cures, partly because of frequent pregnancies, partly because of a seriously infected foot. Money was in short supply, and debts plagued the Mozart household. The composer battled his misfortunes the only way he knew, by concentrating on his work. And even though his income remained low and unpredictable, one masterpiece after another sprang from his untiring mind: the late quintets, the three last symphonies, the Clarinet Concerto, the Piano Concerto in B-flat, *Die Zauberflöte*, the Requiem; and further masterworks were in the making, for Mozart left behind an astonishing number of drafts and sketches.

In spite of his financial and professional difficulties, Mozart did not live his final years in tragic isolation. He hated to be alone—just taking a meal by himself made him unhappy, especially when Constanze was away at Baden, a health spa near Vienna. So, for better or worse, Mozart enjoyed the company of other musicians, text writers, and singers both male and female. In 1790, he even participated in a group composition, a singspiel called *Der Stein der Weisen* (The Philosopher's Stone), written, sung, and produced by a number of his friends; they, in turn, were on hand when he presented his own great magic show, *Die Zauberflöte*. Mozart was artistically and socially active until the last days of his life, and when death came he was not at all prepared to lay down his pen and leave this world.

Mozart's letters from these last years tell of his professional and personal ups and downs with remarkable veracity. The tone of the letters shifts constantly between seriousness and lightheartedness, dejection and optimism, lament and humor. There is, for instance, his famous letter to his father, when Leopold lies seriously ill, which shows Mozart as a man of composure and wisdom. But there are also, during the same period, frequent requests for money that show him with very little composure, literally begging for whatever he could get. While in Frankfurt on his disastrous trip, he writes to Constanze of his discouragement and his bewildering feelings of coldness and confusion, but when he is back in Vienna, poorer than ever, he seems to forget all debts and worries and instead fills his letters to Constanze with funny, nonsensical, melodious incantations. Contradictions are everywhere evident in the last years of Mozart's life and letters. And in his music. The jubilant C-major and the tragic G-minor quintets are poles apart in mood and drama, yet they were written within one month of each other; in his serenades *Eine kleine Nachtmusik* (A Little Night Music) and *Ein musikalischer Spaß* (A Musical Joke), we encounter perfection and parody virtually side by side; and Sarastro and Papageno, wise man and child of nature, are both the opposing and the unifying forces in *Die Zauberflöte.*

Radiating beneath the contrasts, opposites, and modes of contradiction, we can detect not only a spirit of conciliation but also a certain lightness and playfulness that are apparent throughout Mozart's last communications. In his penultimate letter to Constanze, Mozart describes a prank he played on the unsuspecting Schikaneder, who was singing the part of Papageno in *Die Zauberflöte.* He felt the urge, Mozart writes, to play the glockenspiel himself, secretly. He sneaked backstage, and when it was time for Schikaneder to sing the aria with the glockenspiel (by now an audience favorite), the sound of the glockenspiel came not from the orchestra but from the back of the stage. Schikaneder turned around and there, in the wing, stood Mozart, an impish musician filled with delight and mischief, sounding the bells of the glockenspiel. The image is fitting and enduring, for it gives life to the charms of Mozart's music as well as to the charms, profundity, and lightness of his indomitable spirit.

🐾 *Mozart came to Prague following an invitation by the Society of Great Connoisseurs and Amateurs to conduct his* Le nozze di Figaro *after several very successful performances of the opera at the National Theater in Prague. Mozart and*

Constanze were invited to stay at Count Thun's residence. His letter to Gottfried von Jacquin, his student in Vienna and youngest son of Professor Nikolaus Josef von Jacquin, a well-known botanist, is the only letter preserved from this stay of Mozart's in Prague, which lasted from January 11 to February 8, 1787. The letter to his Viennese friend is remarkable for its detail and humor; Mozart must have been in a lighthearted mood not only in Prague but already on his way there as the game of name-inventing indicates.

To Gottfried von Jacquin,² in Vienna

Prague, January 15, 1787

Dearest friend!—

At last I find a moment to write to you;—I had intended to write four letters to Vienna right after my arrival here, but, alas!—I managed only one—to my mother-in-law; and even that one I got only half done.—My wife and Hofer³ had to finish it.

Immediately after we got here on Thursday, the 11ᵗʰ, at 12 o'clock noon, we had to run and rush to get ready for our luncheon at 1 o'clock. After table Count Thun the Elder⁴ regaled us with Musick performed by his own orchestra; it lasted about an hour and a half.—This kind of *true entertainment* will be everyday fare for me from now on.—At 6 o'clock I drove with Count Canal to the so-called Breitfeld Ball, where the crème de la crème of Prague's beauties gathers.—That would have been something for you, my friend!—I can see you now, running after all the pretty girls and women—running?—No, I mean limping!—Well, I didn't dance and didn't flirt.—The former because I was too tired, the latter because I am naturally bashful;—however, I watched with greatest pleasure how everyone was hopping about with sheer delight to the music of my "Figaro," which had been transformed into Contredanses and German dances; for here they talk of nothing but—"Figaro"; nothing is played, blown, sung, and whistled but—"Figaro"; no opera is seen as much as—"Figaro"; again and again it is—"Figaro"; it's all a great

2. Emilian Gottfried von Jacquin was a friend in whose house Mozart spent many happy hours. Two years younger than Mozart, Gottfried died a year after him, of tuberculosis.
3. Franz de Paula Hofer, a court violinist who often played in Mozart's concerts. He married Constanze's sister Josepha in 1788, so Mozart was now his brother-in-law.
4. Count Johann Joseph Anton Thun, whom Mozart had met in Linz. Count Thun maintained residences in Linz and in Prague and kept his own orchestra.

honor for me.—But to come back to my daily agenda. Since I came home late from the ball and since I was tired and sleepy from the trip, there would be nothing more natural in the world than for me to sleep in, right? well, that's exactly what I did.—So the entire next morning was again spent *Sine Linea*;[5]—and, of course, you mustn't forget the count's high and noble Musick after the noon meal. Furthermore, as they put a pretty good Pianoforte in my room that day, you can easily imagine that I couldn't just leave it standing there in the evening, untouched, without playing it; and from that it follows quite logically that we played a little quartet[6] among ourselves in Caritatis camera,[7] and sang that lovely terzetto "das schöne bandel hammera,"[8] and from there it probably follows that we lost another entire evening *sine Linea*; well, that's exactly what happened.—Now go right ahead and give Morpheus a stiff talking to, for this deity seems to favor both of us here in Prague;—I don't know the reason why, but it's enough to say, we over-slept—we did it gracefully, but we did it.—But we managed to meet Pater Unger at 11 o'clock for a tour of the Imperial Library[9] as well as the General Theological Seminary, viewing everything with utmost interest;—after our eyes had almost fallen out of their sockets for all the sightseeing, we thought we could hear a little Stomach-Aria deep inside us; so we considered it best to move on to Count Canal's lun-cheon table.—The evening came upon us quicker than you might think possible;—anyway, it was time for the opera.—What we heard was "Le gare generose."[10]—As far as the performance of this opera is concerned, I cannot tell you anything special, because I was talking too much; but why was I talking so much, contrary to my habit? Well, perhaps that's the clue.—Basta; that evening, too, was wasted al Solito;[11]—but, at last, today I was lucky enough to find a moment that allows me to inquire about the well-being of your dear parents and of the entire Jacquin

5. "Without writing a line."
6. Probably the Piano Quartet in E-flat, K. 493.
7. I.e., a room "free of charge."
8. "Das schöne Bandel Hammera" (which rhymes with "camera" in the letter) is Viennese dialect for "Das schöne Bändchen haben wir auch" (We also have the pretty ribbon). The reference is to a trio, the so-called Bandel-Terzett, K. 441, a humorous three-part song for soprano, tenor, and bass, which Mozart composed in 1783 and dedicated to Gottfried von Jacquin.
9. Kaiserliche und königliche Bibliothek.
10. By Giovanni Paisiello.
11. "As usual."

household.—I hope and wish with all my heart that all of you are as well as we are here.—I must tell you frankly that, although I am receiving all possible courtesies and honors here, and Prague is indeed a very beautiful and pleasant place, I long very much to be back in Vienna; and believe me, the major object of my longing is *your* Family.—When I think that after my return to Vienna I can enjoy the pleasure of your dear company only for a short while and then will have to do without that pleasure for a long time—maybe forever[12]—I feel the full measure of the friendship and respect I have for your entire family.—Now farewell, my dearest friend, my dearest Hinkiti Honky!—For that's your name and I want you to know that. On our journey here we invented names for everyone; here they are: *I* am Pùnkitititi.—*My wife* is Schabla Pumfa. *Hofer* is Rozka-Pumpa. *Stadler*[13] is Nàtschibinìtschibi. *Joseph, my servant*, is Sagadaratà. *My dog Gauckerl* is Schamanuzky.—Mad.*me* Quallenberg is *Runzifunzi.*—Mad.*selle* Crux *is* Ps.—Ramlo *is Schurimuri.* Freystädtler, *Gaulimauli.* Please be so kind and tell him that's his name.—Well, adieu for now. My concert will take place next Friday, the 19th, at the theater;[14] I will probably have to give a second one, which *unfortunately* will prolong my stay here. Please give my Respects to your worthy parents and embrace your brother 1000 times; we might call him Blatteririzi.—And I kiss the hand of your sister, Sig.*ra* Dinimininimi, 100000 times; urge her to practice hard on her new piano—but this reminder is actually quite unnecessary—for I must confess that I've never had a female pupil who has been as diligent and eager as she is.— In fact, I am very much looking forward to giving her lessons again in my own inadequate fashion.—Apropos, if she wants to come here tomorrow—I'll be in at 11 o'clock for sure.—

Well now, it's about time to close?—isn't it?—yes, you're probably thinking, it's been time for quite a while now.—Farewell, dearest friend!—Sustain me with your wonderful friendship—write soon— really soon—and in case you are too lazy to do it, call on the services of a clerk and dictate your letter;—but it won't flow from the heart

12. Mozart was thinking of going on a concert tour to England; however, the trip never materialized.
13. Anton Paul Stadler, an excellent clarinetist for whom Mozart wrote the Clarinet Quintet in A major, K. 581, and, in 1791, the Clarinet Concerto in A major, K. 622.
14. Mozart's Symphony no. 38 in D major ("Prague"), K. 504, was performed at this concert.

unless you write it yourself; well—I shall see whether you are as much
my friend as I am yours, and will always be.

Mozart

P.S. Please address the letter that
you might *perhaps* write to me:
At Count Thun's Palais.
My wife sends her kind regards to the entire Jacquin Family,
and so does Herr Hofer.

N.B. On Wednesday I shall see and hear "Figaro" here—if I haven't
become deaf and blind by then.—Maybe I won't get that way until after
the opera—

*It has been said that the humorous inventions of new names reflect Mozart's pho-
netic perception of the Czech language, which he did not speak or understand (Larry
Wolff, 55–70); other interpretations point to German origins of the names—e.g.,
"Pùnktititi" as a reference to Mozart's own "punkerte" (small, roundish) figure.
The truth may lie somewhere in between, for the names may well indicate a con-
fluence of Viennese dialect and an outsider's perception of Czech. Whatever their
origin and meaning, these imaginative names show that Mozart's sense of humor
and verbal fun were still intact.*

*Mozart's plans of going on a concert tour in England were encouraged by his
English friends in Vienna—Nancy Storace, Thomas Attwood, Michael O'Kelly
(born in Dublin)—but discouraged by his father, who refused to take care of his
two children. Nevertheless, Mozart tried to prepare himself by taking English lessons
from Johann Georg Kronauer, a teacher of languages in Vienna, as well as a
Mason. Whether Mozart's entry into Kronauer's "Family Album" (Stammbuch) is
original or an English quotation has not been determined, but its holistic message of
patience must have appealed to him, because he was always in such a hurry.*

To Johann Georg Kronauer, in Vienna

Entry into the Family Album

Vienna, March 30, 1787

Patience and tranquillity of mind contribute more tu cure our distempers as the whole art of Medicine.—

Vienna, 30ᵗʰ March 1787. Your true and sincere Friend and Brother.

Wolfgang Amadè Mozart

Member of the very Hon. New-Crowned Hope in the Orient of Vienna.

Leopold Mozart died May 28, 1787, in Salzburg and was buried there in the St. Sebastian Cemetery. Although he had been ill for a while, his death came suddenly and took everybody by surprise; Mozart did not have a chance to travel to Salzburg to see his father once more. The sentiments expressed in Mozart's last letter to his father reflect the thinking of Freemasonry as well as the philosophy of Moses Mendelssohn, whose tract Phaidon, or The Immortality of the Soul *(1767) was found among Mozart's books.*

To his father, in Salzburg

Vienna, April 4, 1787

Mon tres cher Père!—

I find it really annoying that my letter did not get to you, because of a stupid carelessness by Mad.ᵐᵉ Storace;[15]—I wrote you in that letter, among other things, that I hoped you had received my last letter—but since you make no mention of that letter at all—it was my 2ⁿᵈ one to you from Prague—I don't know what to think anymore; it is quite possible that one of Count Thun's servants thought it a nifty idea to pocket the postage money himself;—I would rather pay double the amount for postage than to think that my letters have perhaps fallen into the wrong hands.—Ramm and the 2 Fischers—that is, the bass singer and the oboist from London—were here during the Lenten Season; if the latter did not play any better when we heard him in Holland than he is

---

15. Mad.ᵐᵉ Storace, the mother of the singer Nancy Storace, was supposed to deliver a letter to Leopold in Salzburg, but she apparently misplaced it.

playing now, he certainly does not deserve the Renomeè he has.—*But just between you and me*—I was then at an age when I was not competent to make a judgment—I only remember that I thought he was great, as did the rest of the world;—which is quite natural if one considers that musical taste has drastically changed since that time;—is he perhaps following the rules of an old school?—No!—To put it in one word, he is playing like a Miserable student.—Young *Andrè*, Fiala's pupil, *is playing* a thousand times better.—And then the Concerts—of his own Compositions!—Each Ritornello lasts a quarter of an hour—until, at last, the hero appears—lifts up one leaden foot after another—and bangs them down, one after another, on the floor—his tone is entirely nasal and his sustained notes are like a tremulant on the organ. Would you have pictured him that way? Well, it's the Truth—but a Truth I share only with *you*.—This very moment I have received some news that distresses me very much—this all the more as I gathered from your last letter that you were, thank god, doing very well;—but now I hear that you are really ill! I need not tell you how much I'm longing to hear some reassuring news from you yourself; and, indeed, I confidently expect such news— although I have made it a habit to imagine the worst in all situations— as Death, if we think about it soberly, is the true and ultimate purpose of our life, I have over the last several years formed such a knowing relationship with this true and best friend of humankind that his image holds nothing terrifying for me anymore; instead it holds much that is soothing and consoling! And I thank my god that he has blessed me with the insight, you know what I mean,[16] which makes it possible for me to perceive death as the *key* to our ultimate happiness.—I never lie down at night without thinking that perhaps, as young as I am, I will not live to see another day—and yet no one who knows me can say that I am morose or dejected in company—and for this blessing I thank my Creator every day and sincerely wish the same blessing for All my fellow human beings.—I wrote to you my thoughts about such matters in the letter that Mad.^me Storace packed with her things by mistake; these thoughts were occasioned by the untimely death of my dearest and best friend, Count von Hatzfeld;[17]—he had just turned 31; my age—but I do

16. A reference to Mozart's Freemasonic thinking about death, views he assumes his father is familiar with, since Leopold had also joined Mozart's lodge in Vienna.
17. Count August Clemens Ludwig Maria von Hatzfeld was canon of the cathedral at Eichstädt; Mozart had met him the year before in Vienna.

not grieve for *him*—only for myself and all those who knew him as well as I did.—I hope and wish that, while I am writing these lines, you have improved already; but should you not have gotten better, against all expectations, I beg you . . .[18] do not keep it from me, but tell me the whole truth or have someone write it to me, so I can be in your arms as quickly as is humanly possible; I beseech you by all that's—sacred to both of us.—However, I do expect to receive soon a reassuring letter from you; and it is in this soothing expectation that I, together with my wife and Carl,[19] kiss your hands 1000 times and remain Forever

your most obedient son
W. A. Mozart

📖 *The month of April 1787 was, indeed, hectic, confusing, and painful for Mozart. It was the month that a sixteen-year-old musician from Bonn, Ludwig van Beethoven, came to Mozart for lessons but had to return to Bonn after only two weeks because his mother had fallen ill. It turned out to be the only meeting between Mozart and Beethoven. Also, the Mozarts moved from Schulerstraße to less expensive quarters on Landstraße, no. 224 (today, nos. 75 and 77); Mozart himself became seriously ill with kidney problems and was treated by his childhood friend Dr. Sigmund Barisani, who died five months later at the age of twenty-nine.*

To his sister, in St. Gilgen

Vienna, June 2, 1787

Dearest Sister!

You can well imagine how Painful the sad news of our dear father's sudden death was for me, after all, our loss is equally great.—Because I cannot possibly leave Vienna at this time, which, even if I could, would be more to embrace you than for any other reason, since the estate of our dear late father hardly warrants it, I must confess that I share entirely your opinion regarding a public auction.[20] I would, however, like to see an inventory before it takes place, so I could select a few items for

---

18. The points are by Mozart.
19. Mozart's son, Carl Thomas, who was born on September 21, 1784.
20. Such a public auction took place at the end of September 1787 at the Tanzmeisterhaus in Salzburg, Leopold's home for fourteen years.

myself;—but if there is a *dispositio paterna inter liberos*,[21] as Herr von d'Yppold says in his letter,[22] I need to know what's in that disposition before I can decide about anything else.—Therefore, at this point, I simply expect to receive an accurate copy of that writ, and then, after a brief review, I will let you know what I think without delay.—Please, be so kind and give the enclosed letter to our true and good friend Herr von d'Yppold.—As he has shown such friendship toward our family on so many occasions, I hope he will do me yet another service of friendship and be *my representative* in all necessary proceedings. Farewell, dearest sister! I am Forever your

faithful brother
W. A. Mozart

📝 *Mozart's poem on the death of his beloved pet bird, Vogel Star, is humorous, bittersweet, and self-reflective at a time of great loss and grief. His father had passed away, a close friend had died young, and he himself was deeply involved in* Don Giovanni, *his darkest comedy.*

Mozart's poem for his dead starling

Here rests a bird called Starling,
A foolish little Darling.
He was still in his prime
When he ran out of time,
And my sweet little friend
Came to a bitter end,
Creating a terrible smart
Deep in my heart.
Gentle Reader! Shed a tear,
For he was dear,
Sometimes a bit too jolly
And, at times, quite folly,
But nevermore

---

21. A last will and testament. It appears that Leopold *did* leave a will, which, however, was never found (see Halliwell, 545–64).
22. Franz Armand d'Ippold, a friend of the family, had informed Mozart of his father's death. He had also been a serious suitor for Nannerl, but Leopold had turned him down.

A bore.
I bet he is now up on high
Praising my friendship to the sky,
Which I render
Without tender;
For when he took his sudden leave,
Which brought to me such grief,
He was not thinking of the man
Who writes and rhymes as no one can.
June 4, 1787.

Mozart.

To his sister, in St. Gilgen

Vienna, June 16, 1787

Dearest, most beloved sister!

I did not really notice that it wasn't you who informed me about our dear father's death, which came upon me so unexpectedly, because I could easily guess why.—May God have taken him to Himself!—Be assured, my Dear, that if you desire a kind, loving, and protective brother, you will always find one in me whenever you need one.—My dearest, most beloved sister! if you were still single and unprovided for, all this would not be necessary. I would most gladly leave everything to you, as I have thought and said a thousand times before; but because the property is now of no use to you, yet, on the other hand, of considerable value to me, I regard it my duty to think about my wife and child.[23]

Johann von Berchtold zu Sonnenburg, Nannerl's husband, offered Mozart 1,000 gulden as a settlement of his inheritance claims. The offer seemed fair, and Mozart accepted it. In his letter of agreement Mozart refers to Michael Puchberg, a wealthy Viennese merchant and talented amateur musician, to whom Mozart would turn again and again for loans. Puchberg had his office in a building belonging to Count Walsegg-Stuppach, the man who would anonymously commission Mozart to write a requiem in 1791.

23. The letter ends here without a conclusion.

To Johann von Berchtold zu Sonnenburg, in St. Gilgen

Vienna, September 29, 1787

Dearest brother!—

In a hurry!—I am delighted about our amicable settlement. When you are ready to send the bill of exchange, please address it to Herr Michael Puchberg, *The Count Walsegg House, at the Hohen Markt.* He is authorized to receive the money because I will be leaving for Prague very early on Monday morning.—Farewell; kiss my dear sister 1000 times for both me and my wife and be assured that I shall always remain your very sincere brother

W. A. Mozart

Mozart and Constanze set out for Prague on October 1, 1787, for the premiere of Don Giovanni, *which was scheduled for October 14. They arrived in Prague on October 4 and took quarters at the inn Zu den drei Löwen (The Three Lions). Their three-year-old son, Carl Thomas, stayed behind either with Constanze's mother or in a boarding school.*

The premiere of Don Giovanni *took place on October 29, 1787, at the Nostiz National Theater in Prague. Mozart and his librettist, Lorenzo da Ponte, who had come to Prague on October 8 to finalize the text, had worked hard to finish the opera. A day before the premiere, Mozart entered into his* Catalog of Works, *"28ᵗʰ of October. In Prague. Il diβoluto punito, o, il Don Giovanni, opera Buffa in 2 Atti."The opera was a huge success. One of the local papers wrote, "Connoisseurs and musicians say that Prague had never heard the like. Herr Mozard [sic] conducted in person; when he entered the orchestra he was received with threefold cheers, which again happened when he left" (Deutsch,* Documentary, *303).*

To Gottfried von Jacquin, in Vienna

Prague, October 15, 1787

Dearest friend!—

You're probably thinking that my Opera has been performed by now—well—you are a bit mistaken there; first of all, the stage personnel here is not quite as capable as the personnel in Vienna when it comes to learning an opera like this one in so short a time.

Second, I found on my arrival here that very few preparations and arrangements had been made for it, and it would have been totally impossible to have the opera ready on the 14th, which was yesterday.—So, they gave my "Figaro" instead, yesterday, in a fully illuminated theater, and I myself was conducting.—. . . "Don Giovanni" is now scheduled for the 24th.

October, 21st: "Don Giovanni" had been set for the 24th, but one of the singers, who was taken ill, has caused another delay;—since the company is small, the Impreßario has to be constantly concerned about sparing his people as much as possible so that he won't be plunged by some unexpected illness into the most critical of all critical situations: not to be able to stage a performance at all!—therefore, everything here is quite a bit slower because the singers are too lazy to rehearse on opera days and the manager is too timid and fearful to push them—but what's this?—is it possible?—what visions are coming before my ears, what am I hearing with my eyes?—A letter from—I am rubbing my eyes until they hurt—the letter is—the devil take me † god protect me †—it's from you;—if winter weren't sitting before my door, I would kick in the stove; but since I need my stove quite early this year and since I will probably still need it in the days ahead, you will permit me to express my surprise in a more restrained manner by simply telling you in a word or two that I am exceedingly delighted to get some news from you and your dear family.—

October 25th.—Today is the eleventh day that I began scribbling on this letter;—you can see from it that there is no lack of good will—whenever I find a moment I paint another small piece of it—unfortunately, I cannot stay with it—because my life belongs to other people—and not enough to myself; I don't need to tell you that this is not my preferred way of life.—

The opera will be performed for the first time on Monday, the 29th; I shall give you an account of it the very next day.—As far as the Aria is concerned, let me just say, it's not possible right now to send it to you—for reasons that I will tell you in person.—. . . Farewell for now;—please kiss the hand of your gracious mother for me and give my warmest regards to your sister and brother, and rest assured that I shall always remain

> your true friend and servant
> W. A. Mozart

To Gottfried von Jacquin, in Vienna

Prague, November 4, 1787

Dearest, most beloved Friend!

I hope you received my letter;—my opera "Don Giovanni" was per-formed on Oct^b 29th, with the greatest of applause.—Yesterday it was given for the 4th time—for my own Benefit.—I think I'll be leaving here on the 12th or 13th; after I get back I'll bring you the Aria so you can have it right away and sing it; NB, *just between you and me;*—I so wished that my good friends, particularly Bridi and you, could be here just for one evening to share in my great happiness here!—Maybe my opera will be performed in Vienna after all?—I certainly hope so.—They are doing their best here to persuade me to stay a few months and write another Opera,—but I can't accept the offer, no matter how flattering it is.— Well now, dearest friend, how are things?—I hope that *all* of you are as fit and well as we are;—I'm sure you are not lacking in pleasant dis-tractions, dearest friend, because you have everything that you *at your age* and *in your situation* could possibly wish for!—all the more as you seem to be leaving behind your previous somewhat *restless lifestyle;*—aren't you persuaded a little more each day by the Truth of my little lectures to you?—don't you think that the pleasures of unstable and capricious love affairs don't even come close to the blessings of true affection?—I am sure that deep in your heart you are often grateful for my edifying lectures!—Indeed, you have it in you to make me proud;—but all jok-ing aside.—You do owe me some thanks if you proved yourself worthy to Mad.^selle N——,[24] after all, I played a not so insignificant role in your moral improvement and conversion.—My great-grandfather used to say to his wife, my great-grandmother, who said to her daughter, my grand-mother, who in turn said to her daughter, my mother, who told her daughter, my sister, that to speak agreeably and beautifully was a high form of art, but to cease talking at the right moment was perhaps no less a high form of art—I, therefore, will follow the advice of my sis-ter, who derives her wisdom from our mother, grandmother, and great-grandmother and will come to an end not only with my moral ram-blings but with my entire letter.

24. Probably Marianne von Natorp, one of the two sisters to whom Mozart dedicated his Piano Sonata for Four Hands, K. 521.

November 9th:—What surprise, what pleasure, I just received your 2nd letter;—if it is necessary to assure you of my friendship by sending you the "Lied" in question, you'll have no reason to doubt any longer;—here it is.[25]—I do hope, however, that you are convinced of my true friendship even *without this Lied,* and in this hope I remain Forever

your sincerest friend
W. A. Mozart

To his sister, in St. Gilgen

Vienna, December 19, 1787

Dearest Sister!

I most sincerely beg your forgiveness for having kept you without an answer for so long.—You probably know by now that I composed "Don Juan" in Prague and enjoyed the greatest possible applause—but you probably don't know that His Majesty, the Emperor, has taken me into his services.[26] I am certain that you welcome this news.—Would you please send me as quickly as you can the little wooden box containing my scores;—and as far as *my own* recent clavier music is concerned, please write down the themes of the pieces that I sent you from Vienna and let me have the list so I won't send you things twice.—This will be of help to both of us.—

Farewell, dear Sister, and do write—if I don't always reply right away, blame it not on my negligence but on my heavy work schedule.—adieu.—I embrace you with all my heart and remain Forever your sincere and loving brother

W. A. Mozart

P.S.—1000 little kisses from my wife who is expecting her confinement any day now.[27]—And all the best for your husband from both of us.

25. A song, K. 530, which Mozart had written for Gottfried von Jacquin.
26. Mozart was appointed Imperial and Royal Chamber Composer (k. k. Kammer-Kompositeur) to Joseph II on December 7, 1787, with an annual salary of 800 gulden. Gluck, his predecessor in this post, had received 2,000 gulden a year.
27. Mozart and Constanze's fourth child, Theresia Constanzia Adelheid Friederika Maria Anna, was born on December 27, 1787, and died on June 29, 1788.

🖎 *In the course of three and a half years, Mozart wrote more than twenty letters to Michael Puchberg, a Viennese merchant and Masonic brother. All letters contain requests for financial help, and Puchberg responded positively to almost all the requests, although not always with the full amount Mozart asked for. In this case, Puchberg noted on Mozart's letter, "sent 100 fl."*

To Michael Puchberg, in Vienna

Vienna, June 1788

My dearest Brother![28]

Your true friendship and brotherly love give me the necessary courage to ask you a big favor;—I still owe you 8 *ducats*[29]—but at present I am not only unable to pay it back, but my trust in you is so great that I dare ask you to help me out with another 100 gulden until next week (when my concerts start at the Casino)[30]—by that time I will definitely have received my subscription money[31] and can easily pay you back the 136 gulden, together with my warmest thanks.

I take the liberty of enclosing 2 tickets that I ask you (as a Brother) to accept without payment since I will never be able to repay sufficiently the friendship you have shown me.

I beg you once more to forgive my obtrusiveness and remain, with best regards for your esteemed wife, in friendship and brotherly love.

Your most devoted Brother
W. A. Mozart

🖎 *There seem to have been two major reasons for Mozart's pressing need for money at this time: one was the slow and irregular flow of income from subscriptions and performances; the other was the increase in expenses for doctors and medication for Constanze, who, partly because of frequent pregnancies, was in poor health.*

28. Michael Puchberg was a Freemason like Mozart and, therefore, a "brother."
29. I.e., 36 gulden.
30. The Casino was a new concert hall in the Spiegelgasse, where Mozart was planning a series of concerts; they apparently did not materialize.
31. Mozart had offered three string quintets—in C minor, K. 406, in C major K. 515, in G minor, K. 516—for subscription, but, even though he extended the deadline, they failed to bring in the much needed cash.

To Michael Puchberg, in Vienna

Vienna, before June 17, 1788

Most Honorable Brother of the Order,
dearest and best friend!—

The firm conviction that you are *my true friend* and that you know me as a *man of honor* encourages me to open my heart to you and submit the following request.—I shall come right to the point, with my usual frankness and without any pretenses.—

If you would have the kindness and friendship to support me for 1 or 2 years with 1 or 2 thousand gulden at a suitable rate of interest, you would help me keep my field and plow![32] You probably know yourself as a matter of *experience* and *truth* how dreadfully hard, indeed, how impossible it is if you have to depend on your livelihood from one irregular income to the next; without a *certain minimum capital*, it is impossible to keep one's affairs in order.—with nothing you can create *nothing*;—if you will do this service of friendship for me, I would be able, *primo*, to pay my bills at the *proper time*, in other words, with a certain ease, whereas at present I have to *postpone* my payments and then spend my *entire income* all at once, often at a *most inconvenient time.*—*Secondo:* I would be able to work with a *freer mind* and *lighter heart* and consequently *earn* more.—As to securities, I don't imagine that you would have any doubts!—you know my situation quite well—and you know my *sincerity!*—And as far as the subscription is concerned, don't worry about it; I am currently extending the deadline by several months;[33]—I think there'll be more subscribers from *abroad* than from around *here.*—

I have now opened my whole heart to you in a matter of great importance to me, in other words, I have shown myself as a *true brother*—after all, one can be totally frank only with a *true* brother.—Now I am looking forward to your answer—a *favorable answer;*—I don't know— but I see you as *the kind of man* who, like myself, supports his friend, his *true friend*, and brother, I mean his *true brother*, if at all possible.—If, however, you cannot spare such a sum right now, I beg you to lend me *at least a couple of hundred gulden* until Tomorrow because my landlord in the Landstrasse was pressing me so hard that I had to pay him all at once

---

32. "Field and plow" (*Acker* and *Pflug*) is a wonderful rural metaphor for the essentials of life.
33. The sale of subscriptions, which was handled by Puchberg's office, went very slowly.

in order to avoid unpleasantness; and that has brought my finances into complete disarray!—We'll be sleeping tonight for the first time in our new lodgings where we are going to be this coming *summer* and *winter;*—basically, it's all the same to me, if anything it's an improvement. I don't have much business in town anyway and, because I'm not interrupted as much by visitors, I shall have more time and leisure for work;—if I need to go downtown on *business,* which happens rarely enough, any cabbie will take me there for 10 kreuzer, and, after all, our quarters are less expensive, and *more pleasant* in spring, summer, and fall—because I also have a garden.—Our apartment is in the Waringergasse, at the Three Stars, No. 135.[34] Please take my letter as a true sign of my complete confidence in you, and do remain my friend and brother Forever as I will be yours unto death

> Your true, most cordial
> friend and brother,
> W. A. Mozart

P.S. When are we going to make a little Musique at your house again?—I have written a New Trio.[35]

Michael Puchberg did not respond affirmatively to Mozart's request for a larger sum of money, but he did send 200 gulden on June 17, 1788.

In spite of an onset of melancholy and pessimism—Mozart calls it "black thoughts"—he was was extremely productive in his new suburban environment, composing during that spring and summer a number of major works, among them the Piano Trios in E major, K. 542, and in C major, K. 548; the delightful "Sonata facile," K. 545; the Adagio and Fugue in C minor, K. 546; and his three great and last symphonies, no. 39 in E-flat major, K. 543, no. 40 in G minor, K. 550, and no. 41 in C major ("Jupiter"), K. 551.

34. The Mozarts had moved from their apartment in the Landstraße already in the beginning of December 1787. After a short stay in the inner city, they moved again on June 17, 1788, to the suburbs, this time to the suburb of Alsergrund, Währingerstraße, no. 135 (today in the Eighteenth District, northwest of the city).
35. Trio for Piano, Violin, and Cello in E major, K. 542.

To Michael Puchberg, in Vienna

Vienna, June 27, 1788

Most Honored Brother of the Order,
Dearest best Friend!

I thought I would come into town myself one of these days and be able to thank you in person for the kindness you have shown me—but at the moment I wouldn't even have the heart to come before you, as I have to admit that it is not possible for me right now to pay back the money you lent me; instead, I must beg you to be patient a little longer!—I am indeed very troubled about the fact that you are not in a position to help me out in the manner I had wished!—My circumstances are such that I will have to borrow money no matter what.— But, good Lord, whom can I trust?—No one but you, my dearest friend!—If at least you could give me a friendly hand in procuring a sum of money through some other channel!—I'll be glad to pay interest and whoever will lend me the money has, I believe, sufficient securities in my character and through my salary;[36]—I'm truly sorry to be in such a dilemma, but this is the very reason why I wished I could raise a *substantial sum* for a *somewhat longer period* just so this sort of thing could be prevented.—. . .

Do come for a visit; I am always at home;—I have done more work in the 10 days that I've been living here than in 2 months at my previous place, and if I weren't beset so frequently by black thoughts (which I have to chase away forceably), things would be still better because my apartment is pleasant,—comfortable—and—*inexpensive!*—Well, I don't want to take up your time with my twaddle any longer, so I'll be *quiet* now—and remain *hopeful.*

Ever your obliging servant
and true friend and Brother of the Order
W. A. Mozart

---

36. Mozart is undoubtedly referring to his salary of 800 gulden as newly appointed courtly chamber composer.

To his sister, in St. Gilgen

Vienna, August 2, 1788

Dearest sister!

You have every right to be angry with me!—but will you still be angry after receiving my newest piano pieces with this mail coach?—Oh, not really!—Well, I do hope my package will make up for everything.—

I am sure you know that I wish you well every single day, so I hope you will forgive me that I am limping in with my late congratulations for your Name Day;—dearest Sister,—I wish you from the bottom of my heart and from the depth of my soul all the things you wish for yourself—*Punctum!* . . .

Now I have a favor to ask of you;—I would appreciate it very much if Haydn could lend me for a little while the 2 *Tutti-Masses* and the *Graduali* he composed;[37]—I would return them with gratitude.—It's now a year since I wrote to him and invited him to come and stay with me, but he has never answered me;—so, as far as answering letters is concerned, he seems to have a lot in common with me, don't you agree?—It would be a real help to me if you could do the following: invite him out to your place in St. Gilgen and play some of my New pieces for him—he can't possibly dislike the Trio and quartet.[38]—adieu, dearest sister!—As soon as another bunch of my recent compositions has accumulated, I'll send it to you;—I remain forever

your sincere brother
W. A. Mozart

P.S. To answer your question about my service: the emperor has appointed me into his chamber,[39] in other words, he has given me an official title; *right now* I receive a salary of only 800 gulden.—but no one else in the chamber earns *as much.*—On the advertisement that was posted for the premiere of my Prague opera "Don Giovanni" (which will be given again today), . . . it says: *The Musick is by Herr Mozart, Kapellmeister in actual service of His Majesty, the Emperor.*

---

37. It is not known which "Tutti-Masses" and "Graduali" by Michael Haydn Mozart had in mind.
38. Probably the Piano Trio in E major, K. 542, and the Piano Quartet in E-flat major, K. 493.
39. "Chamber" means court here—i.e., Mozart was entitled to call himself court composer (Kammer-Kompositeur).

🐝 *Franz Hofdemel was a clerk in the Vienna law courts. He was also in the process of becoming a Freemason, and when Mozart suggests they "shall soon be able to call each other by a more beautiful name," he means the name of "brother." Mozart was in need of money because he was about to travel to Berlin with Prince Karl Lichnowsky. Hofdemel lent the requested 100 gulden against a promissory note.*

To Franz Hofdemel, in Vienna

Vienna, end of March 1789

Dearest friend!——

I am taking the liberty of asking you without much ceremony for a favor.——If you could or would lend me 100 gulden until the 20th of next month, I would feel much obliged.——On the 20th I will receive the quarterly installment of my salary and shall be able to repay my loan, with many thanks.——

I relied too much on the sum of 100 ducats due to me from abroad.[40]——Since I have not received this sum yet, although I expect it any day now, I have left myself a bit short of cash and need some money *right at this moment.* I put my trust in you because I am completely convinced of your friendship.——

We shall soon be able to call each other by a more beautiful name!——for your proceedings are nearing their end.[41]

Mozart.

🐝 *On December 6, 1791, on the day of Mozart's burial, Franz Hofdemel attempted to kill his wife, Maria Magdalena, who may have been one of Mozart's pupils. Hofdemel committed suicide afterward. The incident gave rise to rumors that Mozart had had an affair with Maria Magdalena.*

🐝 *Mozart was preparing for a journey to Berlin via Prague, Dresden, and Leipzig, in the hope of getting commissions, especially from the king of Prussia. He was accompanying Prince Karl Lichnowsky, son-in-law of Countess Thun (and later friend and supporter of Beethoven), who was traveling to the Prussian court. Mozart's poem "On a Journey to be Taken" was written before their departure.*

40. Mozart may be referring here to his contractual payment for *Don Giovanni* from the Prague National Theater.
41. Probably the proceedings for Hofdemel's novitiate in the Masonic brotherhood.

To his wife, in Vienna

Vienna, before April 8, 1789

On a Journey to be Taken.

When I travel to Berlin in	Style
I hope to gain honor and	Fame,
yet the applause will not make me—	smile,
for you, my dear, cannot enjoy the	same;
But at our wiedersehen I already	know,
we'll be hugging and kissing with burning	Desire!
Meantime, though, tears of sorrow will	flow
splitting our hearts into patience and	Fire.

Mozart and Prince Lichnowsky left early on April 8; they headed into Moravia and made their first stop at Budwitz (Moravské Budějovice; Czech Republic), some fifty kilometers northwest of Vienna.

To his wife, in Vienna

Budwitz, April 8, 1789

Dearest little Wife!

While the prince is off bargaining for fresh horses, I am seizing this opportunity with great pleasure to write you, dearest little wife of my heart, a few quick words.—How are you?—Are you thinking of me as often as I am thinking of you?—I look at your portrait every few minutes—and cry—half out of joy, half out of sorrow!—Please look after your health, which is so dear to me, and stay well, my darling!—And don't worry on my account, because I am suffering no hardships on this trip—no adversities—except your *absence*—which, as it can't be helped, simply must be endured.—I am writing this with tears in my eyes;— adieu—I'll write more from Prague—and I'll also write more legibly because I won't have to be in such a rush—adieu—I kiss you most tenderly a Million times and remain Forever your

stu—stu[42]—Mozart,
faithful unto death.

42. Meaning unknown.

Give Karl a kiss from me, and my regards to Herr und Frau von Puchberg—more next time.

To his wife, in Vienna

Prague, April 10, 1789

Dearest and best little wife of mine!

We arrived safely today at noon, half past one. I trust you have received my brief note from Budwitz in the meantime.—Let me give you a report from Prague: we're staying at the inn The Unicorn; after I had a shave, my hair done, and gotten dressed, I drove to Herr von Canal, thinking I would have lunch with him; but as my way led by the Duscheks' house,[43] I stopped there to call on them—and I learned that Madame had left for Dresden yesterday!!!—So I'll be seeing her there. Herr Duschek was lunching at Leliborn's, where I ate occasionally too.—So I drove there directly.—I asked that Herr Duschek be called outside, pretending to be someone who needed to speak with him; well, you can imagine his delight;—so I, too, lunched at Leliborn's.—. . . One more thing:—Ramm came through here and returned home a week ago. He had come from Berlin and said that the king[44] had asked him several times pointedly whether he thought it was certain that I would come, and since I was not appearing on the scene, he said at another occasion: I fear he is not coming.—Ramm felt very uneasy about it and tried to assure him of the contrary.—Judging from all this, my prospects in Berlin ought to be pretty good.—I'm about to take the prince to Herr Duschek, who is expecting us, and at 9 o'clock this evening we'll be off to Dresden; we'll arrive there tomorrow morning.—

Dearest little wife! I am so longing to hear from you—maybe I'll find a letter from you in Dresden! Oh, dear God! make my wish come true! After receiving this letter, you will have to write to Leipzig, poste restante, of course;—adieu—dearest, I must close now, otherwise I'll miss the mail.—Kiss our Karl a thousand times for me; I am, kissing you with all my heart, your ever faithful Mozart.

43. Franz Xaver Duschek (Dušek), a composer, and Josepha Duschek (Dušek), a singer, whom Mozart had first met in 1777 in Salzburg.
44. Friedrich Wilhelm II of Prussia; he was a nephew of Frederick the Great and, like his uncle, was musical and played the cello.

P.S. All kinds of greetings to Herr and Frau Puchberg; I will have to wait until I'm in Berlin to write and thank him.—Adieu, aimez moi et gardes votre santè si chere et precieuse a votre epaux.[45]

To his wife, in Vienna

Dresden, April 13, 1789
at 7 o'clock in the morning

Dearest and best little wife of mine!

We expected to be in Dresden by Saturday, after the midday meal, but we didn't arrive until yesterday, Sunday, at 6 o'clock in the evening;— that's how bad the roads are.——

Right after my arrival I went to call on the Neumans,[46] where Mad.^me Duschek is staying to bring her a letter from her husband.— Their apartment is on the 4th floor off the corridor and from her room you can see anyone who comes to the house;—when I came to the door, Herr Neumann was already awaiting me and inquired with whom he had the honor of speaking;—I answered: I'll tell you in a moment, but first be so kind and ask Mad.^me Duschek to come to the door so I won't spoil my surprise; but at that instant Mad.^me Duschek stood before me because she had seen me from the window and had said: someone is coming to the house who looks like Mozart;—of course, everybody was delighted.—. . .

Dearest little wife, if I only had a letter from you!—if I wrote you all the things I'm doing with your *portrait*, you'd certainly laugh.—for example, when I take it out of its prison,[47] I say: Grüß dich gott, Stanzerl!—grüss dich gott, grüss dich gott;—Spitzbub;—knaller-baller;—Spitzignas—bagateller—schluck und druck![48]—and when I put it back in its case, I slide it in very slowly saying all the while: Stu!—Stu!—Stu!—but with a *certain emphasis* that is appropriate for such a meaningful word; and at the very last second I say quickly: gute Nacht, Mauserl, schlaf gesund.[49]—Well, I think what I've written here is pret-

45. "Adieu, I love you, and take good care of your health, so dear and precious to your husband."
46. Johann Leopold Neumann was secretary to the Saxon War Council; he also wrote and translated opera texts. His wife was an excellent pianist.
47. The case of the portrait.
48. Sweet utterings without meaning: "Hello, dear Constanze,—good to see you, good to see you;—oh, you thieving little rogue;—slam—bang!—you there with that pointed nose—just a bagatelle—gag and swallow!"
49. "Good night, little mouse, sleep well."

ty stupid, at least as far as the outside world is concerned,—but for the two of us, who love each other dearly, it's not stupid at all.—Today is the 6th day that I've been away from you, and, Heavens, it seems like a year to me.—

You may sometimes find it hard to read my letters because I have to write in haste and, therefore, somewhat poorly;—adieu, my dearest, my one and all!—The carriage has arrived—but this time I can't shout: bravo! the carriage is here! but rather—*Male!* [50]—Farewell, love me always as I love you; I kiss you most tenderly a Million times and remain as ever your

husband who loves you tenderly
W. A. Mozart

Mozart's lengthy letter from Dresden was addressed to "Constance de Mozart," at the "Hohen Markt im Walseckischen Hause." This was the address of the Puchbergs, and it can be assumed that Constanze stayed with the Puchbergs while Mozart was traveling. It is also interesting to note that Mozart, in writing to Constanze, sounds more and more like his father: be more specific in your letters, watch your conduct, do not bring dishonor to the family. However, for all his insistence on details and honor, he himself left out a significant detail in his letter: he neglected to mention that the "pretty snuffbox" from the elector of Saxony contained 100 ducats.

To his wife, in Vienna

Dresden, April 16, 1789
At half past 11 o'clock at night

Dearest and best little wife of mine!

What?—still in Dresden?—Yes, my dear;—let me tell you every-thing in detail.—Monday, the 13th, after having breakfast with the Neumanns, we all went to the court chapel and heard a mass composed by Naumann[51] who also conducted:—very Mediocre!—We were sitting in a choir section facing the orchestra;—suddenly Neumann nudged me and then introduced me to Herr von König[52] who is Director de plaisirs, I should say of the sad plaisirs, of the Elector.[53] He was exceed-

---

50. "Oh, dread!"
51. Johann Gottlieb Naumann, composer and Kapellmeister in Dresden.
52. Friedrich August von König, director of entertainment at the Dresden court.
53. Friedrich August III, elector of Saxony.

ingly polite and to his question whether I wouldn't wish to play before his Highness, I replied that it would be a great honor for me, however, since I was not traveling alone, I couldn't delay my departure;—and that's the way we left it.—My princely travel companion invited the Naumanns[54] and Mad.[me] Duschek to lunch.—While we were at table, I received a message that I was to play at court the following day, Tuesday, the 14th, at 6 o'clock in the evening—this was quite out of the ordinary, for it is difficult here to get an invitation to play; and, as you know, I wasn't counting on it at all.— We had gotten a quartet together at our hotel, l'hotel de Boulogne;[55]—the group included Antoine Tayber, who, as you know, is organist here, and Herr Kraft, a cellist, who is here with his son; he is in the service of Prince Esterhazy. I introduced the Trio I wrote for Herr Puchberg[56] at this little musicale—and we played it quite decently; Duschek sang a number of arias from "Figaro" and "Don Juan."—The next day I played my New Concerto in D at court;[57] and the following day, Wednesday, the 15th, in the morning, I received a very pretty snuffbox.—Afterward we had lunch at the house of the Russian ambassador, where I spent a lot of time at the piano.—After lunch we decided to try out the organ in the church.—At 4 o'clock we were on our way.—Naumann was there too;—You should know also that a certain *Häßler*,[58] who is an organist from Erfurt, is visiting here; and he was there as well. He is a pupil of a pupil of Bach.[59]—His strength is the organ and the Clavier (Clavichord).—Well, the people here think because I am from Vienna, I'm not familiar with their style and technique of organ playing.—So I sat down at the organ and played.—Prince Lichnowsky, who knows Häßler quite well, persuaded him with some difficulty to play also.—I tell you, the special strength of this Häßler consists in his footwork, which, however, is not really such a big thing, because the pedals here are arranged stepwise; apart from that he has simply memorized a few harmonies and modulations of old Sebastian Bach, but he is not able to execute a fugue properly;—

54. Mozart wrote "Naumanns" but meant the Neumanns from Dresden.
55. Mozart means the Hôtel de Pologne in Dresden, where he and Prince Lichnowsky were staying.
56. Divertimento for Violin, Viola, and Cello, K. 563. The trio was performed at the Hôtel de Pologne; Mozart probably played the viola part.
57. Piano Concerto in D major ("Coronation"), K. 537.
58. Johann Wilhelm Hässler, organist at Erfurt.
59. Johann Sebastian Bach.

his play is not solid—in other words, he is far from being an Albrechts-berger.[60]—Afterward we decided to go back to the house of the Russian ambassador so that Häßler could hear me play on the forte piano;—Häßler played too.—I must say, Mad.^selle Auerhammer is just as good, so, as you can well imagine, my esteem for him sank considerably.—Then we went to the opera;—it is Wretched.—Do you know who is among the singers here?—Rosa Panservisi[61]—you can imagine how delighted she was to see me.—. . . After the opera we went home; and now comes the happiest moment of my day; there was a letter from you, dearest, the letter I had so ardently longed for!—My dear Beloved!—Duschek and Neumann were with me as usual, but I went triumphant-ly to my room, kissed the letter innumerable times before I opened it, then—I devoured it more than I read it.—. . .

Dearest Little wife, I have a number of requests to make:—

1.mo I beg you not to be sad;

2.do that you *take good care of your health* and *be careful* when you go out into those spring breezes.

3.^tio that you don't go out walking by yourself—but best of all—don't *go out walking at all*.

4.to that you feel completely assured of my love.—I haven't written you a letter yet without putting your portrait before me.

6.to et ultimo, I'm asking you to please be a little more detailed in your letters.—. . .

5.to I beg you to think not only of *your and my honor* in your conduct, but even of just the *appearance* of it.—Please don't be annoyed by this request.—You should love me all the more for being so concerned about honor.

Now farewell, dearest, my truly beloved!—Remember that every night before going to bed I talk to your portrait for a good half hour, and when I wake up I do the same.—We'll be leaving the day after tomorrow, on the 18th;—*from here on write to Berlin, poste restante.*

Oh, stru! stri!—I kiss you and squeeze you 1095060437082 times; this will help you to practice your pronunciation. I am forever

> your most faithful husband and friend
> W. A. Mozart

---

60. Johann Albrechtsberger, second court organist in Vienna.
61. "Rosa Panservisi" is Rosa Manservisi, who had sung in Mozart's *La finta giardiniera* in 1775.

🖎 *On May 12, 1789, in the evening, Mozart gave a concert at the famous Gewand-haus concert hall in Leipzig. His program included two piano concertos, no. 18 in B-flat, K. 456, and no. 25 in C, K. 503.*

To his wife, in Vienna

Leipzig, May 16, 1789

Dearest, most beloved little wife of my heart!—

What?—still in Leiptzig?[62]—True, in my last letter from the 8ᵗʰ or 9ᵗʰ I wrote I would be leaving that same night at 2 o'clock, however, the numerous requests of my friends made me decide . . . to stay and give a concert here on Tuesday, the 12ᵗʰ.—Well, the concert was a splendid success as far as applause and honors go, but it was all the more disappointing in terms of income. Mad.ᵐᵉ Duschek, who is here also, sang in the concert;—the Neumanns from Dresden are here as well—and the pleasure of being in the company of such dear and wonderful people, who all send their best to you, has delayed my departure as well.—I did want to leave yesterday but couldn't get horses—the same was the case today;—everybody is traveling somewhere *right now;* and there is an unusually large number of travelers;—but tomorrow morning at 5 o'clock, we are finally off! . . .

It appears I will *have* to stay at least a week in Berlin;—this means that in all likelihood I won't be back in Vienna before the 5ᵗʰ or 6ᵗʰ of June;—that's in about 10 or 12 days after you receive this letter. . . .

Farewell, dearest wife, *please fulfill all the requests I sent you in my last letter, my motivation for sending them is love, true and genuine love—love me as much as I love you;*—I am Forever

your only true friend
and faithful husband
W. A. Mozart

🖎 *On May 19, 1789, Mozart anonymously attended a performance of* Die Entführung *in the Royal National Theater in Berlin. The German writer Ludwig Tieck, who saw Mozart that evening before the performance without recognizing him, described him as "small, rapid of movement, restless, and with shy eyes."*

---

62. This was Mozart's second visit to Leipzig; he had returned there from Potsdam.

A week later, Mozart played before King Friedrich Wilhelm II of Prussia at the royal palace. It is assumed that afterward Mozart received a commission from the king to compose six easy piano sonatas for Princess Friederike, the king's daughter, and six string quartets for the king himself. Of the piano sonatas, Mozart finished only one: the D major, K. 576. The sonata never reached the princess, which may be just as well because it is one of his most demanding piano sonatas; it is also his last. Of the quartets, Mozart finished three: the D major, K. 575, the B-flat major, K. 589, and the F major, K. 590. They are known as the "Prussian" Quartets.

To his wife, in Vienna

Berlin, May 23, 1789

Dearest, best and most precious little wife of mine!—

I was overcome with joy when I received your letter of the 13th;—but just this moment I also received a letter you had mailed even before, on the 9th; it had gone to Leipzig and had to make its way back to Berlin.— The first thing I want to do right now is to count up all the letters I have written to you and then count the ones I have received from you.—

I wrote to you on April 8th from the Postal station at Budwitz.—
on April 10th from Prague.
on the 13th and 17th from Dresden.
on the 22nd (in French) from Leipzig.
on April 28th and May 5th from Potsdam.
on the 9th and 16th from Leipzig.
on the 19th from Berlin.
and now this one on the 23rd.
That makes 11 letters altogether.

I received from you the letter of April 8th—on the 15th in Dresden.
of the 13th—on the 21st—in Leipzig.
of the 24th—on May 8th in Leipzig; when I returned.
of May 5th—on the 14th—again in Leipzig.
of the 13th—on the 20th—in Berlin.
and the letter of the 9th—on the 22nd—in Berlin.
That adds up to 6 letters.

As you can see, there's a gap between April 13ᵗʰ and April 24ᵗʰ; there-fore, one of your letters must have been lost during that period, and because of it I had to be without mail for 17 days. . . . The queen[63] wants to hear me play on Tuesday; *but I don't think much will come of it;*—I noti-fied them of my presence only because it is the custom here, and if I hadn't, she would take it as an affront.—My dearest little wife, when I return, you'll have to be content with seeing *me* rather than *money.*—100 Friedrichs d'or are not 900 gulden but 700.[64]—at least that's what I am told.—2ⁿᵈ, Lichnowsky left early because he was in a hurry; conse-quently I have to pay for everything myself in this very expensive town of Potsdam;[65]—3ʳᵈ, I had to lend him 100 gulden because his purse was getting very slim—I couldn't refuse him very well, and you know why.—4ᵗʰ, my concert in Leipzig did not bring much, just as I had pre-dicted, therefore, I made a 32-mile round-trip almost for nothing.[66] It was all Lichnowsky's fault because he gave me no peace, I simply had to go back to Leipzig.—At any rate—I'll tell you more when I get home.—. . . Thursday, the 28ᵗʰ, I shall leave for Dresden, where I'll stay overnight; then on June 1ˢᵗ I'll sleep in Prague, and on the 4ᵗʰ—the 4ᵗʰ?—*I'll be sleep-ing with my dear little wife;*—Spruce up your sweet little nest because my little rascal here really deserves it, he has been very well behaved but now he's itching to possess your sweet . . .[67] Just imagine that little sneak, while I am writing he has secretly crept up on the table and now looks at me questioningly; but I, without much ado, give him a little slap—but now he is even more . . . ;[67] well, he is almost out of control—the scoundrel. I hope you will take a carriage and come out to meet me at the first postal station?—I shall arrive on the 4ᵗʰ at noon.—. . .

I kiss you one Million times and am Forever your faithful husband
W. A. Mozart.

63. Queen Friederike of Prussia.
64. 100 friedrich d'or had a value of between 600 and 1,000 gulden, depending on the region.
65. Potsdam, with its palace Sans Souci, was the summer palace of the Prussian royal family.
66. Mozart wrote "32 Meilen" (32 miles); since a German mile in the eighteenth century varied between 7 and 9 kilometers, it is indeed the approximate round-trip distance between Berlin and Leipzig (290 km).
67. The points are presumably by Mozart.

To Michael Puchberg, in Vienna

Vienna, July 12, 1789

Dearest and best friend!
and Most Honorable Brother.

Oh, God! The situation I am in, I wouldn't wish it on my worst enemy; and if you, my best friend and brother, forsake me, I, *hapless and blameless as I am,* will be lost together with my poor, sick wife and child.—I had wished to pour out my heart to you last time I was at your house—but I didn't have the heart to do it!—and I would not have the courage even now—indeed, I can do it only with a trembling hand in writing—and I wouldn't even dare to put it in writing—if I didn't know that you know me well, know about my circumstances, and are completely convinced of my *innocence* in this wretched and most distressing situation. Oh, God! instead of thanking you, I come to you with new requests!—instead of paying off my debts, I come asking for more. If you can see into my heart, you know how anguished I am about this. I probably won't need to tell you once again that this unfortunate illness[68] is slowing me down with my earnings, but I will tell you that in spite of my miserable situation I had decided to go ahead and give subscription concerts at my house so that I can at at least take care of my expenses, which are considerable and frequent, for I was sure of receiving your friendly help and support; but this plan isn't working either;—fate is against me, *but only in Vienna,* I cannot earn any money even when I want to; for 2 weeks now I have sent around a list for subscriptions, and there is only one name on it: *Swieten!* [69]—. . . In the meantime I'm composing 6 easy piano sonatas for Princess Friederika and 6 quartets for the King, which I am going to have engraved at my own expense at Kozeluch's;[70] the 2 dedications will bring in something as well. Besides, in a couple of months my fate will be decided in *other things* as well, therefore, you are not risking anything; it's now up to you, my one and only friend, whether you will or can lend me another 500 gulden?—I would suggest

---

68. Constanze's bone infection seems to have been fairly serious. The Mozart family physician, Dr. Thomas Franz Closset, recommended sulfur baths in Baden, a spa near Vienna.
69. Baron Gottfried van Swieten, Mozart's steady friend and supporter.
70. The quartets were not engraved by Leopold Koželuch, a Viennese engraver, but were published shortly after Mozart's death by Artaria & Co. as Opus 18; they were printed without a dedication to the Prussian king.

that until my affairs are settled I'll pay you back 10 gulden a month, then (as matters will turn around in a couple of months) return the whole sum to you with whatever interest you wish to charge and, at the same time, acknowledge myself as your debtor for life. . . .

Forever your most deeply obliged servant, true friend and brother W. A. Mozart.

At home, July 14th, 1789.

Oh, God!—I can hardly make up my mind to send this letter!—but I must!—If it weren't for this illness, I wouldn't be forced to be so shameless before my one and only friend;—yet, I hope for your forgiveness, for you know both the good and *the bad of my situation.* The bad is only temporary, the Good, however, will endure once the Bad has been overcome.—Adieu!—Forgive me, for God's sake, do forgive me!—and Adieu!—

To Michael Puchberg, in Vienna

Vienna, July 17, 1789

Dearest and best friend
and most honorable Brother

You must be very angry with me because you are not giving me any answer!—When I compare the evidence of your friendship and my new request, I find that you are completely right. But when I compare my misfortunes (for which I am not to blame) with your friendly disposition toward me, I find that I deserve—an excuse. Since I have already written to you in complete frankness, my best friend, all the things that burden my heart, I would only repeat myself today; but let me add the following: 1st, I wouldn't require such a big sum if I didn't have to face the horrid expenses for my wife's treatment, especially if she has to go to Baden; 2do, as I am certain that my circumstances will change for the better very soon, it doesn't matter to me how big a sum I will have to pay back; therefore, at this moment, I would prefer to borrow a larger amount. 3rd, I beg you with all my heart, if you find it impossible to help me with such a large sum right now, to bring your friendship and brotherly love to bear and help me *just for the moment* with *whatever you can spare!*—I am really in need of it!—Surely you don't doubt my honesty, you know me too well for that; nor can you mistrust my words, my con-

duct, and my way of life because you are well acquainted with it,—so—
if you pardon me for my frankness, I am convinced that only your own
inability could prevent you from helping me, your friend; but if you can
and will quiet my mind, I shall give thanks to you as my savior even
beyond my grave—for you will have helped procure for me my future
happiness;—if you cannot do it—I beg and entreat you to help me, in
God's name, *with whatever support you can give me right now,* or, at least, to help
me with advice and consolation.

Forever your obliging servant

Michael Puchberg sent 150 gulden on July 17, the day he received Mozart's letter.

To Michael Puchberg, in Vienna

Vienna, second half of July 1789

My dearest Friend and Brother!

Since the time you rendered me such a great service of friendship,
I have lived in such *Misery* that I was not only unable to go out but
couldn't even write—out of sheer grief.—

Constanze is feeling better at the moment; if she weren't suffering
from *bedsores,* which adds to her misery, she would actually be able to
sleep;—there is some concern that her bone might become infected;—
but she is astonishingly resigned to her fate and is awaiting improvement or death with true philosophical equanimity; I'm writing this with
tears in my eyes.—If it's possible for you, dearest friend, pay us a visit;
and if you *can,* give me help and advice in word and deed regarding *the
matter we talked about.* [71]

To his wife, in Baden

Vienna, before mid-August 1789

Dearest little Wife of mine!—

I was overjoyed to get your dear letter—and I hope you received my
2nd one yesterday with the decoctum, the electuary, and the ants' eggs I

71. Probably Mozart's continued effort to obtain a position at court.

sent along.[72]—I myself shall set sail tomorrow morning at 5 o'clock to visit you;—if it weren't for the joy of seeing you and holding you in my arms, I wouldn't come out to Baden just now, because "Figaro" is going to be staged again soon, and since I am to make some changes, I'll need to be here for the rehearsals[73]—so I'll probably have to come back into town on the 19th—but to stay around here until the 19th *without you*, that's quite impossible for me;—dearest little wife!—let me talk candidly:— you have no reason whatever to be sad—you have a husband who loves you, who does everything he possibly can for you—and as far as your foot is concerned, all you need is to be patient and I'm sure everything will be fine;—and, you know, I am glad when you are having fun—I truly am—I only wished you wouldn't lower yourself so much at times—you are a bit too familiar with N.N.[74] . . . A Woman has to always behave properly—otherwise people will talk—Dearest!—forgive me for being so frank, but it is necessary for my peace of mind as well as our happiness together—just remember that you yourself confessed to me once that you *give in too easily*—and you know what the conse- quences are—so do remember the promise you gave me—Oh, dear God!—make an effort, my love!—be merry and happy and loving *with me*—and don't torture yourself and me with unfounded jealousy—trust in my love, for you do have full proof of it!—And you'll see how happy we'll be together and, believe me, only a woman's proper conduct can tie a man firmly to her—adjeu—tomorrow I shall be kissing you most tenderly.

Mozart.

🕮 *In spite of persistent debts, Constanze's illness, and the death of Mozart's fifth child, Anna Maria, who died within a day of her birth, Mozart wrote some of his most extraordinary works at this time. In September 1789, he composed the Clarinet Quintet in A major, K. 581; during the winter of 1789–90, he wrote Così fan*

72. These items seem to be home remedies for Constanze, except perhaps the ants' eggs, which were used as bird feed. "Decoctum" was a decoction, i.e., some kind of extract (Absud), and electuary (Latwerge) consisted of a mix of powder, syrup, and prune juice, which was used as a laxative.
73. August 29, 1789, saw the first performance of a revival of *Figaro* at the Burgtheater, and Mozart had indeed written two new soprano numbers, the rondo "Al desio di chi t'adora," K. 577, and the aria "Un moto di gioia," K. 579, for Adriana Ferrarese del Bene, who sang Susanna. Catarina Cavalieri sang the countess; Joseph Weigl conducted.
74. Identity unknown. Points are by Mozart.

tutte *(All Women Are Like This)*, his third and final opera based on a libretto by Lorenzo da Ponte.

To Michael Puchberg, in Vienna

Vienna, during December 1789

Most Honorable Friend
and Brother of the Order!

Don't be alarmed about the content of this letter;—only to you, my best friend, because you know my circumstances intimately, do I have the courage to open my heart completely.—Next month I will receive 200 ducats[75] for my opera from the theater management (such is our present agreement);—if you could lend me 400 gulden until then, you would be rescuing your friend from the greatest embarrassment, and I will give you my word of honor that you'll have the money back at the agreed-upon time in cash and with all my gratitude. I would have been able to stretch my money until then, in spite of the big expenses I have every day, if it weren't for the fact that New Year is upon us and I have to pay off the Apothecaries and the Doctors (whom we don't need anymore) in full if I don't want to lose my credit.—. . . I beg you, pull me from my unhappy state just one more time; as soon as I get the money for the opera, you shall have your 400 gulden with absolute certainty;—and I hope to convince you that by next summer I can (because of my work for the King of Prussia) show you the full extent of my honesty.—Tomorrow evening we can't get together as planned—I have too much work to do—if you happen to see Zisler, please let him know.—But I am inviting you (and you alone) on Thursday at 10 o'clock in the morning to my place for a small opera rehearsal;[76]—I'm inviting only you and *Haydn.*[77]—I will tell you in person about some of Salieri's intrigues, which, however, have already misfired—adjeu,

Forever your
grateful friend and Br.
W. A. Mozart.

75. The opera for which Mozart expected 200 ducats (900 gulden) was *Così fan tutte,* which had been commissioned by Joseph II; it premiered on January 26, 1790.
76. A private rehearsal of *Così fan tutte.*
77. Joseph Haydn.

🖎 *Joseph II died on February 20, 1790, and his brother Leopold, grand duke of Tuscany, succeeded him to the throne of Austria, Hungary, and Bohemia. Mozart had great hopes that Leopold would appoint him Kapellmeister or at least deputy Kapellmeister to the court in Vienna. Typically, Mozart immediately saw "agreeable prospects" where there were none. As it turned out, Leopold had even less use for Mozart than Joseph II did.*

To Michael Puchberg, in Vienna[78]

Vienna, end of March or beginning of April 1790

I am sending you herewith, dearest friend, the Life of Händel.[79]— When I returned home from visiting you the other day, I found the enclosed note from Baron Swieten.[80] You will gather from it, just as I did, that I now have more cause to be hopeful than ever before.—I am standing at the threshold of my fortune;—if I cannot make use of such an opportunity now, it will be gone forever. Yet, my present circumstances are such—that, in spite of these agreeable prospects, I must abandon all hope of future happiness, unless I receive help from a good friend in the meantime.—You may well have noticed some signs of melancholy in me lately—and only the all too frequent kindnesses that you have rendered me have kept me silent. But now I call on you once more and for the last time in this most desperate moment, which may determine my entire future happiness, and I call on you with full confidence in your friendship and brotherly love, which you have shown me so often, to help me to the maximum of your own ability. . . . In short!—My future happiness rests in your hands—follow your noble heart—do whatever you can possibly do and keep in mind that you are helping a fair-minded man who will be forever grateful to you and whose problems are all the more painful for him because they involve you and not just himself!—

Mozart.

78. The letter lacks a formal address.
79. Probably the *Memoirs of the Life of the late G. F. Handel*, by John Mainwaring (1760), which had appeared in German in a translation by Johann Mattheson.
80. Baron van Swieten's note referred either to further commissions for reorchestrating works by Handel (Mozart had already done *Acis and Galatea* and *The Messiah* in 1789; he reorchestrated *Alexander's Feast* and *Ode on St. Cecilia's Day* in 1790) or to upcoming changes at the Habsburg court as a result of the death of Joseph II.

To Michael Puchberg, in Vienna

Vienna, beginning of May 1790

Dearest and best friend
and Brother!—

I am so sorry that I am unable to go out and talk with you myself; but my toothache and headache are still too painful and, generally speaking, I feel rather out of sorts. What you are saying about accepting a few good pupils is exactly what I've been thinking myself, but I wanted to wait until we are in our new apartment because I would like to give my lessons at home;[81] in the meantime, would you please spread the word that I am thinking of taking more students?—another thing I am planning to do is to give subscription concerts at my house during the 3 months of July, June, and August; so it's only my present situation that is getting me down.—When I move from here, I will have to pay 275 gulden toward my new apartment—besides, I need something to live on until my concerts are set to go and the quartets I'm working on are ready for the engraver.[82] If only I had 600 gulden in my hands, I could work in peace—for, alas! one must have peace.—What worries me most right now is a debt I have at a fashion shop at the Stock am Eisen;[83] the owner was satisfied at first, knowing that I couldn't pay him immediately, but now he is making serious and impatient demands for the money I owe him; the sum is 100 gulden.[84] I truly wished I could get this particular annoyance off my back.—So now I have sincerely confessed everything, and I beg you to do whatever is within your ability and and true friendship.

Forever yours
Mozart.

The following is a draft for a letter by Mozart to Archduke Francis, brother of Leopold II, who had succeeded Joseph II. Mozart sought to enlist the help of the archduke in his quest for a position at court under Leopold, who is referred to as "king" here because he had not yet been crowned emperor. Some words and sentences

81. The Mozarts moved on September 30, 1790, to Rauensteingasse no. 970 (now no. 8). It turned out to be Wolfgang Mozart's last lodging.
82. The string quartets commissioned by Friedrich Wilhelm II of Prussia.
83. Stock am Eisen is a small square near St. Stephen's Cathedral.
84. Puchberg sent 100 gulden.

were crossed out by Mozart, and the ellipses are in the original. It is not known whether Mozart ever sent a petition to Leopold; if he did, it was ignored.

To Archduke Francis of Austria, in Vienna

Vienna, first half of May 1790

Your Royal Highness

I am so bold as to beg your Royal H. to be so gracious and speak on my behalf to His Majesty, the King, with regard to my most humble petition to his gracious Majesty.—My quest for Honor, love of my work, and the conviction that I possess the necessary knowledge are the compelling reasons why I dare apply for the post of second Kapellmeister, especially as the very capable Kapellmeister Salieri has never devoted himself to the ecclesiastical style in music, whereas I have thoroughly acquainted myself with that style since my youth. Moreover, the modest renown that the world has accorded me on account of my playing the Piano-forte encourages me to ask His Sublime Majesty for the favor of graciously entrusting the musical education of the Royal Family to me.—

Convinced that I am addressing herewith the worthiest and for me most gracious [benefactor] intermediary, I hope for everything, and am prepared to prove through constant zeal, loyalty, and— . . . I remain in sincere confidence—and will [not] . . . in my services . . . convinced that . . .

Joseph Eybler, a young music student, assisted Mozart with the rehearsals of Così fan tutte; *he was also the first of Mozart's pupils to be asked by Constanze Mozart to complete the* Requiem *after Mozart's death because she knew that Mozart had thought highly of him. Eybler eventually succeeded Antonio Salieri as court Kapellmeister in Vienna (the post Mozart had aspired to), and in 1834 he was enobled, becoming Joseph Leopold Edler von Eybler.*

Letter of Recommendation for Joseph Eybler, Vienna

I, the undersigned, attest herewith that the bearer of this letter, Herr Joseph Eybler, is a worthy pupil of his famous teacher, Herr Albrechtsberger; I consider him a well-trained composer, as skilled in the style of chamber music as in church music, fully experienced in the art of song and completely accomplished as an organist and clavier player. In short, I regard him as a young musician of such quality that I can only regret there are so few of his kind.

Vienna, May 30th, 1790.

Wolfgang Amadè Mozart
Kapellmeister in Imperial Services.

📖 *Mozart, who seemingly composed effortlessly all his life, makes a rare comment here about what "hard work" he had to put into composing the "Prussian" Quartets.*

To Michael Puchberg, in Vienna

Vienna, before or on June 12, 1790

Dearest Friend and Bro. of the O.—

I am in town to conduct my opera.[85] My wife is feeling a little better—her pains have begun to subside a bit; but she'll have to take 60 baths;—so she'll have to make another pilgrimage out there later in the year;—may God grant that it will help.—Dearest friend, if you could help me with my most urgent expenses, please do it;—to save money I'm staying here with her at Baden and come into town only when it is absolutely necessary.—I am forced to sell my quartets,[86] all that hard work, for a trifle, just to get some cash into my hands and meet my immediate obligations.—I have also begun to compose some Clavier sonatas with that in mind.[87]—Adieu—send me whatever you can spare.—One of my masses will be performed at Baden tomorrow.[88] Adjeu—it's about 10 o'clock.

Forever yours,
Mozart

P.S. Would you kindly send along my viola.

---

85. Mozart's *Così fan tutte* had been performed five times in January and February; it was now staged again with Mozart conducting. All in all, *Così fan tutte* had ten performances in Vienna during Mozart's lifetime.
86. K. 575, 589, 590.
87. There are only fragments of these intended sonatas.
88. Probably the Mass in C major ("Coronation"), K. 317.

🖎 *Mozart's brief communication of August 14 may well be the most poignant of his letters to Michael Puchberg. Some of the letters to Puchberg seem exaggerated and, at times, calculated for effect, but this short note about being "sick and full of worry and grief," leaves no doubt that Mozart's pains and problems were real.*

To Michael Puchberg, in Vienna

Vienna, August 14, 1790

Dearest friend and bro.

As tolerable as I felt yesterday, as bad am I feeling today. I couldn't sleep all night for pain; I must have gotten too hot yesterday with all my running about and then caught a chill without realizing it; just imagine my situation: sick and full of worry and grief—such a condition will surely slow down any recovery.—I'm expecting some help in a week or two—that's for certain—but right now I am in need.—Couldn't you help me out with a trifle?—Anything would be a help just now—you would, at least for the moment, bring some consolation to your

true friend, servant, and br.
W. A. Mozart.

🖎 *Mozart left Vienna on September 23, 1790, for Frankfurt am Main to attend the coronation of Leopold of Austria as emperor of the German realm. In contrast to other Viennese musicians, Mozart had not been invited to the festivities, so he made the trip on his own with borrowed money. He was accompanied by one of his brothers-in-law, the violinist Franz de Paula Hofer, and his manservant, Joseph. It is not entirely clear what Mozart thought he would gain from such a journey, but he must have expected to get commissions, give concerts, and investigate possibilities for an appointment outside Vienna.*

To his wife, in Vienna

Frankfurt am Main, September 28, 1790

Dearest and most beloved little wife of mine!

We just arrived here a moment ago—it's 1 o'clock noon—so it took us only 6 days.—We could have speeded up our travel if we hadn't rested 3 times at night.—Now we have just alighted at an inn in the suburb of Sachsenhausen and can count ourselves extremely fortunate to have found a room.—We don't know how things will proceed from here, whether we can stay together or whether we'll have to go our separate ways.—If I can't find a lodging somewhere that won't cost me anything and I find the inns around here not too expensive, I'll certainly stay here. I hope you have received my letter from Efferding[89] all right; I could not write more from the road, because we stopped rarely and then only long enough to get some rest.—

The journey was very pleasant, we had good weather save for one day—and this one day did not inconvenience us, because my carriage—I should like to give it a kiss—is simply wonderful.—We had a splendid midday meal in Regensburg with divine table music for entertainment, heavenly service, and a delicious Mosel wine.—We had breakfast in Nürnberg—what an ugly town[90]—and in Würzburg—a beautiful, magnificent town—we fortified our expensive stomachs with coffee.— Food was pretty good everywhere—only once, in Aschaffenburg, 2½ postal stations from here, we encountered an innkeeper who fleeced us thoroughly.—I'm longing for news from you about your health, and about our financial situation, etc.—I'm determined to do as well here as I possibly can; and I'm eagerly looking forward to be back home with you again;—what a wonderful life we're going to have—I want to work—indeed work very hard—so that we'll never again get into such dreadful straits through unforeseen circumstances. I should like it if you'd ask Stadler to see to it that . . .[91] will come and speak to you about this matter.—His last suggestions were that someone could advance the money—1000 gulden in cash and the rest in cloth—on Hofmeister's[92] draft alone.—This way everything could be paid off and there would even be a little left over so that after I get back I would be able to completely concentrate on my *work*.—The whole matter could be settled by a friend who has my charta bianca.[93] Adieu, I kiss you 1000 times.

Forever your Mzt

---

89. Eferding near Linz, Austria.
90. Mozart's lack of appreciation of medieval Nürnberg is rather typical of eighteenth century (i.e., pre-Romantic) taste; apparently he did not care for half-timbered houses, which was the prevailing style in Nürnberg.
91. The clarinetist Anton Stadler. The points are by Mozart.
92. Franz Anton Hoffmeister, a Viennese publisher, who on occasion advanced money to Mozart.
93. "Carte blanche."

To his wife, in Vienna or Baden

Frankfurt, September 30, 1790

Dearest little Wife of my heart!

If only I had a letter from you, everything would be all right.—I hope you received my letter from Efferding and one from Frankfurt.— I told you in my last letter to talk to Ribisel Face;[94]—I would prefer it, just to be on the safe side, if I could raise 2000 gulden on the draft by H . . .[95]—but you'd have to give some other reason, for example, that I have some business deal in mind, but you don't know exactly what.— Dearest, I have no doubt that I shall get something going here, but it won't be as easy as you and some of our friends think.—It's true, I'm known and respected here; but, well—No—let's just see what happens.—In any case, I do prefer to play it safe, that's why I would like to conclude this deal with H . . . because I would get some money into my possession without having to pay any out; all I would have to do then is *work*, and I shall be only too happy to do that for my little wife.— When you write to me, always address your letter: *Poste restante.*—. . .

Since I don't know whether you are in Vienna or Baden at present, I'm addressing this letter to Mad.^me Hofer.[96] I get all excited like a child when I think about being with you again—if people could see into my heart I should almost feel ashamed. Everything is cold to me—ice-cold.—If you were here with me, maybe I would find the courtesies people are showing me more enjoyable,—but as it is, it's all so empty— adieu—my dear—I am Forever

your Mozart who loves you
with his entire soul.

A promissory note by Mozart

Vienna, October 1, 1790

I, the Undersigned, Wolfg. A. Mozart, Court Kompositeur in Vienna, testify and acknowledge herewith for myself, my heirs and

---

94. *Ribisel* means "red currant" in Austria, so Mozart is saying "Red-currant Face"; it is assumed that the person who had such a distinctly red face was the clarinetist Anton Stadler.
95. The points are by Mozart; "H" probably stands for Hoffmeister.
96. Josepha Hofer was Mozart's sister-in-law.

descendants, publicly and in due legal form, that the honorable Herr Heinrich Lackenbacher, licensed merchant in Vienna, has lent me upon my request and for my present needs a sum of 1000 fl. (that is to say, One Thousand Gulden), in regular currency, that is in Imperial Austrian pieces of twenty Kreutzer in Silver current at the Twenty-Gulden Standard at 3 pieces to one silver Cologne mark, and that I received this sum in cash without any deductions. I not only acknowledge herewith due receipt of this loan but also bind myself, my heirs and descendants to repay this capital to the above-named Lender or his heirs at the end of two years *a Dato*. . . .

As security for the Capital and the interest I pledge the Lender all my Goods and Chattels.

In witness thereof my and the invited witnesses' own signatures. Enacted in Vienna, October 1, 1790.

Mathias Brünner   Anton Heindl   W. A. Mozart
Witness   Witness

The promissory note shows that Mozart had pawned his furniture (goods and chattels) to raise money for his trip to Frankfurt. The note is not in Mozart's hand, and since it is dated October 1, when Mozart was in Frankfurt, it must have been written in Vienna and signed by him after his return. The loan seems to have been guaranteed by the publisher Franz Anton Hoffmeister. It is assumed that Mozart repaid the loan, because Herr Lackenbacher, the lender, is not listed as one of Mozart's creditors after his death.

To his wife, in Vienna

Frankfurt, October 8, 1790

Dearest, most beloved little wife!—

I now have 3 letters from you, my love,—one from September 28th, which arrived this moment;—but I haven't received the one you sent with Herr von Alt; I'll check with le Noble about it immediately.—You should have 4 letters from me by now, this one here is the 5th. Now you won't be able to write to me anymore to this address, because by the time you read this letter I will probably no longer be here; I intend to give my concert on Wednesday or Thursday and then on Friday— tschiri tschitschi—I will be out of here in a hurry.—Dearest wife! I hope you have attended to the business I wrote to you about—and are still working on it; I am pretty certain that I won't make enough money here to be in a position to repay 800 or 1000 gulden right after I return.— . . . Please see to it that our business deal with H. will be concluded;—that is if you want me to come back right away.—If you could only see into my heart—there is a struggle going on between my wish, my desire, to see you soon and hold you in my arms and, on the other hand, the wish to bring home a lot of money;—sometimes the thought comes to my mind that I should perhaps travel *farther afield*— but whenever I came close to making such a decision, it instantly occurred to me that I would deeply regret it if I had stayed away from my dear wife for such an indefinite and perhaps even *fruitless* period—I feel as if I'd been away from you for years already;—believe me, my love—if you were here with me, I could perhaps make such a decision more easily— but as it is—I've become so accustomed to you—and I love you too much for being able to endure a lengthy separation—besides, all this talk about Imperial Cities is nothing but boastful chatter.—To be sure, I am famous, admired, and popular, but people here are even greater skinflints than the Viennese.—If my concert will have any kind of success, it'll be thanks to my *name*—the Countess Hatzfeld[97] and the Schweitzer family,[98] who are doing everything they can on my behalf.— But I shall be glad when it is all over.—If I work hard in Vienna and take more pupils, we'll be able to live quite comfortably; nothing can persuade me to think otherwise, except perhaps a *good appointment* at some court.—

Please do your best to settle our business affair with *Hofmeister* and get the help of *Ribisel Face* or *someone else;* and also spread the word that I intend to take more pupils; then we'll be all right. Adieu—my dearest—you'll receive more letters from me, but, sadly, I cannot get any more from you.—

Love me forever,
Mozart

The coronation is tomorrow.—
Take care of your health—and be careful when you go *walking. Adieu.*

---

97. Probably Sophie von Hatzfeld, née Coudenhoven.
98. The family of Franz Maria Schwei(t)zer, a wealthy Frankfurt banker.

The coronation of Leopold II took place on October 9, 1790. Music for the festiv-
ities was provided by the court musicians of the elector of Mainz as well as by the
musicians from the Viennese court under their two Kapellmeisters—Antonio
Salieri and Ignaz Umlauf. Mozart's own concert took place on October 15 at the
Great Municipal Playhouse of Frankfurt (Stadtspielhaus). Mozart performed the
Piano Concerto no. 19 in F, K. 459, and the Piano Concerto no. 26 in D, K.
537. The latter was his most recent concerto (first performed in Dresden), given the
nickname Coronation because Mozart performed it at this time in Frankfurt.
Mozart's concert included one of his symphonies and several of his arias. Francesco
Ceccarelli, his old friend from Salzburg, was one of the singers. A second concert
never materialized.

To his wife, in Vienna

Frankfurt, October 15, 1790

Dearest little wife of my heart!—

I still have no answer to any of the letters I wrote to you from
Frankfurt; it worries me quite a bit;—my concert took place today at 11
o'clock; it was a splendid success from the point of view of acclaim but
rather meager in terms of money.—As luck would have it, some prince
was giving a big dinner just at the time of the concert and the Hessian
troops were out on a large-scale maneuver.—Some such obstacle has
been plaguing me every day during my stay here. . . . Yet, in spite of it
all, I was in such good spirits and delighted my audience so much that
they pleaded with me to give another concert this coming Sunday.—So
I'll be leaving on Monday.—I have to close now if I don't want to miss
the mail coach.—I can see from your letters that you haven't received
any of my letters from Frankfurt, and I have written 4 already—and
then I seem to detect a little bit of doubt in my promptness or rather
my eagerness to write to you—and that really hurts. Surely you know
me better than that—Oh, dear God! just love me half as much as I love
you, and I'll be content.

Forever yours,
Mozart.

To his wife, in Vienna[99]

Mainz, October 17, 1790

P.S. When I wrote the foregoing page, one tear after another fell on my paper; but I must cheer up—catch them—there's an amazing number of kisses flying about. . . .[100] what the devil!. . . . I see a whole bunch of them. . . . ha! ha!. . . . I've just caught 3!—how delicious they are!—You can still reply to this letter, but you'll have to address it to Linz, *poste restante;*—that would be safest.—Since I don't know for sure whether or not I'll be traveling by way of Regensburg, I can't tell you anything definite.—Just write on the envelope that the letter should be held until someone calls for it.—Adieu—my dearest and best little wife—take care of your health—and don't go into town on foot—let me know how well you like the new apartment—adieu, I kiss you a Million times.

The baroque gardens of Schwetzingen were as much a tourist attraction in Mozart's time as they are today; Mozart must have enjoyed baroque and rococo settings, for he had been to the gardens twice before, in 1763 and in 1777.

To his wife, in Salzburg

Mannheim, October 23, 1790

Dearest and best little wife of my heart!—

Tomorrow we are going to Schwetzingen to visit the gardens.—This evening "Figaro" will be given here for the first time—and the day after tomorrow we'll be on our way again. Actually, "Figaro" is the reason why I am still here—because the entire cast begged me to stay long enough that I could help them with the rehearsals, and that's also the reason why I can't write as much as I would like to, because it's time right now to go to the dress rehearsal—indeed, the first act is probably over already;—I hope you got my letter of the 17th from Mainz all right—the day before we left I played before the Elector[101] and received a measly 15 Carolin;[102] make sure that everything goes well with H.—I

99. This postscript was separated from a letter that is presumably lost.
100. All the points are by Mozart.
101. Friedrich Karl Joseph Freiherr von Erthal.
102. About 165 gulden.

hope to embrace you for sure in 6 or 7 days after you receive this letter—but you'll still get some news from me from Augsburg, Munich,
and Linz—of course, you can't write to me anymore, except I might
still get a letter from you in Linz if you write immediately after getting
this one. Please try it.—Farewell for now, dearest little wife! I kiss you
1000 times and I am forever and unalterably

your faithful husband
Mozart.

When Elector Karl Theodor of the Palatinate became elector of Bavaria, in 1778,
he moved his residence, including his famed Mannheim orchestra to Munich. On his
way back to Vienna, Mozart visited some of these "old friends from Mannheim"
whom he had first met in 1777 on his way to Paris. He was clearly elated to be
in the company of such excellent musicians and good friends.

To his wife, in Vienna

Munich, before November 4, 1790

Dearest, most beloved wife of my heart!

What pains me most is that I will have to wait until Linz in order
to get some news from you. Patience! If one doesn't know how long one
will be staying in one or the other place, one simply can't make any definite arrangements. Even though I had wanted to remain here a bit
longer, with all my old friends from Mannheim, I nevertheless thought
I'd stay only one day; but now I will have to remain until the 5th or 6th
because the Elector[103] has requested that I perform at a concert that he
is giving in honor of the King of Naples.[104] That's an honor indeed.—
And what an honor it is for the court of Vienna that the King of
Naples has to hear me in a foreign country.[105] You can well imagine that
I am having a great time here with the Cannabichs, La Bonne, Ramm,
Marchand, and Brochard; and of course, I'm telling them a lot about
you and how much I love you.—I am so looking forward to seeing you,
for we have lots to talk about; I am thinking that next summer I'd like

103. Karl Theodor, elector of Bavaria.
104. King Ferdinand IV and Queen Maria Carolina of Naples.
105. Mozart is alluding to a visit by the king and queen of Naples in Vienna; during their stay in
September 1790, Salieri and Haydn were called on to perform but Mozart was not invited.

to come here with you, my love, so you could try out different Baths and, besides, be entertained and get some exercise; a change of air would do you good, just as it agrees with me very much. I'm already excited about the idea and all my friends here love it.

Forgive me for not writing as much as I would like to, but you can't imagine what fuss they are making about me here.—Right now I'm on my way to Cannabich; if I'm right in my calculations, I can't get a reply to this letter anymore. So farewell, my love, I kiss you a Million times and I am Forever

your Mozart who loves you.

To the city council of Vienna

Vienna, beginning of May 1791

Most Honorable and Wise City Council of Vienna!

When Herr Kapellmeister Hofmann was stricken ill, I considered taking the liberty of applying for his post in view of the fact that my musical abilites and achievements as well as my compositional skills are well known abroad and my name is held in some esteem in the world; in addition, I have the honor of holding an appointment as composer at the Court of Vienna for several years now. I was confident, therefore, not to be unworthy of this post and to gain favorable consideration by this most learned City Council.

Kapellmeister Hofmann, however, has regained his health, and as I wish and hope with all my heart that he will live a long life, it occurred to me that it might be beneficial to the Cathedral as well as the City Council if I were appointed as an unpaid assistant to the Herr Kapellmeister, who is advanced in years, and thereby gain the opportunity to assist this worthy man in his duties, thus acquiring the approbation of so wise a City Council by my actual participation in the services for which I deem myself well qualified since I am trained in both the secular and the ecclesiatic styles of music.

Your most humble Servant,
Wolfgang Amadé Mozart
Imperial and Royal Court Composer

🕮 *Leopold Hofmann was Kapellmeister of the Cathedral of St. Stephen's. Mozart's petition to the city council of Vienna to serve as Hofmann's assistant was first rejected on the grounds that Herr Hofmann had "not asked for an assistant." A month later, however, the petition was granted, and Mozart was appointed as Hofmann's unpaid assistant. Mozart, of course, was hoping to succeed to the post of Kapellmeister at St. Stephen's, which would have brought him 2,000 gulden a year; but he never did, because Hofmann outlived Mozart by more than a year.*

🕮 *Mozart enjoyed communicating with Constanze in French on occasion. She spoke and wrote French with some fluency.*

To his wife, in Baden

Vienna, June 6, 1791

Ma trés chere Epouse!

J'écris cette lettre dans la petite Chambre au Jardin chez Leitgeb[106] ou j'ai couché cette Nuit excellement—et J'espére que ma chere Epouse aura paßée cette Nuit außi bien que moi, j'y paßerai cette Nuit aussi, puisque j'ai congedié Leonore,[107] et je serais tout seul á la maison, ce qui n'est pas agreable.[108] . . .

I received your dear letter this very moment and see from it with great pleasure that you are well and in good spirits—Mad.e Leitgeb helped me put on my necktie today; but how!—dear god!—all the while she was helping me, I kept saying: no. *she does it this way!*—but to no avail.—I'm so glad you're enjoying a good appetite—but who eats a lot, has to sh . . . a lot!—No, has to walk a lot, I wanted to say.—I wished you wouldn't go for long walks without me.—Please, follow my advice, it comes from the heart, truly. Adieu—my love—my one and only!— catch them in the air—2999 and ½ little kisses are flying around, they are all from me and waiting to be snapped up.—Now I'm whispering something into your ear — — — — — now you into mine — — — more—and more — — finally we are saying;—it's all because of

---

106. Joseph Leutgeb, formerly a horn player in the Salzburg court orchestra, now lived in Vienna.

107. The Mozarts' maidservant, whom Mozart had just fired.

108. "My dear wife! I am writing this letter in a little garden house at Leitgeb's, where I slept very well last night.—I hope that my dear wife spent the night as well as I did, I am going to be here this evening also, for now that I have given Leonore notice, I would be all alone in the house, and that's not to my liking."

Plumpi-Strumpi—and you can imagine anything you want—that's just what makes it so much fun—adieu—1000 tender kisses and Forever yours,

Mozart

To his wife, in Baden

Vienna, June 11, 1791

Ma très chère Epouse!—

Criés avec moi contre mon mauvais sort!—Mad^{selle} Kirchgessner[109] ne donne pas son Academie Lundi!—par consequent j'aurais pu vous posseder, ma chère, tout ce jour de Dimanche—mercredi je viendrai sûrement.[110]—

I must hurry because it's already a quarter to 7—and the mail coach leaves at 7 o'clock—take care when you bathe so that you don't slip and fall, and don't do anything alone—also, if I were you, I would skip a day once in a while, don't go into this thing too intensely. I hope someone was able to keep you company during the night.—What I wouldn't give to be able to join you in Baden instead of sitting around here.— Out of sheer boredom I composed an aria for my opera today.[111] I got up at half past four this morning—and I managed to open up my clock—I do hope you're impressed!—but I wasn't able to wind it up, because I didn't have the key; isn't that a sad story?—schlumba!—now here's another word that makes you Think—at any rate, I wound up the *big clock* instead. Adieu—My Love!—today I'll be eating at Puchberg's— I kiss you 1000 times and say, while thinking of you: "Death and Despair were his Reward!"[112]

Your husband, who loves you tenderly forever and ever,
W. A. Mozart.

---

109. Maria Anna Antonia Kirchgäßner was a blind performer on the glass harmonica. Mozart, who had been familiar with the instrument ever since 1764, when he heard Marianne Davies in London, had written the Adagio in C, K. 356, for Kirchgäßner and, more recently, the Adagio and Rondo in C minor for Glass Harmonica, Flute, Oboe, Viola, and Cello, K. 617. Kirchgäßner had given a concert in Vienna on June 10, but the one Mozart is referring to was postponed to August 19; at that time K. 617 was performed.
110. "Cry with me against my fate!—Mad^{selle} is not having her concert on Monday!—So I could have been with you all day Sunday—Tuesday I shall be there for sure."
111. *Die Zauberflöte.*
112. "Tod und Verzweiflung war sein Lohn," duet from *Die Zauberflöte,* act 2, scene 3.

Tell Carl to behave,
and kiss him from me.[113]
(Take an electuary if you are constipated—but not otherwise.)
(And be careful in the morning and evening when the air is chilly.)

Emanuel Schikaneder, the librettist for Mozart's Die Zauberflöte, *had taken the text for his libretto from a fairy tale called "Lulu oder die Zauberflöte" (Lulu, or the Magic Flute) by Jakob August Liebeskind. By coincidence, another librettist, Joachim Perinet, had taken the same fairy tale as a subject for a singspiel by the Viennese composer Wenzel Müller called* Kaspar der Fagottist *(Kaspar, the Bassoonist). The Müller-Perinet singspiel had already begun a successful run at the Leopoldstädter Theater, when Mozart and Schikaneder were still finishing their* Zauberflöte. *This unforeseen circumstance may have caused Schikaneder to make some last-minute changes in his plot, but Mozart, it seems, was unconcerned.*

To his wife, in Baden

Vienna, June 12, 1791

Dearest and most beloved little wife!

And why did I not get a letter last evening? So that I must worry even more about your baths?— . . . If there had been only one soul to keep me company and console me a little.—It's not at all good for me to be alone when I am preoccupied with something.— . . . To cheer myself up I went to the theater to see the Kasperle in the new opera *Der Fagottist*, which is creating such a commotion—but actually there's nothing to it.— . . . If I only had some news from you!—it's now half past 10 and we'll be eating at 12 o'clock! Well, the clock is now striking 11, so I can't wait any longer! Adieu, my dear little wife, love me as I love you; in my thoughts I'm kissing you 2000 times.

Sunday.

Forever yours,
Mozart.

---

113. Constanze had taken their six-year-old son, Carl Thomas, with her to Baden.

🐚 *The letter of June 25 is Mozart's last letter to Michael Puchberg. In the course of three years, the Viennese merchant had sent a total of 1,415 gulden to Mozart. In this case, too, Puchberg sent 25 gulden. It is not clear whether Mozart repaid Michael Puchberg all the money he had borrowed, but he certainly paid him back handsomely in his own currency by dedicating to him his last and most magnificent divertimento, the Trio for Strings, K. 563.*

To Michael Puchberg, in Vienna

Vienna, June 25, 1791

Dearest and best Friend!
Most Honorable Br.

I had to forgo the pleasure of seeing you today because I had some business matters to attend to; but I do have a request;—my wife wrote to me that she was made aware that they (at Baden) would like to see some money for her room and board and, although they cannot really insist on it, she is asking me to send some. I thought that the bills would be settled at the end when it was time for her to come home; so I find myself right now in a dilemma. I don't wish to expose my poor wife to any embarrassment—and yet it is pretty impossible for me to spare anything at the moment. If you, dearest friend, could help me with a small sum, which I could send her right away, you would oblige me very much.—It's anyway only a matter of a few days until you'll receive 2000 gulden in my name—from which you can pay yourself back immediately.

Forever yours,
Mozart

To his wife, in Baden

Vienna, June 25, 1791

Ma trés chere Epouse!—

This very minute I received your letter, which has given me such extraordinary joy.—Now I'm already eagerly awaiting the next one so I can find out whether the baths are really doing you any good.—I am sorry I couldn't be out there yesterday to hear that beautiful Musique of yours, not so much because of the Musique, mind you, but because it would have made me happy to spend the day with you.—Today I played a trick on———;[114] I first went to the Rechbergs—the lady of the house sent her daughter upstairs to deliver the message that an old friend from Rome had arrived to see him—he had been looking all over town but hadn't been able to find him!—He sent back a message requesting that I should please wait a little while. In the meantime the poor fool got all dressed up in his most elegant suit, as if it were *Sunday,* and he had his hair beautifully done—well, you can just imagine how much fun we had with him afterward.—I just have to have somebody around I can make fun of—isn't it so?—*Snai*—And where did I sleep?—at home, of course—in fact, I slept very well—although the mice kept me pretty good company—and I had a regular discourse with them.—I was already up before five o'clock.—By the way, my advice for you is not to go to Mass tomorrow—it seems to me that the peasant lads are a bit too rude.— . . .

Don't forget what I told you about the morning and evening air— and about bathing too long, etc., etc.—and give my regards to Count and Countess Wagensperg—adieu—in my thoughts I'm kissing you 1000 times, I am Forever yours,
Vienna, June 25th 1791

Mozart

P.S. It would probably be good for Carl if you'd give him some rhubarb.—

Why didn't you send me that long letter?—Well, here's one for him—I most certainly hope that he'll answer me.—catch—catch— bis—bis—bs—bs—lots of little kisses are flying through the air for you — — — *bs*—here is one more tottering after the others.—

Just this moment I received your second letter.—Do be *careful* with your baths!—and sleep *more*—and not so *irregularly!*—otherwise I worry about it.—I am worried as it is.

114. A name was crossed out.

To his wife, in Baden*

Vienna, July 2, 1791

Ma trés chere Epouse!—

I hope you are feeling just fine;—I was thinking about all your pregnancies and I remember that you *rarely* had any morning sickness.[115]—maybe the baths are making you too weak?—I wouldn't want to wait for the *evidence;* it would be too sad;—my advice is to stop taking baths now! if you did, it would really ease my mind.—Today is the day to skip one, but I bet my little wife has been to the bath already?—*seriously*—I would rather that you make them up later in the year! I hope you received my first brief letter.

Please tell Süssmayer, that knucklehead, to send me the score of the first act, from the introduction to the *finale,* so I can orchestrate it; if he would get everything together today, so it could be on the first mail coach tomorrow morning, I would have it at noon.—A couple of Englishmen just called on me; they didn't want to leave Vienna without making my acquaintance—but that's not true—they really wanted to get to know Süssmayer, the famous Man, and came to me only to inquire where he was living, for they had heard I was fortunate enough to enjoy his favor.—I told them to go to the Ungarische Krone[116] and wait there until he came back from Baden!—Snai!—They want to hire him as a lamp cleaner.

I am so eager to have some news from you; . . . farewell—adieu, one thousand kisses, and a thousand boxes on the ear for that lacci bacci.[117]

Forever yours,
Mozart

---

* See facsimile, plate no. 16.

115. Constanze was in her sixth pregnancy in nine years of marriage. So far only one of her children, Carl Thomas, had survived. The new baby, Franz Xaver Wolfgang, was born on July 26, 1791; he, too, would survive and become a musician, later calling himself Wolfgang Amadeus Mozart.

116. The Ungarische Krone (Crown of Hungary) was a favored restaurant for Mozart, Süssmayr, and (later) Franz Schubert. Mozart continually misspells Süssmayr's name as Süssmayer.

117. Probably Süssmayr; "lacci bacci" seems to be Mozart's own creation, and more for sound than meaning.

To his wife, in Baden

Vienna, July 6, 1791

Dearest, most beloved little wife!—

Your message about receiving the money I sent safely gave me indescribable comfort;—but I don't recall writing that you should settle *everything!* how could I, sensible fellow that I am, write such a thing?—if it's true—I must have been very absentminded!—which, of course, is quite possible, because I have a lot of things spinning around in my head.—What I thought I had told you was to take care of the *baths* only;—the rest of the money is for your own use—and what we still owe—I already made a list of expenses—I shall take care of it myself when I get out there.—Right now Blanchard[118] will either *go up* in his balloon—or fool the Viennese for a 3rd time!— . . .

You cannot really make me happier than when you are having fun and feel relaxed!—as long as *I know for sure* that you have everything you need—then all my efforts become a thing of joy and pleasure;—the most miserable and perplexing situation in which I may find myself becomes unimportant compared with knowing that you are *well* and in a *happy* mood.—and now farewell!—make good use of your fool[119] at dinner time—think and talk about me—and love me as I love you, and be my Stanzi Marini[120] forever, just as I will always be your

Stu!—Knaller paller—
schnip—schnap—schnur—
—Schnepeperl
snai!—

Give N. N.———[121] a box on the ear
and tell him you were swatting a fly
that I had seen sitting on his face!—adieu,
catch—catch — — bi—bi—bi—
3 little kisses, sweet as sugar,
are buzzing around and coming your way!—

118. Jean-Pierre Blanchard was the first to cross the English Channel in a balloon. Here he attempted to "go up" from the Prater, the Viennese amusement park; he succeeded on July 6 (see Mozart's next letter) and sailed with his balloon *Montgolfiere* from Vienna to Groß-Enzersdorf, a village nearby.
119. Probably Süssmayr.
120. Another Mozartian creation; "Stanzi," of course, is Constanze.
121. A name was crossed out. The identity of N. N. is not clear, but sometimes, as for instance here, it seems to stand for Mozart's pupil Süssmayr, who also spent some time in Baden.

Mozart's last opera, Die Zauberflöte, *was nearly finished when his work was interrupted by the commission of a requiem mass from a mysterious messenger on behalf of an anonymous patron, Count Walsegg von Stuppach, who commissioned the mass in honor of his wife, who had recently died. Count Walsegg did not reveal his identity, because he wanted to proclaim the mass as his own composition. At the same time, Mozart received a commission from Prague for a festival opera for the coronation of Leopold II as king of Bohemia. The opera was* La clemenza di Tito, *an opera seria, based on a text by Pietro Metastasio.*

To his wife, in Baden

Vienna, July 7, 1791

Dearest, most beloved little wife of mine!

You'll have to pardon me that at present you're receiving only *one* letter a day from me. The reason is: I have to keep N. N. in captivity, can't let him get away—I'm at his place every day at 7 o'clock in the morning. I hope you received my letter from yesterday all right—I did not go to see the balloon; for one thing, I can use *my own* imagination for visualizing it, for another, I didn't think he would make it this time either—but now the Viennese are really cheering!—now they are as full of praise as they had been full of derision before.— . . .

Now I wish nothing more than to get everything settled here, just so I can be with you again; you can't imagine how slowly time has been passing without you!—I cannot describe to you what I feel, but there's a sort of emptiness—which hurts somehow—a certain longing that is never fulfilled and therefore never stops—it's always there—and even grows from day to day;—when I think of how merry we were and how much like children when we were at Baden together—and what sad and tedious hours I am spending here now,—not even my work gives me joy anymore, because I am so used to taking a break now and then and have a little chat with you; but this kind of pleasure is unfortunately denied me right now—and when I go to the piano and sing something from my opera,[122] I have to stop at once—it makes me too emotional—Basta! . . . Adieu, dearest wife of mine,

Forever yours,
Mozart.

122. *Die Zauberflöte.*

Anton Stoll was a schoolteacher and choir master at the spa of Baden. Mozart not only befriended him but wrote the motet "Ave verum corpus," K. 618, for him at Baden on June 17, 1791. Here Mozart is having fun with both Stoll and Süssmayr.

To Anton Stoll, in Baden

Vienna, July 12, 1791

Dearest Stoll!
good old troll!
you sit in your hole
drunk as a Mole!—
But you're touched in your soul
by music's sweet flow.

I have a favor to ask of you, and that is, would you be so kind as to send me tomorrow with the very first mail coach my Mass in B♭[123] (the one we did last Sunday), together with the Gradual in B, *Pax vobis*, by Michael Haydn—which we performed also.—Please understand, I do not need the scores, just the voice parts;—it's because I've been asked to conduct a Mass in a church here.—Don't think for a moment this is an excuse to get my Mass back—if I weren't happy to see it in your hands, I would not have given it to you in the first place.—On the contrary, it is a pleasure for me to be able to do you a favor.—I have to absolutely rely on you in this matter, for I have given my word.

Mozart.

On the reverse side of the letter, Mozart wrote the following message in a feigned hand pretending to be his pupil Süssmayr:

Dearest Herr von Schroll!
Don't let us down or we shall be sitting in muck; my sensitive and delicate handwriting will attest to the truth of Herr von Mozart's request, therefore—either he gets the Mass and the Gradual by Mich Haydn, or there will be no more news about his opera.

123. Probably the Missa brevis in B♭, K. 275.

We shall return everything immediately. Please be so kind and kiss the hand of my dear Theresa for me, if not—we'll be enemies forever!—Your handwriting must be witness thereof, just as mine serves as such now. So, you shall definitely have Michl Haydn's Mass, which I have already requested from my father. And remember, a Man keeps his word!

> I remain your
> true friend
> Franz Süssmayer,
> Shithead.

From the Outhouse, July 12

La Clemenza di Tito *premiered in Prague on September 6, 1791. Mozart, who had completed the opera in a carriage on his way to Prague, returned to Vienna exhausted. Still, he finished his grand German opera,* Die Zauberflöte, *which premiered on September 30. He himself conducted from the clavier, Emanuel Schikaneder played Papageno, and Mozart's sister-in-law Josepha Hofer sang the Queen of the Night.*

To his wife, in Baden

> *Vienna, October 7 and 8, 1791*
> *Friday at half past 10 o'clock at night.*

Dearest and best little wife of mine!—

I've just come back from the opera;—it was full as ever.—The Duetto *Man and Wife*[124] and the Glockenspiel in the first act had to be repeated as usual—the same was true of the boys' trio in the 2nd act,[125] but what really makes me happy is the *Silent applause!*—one can feel how this opera is rising and rising. But now to my daily life: right after you sailed off I played 2 games of billiards with Herr von Mozart; he is the fellow who wrote the opera for Schikaneder's theater. Then I sold my old nag for 14 ducats,—after that I had Joseph get *Primus* to fetch me some black coffee, with that I smoked a glorious pipe of tobacco. Then I orchestrated almost the entire Rondó of the Stadler concerto.[126] In the

124. "Mann und Weib," the duet between Pamina and Papageno, act 1, no. 7.
125. Act 2, no. 16.
126. Third movement of the Clarinet Concerto in A, K. 622, written for Anton Stadler.

meantime I received a letter from Stadler from Prague;—the Duschecks are all fine—it seems that Mad.^{me} Duscheck never received any of your letters—but that's hard to believe!—at any rate—they already know how well my German opera has been received here.—

It's the strangest thing, but the same evening that my new opera was given here for the first time with such applause, Tito[127] had its final performance in Prague, also with extraordinary applause.— . . .

At half past five in the afternoon I went through the Stubenthor[128]—and took my favorite walk along the Glacis[129] to the theater.— But hold on, what do I see?—what do I smell?—it's Don Primus with the Cutlets!—che gusto![130] I am now eating to your health—the clock is striking 11 o'clock;—perhaps you are asleep already?—St! St! St!—I don't want to wake you!—

Saturday, the 8th— . . . Adieu, dearest little wife!—the mail coach is about to leave—I hope for sure to get something from you today, and in such sweet anticipation I kiss you 1000 times and am Forever your

loving husband
W. A. Mozart

To his wife, in Baden

Vienna, October 8 and 9, 1791
Saturday night at half past 10 o'clock.—

Dearest and most beloved little wife!—

With greatest delight and joy I found your letter waiting for me when I returned from the opera;—the opera was performed again to a full house with the usual applause and repetition of numbers, even though Saturday is always a bad day for opera because it is postal day;—it will be given again tomorrow but not on Monday—therefore, Süssmayer will have to bring in Stoll, if he wants to see it, on Tuesday, when it will be performed *for the first time* again—I'm saying *for the first time* because it will probably be given several times in succession.—

127. *La clemenza di Tito.*
128. The Stubenthor was one of the old fortified gates of Vienna (also called Hungarian Gate).
129. Glacis is an area outside and along the city wall that Joseph II had improved by planting trees to create a shady walkway.
130. "How delicious!"

I have just consumed a delicious piece of sturgeon, which Don Primus, that faithful servant, served me—and since I am having a rather healthy appetite today, I sent him off to bring me, if possible, another slice.—In the meantime I shall continue with my letter to you.—This morning I worked with such concentration that it was suddenly half past 1 o'clock and I was late for my noon meal—so I dashed off to Hofers', simply because I didn't want to eat alone—and I found Mama[131] there. After table I went back home and continued working until it was time to go to the opera. Leitgeb has asked me to take him a second time, and I did.—Tomorrow I shall take *Mama;*—Hofer has already given her the libretto to read;—in Mama's case we'll probably have to say: she is *seeing* the opera, not she's *hearing* it;— . . .[132] had a box this evening and applauded *everything* vigorously; but He, that Know-it-all, proved to be a real *Bavarian;* I couldn't stay with them or I would have been tempted to call him an ass;—unfortunately, I just happened to be in their box when the 2nd act started, and it begins with a solemn scene.—He laughed at everything; at first I was patient enough to draw his attention to some of the lines, but—he just laughed;—well, it was too much for me—I called him a real *Papageno* and left the box;—but I don't think this Nitwit understood what I meant—so I went to another loge, occupied by Herr Flamm and his wife, and there I could enjoy the opera fully, and I stayed to the end;—except when Papageno's aria with the Glockenspiel came on, at that moment I went backstage because today I had a kind of urge to play the Glockenspiel myself.—So I played this joke: just when Schikaneder came to a pause, I played an arpeggio—he was startled—looked into the scenery and saw me—the 2nd time he came to that spot, I didn't play—and this time he stopped as well and did not go on singing—I guessed what he was thinking and played another chord—at that he gave his Glockenspiel a slap and shouted *"shut up!"*—everybody laughed.—I think through this joke many in the audience became aware for the first time that Papageno doesn't play the Glockenspiel himself.—By the way, you can't imagine how charming the music sounds when you hear it from a box close to the orchestra—it sounds so much better from there than from the balcony.—As soon as you come back, you'll have to try it out.—

131. Maria Caecilia Weber, Constanze's mother.
132. A name was crossed out.

Sunday, at 7 o'clock in the morning.—I slept very well and hope that you also slept well.—I relished the half capon that my friend Primus brought me.—At 10 o'clock I will go to Mass at the church of the Piarists because Leitgeb told me that I could have a conference with the *Director* at that time.[133]—I'll stay there for lunch. . . .

I am coming out to Baden next Sunday for sure—then we can go out to the Casino and on Monday we'll come home together.— . . . Farewell, my dear!—I kiss you a Million times and am Forever your

Mozart

To his wife, in Baden

Vienna, October 14, 1791

Dearest and best little wife,

Yesterday, Thursday, the 13th, Hofer and I drove out to see Carl;[134] we had lunch there and afterward drove back; at 6 o'clock I fetched Salieri and Mad.[me] Cavalieri with a carriage and took them to my box—then I quickly drove back to pick up Mama and Carl, who were waiting for me at Hofer's. You can't believe how sweet they both were—and how much they enjoyed not only my music but the libretto and everything.—Both of them told me it was an *opera* fit to be played at the grandest festivity, before the greatest monarch—and they would certainly go and see it more often because they had never seen a more beautiful and more pleasant spectacle.—Salieri listened and watched with great attention, and from the overture all the way through to the final chorus there was not a single number that did not elicit from him a "bravo" or "bello." He and Cavalieri went on and on thanking me for doing them such a great favor. They had wanted to see the performance yesterday but would have had to get their seats by 4 o'clock—so, this way, they were able to see and hear it all without being rushed.—After the performance I took them home and then had supper with Carl at Hofer's.— Then the two of us drove home, and we both slept heavenly. Carl was so delighted that I had taken him to the opera.—He looks great;—he couldn't be at a better place for his health, but everything else is unfortunately pretty bad out there!—the place is probably all right for pro-

133. Mozart wanted to register his son Carl Thomas at the Piarist church school.
134. Carl Thomas was attending a boarding school in the Viennese suburb of Perchtoldsdorf.

ducing some fine peasants for the world!—but enough of it; I had Carl excused from school until Sunday after lunch because his serious studies (Heaven help him) will not begin until Monday; I told the school that you would like to see him—and tomorrow, Sunday, I shall come out to Baden with him for a visit—then either you can keep him there or I'll take him back to Hecker[135] after lunch.—Think about it! I don't believe that his education will go down the drain if he stays out of school for a month,—and in the meantime, maybe something will come of my talks with the Piarists; they are considering his acceptance.— Apart from all that, Carl is neither worse nor better than he was before; he has the same bad manners, likes to get attention as always, enjoys learning *even less* than before because all he does out there is to go walking in the garden, 5 hours in the morning and 5 hours in the afternoon; he told me that himself; in other words, the children are not doing anything, except eating, drinking, sleeping, and going for walks. Leitgeb and Hofer are here with me right now;—the former will stay and eat with me; in fact, I've sent my faithful comrade Primus already to fetch us a meal from the Bürgerspital.—I'm really quite satisfied with Primus; he let me down just once, forcing me to sleep over at Hofer's, which annoyed me very much because they get up too late for my taste. I am happiest at home because I can follow my own established order; that one incident had put me in a pretty bad mood. Yesterday I wasted a whole day going out to Bernstorf;[136] that's also the reason why I couldn't write to you—but it is unforgivable that you haven't written to me in 2 days; I hope to hear from you today for sure, and tomorrow I expect to speak with you myself and kiss you with all my heart.

Farewell, Forever yours
Mozart

I kiss Sophie a thousand times;[137] with N. N. do whatever you like. Adieu.

As far as is known, the letter of October 14, 1791, is Mozart's last letter. It is a routine message to Constanze filled with excitement about the success of Die

135. Wenzel Bernhard Heeger, headmaster of Carl's school.
136. Mozart means Perchtoldsdorf.
137. Constanze's younger sister, who was visiting at Baden.

Zauberflöte *and with concerns about a good school for his little son Carl.* *Nothing in the letter indicates that Mozart was ill or depressed, although he became* *progressively weak and feverish as he continued with his work on the* Requiem. *Early in December, he became partially paralyzed but was able to discuss the com-* *pletion of the* Requiem *with his pupil Süssmayr. He died in the early hours of* *Monday, December 5, 1791, of complications arising from a chronic kidney ail-* *ment, acute rheumatic fever, and a streptococcal infection. On December 6, his body* *was consecrated in the Chapel of the Cross (Kreuzkapelle) in St. Stephen's* *Cathedral and taken by hearse to the cemetery of St. Marx, six kilometers outside* *of Vienna. Mozart was buried in an unmarked communal grave; no mourners were* *present at the graveside.*

Epilogue

MOZART'S LETTERS are unique and wonderfully idiosyncratic: unique in that no matter how often we read them, they come to us fresh and alive, filled with incredible energy and imagination; idiosyncratic in that he had his own view of the world, a Mozartian view, which was not entirely inaccurate, but not always realistic or objective. His outlook was tempered by his personal feelings and perceptions, making everything he wrote intriguing and compelling.

When we enter into Mozart's epistolary realm, we step into an area of complete privacy. Mozart did not write his letters for publication, and each time we read a letter, we are eavesdropping on a personal conversation. Yet we must be grateful to Leopold, Nannerl, Constanze, and, perhaps most of all, Bäsle for preserving Mozart's correspondence and making most of it available to the public, for it enables us to gain access—limited, to be sure—to a composer who has repeatedly been described as difficult to characterize and hard to know.

It may well be true that Mozart hides behind his words and music, or that he played games with his correspondents; but we, the readers of his letters, receive at least two messages from him about his life and character. The first is his work ethic and his power of concentration. Previous generations may have thought of him as carefree and divine, but we can surmise from his letters that he worked hard and constantly. The second message is his enthusiasm for writing letters. Mozart loved words: he loved writing them, creating them, toying with their sounds and meanings. There was nothing he would not talk about in his letters—travels, performances, money problems, affairs of the heart, moments of exuberance, times of anguish—but often he wrote just for the sheer fun of writing.

Music is, of course, the most frequently recurring theme in Mozart's correspondence. More than three-quarters of his letters show references to music, whether passing remarks about fellow artists or full-scale reports from his workshop. What is special, however, and endearingly Mozartian, is the way he talks about some of his musical inspirations and the way he humanizes the compositional process. When writing about his craft, Mozart rarely uses professional terminology. Not only is his language utterly simple and nontechnical, but his musical creations become live beings that march, walk, sigh, sleep, drag their feet, and use the bathroom. Tonalities relate to each other not in consonance or dissonance but as friendly and unfriendly neighbors. An improvisation is called not allegro or rondo but a "merry little thing" that is taken for a walk by Herr Mozart and returned to home base, "assbackwards." And when he plays parts of his singspiel *Die Entführung* for Countess Thun in Vienna, he avoids the word *vorspielen* (playing through) in favor of *vorreiten* (prancing through), as if he had invited the countess to a horse show.

Mozart's letters allow us to see a composer who not only lived his work every minute of his life but also enjoyed expressing himself in words. It is through these words, these uniquely vibrant, down-to-earth, concrete expressions, that we can see the composer as a creative artist who, in spite of the abstract nature of his craft, has a rich and profound connection with all things human. Mozart's letters reveal his extraordinary humanity—as does every note of his music.

A Chronology
of Mozart's Life

CHRONOLOGY OF BIOGRAPHICAL DATES, JOURNEYS,
AND MAJOR COMPOSITIONS

1719   November 14, Johann Georg Leopold Mozart is born in Augsburg (d. May
28, 1787, in Salzburg).

1720   December 25, Maria Anna Walburga Pertl is born in St. Gilgen, near Salzburg
(d. July 3, 1778, in Paris).

1751   July 30, Maria Anna Walburga Ignatia (Nannerl) Mozart is born in Salzburg,
fourth (and first surviving) child of Leopold and Maria Anna (d. October
29, 1829, in Salzburg).

1756   January 27, Johannes Chrysostomus Wolfgangus Theophilus (Lat. Amadeus,
Ger. Gottlieb) Mozart is born in Salzburg, seventh (and only other surviving) child of Leopold and Maria Anna (d. December 5, 1791, in Vienna).

1761   Wolfgang's first composition: Andante for Piano, K. 1a.

1762   January 12–beginning of February, Leopold and the two children travel to
Munich; Wolfgang and Nannerl perform at court before the elector of
Bavaria, Maximilian III, Joseph.
September 18–January 5, 1763, the entire Mozart family travels to Vienna and
Pressburg (today Bratislava). Both children perform before Emperor
Francis I and Empress Maria Theresa of Austria. Wolfgang falls ill during the
trip (streptococcal infection). After his return to Salzburg, he contracts rheu-
matic fever.

1763   June 9–November 29, 1766, the Mozart family undertakes a grand tour of
Europe. Major stops: Paris, London, and The Hague. The Mozarts are invited to the court of King Louis XV at Versailles; Baron von Grimm writes
about Wolfgang, the wunderkind, in his *Correspondence littéraire*. In London, the
family is received by King George III and Queen Sophie Charlotte; Wolfgang
performs with Johann Christian Bach and takes singing lessons from the castrato Giovanni Manzuoli. On their return trip, both children come down

with typhoid fever; at the end of the journey (in Munich), Wolfgang has another bout with rheumatic fever. On November 29, 1766, after three and a half years of travel, the Mozarts arrive back in Salzburg.
Compositions: Sonatas for Violin and Piano, K. 6–9, Sonatas for Piano, Violin (or Flute), and Cello, K. 10–15; the first symphonies, K. 16–19 and 22.

1767   September 11–January 5, 1769, the Mozart family travels to Vienna and Brünn (today Brno). Both children come down with smallpox in Olmütz (today Olomouce) but survive. In January 1768, the Mozarts have an audience with Empress Maria Theresa and her son, the newly appointed Emperor Joseph II.
Compositions: *Bastien and Bastienne*, K. 50, a singspiel; *La finta semplice*, K. 51, an opera buffa.

1769   November 14, Wolfgang, at age thirteen, is appointed violinist and third concertmaster (without pay) at the court orchestra in Salzburg.
December 13–March 28, 1771, first Italian journey. Wolfgang travels with his father to Milan, Bologna, Florence, Rome, Naples, and Venice. In Bologna, he meets with Padre Giovanni Battista Martini, famous music theorist, who gives him a certificate of excellence; in Rome, he writes down from memory Gregorio Allegri's *Miserere;* in Naples he meets the English ambassador, Sir William Hamilton and his wife, Catherine. On July 5, 1770, he receives the Order of the Golden Spur from Pope Clement XIV, and he is awarded diplomas of membership from the Accademias Filarmonica in Bologna and Verona.
Compositions: Quartet in G major, K. 80 (Mozart's first string quartet, completed at an inn at Lodi), *Mitridate, rè di Ponte*, K. 87, an opera seria, written for the Teatro Regio Ducal in Milan.

1771   August 13–December 15, second Italian journey. Wolfgang is commissioned to write an opera for the occasion of the marriage of Archduke Ferdinand of Austria to Princess Maria Beatrice Ricciarda of Modena. Wolfgang travels to Milan with his father to compose the opera.
Compositions: *Ascanio in Alba*, K. 111, an opera seria.

1772   March 14, Count Hieronymus Colloredo becomes prince archbishop of Salzburg.
Compositions: *Il sogno di Scipione*, K. 126, an opera seria (written in honor of the new archbishop). August 21, Wolfgang is named concertmaster (with an annual salary of 150 gulden) at the court orchestra in Salzburg.
October 24–March 13, 1773, third Italian journey. Wolfgang receives a commission to write an opera for the Teatro Regio Ducal. He and Leopold travel to Milan for a third and final time.
Compositions: *Lucio Silla*, K. 135, an opera seria; Divertimentos, K. 136–138.

1773   January 17, Mozart composes the Motet "Exsultate, jubilate," K. 165, for the castrato Venanzio Rauzzini, who sings it at the Church of the Theatines in Milan.

July 14–September 26, Wolfgang travels with his father to Vienna. They have an audience with Empress Maria Theresa and visit Dr. Franz Anton Mesmer, famed doctor of magnetism. After returning to Salzburg, the Mozarts move from Getreidegasse no. 225 (today no. 9), where Nannerl and Wolfgang were born, to the Tanzmeisterhaus at Hannibal (today Makart) Square in Salzburg. Compositions: String quartets, divertimentos, and symphonies: among them, "little" G-minor Symphony, K. 183; Piano Concerto no. 5 in D major, K. 175, Mozart's first original piano concerto.

1774   December 6–March 7, 1775, Wolfgang is commissioned to write *La finta giardiniera*, an opera buffa, for the Munich carnival season. Father and son travel to Munich for the premiere, which is on January 13. Wolfgang suffers from a dental abcess.
Compositions: Symphony no. 29 in A major, K. 201; *La finta giardiniera*, K. 196.

1775   Wolfgang is nineteen and in Salzburg. He is extremely productive.
Compositions: *Il rè pastore*, K. 208, *dramma per musica*; "Misericordias Domini," K. 222, an offertory; Piano Sonatas nos. 1–6, K. 279–284; Violin Concertos nos. 1–5, K. 207, 211, 216, 218, and 219.

1776   Wolfgang remains in Salzburg.
Compositions: Divertimento in F major ("Lodron"), K. 247; Serenade in D major ("Haffner"), K. 250.

1777   September 23–ca. January 15, 1779, Wolfgang undertakes a sixteen-month journey to find "employment or make money"; it is his first trip without "papa"; he is accompanied by his mother, Maria Anna. Major stops: Munich, Augsburg, Mannheim, and Paris. Wolfgang meets his cousin, Maria Anna Thekla Mozart, the Bäsle, in Augsburg, and falls in love with Aloysia Weber, a young singer, in Mannheim. Maximilan III dies in Munich; the new elector of Bavaria will be Karl Theodor of the Palatinate.
Compositions: Piano Concerto in E-flat ("Jeunehomme"), K. 271 (January, before the journey); Piano Sonata in C major, K. 309; "Alcandro lo confesso," K. 294, concert aria for Aloysia Weber.

1778   July 3, Maria Anna Mozart dies in Paris, probably of typhus. She is buried in the Cimetière de Saint-Eustache in Paris. Wolfgang returns to Salzburg via Mannheim and Munich, searching for Aloysia, who is now employed at the court theater in Munich. Wolfgang apparently proposes marriage, but Aloysia rejects him.
Compositions: Symphony no. 31 in D major ("Paris"), K. 297; Concerto for Flute and Harp in C major, K. 299; Sonata for Piano and Violin in E minor, K. 304; Piano Sonata in A minor, K. 310.

1779   Wolfgang returns to Salzburg. He accepts a position as court organist with an annual salary of 450 gulden.

Compositions: Mass in C major ("Coronation"), K. 317; *Vesperae solennes de confessore* in C major, K. 339; Sinfonia concertante for Violin and Viola in E-flat, K. 364.

1780   November 5, Mozart leaves Salzburg (unknowingly for good). He travels to Munich to complete *Idomeneo,* an opera seria, commissioned by the court theater of Munich. Aloysia Weber marries the actor Joseph Lange and moves to Vienna.
November 29, Empress Maria Theresa dies in Vienna.
Compositions: *Idomeneo, rè di Creta,* K. 366.

1781   January 29, premiere of *Idomeneo.* Leopold and Nannerl come to Munich for the premiere. Mozart is ordered by Archbishop Colloredo to join him in Vienna; he obeys but within two months breaks with the archbishop. Against his father's wishes, Mozart decides to stay in Vienna as a freelance composer and performer.
Compositions: Eight Variations for Piano in F major, K. 352; Concerto for Two Pianos in E-flat, K. 365.

1782   January, death of Johann Christian Bach in London. Mozart deepens his knowledge of the music of Johann Sebastian Bach and George Frideric Handel at the house of Gottfried van Swieten. August 4, Mozart marries Constanze Weber, sister of Aloysia, in St. Stephen's Cathedral in Vienna.
Compositions: *Die Entführung aus dem Serail,* K. 384, a singspiel; Symphony no. 35 in D major ("Haffner"), K. 385; Prelude and Fuge in C major, K. 394; String Quartet no. 14 in G major, K. 387.

1783   Mozart meets Lorenzo da Ponte, his later librettist for *Le nozze di Figaro, Don Giovanni,* and *Così fan tutte,* at the house of his landlord, Baron von Wetzlar. He gives a concert at the Burgtheater with Aloysia.
June 17, Wolfgang and Constanze's first child, Raimund Leopold, is born; he dies on August 19, while the Mozarts are visiting in Salzburg (end of July to end of November). Constanze sings one of the soprano parts in Mozart's C-minor Mass at St. Peter's Church in Salzburg.
Compositions: Piano Concertos nos. 11–13, K. 413–415; Horn Concerto in D major, K. 412; Mass in C minor, K. 427; String Quartets nos. 15 and 16, K. 421 and 428; Symphony in C major ("Linz"), K. 425.

1784   February 9, Mozart establishes a thematic catalog of his works. First entry: Piano Concerto no. 14 in E-flat, K. 449.
August 23, Nannerl marries Johann Baptist von Berchtold zu Sonnenburg, widowed civil servant in the bishopric of Salzburg, residing at St. Gilgen, near Salzburg. Wolfgang and Constanze's second (and first surviving) child is born: Carl Thomas (d. October 31, 1858, in Milan). In December, Mozart becomes a Freemason in the lodge Benevolence (Zur Wohltätigkeit).
Compositions: Six piano concertos, including no. 19 in F major, K. 459; Piano Quintet in E-flat, K. 452; String Quartet no. 17 in B-flat ("Hunt"), K. 458.

1785   In February, Leopold visits Wolfgang and Constanze in Vienna. Mozart performs two piano concertos in public with his father in the audience. Leopold
returns to Salzburg in May. Mozart begins work on *Le nozze di Figaro*.
Compositions: Publication of six string quartets (K. 387, 421, 428, 458, 464,
and 465) dedicated to Joseph Haydn, the "Haydn" Quartets; Piano Concerto
no. 20 in D minor, K. 466; Piano Concerto no. 21 in C, K. 467; Piano
Concerto no. 22 in E-flat, K. 482; *Die Maurerfreude*, K. 471, Masonic cantata;
Fantasia for Piano in C minor, K. 475; "Das Veilchen" (text by Goethe), K.
476; Sonata for Piano and Violin, in E-flat, K. 481.

1786   May 1, *Le nozze di Figaro* premieres at the Burgtheater in Vienna. The Mozarts'
third child, Johann Thomas Leopold, is born and dies. Mozart suffers from
headaches and stomach cramps.
Compositions: *Le nozze di Figaro*, K. 492, opera buffa; Piano Concerto no. 23 in
A, K. 488; Piano Concerto no. 24 in C minor, K. 491; Piano Concerto no. 25
in C, K. 503; Quartet for Piano and Strings in E-flat, K. 493; Horn Concerto
in E-flat, K. 495; Symphony no. 38 in D ("Prague"), K. 504.

1787   January, *Figaro* is performed at the Prague National Theater in Mozart's presence. *Don Giovanni* is commissioned. Mid-March, the sixteen-year-old
Beethoven comes to Vienna to study with Mozart; he returns to Bonn with-
in weeks because his mother falls ill. May 28, Leopold Mozart dies in
Salzburg and is buried at the cemetery of St. Sebastian.
October 29, *Don Giovanni* premieres in Prague. Mozart is appointed "cham-
ber music composer" by Joseph II with an annual salary of 800 gulden.
Compositions: *Don Giovanni*, K. 527, an opera buffa; String Quintet in C, K.
515; String Quintet in G minor, K. 516; *Ein musikalischer Spaß*, K. 522; *Eine kleine
Nachtmusik*, K. 525.

1788   May 7, *Don Giovanni* is performed in Vienna for the first time (Aloysia sings
Donna Anna). Short of cash, Mozart arranges music by George Frideric
Handel for Baron van Swieten; he also begins borrowing money from the
Viennese merchant Michael Puchberg.
Compositions: The last three symphonies: no. 39 in E-flat, K. 543; no. 40 in
G minor, K. 550; no. 41 in C ("Jupiter"), K. 551; Divertimento for String Trio
in E-flat, K. 563.

1789   April 8–June 4, Mozart travels to Prague, Dresden, Leipzig, Potsdam, and
Berlin in search of commissions. He probably receives a commission from
King Friedrich Wilhelm II of Prussia for six string quartets and six easy piano
sonatas (the latter for the king's daughter, Princess Friederike Charlotte).
The Mozarts' fifth child, Anna Maria, is born, but lives only one hour.
Constanze falls ill with a varicose ulcer and visits the sulfur baths at Baden,
near Vienna.
Compositions: String Quartet no. 21 in D major, K. 575; Piano Sonata in D
major, K. 576; Quintet for Clarinet and Strings in A major, K. 581.

1790   February 20, Emperor Joseph II dies and is succeeded as king and emperor by his brother, Leopold II, former grand duke of Tuscany.

September 23–November 10, although not officially invited, Mozart travels to Frankfurt to participate in the coronation of Leopold II as Emperor of the Holy Roman Empire of the German Nation. Mozart gives concerts in Frankfurt, Mainz, and Munich, with very modest financial results.

Compositions: *Così fan tutte*, K. 588, an opera buffa; String Quartet no. 22 in B-flat, K. 589; String Quartet no. 23 in F major, K. 590; String Quintet in D major, K. 593.

1791   January, Mozart composes his last piano concerto, no. 27 in B-flat major, K. 595, which he performs on March 4. In May, Mozart begins to compose *Die Zauberflöte*. July 26, the Mozarts' sixth (and second surviving) child, Franz Xaver Wolfgang (d. July 29, 1844, in Carlsbad—today Karlovy Vary) is born. Mozart journeys to Prague with Constanze for the last time, to conduct a performance of *Don Giovanni* and his new opera *La clemenza di Tito*, written in honor of Leopold II as king of Bohemia. September 30, *Die Zauberflöte* premieres at the Theater auf der Wieden in a suburb of Vienna. Feverish work on a requiem mass, commissioned by a stranger.

November–December, Mozart suffers chronic renal failure. November 20, a fatal illness sets in: probably acute rheumatic fever brought on by a streptococcal infection. December 5, shortly before one in the morning, Mozart dies, at the age of thirty-five. Present at his bedside are Constanze, her sister Sophie, and the attending physician, Dr. Thomas Closset. December 6, Mozart is buried in an unmarked grave at St. Marx cemetery in the outskirts of Vienna.

Compositions: String Quintet in E-flat major, K. 614; "Ave verum corpus," K. 618, a motet; *Die Zauberflöte*, K. 620, a singspiel; *La clemenza di Tito*, K. 621, an opera seria; Clarinet Concerto in A major, K. 622; Requiem, K. 626.

Selected Bibliography

Letters and Reference Works

Anderson, Emily, trans. *The Letters of Mozart and His Family.* 3rd ed. New York: W. W. Norton, 1985.

Bauer, Wilhelm A., Otto Erich Deutsch, and Joseph Heinz Eibl, eds. *Mozart: Briefe und Aufzeichnungen.* Gesamtausgabe der Internationalen Stiftung Mozarteum, Salzburg. 7 vols. Kassel: Bärenreiter Verlag, 1962–75.

Blom, Eric, ed. *Mozart's Letters.* Baltimore: Penguin Books, 1956.

Deutsch, Otto Erich, ed. *Mozart: A Documentary Biography.* Translated by Eric Blom, Peter Branscombe, and Jeremy Noble. Stanford: Stanford University Press, 1965.

Eibl, Joseph Heinz, ed. *Wolfgang Amadeus Mozart: Chronik eines Lebens.* 2nd ed. Kassel: Bärenreiter Verlag; Munich: Deutscher Taschenbuch Verlag, 1977.

Eibl, Joseph Heinz, and Walter Senn, eds. *Mozarts Bäsle-Briefe.* 4th ed. Munich: Deutscher Taschenbuch Verlag, 1991.

Eisen, Cliff. *New Mozart Documents: A Supplement to O. E. Deutsch's Documentary Biography.* Stanford: Stanford University Press, 1991.

Geffray, Geneviève, trans. *W. A. Mozart: Correspondance.* 7 vols. 2nd ed. Paris: Harmoniques, Flammarion, 1986–99. [French translation of the Bauer/Deutsch/Eibl complete edition, *Mozart: Briefe und Aufzeichnungen*]

Köchel, Ludwig Ritter von. *Chronologisch-thematisches Verzeichnis sämtlicher Tonwerke Wolfgang Amade Mozarts.* 6th ed. Edited by Franz Giegling, Alexander Weinmann, and Gerd Sievers. Wiesbaden: Breitkopf and Härtel, 1946.

Mersmann, Hans, ed. *Letters of Wolfgang Amadeus Mozart.* Translated by M. M. Bozman. London and Toronto: J. M. Dent; New York: E. P. Dutton, 1928.

Nohl, Ludwig, ed. *The Letters of Wolfgang Amadeus Mozart.* 2 vols. Translated by Lady Wallace. London: Longmans, Green, 1865.

Valentin, Erich, ed. *Lübbes Mozart Lexikon.* 2nd ed. Bergisch Gladbach: Gustav Lübbe Verlag, 1985.

Zaslaw, Neal, with William Cowdery, eds. *The Compleat Mozart: A Guide to the Musical Works of Wolfgang Amadeus Mozart.* New York: W. W. Norton, 1990.

Books and Articles

Allanbrook, Wye Jamison. *Rhythmic Gesture in Mozart: Le Nozze di Figaro and Don Giovanni.* Chicago: University of Chicago Press, 1983.

Bär, Carl. *Mozart: Krankheit, Tod, Begräbnis.* 2nd ed. Salzburg: Auslieferung Bärenreiter, 1972.

Barth, Karl. *Wolfgang Amadeus Mozart.* Translated by Clarence K. Pott. Grand Rapids, Mich.: William B. Eerdmans, 1986.

Braunbehrens, Volkmar. *Mozart in Vienna, 1781–1791.* Translated by Timothy Bell. New York: Grove Weidenfeld, 1989.

Bruford, Walter H. *Germany in the Eighteenth Century: The Social Background of the Literary Revival.* Cambridge: Cambridge University Press, 1959.

Clive, Geoffrey. "Mozart and the Daemonic." In *The Romantic Enlightenment.* New York: Meridian Books, 1960.

Da Ponte, Lorenzo. *Memoirs.* Translated by Elisabeth Abbott. New York: Orion Press, 1959.

Davies, Peter J. *Mozart in Person: His Character and Health.* New York: Greenwood Press, 1989.

Einstein, Alfred. *Greatness in Music.* Translated by César Saerchinger. New York: Oxford University Press, 1941.

———. *Mozart: His Character, His Work.* Translated by Arthur Mendel and Nathan Broder. New York: Oxford University Pres, 1962.

Elias, Norbert. *Mozart: Zur Soziologie eines Genies.* Edited by Michael Schröter. Frankfurt: Suhrkamp Verlag, 1991.

Ellison, Cori. "Between the Lines: Mozart in Translation—circa 1991." *Stagebill.* Mozart Bicentennial Issue. New York: Lincoln Center, 1991. Pp. 33–38.

Ermen, Reinhard. Epilogue to *Wolfgang Amadeus schreibt an Maria Anna Thekla Mozart . . . und der nähmliche narr bleibe ich.* Munich: C. H. Beck Verlag, 1990.

Fog, Rasmus. "Havde Mozart Gilles de la Tourete's Syndrom?" *Astra.* Draco Information (an in-house pharmaceutical publication). 1 (1984): 8–12.

Gay, Peter. *Mozart.* New York: Viking Penguin, 1999.

Gunne, Lars. "Hade Mozart Tourettes syndrom?" *Läkartidningen.* 88 (1991): 4325–26.

Halliwell, Ruth. *The Mozart Family: Four Lives in a Social Context.* New York: Oxford University Press, 1998.

Hennenberg, Fritz. *Wolfgang Amadeus Mozart.* Leipzig: Reclam Verlag, 1976.

Hildesheimer, Wolfgang. *Betrachtungen über Mozart.* Pfullingen: Günter Neske, 1963.

———. *Mozart.* Translated by Marion Faber. New York: Farrar Straus Giroux, 1982.

Hilmera, Jiri, Tomislav Volek, and Vera Ptácková. *Mozarts Opern für Prag.* Translated by Lenka Reinerová. 2nd ed. Prague: Theaterinstitut, Prag, 1991.

Hutchins, Arthur. *Mozart: The Man, the Musician.* New York: Schirmer Books, 1976.

Kerman, Joseph. *Opera as Drama.* New York: Vintage Books, 1959.

———. *Listen.* 3rd ed. New York: World Publishers, 1980.

Knepler, Georg. *Wolfgang Amadé Mozart.* Translated by J. Bradford Robinson. Cambridge: Cambridge University Press, 1994.

Konrad, Ulrich, and Martin Staehelin, eds. *Allzeit ein Buch: Die Bibliothek Wolfgang Amadeus Mozarts.* Wolfenbüttel: Herzog August Bibliothek, 1991.

Köpke, Rudolf, ed. *Ludwig Tieck: Erinnerungen aus dem Leben des Dichters nach dessen mündlichen und schriftlichen Mittheilungen.* 2 vols. Leipzig: F. A. Brockhaus, 1855.

Kraemer, Uwe. "Wer hat Mozart verhungern lassen?" *Musica* 30 (1976): 203–11.

Kühn, Arnold. *Mozarts humoristische Briefe.* Saarbrücken: Inaugural-Dissertation, 1960.

Küster, Konrad. *Mozart: A Musical Biography.* Translated by Mary Whittall. New York: Oxford University Press, 1996.

Marshall, Robert L. *Mozart Speaks: Views on Music, Musicians, and the World.* New York: Schirmer Books, 1991.

Leinsdorf, Erich. "What a Piece of Work Is Mozart." *Stagebill.* Mozart Bicentennial Issue. New York: Lincoln Center, 1991. Pp. 62–63.

Nagel, Ivan. *Autonomy and Mercy: Reflections on Mozart's Operas.* Translated by Marion Faber and Ivan Nagel. Cambridge: Harvard University Press, 1991.

Niemetschek, Franz Xaver. *Ich kannte Mozart: Leben des k. k. Kapellmeisters Wolfgang Gottlieb Mozart nach Originalquellen beschrieben.* Prague: In der Herrlischen Buchhandlung, 1798. Reprint. Edited by Jost Perfahl. Munich: Bibliothek zeitgenössischer Literatur, 1984.

Nissen, Georg Nikolaus von. *Biographie W. A. Mozarts.* Leipzig: Breitkopf and Härtel, 1828. Reprint, Hildesheim: Georg Olms Verlag, 1972.

Ochs, Michael. "L.m.i.a.": Mozart's Suppressed Canon Texts." *Mozart-Jahrbuch 1991:* 254–61.

Ortheil, Hanns-Josef. *Mozart: Im Innern seiner Sprachen.* Frankfurt: S. Fischer, 1982.

Panagl, Oswald. "'Ich gute eine wünsche nacht': Mozarts Spiel mit der Sprache." In *Wolfgang Amadeus: Summa summarum.* Edited by Peter Csobádi. Vienna: Paul Neff Verlag, 1990. Pp. 96–100.

Parouty, Michel. *Mozart: From Child Prodigy to Tragic Hero.* Translated by Celia Skrine. New York: Harry N. Abrams, 1993.

Robbins Landon, H. C. *Mozart: The Golden Years, 1781–1791.* New York: Schirmer Books, 1989.

———. *Mozart's Last Year.* New York: Schirmer Books, 1988.

Rosen, Charles. *The Classical Style: Haydn, Mozart, Beethoven.* New York: W. W. Norton, 1972.

Sadie, Stanley. "The Mozart Letters." In *Mozart's Nature, Mozart's World: A Bicentenary Humanties Symposium.* Easthampton, Massachusetts: The Westfield Center for Early Keyboard Studies. 1991. Pp. 8–13.

Schenk, Erich. *Mozart: Sein Leben, seine Welt.* 2nd ed. Munich: Amalthea, 1975.

Schroeder, David. *Mozart in Revolt: Strategies of Resistance, Mischief, and Deception.* New Haven: Yale University Press, 1999.

Seidlin, Oskar. "Ein Brief nebst einer Brief-Interpretation." In *Festschrift für Werner Neuse,* ed. Herbert Lederer and Joachim Zeyppel. Berlin: Die Diagonale, 1967.

Simkin, Benjamin. "The Case for Mozart's Affliction with Tourette Syndrome." *Journal of the Conductors' Guild* 12 (1991): 50–64.

———. "Mozart's Scatological Disorder." *British Medical Journal* 305 (1992): 1563–67.

Stafford, William. *The Mozart Myths: A Critical Reassessment.* Stanford: Stanford University Press, 1991.

Till, Nicolas. *Mozart and the Enlightenment: Truth, Virtue and Beauty in Mozart's Operas.* New York: W. W. Norton, 1992.

Turner, Walter James. *Mozart: The Man and His Works.* New York: Alfred A. Knopf, 1938.

Tyson, Alan. *Mozart: Studies of the Autograph Scores.* Cambridge: Harvard University Press, 1987.

Winternitz, Emanuel. "Gnagflow Trazom: An Essay on Mozart's Script, Pastimes, and Nonsense Letters." *Journal of the American Musicological Society* 11 (1958): 200–16.

Wolff, Christoph. *Mozart's Requiem: Historical and Analytical Studies, Documents, Score.* Translated by Mary Whittall. Berkeley: University of California Press, 1994.

Wolff, Larry. "Mozart's Eastern Europe: Bohemians, Albanians, Wallachians, and Turks." *Halcyon: A Journal of the Humanities* 15 (1993): 55–70.

Index

Note: References marked as footnotes refer *only* to material not mentioned or alluded to in the letters or commentary.

Mozart's Travels

YEARS	MOZART'S AGE	SELECTED STOPS (**bold** indicates longer stay)
1756		Mozart born in **Salzburg**
1762	6	**Munich**
1762–63	6–7	**Vienna**, Bratislava (Pressburg)
1763–66	7–10	Frankfurt, **Paris**, The Hague, **London**, Donaueschingen
1767–69	11–13	**Vienna**, Brno (Brünn), Olomouce (Olmütz)
1769–71	13–15	Wörgl, Innsbruck, Verona, Cremona, **Milan**, Lodi, Parma, **Bologna**, Florence, **Rome**, **Naples**, Turin, Venice
1771	15	Innsbruck, Bolzano (Bozen), Rovereto, Brescia, **Milan**
1772–73	16–17	Bolzano (Bozen), Brescia, **Milan**
1773	17	**Vienna**, Linz, Lambach
1774–75	18–19	Wasserburg, **Munich**
1777–79	21–23	Wasserburg, **Munich**, **Augsburg**, **Mannheim**, Worms, Kirchheimbolanden, Metz, Clermont-en-Aronne, **Paris**, Nancy, Strasbourg, Kaisheim
1780–81	24–25	Wasserburg, **Munich**
1781	25	Mozart moves to **Vienna** in March
1783	27	**Salzburg**, Lambach, Linz
1784		Nannerl moves to St. Gilgen in August
1787	31	**Prague** (two trips)
1789	33	Moraské Budejovice (Budwitz), Dresden, Leipzig, Berlin, Potsdam, Prague
1790	34	Regensburg, Nürnberg, Würzburg, **Frankfurt**, Mainz, Schwetzingen, Munich
1791	35	**Prague**